Withdrawn from
Davidson College Library

Library of
Davidson College

Developing Economies of the Third World

Outstanding Studies of
Economic Development in
Latin America and
the Pacific Rim

Edited by
Stuart Bruchey

A Garland Series

THE STATE AND ECONOMIC TRANSFORMATION

THE TAIWAN CASE

CHIEN-KUO PANG

GARLAND PUBLISHING, INC.
NEW YORK & LONDON
1992

Copyright © 1992 by Chien-Kuo Pang
All Rights Reserved

LIBRARY OF CONGRESS CATALOGING-IN-PUBLICATION DATA

P'ang, Chien-kuo.
  The state and economic transformation : the Taiwan case / Chien-Kuo Pang.
   p. cm. — (Developing economies of the Third World)
  Revision of the author's thesis (Ph. D.—Brown University, 1987).
  Includes bibliographical references (p.   ) and index.
  ISBN 0-8153-0635-0 (alk. paper)
  1. Taiwan—Economic policy—1945–   2. Taiwan—Economic conditions—1945–   I. Title. II. Series.
HC430.5.P37 1992
338.95124'9—dc20
                                91-41620

Designed by Lisa Broderick

Printed on acid-free, 250-year-life paper.
MANUFACTURED IN THE UNITED STATES OF AMERICA

CONTENTS

List of Figures and Tables	*vii*
Glossary	*ix*
Preface	*xi*

Chapter 1 Theory and Methods — 1
- Introduction — 1
- Literature Review and Its Implications for the Present Research — 4
- A Conceptual Framework Derived from the State-centric Approach — 10
- Research Methods — 17
- Data Sources — 18

Chapter 2 An Overview of the Taiwan Case — 21
- Why the State on Taiwan Matters — 21
- Taiwan as a Case to Examine the State and Society — 37

Chapter 3 Constitutional Structure of Economic Policy-making — 50
- The Economic Bureaucracy — 50
- The Executive Yuan Council — 61
- The Central Standing Committee of the KMT (CSC) — 62
- The Legislative Yuan — 71
- A Remark on the Constitutional Structure of Economic Policy-making — 73

Chapter 4 Policy Makers and the Operational Economic Policy-making Structure — 77
- An Introduction to the Operational Economic Policy-making Structure — 77
- The Top Political Leadership — 80
- The Economic Policy Makers — 89
- The Economic Bureaucrats — 104
- The Consulting Economists — 107
- The American Advisors — 110
- The Local Capitalists — 112
- The Transnational Capitalists — 115
- Some Remarks on the Operational Structure of Economic Policy-making — 116

Chapter 5 Formulation and Execution of Economic Policy Before the Late 1950s — 123
Situational Imperatives — 123
Agricultural Policy — 129
Industrial Policy — 147
Fiscal and Monetary Policies — 152
Foreign Trade Policy — 157
The 1950s as a Starting Point — 160

Chapter 6 The Turning Point of Taiwan's Economic Development: 1958-61 — 163
Situational Imperatives — 163
Formulation and Execution of the Foreign Exchange and Trade Reform — 170
Formulation and Execution of the Nineteen-Point Program of Economic and Financial Reform — 177
Formulation and Execution of the Statute for Encouragement of Investment — 187
A Review on the Economic Reforms — 191

Chapter 7 Formulation and Execution of Economic Policy After the Early 1960s — 199
Situational Imperatives — 199
Agricultural Policy — 210
Industrial Policy — 213
Fiscal and Monetary Policies — 225
Foreign Trade Policy — 235
The KMT State's Changing Role in Taiwan's Economic Transformation — 240

Chapter 8 Conclusion — 255
Explaining Policy-making in Taiwan's Economic Transformation — 255
The International Political-Economic Environment — 257
The Taiwanese Society and Its Relationship to the KMT State — 261
The Internal Structuring of the KMT State — 265
What Can Be Learned from the Taiwan Case? — 273

Appendixes — *277*

Bibliography — *295*

Index — *315*

LIST OF TABLES AND FIGURES

Tables

Table 2.1 Major Indicators of Taiwan's Economy	23
Table 2.2 Indicators of Taiwan's Economy by Growth Rates	27
Table 2.3 Employment by Industries	29
Table 2.4 Industrial Origin of Net Domestic Product	31
Table 2.5 Income Distribution of Taiwan Area	33
Table 3.1 Ethnic Background of the Members of the CSC, 1952-1984	66
Table 3.2 Professional Background of the Members of the CSC, 1952-1984	69
Table 4.1 Personnel Evolution of Economic Policy Makers, 1949-1985	91
Table 4.2 A Comparison of the Birthplace and the educational Background of the Economic Planners and the 1957 Members of the CSC	95
Table 5.1 Area and Household Affected by Land Reform	139
Table 5.2 Types of Farm Families Before and After the Land Reform	140
Table 5.3 Changes in the Number of Landowner Families Before and After the Implementation of the Land-to-the-tiller Program	141
Table 5.4 Government Collection of Rice, 1950-1960	145
Table 5.5 Changes in Ratios of Domestic Production to Total Supply	151
Table 5.6 Foreign Transfers and Government Current Surplus	156
Table 6.1 Tax Reduction and Refunds from 1955 to 1979	193
Table 7.1 Private Foreign & Overseas Chinese Investment in Approvals	218
Table 7.2 Tax and Monopoly Revenues	228
Table 7.3 Structure of Tax and Monopoly Revenues	230

Figures

Figure 1.1 The Conceptual Framework	16
Figure 2.1 Organization Chart of the Central Government of the Republic of China	44
Figure 3.1 The Constitutional Structure of Economic Policy-making	50
Figure 3.2 Evolution of the Agency for Economic Planning	56
Figure 3.3 Organization Chart of the Economic Bureaucracy	58
Figure 4.1 The Operational Structure of Economic Policy-making	78

GLOSSARY

AID	(United States) Agency for International Development
CCP	Chinese Communist Party
CEPD	Council for Economic Planning and Development
CIECD	Council for International Economic Cooperation and Development
CSC	Central Standing Committee of the Kuomintang
CUSA	Council for U.S. Aid
EPC	Economic Planning Council
EPZ	Export Processing Zone
ESB	Economic Stabilization Board
ESC	Exchange Settlement Certificate
FETCC	Foreign Exchange and Trade Control Commission
GDP	Gross Domestic Product
GNP	Gross National Product
IDC	Industrial Development Commission of ESB
JCRR	(Sino-American) Joint Commission on Rural Reconstruction
KMT	Kuomintang (Chinese Nationalist Party)
LDC	Less Developed Country
PRC	People's Republic of China
ROC	Republic of China
TNC	Transnational Corporation
TPB	Taiwan Production Board

PREFACE

This book is a revised edition of my Ph. D. dissertation which was submitted in the Department of Sociology at Brown University in May 1987. The analysis of the role of the state and the economic transformation process in Taiwan therefore ends with the year of 1986 basically. Since 1987, there have been a number of critical events and dramatic changes happened on the island. The martial law was lifted on July 15, 1987 and the prohibition on forming new political party was accordingly abolished. Since then, more than fifty new parties have been formed in addition to three originally existant parties. President Chiang Ching-kuo died in January 1988. His death ended the ruling pattern with one supreme leader that had dominated Taiwan's politics for nearly fourty years. A trend of democratization, which was initiated by Chiang Ching-kuo, has speeded up and many reform programs were carried out. In contrast to the zigzag road toward democracy in most developing countries, the democratization process in Taiwan has been quite smooth. Indeed, following the miraculous achievement of economic transformation, Taiwan seems to be able to create a miracle of political development. With all of these changes, there have a lot of things to say about the role of the state and its relationship with Taiwanese society. Unfortunately, we are not able to add them into our analysis. While the contents of the dissertation is basically kept intact, we do bring some statistical data up to date to show the present socioeconomic situation in Taiwan.

There are numerous people to whom I am grateful for enabling me to complete the dissertation. I am deeply indebted to the three professors who served on my committee. I would like to thank Peter Evans, Dietrich Russchemeyer, and Ying-mao Kau both for their patience and for their guidance. This dissertation would not have been possible had it not been for their continuous support and immeasurable help. I owe a special thank you to Professor John C. H. Fei of Yale University. He provided me with many insights and much enthusiastic guidance, almost as if he was also on my committee.

During the 1985-86 academic year, while undertaking field research in Taiwan, I approached many individuals and institutions for data and assistance. I am grateful to them all for their courtesy and cooperation and wish to single out the late Wu Mei-ts'un (former vice minister of Economic Affairs); Wang Tso-jung and Sun Chen of National Taiwan University; Tsiang Sho-chieh of the Chung-hua Institute for

Economic Research; Shih Ch'i-p'ing and Yeh Ming-hsien of the Council for Economic Planning and Development; Huang T'ien-mu of the Ministry of Finance; Diane Ying of *T'ien-hsia tsa-chih* (Commonwealth); Huang Chuan-chuan of *Lien-ho-pao* (United News); Ch'en Ch'en-chung of *Chung-kuo shih-pao* (China Times); Liu Feng-wen; Tsu Sung-chiu; and P'eng Huai-en. I am especially indebted to my former teachers: K. T. Li, who allowed me to audit his course on Taiwan's economic development at National Taiwan University, thereby facilitating my access to a number of important official contacts; Ch'in Hsiao-yi, who gave me permission to gain access to minutes of the Central Standing Committee of the Kuomintang; and Yeh Wan-an, who allowed me to make use of the official files of the Council for Economic Planning and Development.

At one stage or another of my research I received valuable comments from Chalmers Johnson, Thomas Gold, Robert Wade, Allen P. L. Liu, Ramon Myers, Richard Barrett, Hsin-huang Michael Hsiao, Shiau Chyuan-jeng, Lee Pi-han, Hsu Cheng-kuang, Chu Yun-han, and Wu Wen-ch'eng. I gratefully acknowledge the advice and suggestions of each and every one.

Finally, I would like to thank the National Youth Commission and the Institute of Ethnology at Academic Sinica of the Republic of China for supporting my field research in Taiwan.

September 1991   Chien-kuo Pang

CHAPTER 1

THEORY AND METHODS

Introduction

This dissertation purports to show that the *state-centric* approach emphasizing the autonomous and active characteristics of the state and the process of state building, is an analytical cornerstone for examining the socioeconomic development of Taiwan since the retreat of the Kuomintang (KMT, the Chinese Nationalist Party) state from Mainland China in 1949.

During the 1978-79 academic year, while a student at the Graduate Institute of San Min Chu I* of National Taiwan University, I took a course given by K. T. Li (Li Kwoh-ting, a leading architect of Taiwan's economic transformation), entitled "Modern Economic Development and Economic Policy: The Implementation of the *Min-sheng* Principle in Taiwan." The course covered a variety of state policies concerning different aspects of Taiwan's economic development since 1949, such as agricultural policy, industrial policy, fiscal policy, monetary policy, foreign trade policy, energy price policy, the management of state enterprises, and the evolution of the mechanism for economic planning, etc. More than a dozen government officials and scholars who had participated in the policy-making process, were invited to discuss the formulation and execution of corresponding policies. After each speaker had finished the lecture, K. T. Li would make a brief comment, adding more information as to the background and operational actualities of the decision-making.

I learned a lot about the economic policy-making of the KMT state from the course. For example, I got the idea that economic stability was an overriding objective in the KMT state's economic policy decisions. Economic officials payed a good deal of attention to the control of inflation, even at the expense of economic growth. I also got the idea that the character of Taiwan's economy had undergone a dramatic change in the late fifties and early sixties. A series of reforms during this period switched the KMT state's development strategy from import-substitution industrialization to export-led industrialization and

---

* San Min Chu I (the Three Principles of the People, or Sun Yat-senism) are the political doctrines of Sun Yat-sen, founding father of the Republic of China. The three principles are the *Min-tsu* Principle (the Principle of Nationalism), the *Min-ch'uan* Principle (the Principle of Democracy), and the *Min-sheng* Principle (the Principle of People's Livelihood).

prepared the ground for Taiwan's economic takeoff. Moreover, I recognized that economic policy-making is not simply a matter of economic rationality; economic policy decisions made by the KMT state were compounded by political considerations and personnel factors. This course aroused my interest in studying Taiwan's economic development and especially the role of the KMT state in this process.

However, the course also left me with a number of unanswered questions. Knowing that Taiwan has enjoyed one of the highest sustained growth rates in the world and shown outstanding records in income distribution as well as economic stability since 1949, I wondered what were the key factors determining Taiwan's exceptional success. In my attempt to figure out the "correctness" of the KMT state's policies for economic development, I could answer neither the question as to "Why the KMT state was able to adopt and implement this particular set of policies when so many other developing states have been unable to do so," nor "Why the KMT state that seemed so incapable of promoting economic development on the mainland proved so effective on Taiwan?" Above all, I lacked a theoretical framework to organize my knowledge about Taiwan's economic transformation and the role of the KMT state in a systematic manner. These problems had bothered me for some time and had made me hesitant to research further into this subject.

Fortunately, the predicament was resolved via my graduate study in the sociology of development at Brown University. In taking the course "The State as Institution and Social Actor" instructed by Professor Peter Evans, and reading such literature as *Bringing the State Back In* (Evans, Rueschemeyer, and Skocpol, 1985), I learned of a newly emerging discipline in the social sciences–the *state-centric* approach. Appreciating its distinctive method of examining the nature of the state and public policy-making, I believed that I had found a very fruitful analytical tool to unravel those unanswered questions in Taiwan's story. Therefore, with the encouragement of Professors Peter Evans, Dietrich Rueschemeyer, and Ying-mao Kau, I decided to further my study of Taiwan's socioeconomic development through the eyes of this perspective. This dissertation is an initial result of this effort.

There are eight chapters to this dissertation. Chapter I deals with theoretical and methodological issues. It reviews the previous literature on Taiwan's postwar development, introduces the state-centric approach, establishes the analytical framework for the dissertation, and discusses research methods and data sources. Chapter II presents an overview of Taiwan's economic achievement, shows the pivotal role of the KMT state in Taiwan's economic transformation, and depicts the overall structure of the KMT state and the formation of Taiwanese society.

Chapter III and IV describe the organization and personnel involved in the KMT state's economic policy-making process. Chapter III talks about the constitutional structure of economic policy-making by following the formal organizational flow chart of the KMT state. Three major organizations–the economic bureaucracy, the Executive Yuan Council, and the Central Standing Committee of the KMT–are examined. The deficiency of the constitutional structure in explaining the KMT state's economic policy-making leads to the analysis of chapter IV. An operational structure demonstrating the actualities of the KMT state's economic policy-making more vividly is plotted in this chapter. Seven related groups–the top political leadership, the economic policymakers, the economic bureaucrats, the consulting economists, the American advisors, the local capitalists, and the transnational capitalists–are discussed.

Chapters V to VII review the formulation and execution of economic policy from 1949 to 1987. The entire course is broken down into three phases: the period before the late 1950s, the 1958-61 period, and the period after the early 1960s. The period spanning 1958-61 is given a more detailed discussion. The essence of Taiwan's economic transformation during this period was the result of a switch of development strategy from import-substitution industrialization to export-led industrialization. A series of reform programs were carried out during this critical period. These programs dramatically reshaped the character of Taiwan's economy from a relatively closed system to a highly open system and laid down the tracks for Taiwan's subsequent development. Because of this, they deserve attention. Chapter VII also illustrates the changing role of the KMT state amid Taiwan's economic transformation in recent years.

Finally, the concluding chapter summarizes and synthesizes the major findings and arguments of this dissertation. By examining the internal structure of the KMT state, the cultural and structural features of Taiwanese society, the wider international political-economic environment, the interactions among all these components, and their influence on the formulation and execution of the KMT state's economic policy, this dissertation reveals that the KMT state's success in regulating Taiwan's economic transformation is primarily attributable to: (1) the internal coherence of the KMT state apparatus; (2) the high degree of autonomy from Taiwanese society enjoyed by the KMT state;

and (3) favorable international economic and geo-political circumstances pertaining to the earlier period of Taiwan's postwar development. A crucial lesson from Taiwan's developmental experience is that to promote economic development effectively, we need a state which is autonomous and capable enough to carry out transformative policy.

Literature Review and Its Implications for the Present Research

The importance of the state in the process of economic transformation has long been recognized (Polanyi, 1944). As Rueschemeyer and Evans (1985: 44-46) point out, effective state intervention is now assumed to be an integral part of successful economic development even in a capitalist context, though the scholars of different schools may have different views on the role that the state should play and the way that the state should act. A number of theoretical arguments as to why state intervention should be necessary for capitalist economic transformation, summarized by Rueschemeyer and Evans, are worth reiterating briefly here.

It has been argued that economic transformation involves the institutionalization of market exchange which requires a set of normative underpinnings in order to reduce "transaction costs" and allocate resources effectively, and that the state is crucial in offering effective guarantees to these normative underpinnings (North, 1979). At the same time, as Olson (1977: 2) observes, "unless the number of individuals in a group is quite small, or unless there is coercion or some other special device to make individuals act in their common interest, rational, self-interested individuals will not act to achieve their common or group interests." Thus, if there is no institutionalized mechanism such as the state to impose a less atomized rationality, it is likely that collective goods will not be adequately provided, and external diseconomies will not be effectively controlled.

The state is also necessary for breaking through economic monopoly and promoting capital accumulation. In advanced capitalist economies, if the predominant economic actors are comfortable oligopolists and if "market signals" to promote capital accumulation are distorted, the state must intervene to interject entrepreneurship (Holland, 1972). In Third World countries, when the dominant class is a group of agrarian elites who have no structured interest in the transformation of the means of production or a group of industrial elites who are monopoly-seeking security maximizers rather than risk-taking profit maximizers, we need the state to serve as an additional agent of capital accumulation (Skocpol, 1979; Hirschman, 1958). Thus, for those late-comers in economic development, Gerschenkron (1979) discovers the "advantages of economic backwardness." He urges the states in backward countries to introduce the most technologically advanced and large-scale capital-intensive industries in order to leap ahead. Rosenstein-Rodan (1943) develops the idea of the "big push." He advocates that the states in backward countries should bring in required investment in social overheads, primarily the required non-tradable capital-intensive inputs common to all industrial production, such as power and transport. And Hirschman (1958) calls for state intervention to stimulate "unbalanced growth" by introducing key projects that would in turn generate forward and backward linkages throughout the economy.

The importance of the role of the state is particularly striking in the Third World, when we take the evolution of the world capitalist system or the situation of dependency into account. For most LDCs in the postwar era, national development encounters not only the constrains of the internal structure but also the impacts of the external environment (Frank, 1967; Cardoso and Faletto, 1979; Wallerstein, 1979). Given the economic weakness of the national bourgeoisie, the state in the LDC is likely to play a leading role in economic development. On the one hand, the state has to protect the local economy from excessive penetration by foreign capital and encourage local capital accumulation through certain kinds of incentives. On the other hand, it must be able to extract resources from society and deploy this surplus to control the local population in order to attract foreign capital as well as introduce its nation into a niche in the world economy. In certain situations, the state itself may become the primary agent of capital accumulation (Evans, 1979 and 1981; O'Donnell, 1973; Fitzgerald, 1976; Becker, 1983).

Moreover, if wealth distribution rather than accumulation is at issue, the necessity for state intervention is even more clear-cut. Given the empirically unavoidable assumption that market exchange is instituted under conditions of preexisting inequality, there are good reasons to expect the unequal situation to worsen in the absence of some allocational criteria and mechanisms that channel and counteract market forces, not to mention the Marxist predictions of proletarianization and immiseration in the unfettered market. Given actually existing market structures and the historical conditions under which they have arisen, even those who would argue that competitive markets arising in conditions of relative equality might produce equitable distributional results will have to recognize the function of state intervention for distributional goals (Rueschemeyer and Evans, 1985: 46).

In sum, for both the advanced industrial societies and the less developed countries, state policy is assumed to affect the forms and the rate of capital accumulation and to play a major role in determining wealth distribution. In the Third World, where the pressure of accelerating economic development is much stronger but the market mechanism is much weaker than in advanced capitalist countries, the necessity of state intervention becomes even less questionable.

Taiwan's economic system has been identified as a market economy guided by state planning, that is, a mixed economy (Sun, 1981; Li, 1985: 193). In the system, the importance of the role of the state in regulating the economy is undeniable. As a matter of fact, almost all of the previous analyses of Taiwan's economic transformation agree that the KMT state plays a significant role in promoting the economic development on the island. However, there is a disagreement on the nature of this role and the factors that influence the state's ability to act. We can roughly classify these studies into two broad categories: the *economic* perspective and the *sociological* or *political-economy* perspective.

With a few exceptions (Wang, 1978), most scholars adopting the first perspective are neoclassical economists or lean toward neoclassical school (Lin, 1973; Ho, 1978; Fei, Ranis, and Kuo, 1979; Galenson, 1979; Li and Yu, 1983; Tsiang, 1985; Myers, 1986). For these scholars, the major function of the state is to create the external economies necessary for economic growth. This includes accumulating capital which is assumed to be in short supply, building physical and social infrastructures, restricting luxurious consumption, and controlling the population growth. Some plans or strategies may be necessary for regulating economic transformation, but they should not play as important a role as the planning taking place in the socialist world. Basically, economic planning must not violate the operation of the market mechanism, and the role of the state should be auxiliary rather than dominant.

Accordingly, these scholars do not deny that the state has contributed substantially to Taiwan's development; however, they believe that the success of the KMT state is mainly due to its observance of the rules of neoclassical economics. Industrialization proceeds vigorously not because of the state's active involvement in the sector, but because of its progressive withdrawal from intervention to widen the room for the operation of market forces. The favorable performance of Taiwan in income distribution is largely attributed to the indirect effects of a growth-promoting policy, which follows the rule of comparative advantage, rather than to the direct state intervention through tax and relief measures. Taiwan enjoys relative stability in the process of economic transformation because the state cautiously avoids budget deficit and excessive money supply. In a sense, these arguments correctly portray a part of the picture of Taiwan's economic transformation, though sometimes the significance of the KMT state as an active actor is underestimated.

A more serious problem with this perspective is that it usually avoids the issue of the state's relationship to society and how that influences the form of the state's actions and its capacities to implement them. Consequently, although those economists can plausibly pinpoint the rationality of the policies carried out by the state on Taiwan, they cannot tell us why the KMT state was able to adopt correctly these policies while some other states in developing countries were not able to do so. Similarly, although some development strategies were adopted both by Taiwan and by some other LDCs, such as land reform, encouragement of investment, and export expansion, they cannot explain why the state on Taiwan was able to implement them more effectively than the other states.

It is due to these problems that we turn to the second perspective. In contrast to the economic perspective, there are a handful of scholars who stress the role of the state in regulating Taiwan's development (Amsden, 1979 and 1985; Gold, 1981 and 1986; Barrett, 1980 and 1983; Wade, 1984, 1985a and 1985b). While Amsden acknowledges that state intervention in Taiwan does not take the form of heavy protection and price distortion to facilitate industrialization as has taken place in many other Third World countries, she contends that "both in the past and at present, the state in Taiwan has acted as a key agent in the process of capital accumulation: not because it has kept aloof from it, but because it has very much dominated it" (Amsden, 1979: 342). Applying the triple alliance model of Brazilian dependent development proposed by Peter Evans and the concept of autonomous state to Taiwan's development, Gold asserts that the triple alliance model must be modified for the Taiwan case. While the triple alliance in Brazil is characterized by the dominant role of the multinationals and the weak position of the state *vis-a-vis* the local bourgeoisie and the demands of multinationals, the state in Taiwan plays the dominant role among the three. Barrett, on the one hand, accepts the argument of the neoclassical economists that Taiwan's development since 1960 has been primarily capitalist in nature and that the degree of direct state control of industrial development is surprisingly low; on the other hand, he emphasizes that there is a strong state on Taiwan which is highly autonomous from the local bourgeoisis and foreign capitalists in making economic policy. Wade points out that the state actually behaves in a much more aggressive way than free trading principles would justify. "It has been *anticipating,* rather than simply reacting to, changes in Taiwan's international competitive position. And it has been *selecting* between industries and specific products in giving substantial incentives" (Wade, 1984: 65).

Focusing on the role of the state and its relationship to the surrounding social environment both at the intra-national and international levels, the sociological or political-economic perspective seems more capable of explaining why the development of Taiwan and other LDCs took place at different rates and in different forms. It is also likely to give more valid reasons to explain why the state in Taiwan was more effective than the states in other Third World countries in carrying out state intervention. However, this does not imply that the existing works taking this perspective have fully explored the factors or perfectly developed the conceptual framework that can account for Taiwan's development.

One common shortcoming among the works within this second perspective is that they never accord enough analysis to the organization of the state apparatus. While they stress that the state's relationship to society influences the form of state intervention and the capacities of the state to implement it, they never unravel deeply enough how the internal structure and the composition of personnel in the state apparatus on Taiwan shape state policies and influence the state's capacity to undertake such intervention. Although in his new work Gold (1986) has touched on this issue and presented an excellent exposition of how the KMT state manages Taiwan's economic growth and political stability, his discussion on the KMT state's internal structuring remains unsatisfying. We still need to know more about the internal structuring of the KMT state and its relations with the external environment as well as their influence on economic policy-making.

Our concern with the state apparatus and its relationship to society is further justified by the fact that the Taiwan case does not correspond to the arguments underlying two major models of the role of the state in the Third World, namely, those of *state capitalism* and *bureaucratic-authoritarianism* (Canak, 1981; O'Donnell, 1973 and 1978; Dupuy and Truchil, 1979). While both of these theories attempt to link state structure and state policy to a crisis resulting from the exhaustion of an import substitution model of industrialization, the experience of Taiwan has been a smooth policy transition from import substitution to export expansion. In contrast to these two perspectives, which share a focus on the importance of foreign capital as a determinant in shaping the process of economic growth and industrialization, foreign capital has played only a supporting role in Taiwan's development. Although both theories characterize the national bourgeoise as relatively weak and link the expansion of the state to this weakness, Taiwan has experienced a vigorous development of the private sector accompanied by a progressive withdrawal of the state.

In O'Donnell's bureaucratic-authoritarian model, the upsurge of the bureaucratic-authoritarian state is a response to the failure of the representative government to preserve a stable domination in the face of increasing popular mobilization. In order to attract the international capital necessary to increase the vertical integration of industrial structure, the techno-bureaucracy must not only repress the popular sectors but also the national bourgeosie. This is obviously not the case in Taiwan. With widespread improvement in the standard of living and successful inclusionary policies, the relationship between political development toward democracy and economic transformation in Taiwan is relatively positive and steady, or at least, not inverse (Gold, 1981: 306; and 1986: 121; Wei, 1976; Copper, 1984). Indeed, when O'Donnell (1978: 30) suggests that certain of the bureuacratic-authoritarian features should appear in some developing countries in Asia, such as South Korea, Indonesia, and the Phillipines, intentionally or unintentionally, he never mentions Taiwan.

The fact that the Taiwan case is in these different ways at odds with the major theories concerning the role of the state in LDCs suggests that a re-examination of the role of the KMT state in Taiwan's socioeconomic development is necessary to grasp the dynamics underlying Taiwan's success. At the same time, the merits and shortcomings of previous studies tell us that to account for the success on Taiwan, we have to answer the following question: what organizational features of the KMT state apparatus and its relations to the surrounding social structure are responsible for the effective intervention that contributed to Taiwan's socioeconomic transformation? Based on this understanding, we discover that the newly emerged state-centric approach is a very fruitful analytical instrument for our study. A conceptual framework derived from the state-centric approach will help us to figure out: Why did the development of Taiwan and other LDCs occur at different rates and in different forms? Why was the transformation on Taiwan not replicated in other Third World countries? Why was the state on Taiwan able to exercise its intervention more effectively than the states in other developing countries? And what features of the organization of the state apparatus and of its relationship to the surrounding social structure were responsible for such effective interventions?

A Conceptual Framework Derived from the State-centric Approach

During the last decades, an upsurge of interest in *the state* has occurred in the social sciences. The state as an actor or institution has been highlighted by scholars from diverse disciplines. The range of topics varies from the role of states in developing countries to that in advanced industrial societies; from the impact of the state on class formation to that on ethnic relations, women's rights, and modes of social protests; and from the function of the state in economic planning to that in political development as well as in foreign policy-making. Some scholars believe that to explain a variety of social phenomena better, especially public policy-making and social change, we need to "bring the state back in" to its proper central place in analysis (Evans, Rueschemeyer and Skocpol, 1985; Skocpol, 1979; Krasner, 1978; Stepan, 1978). We adopt this perspective, a *state-centric* approach, for the present study.

The state-centric approach is a paradigmatic reorientation of social science research *vis-a-vis* the previous society-centered ways, namely, the *pluralist* approach and the *Marxist* approach, of explaining governmental activities and societal transformation. During the 1950s and 1960s, political science and sociology in the United States were dominated by the pluralist approach. This approach has for its main normative, empirical, and methodological concern the study of individuals who, pursuing their individual economic and political interests, together make up society. Individuals may form into groups, but because they all have a variety of interests, they tend to associate themselves with numerous and different groups whose interests crosscut. A methodological and normative assumption in the approach is that it is undesirable to use the concept of the general good. Instead, individual utility for the constituent members of society is most nearly achieved when individuals are allowed to pursue freely their own economic and political interests (Stepan, 1978: 7). Accordingly, the state is viewed primarily as an arena within which interest groups contend or ally with one another to shape the making of public policy decisions. Those decisions are understood to be allocations of benefits among demanding groups. Research centers on the societal "inputs" to the state and on the distributive effects of "outputs" by the state (Truman, 1951; Easton, 1957; Almond, 1965). The state itself is not taken seriously as an independent actor or active agent (Skocpol, 1985: 4).

The pluralist approach, as a description of the real world, suffers from some obvious limitations. When pluralists examine the determinants of particular public policy decisions, they often find that state managers took initiatives well beyond the demands of the people or electorate and that government agencies rather than social groups are the most prominent participants in the decisions concerning policy-making (Skocpol, 1985: 4). The state in fact plays a pivotal role in setting the agenda and granting access to interest groups and therefore becomes instrumental shaping the input process (Stepan, 1978: 17). Even in fairly democratic polities, state officials can still determine public policy autonomously (Nordlinger, 1981). In addition, if the study of social change, especially national development in the Third World, is at issue, pluralists often discover that concrete international and domestic struggles over state building and autonomous actions by state elites are actually the key factors in shaping societal transformation (LaPalombara, 1963; Binder et al., 1971).

In contrast to the pluralist approach, as Krasner (1984: 224-225) observes, the state-centric approach has the following five characteristics. First, the state-centric approach sees politics more as a problem of rule and control than as one of allocation. It is more concerned with preserving order against internal and external threats than with the allocation of benefits among political actors. Second, the state-centric approach stresses that the state can be treated as a factor in its own right as either an exogenous or an intervening variable. The state cannot be understood as just a reflection of societal characteristics or preferences. Third, the state-centric approach places greater emphasis on institutional constraints, both formal and informal, on individual behavior. Bureaucratic apparatus and legal order can limit, even determine, people's conceptions of their own interest and their political resources. The political outcome cannot be adequately understood as simply the resolution of a vector of forces emanating from a variety of different interest groups. Fourth, the state-centric approach pays more attention to the historical aspect of social phenomena and of state building. It demands researchers that they understand both how institutions reproduce themselves through time and what historical conditions gave rise to them in the first place, since current institutional structures may be a product of some peculiar historical conjuncture rather than of contemporaneous factors, and any historical choice may preclude or facilitate alternative future choices. And fifth, the state-centric approach is more inclined to see disjunctures and stress within any given political system. Political life is characterized not simply by a struggle over the allocation of resources but also periodically by strife and uncertainty about the rules of the game within which this allocative process is carried out.

Another approach is that of the neo-Marxist scholars who, since the mid-sixties have launched a series of debates about "the capitalist state." There are different understandings of the socioeconomic functions performed by the capitalist state among these neo-Marxists. We can roughly classify them into three theses: the *instrumentalism,* the *structuralism,* and the *class struggle* thesis (Gold, Lo and Wright, 1975; Jessop, 1977; Hamilton, 1982: 8-13; Carnoy, 1984; Skocpol, 1985: 5). The "instrumentalism" sees the state in capitalist society as an instrument of dominant class. It assumes that the capitalist state is manipulated by the dominant class through a variety of direct or indirect means, such as recruitment into positions in the state apparatus, membership in advisory committees, campaign financing, lobbying, special relations with congressional and regulatory bodies, and control of the media or the educational system (Domhoff, 1967; Miliband, 1969). The "structuralism" thesis considers the capitalist state as an objective guarantor of production relations or economic accumulation. For the "structuralists," the state is constrained by its position within a given social formation and granted a certain degree of autonomy from the dominant class and society in order to preserve or reproduce that social formation, including the given dominant class structure. In a capitalist society, the state accordingly becomes a guarantor for the capitalist mode of production and the related class structure (Althusser, 1969; Althusser and Balibar, 1970; Poulantzas, 1969 and 1973). The "class struggle" thesis sees the capitalist state as an arena for political class struggle. This thesis argues that in order to cope with general capitalist crises and the expansion of socialism, the capitalist state has to intervene increasingly in the economy as a relatively autonomous mediator of the class struggle inherent in the capitalist accumulation process to main tain the dynamics of capitalist development. Contradictions arising from the various mediating roles of the state itself make the state the principal arena of crisis and the place where the crisis is resolved or exacerbated (Offe, 1973 and 1974; Poulantzas, 1978).

Valuable concepts and questions have emerged from these neo-Marxist debates, such as the concept of the "relative autonomy" of the state. The concept grants the state some possibility to play a role as an independent and active actor. However, at the theoretical level, as Skocpol (1985: 5) argues, all neo-Marxists on the state virtually retain society-centered assumptions. They still keep the basic viewpoint that states are inherently shaped by classes or class struggles and function to preserve and expand modes of production. Many possible forms of autonomous state action are thus ruled out by definitional fiat. "Furthermore, neo-Marxist theorists have too often sought to generalize-often in extremely abstract ways-about features or functions shared by *all* states within a mode of production, a phase of capitalist accumulation, or a position in the world capitalist system. This makes it difficult to assign causal weight to variations in state structures and activities across nations and short time periods, thereby undercutting the usefulness of some neo-Marxist schemes for comparative research" (Skocpol, 1985: 5).

In contrast to the Marxist approach, the state-centric approach assumes that the state can be treated as a relatively independent actor pursuing its own distinctive goals that do not necessary reflect the interests generated from the society (Krasner, 1978; Stepan, 1978; Trimberger, 1978; Skocpol, 1985). The approach challenges the neo-Marxists' conceptualizations of state autonomy by contending that the states may be *conditioned* by socioeconomic structures but are not *shaped* by them. In many cases, political elites might play a predominant role in the "revolution from above." The state, under certain circumstances, could transcend structural boundaries of society to act for the ends opposed to the interests of the dominant class and transform the social structure. In other words, contrasting to both the pluralist and Marxist approaches, the state-centric approach believes that the state is not necessarily a passive recipient of societal pressure though it may have special relations with certain social groups. State policy at any time and place can be considered more or less independent action by the individuals or groups occupying strategic positions in the state apparatus though it may be a response to certain social demands.

Based on these recognitions, we construct a conceptual framework for examining Taiwan's economic transformation as follows. The working definition of the state in this dissertation, following the argument of Rueschemeyer and Evans, is essentially a Weberian one (Weber, 1946). The state is defined as "a set of organizations invested with the authority to make binding decisions for people and organizations juridically located in a particular territory and to implement these decisions using, if necessary, force" (Rueschemeyer and Evans, 1982: 5). It is a continuous administrative, legal, bureaucratic, and coercive system that attempts "not only to structure relations *between* civil society and public authority in a policy but also to structure many crucial relationships *within* civil society as well" (Stepan, 1978: xil).

According to this definition, Rueschemeyer and Evans (1985: 47-48) distinguish four characteristics of the state. In the first place, the state many be an instrument of domination. The overall "pact of domination" is determined by the interrelations between the various parts of the state apparatus, on the one hand, and the most powerful classes or class fractions, on the other. Second, the state may act as a corporate actor. Coherent state action will be a concern of state elites. To mobilize outside support for such an action, state elites may conflict even with dominant interests. Third, the state may be an arena of social conflict. Each state is composed of various departments and many individuals. Despite their interest in unified action, state managers are likely to be divided on substantive goals; they may have different interests, uphold different ideologies, and represent different social forces. In addition, various social groups, both dominant and subordinate, will try to use the state as a means of realizing their particular interests. Therefore, unless social domination is monolithic, state apparatuses in the real life of a society will inevitably becomes arenas of social conflict. And, finally, the state may act somehow as the guardian of the universal interests of the society over which it has jurisdiction. The state's claim of pursuing the "common good" should not be simply dismissed as rhetoric; it actually constitutes a nearly universal role by which the state can obtain hegemonic acceptance, and attract commitments of different strength from state managers as we as from outside groups.

Therefore, while our definition of the state is cast in formal terms of authority and enforcement, we emphasize that "the state *tends* to be an expression of pacts of domination, to act coherently as a corporate unit, to become an arena of social conflict, and to present itself as the guardian of universal interests" (Rueschemeyer and Evans, 1985: 48). Clearly, these tendencies stand in contradiction to each other and cannot be enacted all at once. Our preoccupation with effective intervention of the KMT state in regulating Taiwan's economic transformation naturally focuses attention on the state as a corporate actor. The underlying point is that the efficacy of the state will always depend on the pattern in which these contradictory tendencies are combined, both in its internal structure and in its relation to the social structure as a whole. Applying this premise to the Taiwan case, we thus focus on the following question: what organizational features of the state apparatus and its relation to the surrounding social structure are responsible for the effective intervention we are discussing?

According, our analysis of the conditions underlying the effective intervention by the KMT state on Taiwan can be divided into two major issues. The first focuses on the structuring of the state apparatus itself; the second focuses on the state relationship to society, in particular to the dominant class or social forces. Since there have already been some studies dealing with the issue of the state's relationship to society in the process of Taiwan's development (Amsden, 1979 and 1985; Barrett, 1980 and 1983; Chen, 1981; Gold, 1981 and 1986; Hsiao, 1981; Winckler, 1980a and 1980b), our discussion will pay more attention to the first issue. Moreover, a wider world political-economic context has to be brought in. This is not only because of the fact that, as we have mentioned, Taiwan's development benefited from U.S. aid and a favorable timing in the world economy, but also because, as we will find out, a particular international geo-political context under the hegemony of the United States is a crucial factor to explain the KMT state's development strategy and the very different consequences of Taiwan's dependent development from Latin America's (Cumings, 1984; Evans, 1984: 9-11; Hsiao, 1985b: 6-8).

Thus, if we use the model of systems analysis for policy-making to help us illustrate our argument, the conceptual framework for the present study will be like figure 1.1. In the diagram, the state apparatus is composed of various departments filled with different individuals. It is surrounded by the civil society and the international political-economic system. The factors that may influence policy-making will include the organizational features and personnel composition of the state apparatus, the stratified structure of society, the international economic or geo-political situation, and the interactions among them. An analytic framework linking these components together may help us to understand the socio-political aspect of Taiwan's success, which "was a product of the interaction of a number of forces–economic, political, and social; endogenous and exogenous; constructive and destructive; fortuitous and planned; ideological and pragmatic" (Gold,

16   *THE STATE AND ECONOMIC TRANSFORMATION*

Figure 1.1

The Conceptual Framework

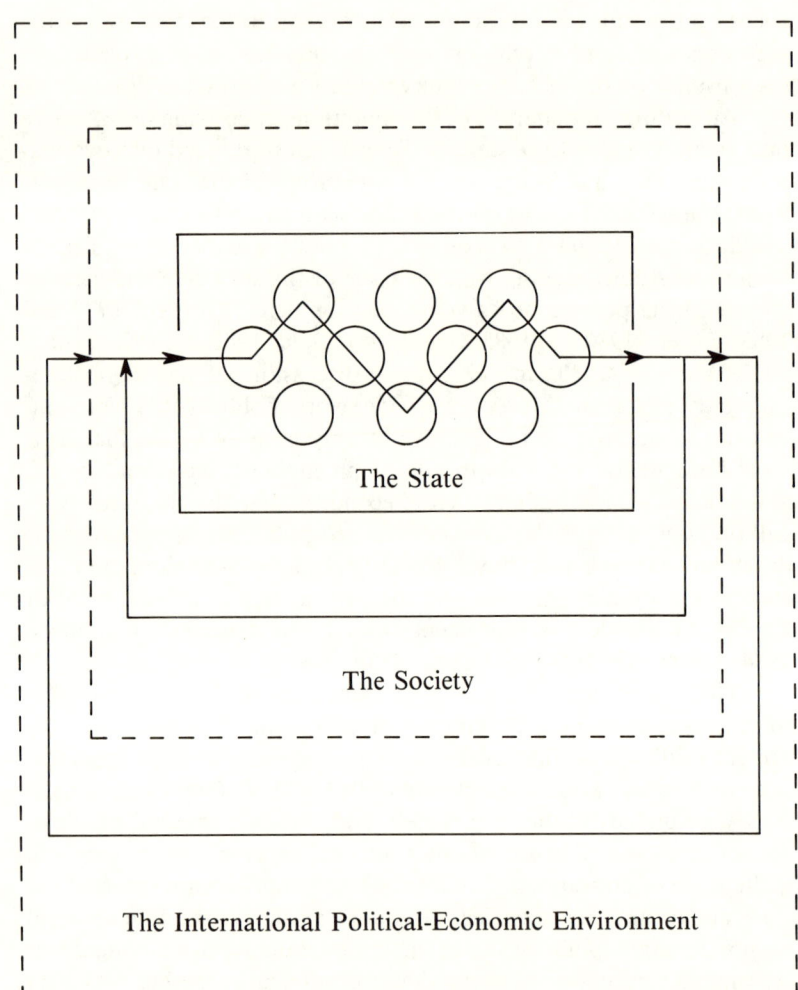

1986: 11).

The two basic concepts of the state-centric approach, namely, *state autonomy* and *state capacities* will always be kept in mind when we proceed with our analysis. To put it simply, the concept of *state autonomy* means that the state may formulate and pursue goals that are not merely reflective of the demands or interests of social groups, classes, or society. The concept of *state capacities* refers to the possibility of the state to implement official goals, especially against the actual or potential opposition of powerful social groups or in the face of recalcitrant socioeconomic circumstances (Skocpol, 1985: 9). We realize that for any state to make effective intervention, a certain extent of *state capacities* and a certain degree of *state autonomy* should be satisfied. Therefore, we will try to figure out the dynamics underlying Taiwan's economic transformation by examining the structures and evolutions of the KMT state, the Taiwanese society, the international environment, and the linkages among them in terms of the concepts of *state autonomy* and *state capacities*.

Research Methods

In a methodological sense, the approach of this dissertation will be both *historical-structural* and *voluntarist*. As far as the historical-structural approach is concerned, we accept Cardoso and Faletto's assertion. In their influential work, *Dependency and Development in Latin America* (1979), Cardoso and Faletto formulate a "historical-structural" perspective to offer what they call a "comprehensive analysis of development." They maintain that social structures are the product of man's collective behavior. Thus, to understand social change, we should emphasize not only the structural conditioning of social life, but also the historical transformation of structures in terms of various human collective behaviors, such as social conflicts, social movements, and class struggles (Cardoso and Faletto, 1979: x). By focusing on historical moments of significant structural change, we can determine how economic relationships and the social structure that underlies them arise as a result of human activity, and how they can be transformed through social action. Cardoso and Faletto do not predict necessary outcomes in their study; they analyze facts and suggest possible alternative lines of development. Their analysis is comprehensive because it examines the continuous interaction among economic, social, political, and ideological variables, at both intra-national and international levels (Gold, 1986: 15). Our study will follow this perspective.

As far as the voluntarist approach is concerned, we do not approve of a "nonvoluntarist, structural" perspective, such as Skocpol puts forth in her exemplary work, *States and Social Revolutions in France, Russia and China* (1979). We believe that human thought and action are the mediating link between structural conditions and social outcomes. To determine the role of the state in economic transformation, we argue that while structural conditions may define the options available to state elites, the decision of what strategies or policies should be adopted in pursuit of development still rests with the state elites. In fact, as we will find out later, in the Taiwan case, where a rather autonomous and capable state dominated its socioeconomic transformation, the ideas of the state managers and their assessments of developmental situation cannot be dismissed.

As to research methods, unobtrusive research and survey research are our main techniques. In addition to integrating written materials into the analytical framework, quite a part of the data and explanations in the dissertation are collected from interviews. To provide a relatively complete picture and present a more balanced explanation to the issues that we are concerned with, we tried to interview as many relevant persons as we could and tried to check and balance the different or opposite viewpoints. Moreover, we construct a number of organizational charts, tables showing the composition and evolution of personnel, as well as statistical tables to help us illustrate facts and search for reasonable explanations.

Data Sources

The sources of data for this dissertation can be listed under five categories: (1) previous literature, (2) official files, (3) minutes, (4) newspapers and magazines, and (5) interviews.

Previous literature. There have already been some writings about policy-making, organizations, and personnel relating to Taiwan's economic transformation. For example, Neil Jacoby's *U.S. Aid to Taiwan* (1966) offers us a detailed exposition of the organizations and utilization of U.S. aid in Taiwan's economic development, K. T. Li's various writings provide a lot of first-hand information about the organizations, personnel, and policy formulation concerning the KMT state's developmental strategies (Li, 1984; Li and Ch'en, 1984a and 1984b). Wang Tso-jung's work presents a somewhat different view from the official stance on Taiwan's economic policy-making (Wang, 1978). Alan Liu's study gives us an analysis of the thinking and doing of the KMT's economic policy makers in depth (Liu, 1986). And the biography of K. Y. Yin, written by Shen Yun-lung (1972), helps us trace back Taiwan's economic development policies in the 1950s and early 1960s. Moreover, a number of books dealing with the backgrounds of the KMT's leaders and economic policy makers as well as the internal structuring of the state have been published in recent years. We also found some information in these publications.

Official files. This category consists of government documents, statistical data, and files of economic policy-making and personnel affairs. We obtained the entire file on the formulation of the Nineteen-Point Program of Economic and Financial Reform, which is helpful to understand the switch of the KMT state's developmental strategy in the late 1950s and early 1960s. While we were not able to gain access to the confidential personnel files of state managers, we located the roster of high-ranking officials and their brief curriculum vitaes from the publications of the Government Information Office and the Secretariat of the Central Committee of the Kuomintang, such as the *China Yearbook*. We also had access to the documents of economic planning and statistical data from the Council for Economic Planning and Development.

Minutes. In addition to some minutes included in the file about the formulation of the Nineteen-Point Program, we secured the minutes of the Central Standing Committee (CSC) of the KMT for the period 1957 to 1963. The minutes are useful to figure out the real situation of the rearrangement of state priorities and the switch of economic policy for national development in Taiwan around that period.

Newspapers and Magazines. We gathered some data from four newspapers: *Chung-yang jih-pao* (Central Daily), the KMT's organ; *Chung-kuo shih-pao* (China Times) and *Lien-ho-pao* (United News), the two biggest private newspapers; and China Post, a private English newspaper in Taiwan. The information office of *Lien-he-pao* has a good collection of the reports on Taiwan's economic issues and policy-making after early 1970s. In addition, several magazines reporting on the economic and financial affairs of the island have been published in recent years. Among them, *Tien-hsia tsa-chih* (Commonwealth) is the most prestigious one and has done some excellent reports on the personnel and organizations of economic policy-making.

Interviews. We have interviewed five kinds of respondents. First are the members or ex-members of the CSC and the persons who are not members of the CSC but have the right to attend the CSC's meetings. Five respondents belong to this first category. Next are the economic policy makers and bureaucrats who were in charge of economic planning or important economic policy-making–twelve interviewees are in this category. The third kind of respondents are the economists who were consultants of the state. Six consulting economists have contributed their views. The fourth kind of respondents are journalists who were responsible for covering economic and financial affairs. Five of them were interviewed. The last kind of respondents are those private entrepreneurs who have intimate connections with state officials and might have influence on economic policy-making–three respondents are in this category. There is some overlap between the respondents in the different categories. For example, one of the economic policy makers and one of the private entrepreneurs are concurrently the members of the CSC. And three consulting economists are former economic bureaucrats. Therefore, a total of twenty-six respondents have been interviewed.

CHAPTER 2

AN OVERVIEW OF THE TAIWAN CASE

Why the State on Taiwan Matters

For more than three decades, Taiwan, the Republic of China (ROC), has enjoyed not only one of the highest sustained growth rates experienced by any country, but has also shown outstanding records in income distribution and economic stability compared to most societies. While many developing countries suffer from economic stagnation or distributional polarization, or both, Taiwan has experienced "growth with equity" in her postwar development (Fei, Ranis, and Kuo, 1979; Prybyla, 1979; Myers, 1986). From 1952 to 1990, her GNP growth rates averaged 8.8% and industry grew 12.0% annually. During the same period, the share of industry in employment climbed from 16.9% to 40.9% while the share of agriculture decreased from 56.1% to 12.9%. The share of industrial production in gross domestic product increased from 19.7% to 42.3% whereas the share of agricultural production decreased from 32.2% to 4.2%. The average annual growth rate of its exports was 21.6% and of its imports, 18.9%; this has generated trade surplus nearly every year since 1971 and huge foreign reserves amounting to U.S. $81 billion by 1990. In the meantime, the *Gini* coefficients measuring income inequality decreased from 0.507 in 1953 to 0.260 in 1980, accompanied with an average inflation rate of 6.4% and an average unemployment rate of less than 1.7% from 1953 to 1990 (Kuo, 1983: 96-97; Myers, 1984: 504-505; CEPD, 1989: 2; CEPD, 1991: 2, 16, 41, and 61-62). Tables 2.1 to 2.5 illustrate some of the indicators of Taiwan's accomplishments. This is a spectacular record by any absolute or relative standard. Taiwan is no doubt one of the most successful cases of economic development in the Third World.

Actually Taiwan's success in a certain sense is a challenge to existing development theories. Its achievement of "growth with equity" runs counter to the experience of most contemporary less developed countries (LDCs) and previous findings of conventional Western economics, which maintain an inverse U-shape relation between growth and equity, that is, as income increases from low levels in a developing society, the distribution of income must first worsen before it can improve (Kuznets, 1955; Lewis, 1955; Adelman and Morris, 1973). Moreover, its particular success of "dependent development" (Chen, 1981; Gold, 1981) contradicts of the arguments of dependency theorists (Amsden, 1979; Barrett and Whyte, 1982), who assert that the dependency situation is the main cause of stagnation, inequality, or both in the Third World (Frank, 1967 and 1969; Dos Santos, 1970; Sunkel, 1973; Amin, 1976).

The achievement on the island appears even more remarkable when we take the disadvantageous conditions for her development into account. Taiwan is an island with an area of 13,840 square miles, about the combined size of the states of Connecticut, Massachusetts, and Rhode Island. Because of her mountainous terrain, only one-fourth of the land area is arable and the natural fertility of her farmland is low. The island had a population of 8,128 thousand in 1952 that increased to 20,359 thousand by 1990. While the population and land are too small to constitute a self-sustained market in terms of economic scale, Taiwan has one of the highest population densities in the world. There were 587 persons per square mile in 1952 which had become 1,471 by 1990. In regard to natural resources, Taiwan is poorly endowed. The only important mineral resource is coal, estimated at about 700 million metric tons, but because of the narrowness and the depth of most seams, merely one-third of the reserve is economically recoverable (Ho, 1978: 1, CEPD, 1991: 3-5). These disadvantages are further complicated by an extremely heavy defense burden during the whole process of development, a high inflation during the earlier period, as well as the two oil price crises and diplomatic isolation in recent years. In view of all of these unfavorable conditions, it seems justified to call Taiwan's accomplishments a miracle.

Of course, Taiwan enjoyed some favorable conditions in the process of her economic transformation. Several factors are frequently cited as special advantages that distinguish Taiwan's development from other LDCs, notably, the Japanese legacy, U.S. aid, the international economic cycle, Confucianism, and its size. Indeed, it seems undeniable that all of these factors to a certain extent and in a certain way participated in Taiwan's postwar economic development. However, as we will see in the following few paragraphs, they cannot explain sufficiently Taiwan's successful experience.

The legacy inherited from the Japanese colonial period is often considered a special contribution to Taiwan's success. The Japanese, in their occupation of Taiwan from 1895 to 1945, brought about many significant changes in Taiwanese society. They undertook a variety of projects to develop the physical, institutional, and human infrastructure on the island: improving transportation and irrigation systems; establishing comprehensive public education and health networks, farmers' associations, and rural credit cooperatives; introducing new

Table 2.1
Major Indicators of Taiwan's Economy

Year	Population[a]	Gross National[b] Product	Per Capita[c] GNP
1952	8,128	17,247	81
1953	8,348	22,951	104
1954	8,749	25,200	110
1955	9,078	29,978	126
1956	9,390	34,403	141
1957	9,690	40,118	160
1958	10,039	44,785	173
1959	10,431	51,677	131
1960	10,792	62,480	154
1961	11,149	69,960	152
1962	11,512	77,049	162
1963	11,884	87,139	178
1964	12,257	101,982	203
1965	12,628	112,433	217
1966	12,993	125,925	237
1967	13,297	145,494	267
1968	13,650	169,446	304
1969	14,335	196,598	345
1970	14,676	226,393	389

1971	14,995	263,554	443
1972	15,289	316,240	522
1973	15,565	410,289	695
1974	15,852	549,400	920
1975	16,150	586,307	964
1976	16,508	702,694	1,132
1977	16,813	823,871	1,301
1978	17,136	989,271	1,577
1979	17,479	1,196,238	1,920
1980	17,805	1,488,953	2,344
1981	18,136	1,764,278	2,669
1982	18,458	1,899,289	2,653
1983	18,733	2,103,261	2,823
1984	19,012	2,368,478	3,167
1985	19,258	2,515,049	3,297
1986	19,455	2,925,772	3,993
1987	19,673	3,288,973	5,275
1988	19,904	3,585,294	6,333
1989	20,107	3,968,975	7,512
1990	20,359	4,349,445	7,997

Source: CEPD, 1986: 6, 24, 38, and 202; CEPD, 1991: 4, 26, 29, 40 and 207.
a. 1000 persons.
b. million new Taiwanese dollars at current prices.
c. U.S. dollars at current prices.
d. million U.S. dollars.

Table 2.1 (continued)
Major Indicators of Taiwan's Economy

Year	Agricultural[b] Production	Industrial[b] Production	Exports[d]	Imports[d]
1952	5,558	3,369	116	187
1953	7,903	4,409	128	192
1954	6,940	5,865	93	211
1955	8,720	6,966	123	201
1956	9,446	8,401	118	194
1957	10,977	10,147	148	212
1958	12,035	11,163	156	226
1959	13,657	14,045	157	231
1960	17,838	16,796	164	297
1961	19,225	18,616	195	322
1962	19,269	21,772	218	304
1963	20,286	26,128	332	362
1964	24,989	30,968	433	428
1965	26,611	34,025	450	556
1966	28,379	38,494	536	622
1967	30,057	48,053	641	806
1968	32,308	58,524	789	903
1969	31,276	72,565	1,049	1,213
1970	35,076	83,530	1,481	1,524

1971	34,455	102,680	2,060	1,844
1972	38,619	131,570	2,988	2,514
1973	49,678	179,893	4,483	3,792
1974	68,279	223,609	5,639	6,966
1975	74,875	235,419	5,309	5,952
1976	80,504	305,443	8,166	7,599
1977	87,875	364,393	9,361	8,511
1978	93,033	448,007	12,687	11,027
1979	102,248	542,210	16,103	14,774
1980	114,556	682,114	19,811	19,733
1981	129,487	807,242	22,611	21,200
1982	147,016	843,022	22,204	18,888
1983	153,289	944,691	25,123	20,287
1984	148,351	1,081,913	30,456	21,959
1985	142,999	1,144,824	30,726	20,102
1986	158,224	1,360,196	39,862	24,181
1987	171,234	1,528,714	53,679	34,983
1988	175,624	1,597,457	60,667	49,673
1989	189,567	1,690,913	66,304	52,265
1990	179,168	1,794,429	67,214	54,716

Table 2.2
Indicators of Taiwan's Economy by Growth Rates

Unit: %

Year	Population	Gross National Product	Per Capita GNP	Agricultural Production	Industrial Production	Consumer Prices	Exports	Imports
1953	3.8	9.3	5.9	15.4	25.4	18.8	35.1	8.7
1954	3.7	9.5	5.8	−0.3	5.7	1.7	−26.9	20.0
1955	3.8	8.1	4.2	2.9	13.0	9.9	32.2	−4.8
1956	3.4	5.5	1.8	5.2	3.5	10.6	52.9	52.6
1957	3.2	7.4	4.0	7.9	12.6	7.5	25.4	9.6
1958	3.6	6.7	3.2	7.3	8.4	1.3	5.1	6.6
1959	3.9	7.7	4.3	1.7	11.9	10.6	47.8	50.2
1960	3.5	6.3	3.1	0.6	14.3	18.5	4.5	28.2
1961	3.3	6.9	3.5	7.3	15.7	7.8	30.9	19.4
1962	3.3	7.9	4.7	3.1	8.0	2.4	11.8	-5.6
1963	3.2	9.4	6.2	1.8	9.2	2.2	52.1	19.0
1964	3.1	12.2	9.1	9.5	21.1	−0.2	30.7	18.5
1965	3.0	11.1	7.9	6.6	16.3	−0.1	3.6	29.9
1966	2.9	8.9	6.1	3.6	15.7	2.0	19.3	11.9
1967	2.3	10.7	7.9	7.1	16.7	3.4	19.5	29.5
1968	2.7	9.2	6.6	7.7	22.3	7.9	23.2	12.1
1969	5.0	8.9	6.6	−1.2	19.9	5.1	33.0	34.3
1970	2.4	11.4	9.0	6.9	20.1	3.6	41.2	25.7

1971	2.2	12.9	10.7	2.8	23.6	2.8	39.1	21.0
1972	2.0	13.3	11.3	4.6	21.2	3.0	45.0	36.3
1973	1.8	12.8	10.7	7.0	16.2	8.2	42.8	43.9
1974	1.8	1.2	-0.7	−0.4	−4.5	47.5	25.2	82.9
1975	1.9	4.9	2.5	−1.4	9.5	5.2	−5.7	−14.7
1976	2.2	13.6	11.4	12.7	23.3	2.5	53.8	27.7
1977	1.8	10.2	8.1	5.5	13.3	7.0	14.6	12.0
1978	1.9	13.6	11.9	0.3	22.5	5.8	31.9	26.1
1979	2.0	8.2	6.4	7.9	6.4	9.8	23.6	30.5
1980	1.9	7.3	5.1	1.1	6.8	19.0	22.9	33.5
1981	1.9	6.2	3.8	−1.4	3.5	16.3	16.5	9.4
1982	1.8	3.6	2.2	1.8	−0.9	3.0	4.2	−5.5
1983	1.5	8.4	6.9	4.0	12.7	1.4	16.3	10.6
1984	1.5	10.6	10.0	3.1	11.8	0.0	19.8	7.0
1985	1.3	5.0	4.1	3.1	2.7	−0.2	1.5	−7.9
1986	1.0	11.6	11.3	−0.3	13.9	0.7	23.2	14.4
1987	1.1	12.3	10.7	8.3	10.7	0.5	13.3	21.5
1988	1.2	7.3	6.6	1.5	4.4	1.3	1.4	27.8
1989	1.0	7.3	6.2	−0.2	3.7	4.4	0.9	−2.6
1990	1.3	5.3	4.1	2.2	−1.0	4.1	3.1	6.2

Source: CEPD, 1989: 2; CEPD, 1991: 2.

Table 2.3
Employment by Industries (Percentage)

Year	Primary Industry	Second Industry	Teritary Industry
1952	56.1	16.9	27.0
1953	55.6	17.6	26.8
1954	54.8	17.7	27.5
1955	53.6	18.0	28.4
1956	53.2	18.3	28.5
1957	52.3	19.0	28.7
1958	51.1	19.7	29.2
1959	50.3	20.3	29.4
1960	49.8	20.5	29.3
1961	49.8	20.9	29.3
1962	49.7	21.0	29.3
1963	49.4	21.3	29.3
1964	49.5	21.3	29.2
1965	46.5	22.3	31.2
1966	45.0	22.6	32.4
1967	42.5	24.6	32.9
1968	40.8	25.4	33.8
1969	39.3	26.3	34.4
1970	36.7	28.0	35.3

1971	35.1	29.9	35.0
1972	33.0	31.8	35.2
1973	30.5	33.7	35.8
1974	30.9	34.3	34.8
1975	30.4	34.9	34.7
1976	29.0	36.4	34.6
1977	26.7	37.6	35.7
1978	24.9	39.3	35.8
1979	21.5	41.8	36.7
1980	19.5	42.4	38.1
1981	18.8	42.2	39.0
1982	18.9	41.2	39.9
1983	18.6	41.1	40.3
1984	17.6	42.3	40.1
1985	17.5	41.4	41.1
1986	17.0	41.5	41.5
1987	15.3	42.7	42.0
1988	13.7	42.6	43.7
1989	12.9	42.2	44.9
1990	12.9	40.9	46.3

Source: CEPD, 1989: 16; CEPD, 1991: 16.

Table 2.4
Industrial Origin of Gross Domestic Product (Percentage)

Year	Agriculture	Industries	Services
1952	32.2	19.7	48.1
1953	—	—	—
1954	—	—	—
1955	29.1	23.2	47.7
1956	27.5	24.4	48.1
1957	27.3	25.3	47.4
1958	26.8	24.8	48.4
1959	26.4	27.1	46.6
1960	28.5	26.9	44.6
1961	27.5	26.6	46.0
1962	25.0	28.2	46.8
1963	23.3	30.0	46.8
1964	24.5	30.4	45.1
1965	23.6	30.2	46.2
1966	22.5	30.6	46.9
1967	20.6	33.0	46.4
1968	19.0	34.4	46.5
1969	15.9	36.9	47.3
1970	15.5	36.8	47.7

1971	13.1	38.9	48.0
1972	12.2	41.6	46.2
1973	12.1	43.8	44.1
1974	12.4	40.7	46.9
1975	12.7	39.9	47.4
1976	11.4	43.2	45.5
1977	10.6	44.0	45.4
1978	9.4	45.2	45.4
1979	8.6	45.3	46.1
1980	7.7	45.8	46.6
1981	7.3	45.5	47.2
1982	7.7	44.4	47.9
1983	7.3	45.0	47.7
1984	6.3	46.2	47.5
1985	5.8	46.3	47.9
1986	5.5	47.6	46.8
1987	5.3	47.4	47.3
1988	5.0	45.7	49.3
1989	4.9	43.6	51.5
1990	4.2	42.3	53.5

Source: CEPD, 1991: 41.

Table 2.5
Income Distribution of Taiwan Area
(by Households)

Year	Lowest[a] Fifth	Second Fifth	Third Fifth	Fourth Fifth	Highest Fifth	Ratio[b]	Gini Coefficient
1953	3.0	8.3	9.1	18.2	61.4	20.47	0.558
1959	5.7	9.7	13.9	19.7	51.0	8.95	0.440
1961	4.5	9.7	14.0	19.8	52.0	11.56	0.461
1964	7.7	12.6	16.6	22.0	41.4	5.34	0.321
1966	7.9	12.4	16.2	22.0	41.5	5.25	0.323
1968	7.8	12.2	16.3	22.3	41.4	5.31	0.326
1970	8.4	13.3	17.1	22.5	38.7	4.61	0.294
1972	8.6	13.2	17.1	22.5	38.6	4.49	0.291
1974	8.8	13.5	17.0	22.1	38.6	4.39	0.287
1976	8.9	13.6	17.5	22.7	37.3	4.19	0.280
1978	8.9	13.7	17.5	22.7	37.2	4.18	0.287
1980	8.8	13.9	17.7	22.8	36.8	4.18	0.277
1981	8.8	13.8	17.6	22.8	37.0	4.21	0.281
1982	8.7	13.8	17.6	22.7	37.3	4.29	0.283
1983	8.6	13.6	17.5	22.7	37.6	4.36	0.287
1984	8.5	13.7	17.6	22.8	37.4	4.40	0.287
1985	8.4	13.6	17.5	22.9	37.6	4.50	0.290
1986	8.3	13.5	17.4	22.6	38.2	4.60	0.296
1987	8.1	13.5	17.5	22.8	38.1	4.69	0.299
1988	7.9	13.4	17.5	22.9	38.3	4.85	0.303
1989	7.7	13.5	17.7	23.1	38.0	4.94	0.303

Source: Kuo, 1983: 96-97; DGBAS, 1990:63; CEPD, 1991: 61-62.
a. Households are divided into five groups of equal size and arranged from the poorest 20% of families to the richest 20% of families.
b. The ratio of the income share of richest 20% of families to that of poorest 20%.

farming techniques and new agricultural varieties; unifying weights, measures, and currency; making investment capital available; and enforcing law and order (Ho, 1971; Gold, 1986: 32-46). During that period, the Japanese removed bureaucratic, legal, and social impediments to economic transformation and created a good investment climate, which undoubtedly was conducive to Taiwan's subsequent development. However, we should point out that although the contribution of the Japanese legacy is unquestionable, it obviously was not a guarantee for Taiwan's later success. Otherwise, Manchuria, where the Japanese had invested much more than in Taiwan (Chao, 1982), should have had a better performance. But this is simply not the case. The counterargument becomes even more convincing as we compare the developments of South and North Koreas. Both societies inherited the Japanese colonial legacy and North Korea received much more investment than its southern counterpart. Nevertheless, there is no doubt that South Korea has until now held the lead. Therefore, it seems justifiable to argue that the Japanese legacy is not a decisive factor, or at least not a sufficient condition, for Taiwan's success. Other factors have supported this legacy's contribution.

U.S. aid is another factor often cited as a crucial component in Taiwan's development. Systematic American aid to Taiwan began in 1951 and continued through 1965. During this period U.S. economic aid, aside from $2.5 billion of military aid, amounted to $1.5 billion, averaging about $100 million per annum. It not only helped Taiwan to overcome inflation and enabled it to accumulate capital, but also augmented the confidence in security and fostered a willingness to invest on the island. In addition, American advisors had assisted the KMT state to improve its budget system and map out several development projects. Taiwan's achievement would have been less spectacular if there had been no U.S. aid (Jacoby, 1966; Ho, 1978: 111-120). As a matter of fact, both the officials and scholars in Taiwan have never denied the importance of U.S. aid for Taiwan's development (Wang, 1978: 124-129; Li and Ch'en, 1984a: 30-35). However, there is no compelling reason to believe that American aid might fully explain Taiwan's accomplishments. Many countries received more economic aid per head than Taiwan; these included South Vietnam, South Korea, Zaire, Turkey, Egypt, Cyprus, Israel, Jordan, Yugoslavia, Cuba, and France's colonies or former colonies in Africa (Little, 1979: 457-458). But few can match Taiwan's record. In fact, Taiwan is the first recipient "graduating" from the U.S. aid program. Her growth pace did not slow down after the "graduation." If the level of economic aid were a sufficient condition for economic growth, it would be difficult to explain the disappointing performances of many other LDCs which have received comparable economic aid for much longer. If the level of economic aid is the necessary condition for economic growth, then attention should be directed to intervening and contingent variables that bring the effect of U.S. aid in facilitating Taiwan's development fully into play (Gregor, Chang and Zimmerman, 1981: 87-89). What are these variables?

Taiwan's economic development also could take advantage of a favorable timing of the world economy. The major dynamics of economic growth on the island since the mid-1960s has been the rapid booming of its manufactured exports. When Taiwan undertook the critical switch of its development strategies from import-substitution industrialization to export-led industrialization in the mid-1960s, the world economy was extremely conducive to trade and exports (Hsiao, 1985: 5). The market in the advanced industrial societies, especially the United States, after having experienced high growth, increase of wage rates, and the loss of competitiveness in labor-intensive manufactured goods, was readily accessible to manufactured exports from the LDCs. Taiwan was lucky enough to join in at such a favorable time. In this sense, Taiwan's success is to a certain degree merely a free ride on the prosperity of the world economic cycle. However, the question is that while the opportunity was fairly open to every developing country, why only few economies, namely, the so-called "Four Little Dragons of East Asia," including Taiwan, South Korea, Hong Kong, and Singapore, took full advantage of such timing. Although many developing countries adopted industrial deepening as the next step for economic development after the exhaustion of import-substitution industrialization, why did Taiwan shift its way to export-led industrialization? It is obvious that to grasp the favorable timing, some measures had to be taken. Then, who is responsible for adopting those measures?

In recent years, Confucianism has been widely recognized as a special feature in Taiwan and East Asia's development (Kahn, 1979; Hofheinz and Calder: 1982: 41-52; Berger, 1983; King, 1985; Fei, 1986). The cultural elements of Confucian ethics, such as thrift, diligence, respect for educational achievement, avoidance of overt conflict in social relations, loyalty to hierarchy and authority, and stress of order and harmony, are believed to have something to do with Taiwan's dynamic economic transformation (Hsiao, 1985: 12). Weber's argument that Confucianism impeded the development of capitalism in China has been challenged by many scholars (Weber, 1964; Berger,

1983; King, 1985). We agree that Confucianism seems to have some positive effects on economic development in terms of its related ethics and values toward family, work, and organizational authority. However, we should argue that Confucianism itself cannot fully explain the Taiwanese or East Asian miracle. Otherwise, how can we explain the very different achievements in Taiwan and Mainland China as well as in South and North Koreas, given the fact that they have exactly the same cultural heritage? In fact, many Chinese officials and scholars are still complaining about the incompatibility between some Chinese cultural traits and modern economic activity (Li, 1976: 12-19 and 1986a; Wang, 1983: 165-176; Yu, 1983). To mediate the relationship between Confucianism and the energetic economic development, we need extra-mechanism. Then, what is the mechanism?

One final argument claims that Taiwan's economic development benefits from the small size of her economy because it is easier to handle. We can rebut this argument by simply pointing to the fact that there are many small economies in the world which share similar conditions with Taiwan, such as Sri Lanka, Cuba and the other Caribbean countries, but none are able to match Taiwan's record. This makes it unnecessary to develop the argument that there are also disadvantages of a small economy. We believe that size or geography by itself is neither necessary nor sufficient for rapid economic growth. There must be mediating factors between a favorable environment and economic development (Liu, 1986: 20). Again, what are the mediating factors?

The state is the clue to resolve the puzzle. When we recognize that all of the factors mentioned above to a certain extent and in a certain way have contributed to Taiwan's economic development, we also discover that to bring all of these advantages together and make them have full meaning, we must put the state at a pivotal position and regard it as a key variable. It is the state that brings the advantages for Taiwan's economic development fully into play. If the KMT state had not been able to succeed the Japanese legacy properly, utilize U.S. aid effectively, make a timely shift of its development strategy, adopt suitable socioeconomic institutions that mediate the relationship between Confucianism and economic growth, as well as make use of the advantages and overcome the disadvantages of a small economy, the Taiwan miracle would hardly have been possible. In other words, the economic accomplishments on Taiwan should be attributed largely to the effective intervention and policy-making by the state. To understand Taiwan's development fully, the role of the KMT state must be analyzed.

Taiwan as a Case to Examine the State and Society

State Building and Social Formation before 1945

Taiwan is an ethnically homogeneous society in a comparative sense, though there have been ethnic or subethnic conflicts on the island (Gates, 1981; Lamley, 1981). Most of the people in Taiwan came from the Fukien and Kwangtung provinces of Mainland China. Settlers from the mainland began arriving in the Christian era and started to come in large numbers in the seventeenth century. The aborigines, who make up about 1.7% of Taiwan's current population, were pushed into the mountains by the subsequent waves of Chinese immigrants. The immigration continued until the Japanese occupation in 1895 and was resumed in 1945 when the Japanese departed. The coming and going between Taiwan and the mainland was cut off soon afterwards, however, because of the confrontation between the KMT and the Chinese Communist Party (CCP); the latter having finally taken over the mainland in 1945. The last wave of the people from the mainland was comprised of more than one million refugees who followed the KMT state arriving in Taiwan in 1949-50. Aside from the aborigines, the people descended from those who reached Taiwan before 1945 are usually referred to as "Taiwanese." They make up a little more than 80% of the current population in Taiwan. The people who arrived in Taiwan after 1945 are usually called "mainlanders." They make up about 15 to 17% of the population (Republiteratlic of China 1986: 45 and 159-160).

Taiwan became a protectorate of the Chinese empire in 1206, but the empire made no effort to lay claim to the island. The Dutch arrived in 1624. They established a branch of the Dutch East India Company in the south of Taiwan. The Dutch occupation of Taiwan was part of Holland's expanding global mercantile activities. The branch provided a jumping off point for trade with China and Japan and served as a base to compete in commerce, war, and missionary work with the rival Spanish and Portuguese. In the middle of the seventeenth century, a general of the Ming Court, Cheng Ch'eng-kung, expelled the Dutch and established his base on Taiwan to resist the Manchus, who overthrew the Ming Court and established the Ch'ing Dynasty. The

Cheng authorities exerted great efforts to develop the island's economy. In spite of Manchu policies prohibiting emigration and moving Fukienese away from the coast to prevent them from supporting Cheng, large numbers of Chinese moved to Taiwan. When the Cheng period was ended by the Manchus' invasion in 1683, there were an estimated 100,000 mainland Chinese there. The Cheng authorities had also set up the institutional, social, and cultural foundations of Chinese civilization on the island (Hsu, 1980a).

The role of the Ch'ing government in developing Taiwan was minimal before the mid-nineteenth century. The Manchus made Taiwan only a prefecture attached to Fukien province. The quality of officials sent from Peking was notoriously poor and many spent very little time on the island. Partly due to the absence of effective state control and partly due to the violent nature of the pioneers, Taiwan suffered from social unrest for a long time. The settlers grouped themselves according to the same surnames, place of worship, dialect, or belief in a common deity. Voluntary associations took charge of water control and mutual aid, and participated vigorously in armed battles. Into the nineteenth century, as families formed and permanent settlements grew, life in Taiwan increasingly resembled that on the mainland. Most of the settlers engaged in agriculture, but there were numbers of traders and fishermen. The land tenure pattern in much of Taiwan was a "three-tier" system. The top level was held by the absentee landlords residing in Taiwan's urban areas or on the mainland. The middle tier consisted of tenant landlords while tenants were at the bottom. About 75% of the land was tenant-cultivated in northern Taiwan, somewhat less elsewhere. The tenancy rate was high in Taiwan as compared with the mainland. Rice, sugar, tea, and camphor were major exports, which were sold mainly to the mainland in exchange for manufactured goods like textiles and opium. Ports and commercial centers gradually developed. As the population filled out the island and engaged in exchange relations, much of the violent subethnic rivalry subsided. Large landowning families diversified their commercial interests into activities such as trade, retailing, and camphor processing. A new stratum of compradors emerged to deal with the foreign traders. Schools were established and a *literati* class began to appear (Hsu, 1980b; Wickberg, 1970 and 1981; Gold, 1986: 25-29).

The global political-economic context changed radically since the mid-nineteenth century and influenced the Manchus' policy toward Taiwan. Starting from the Opium War in 1842, the foreign powers began to enter the China market aggressively. Taiwan was also one of the targets. Four treaty ports were opened by the terms of the 1862 Treaty of Tientsin. In the process, the Ch'ing Court became increasingly aware of the strategic value of the island as the front line of defense of the motherland. Competent officials were sent to Taiwan to take charge of Taiwan's development. Among them, General Liu Ming-chuan, who served on the island from 1884 to 1891, was the most prestigious one. He instituted many reforms in Taiwan's administration, infrastructure, and economy. Taiwan, inhabited by population of 2.5 million at the time, was upgraded to provincial status in 1887. But the Ch'ing Court was not able to further develop this frontier island. In 1985, Taiwan was ceded to Japan as one of the spoils of the First Sino-Japanese War (Kuo, 1973).

The colonial occupation of Japan on Taiwan can be divided into three periods: (1) 1895 to 1919, the harsh period of consolidating political control and reshaping the economy to make it suit the needs of Japan; (2) 1919 to 1936, a relatively liberal interlude characterized by civil administration and demands for home rule; and (3) 1937 to 1945, renewed military rule and forced assimilation as Japan prepared for, waged, and lost the world war (Gold, 1986: 34). During the first period, the Japanese established a structure of control to suppress resistance by the islanders and ensure their hegemony. The supreme authority was the Government-General headed by a military officer. The governor-general had extensive political, bureaucratic, military, and legislative powers over the colony. Only Japanese held the top posts at all levels of government. A pervasive police system was set up to supervise local activities; however merely one-sixth of the police force were local people, and no Taiwanese was appointed above the rank of captain. By extending their effective control throughout the island and penetrating down to the village, the Japanese removed many of the elements that had traditionally fostered the rise of local strongmen beyond state control (Gold, 1986: 35-36).

Employing tight state control, the Japanese tried to develop Taiwan as an agricultural appendage to their home country. A land survey was completed in 1904 and a land reform was instituted the following year. The absentee landlords at the top of the three-tier system were forced to give up claims to rent in exchange for government bonds. The tenant landlords in the middle tier were made the legal owners of the land and directly responsible for taxes. The land reform intended to tie peasants closer to the land so as to increase productivity but did not seek to alter fundamentally the relations of production in the countryside. There was no redistribution of land. Actually the Japanese used the police and administrative means to preserve the rural social structure. The farmers' associations were organized as an instrument of control and a channel for new agricultural technology and capital. Education was another instrument to assimilate the Taiwanese and control the whole society. A compulsory six-year elementary school system was set up to impart basic literacy and skills to Taiwanese children and to indoctrine them in loyalty to Japan and the emperor. Educational opportunities beyond primary school were limited, however. The educational policy aimed at eliminating the traditional teaching and administrative functions of the remaining Chinese *literati*. Meanwhile, the colonial state used monopoly licenses and other economic privileges to win the allegiance of influential Taiwanese. But while allowing Taiwanese to participate in commercial activities, the Japanese used legal and economic means to prevent all but a handful of top collaborators from entering the modern industrial sector. Capitalist institutions such as banks, legal protection of private property, limited liability companies, and so on were introduced to benefit Japanese investors and workers. The Taiwanese in general were related to the periphery of the capitalist mode in their own society (Ho, 1971; Gold, 1986: 36-39).

Taiwan received her first civilian governor-general in 1919. From 1920 onwards, Japanese law was to be applied as much as possible on the island though the governor-general still retained the power to determine the limits of its applicability. At the same time, Advisory councils were established at provincial and local levels. In 1921, the governor-general included nine Taiwanese in his Consultative Council. The restriction of preventing Taiwanese from entering the modern industrial sector was partly lifted. The measures of assimilation were extended to postprimary vocational training and integrated into all postprimary schools. Thousands of youths continued to seek higher education in Japan and some chose law, business, and politics, which were unavailable to them at home. Exposed to currents of thought in Japan, which were not accessible through Taiwan's controlled press, many Taiwanese youths acquired a new political consciousness. After returning to Taiwan, they and other intellectuals formed several organizations to press for local autonomy and elections. They also organized workers and peasants to demand for more benefits and rights. Japanese tactics in reaction to these struggles ranged from suppression of organizations to planning a new program in 1935 for Taiwan's partial autonomy, including elections. Nevertheless, a military man assumed the governor-general's post in the following year and political movements were terminated as the war atmosphere intensified (Gold, 1986: 41-42).

The war changed the Japanese policy toward Taiwan's development. Japan launched a total war with China in July, 1938. She signed the Tripartite Pact with Nazi Germany and Fascist Italy in September, 1940 and began invading Southeast Asia in 1941. Taiwan was now to serve as the stepping stone to the South Seas. This meant that in addition to producing rice and sugar, Taiwan would set up somewhat of a heavy industry that could process raw materials coming from Southeast Asia to serve the imperial war machine. Taiwan was also expected to increase self-sufficiency in consumer goods. To accomplish this, the major Japanese *zaibatsu* and expatriate firms worked closely with Japanese authorities to facilitate Japanese immigration to the island and establish economic links between Taiwan, South China, and Southeast Asia. Industrial chemicals, ceramics, aluminum, machine tools, and textiles were introduced at the time. As a part of the industrial mobilization, Taiwanese-owned modern enterprises were merged into Japanese firms. Economic control was thus concentrated almost entirely in Japanese hands. In addition, the Japanese militarized the island's political and social spheres; police organs were expanded; dissent and social activism were suppressed; forced assimilation measures were implemented; and Taiwanese were pressed into service at the front as soldiers and laborers (Gold, 1986: 43-44). Japanese hopes of building Taiwan into an industrial bridgehead to Southeast Asia and South China, however, never materialized. From late 1944, Taiwan sustained bombing by the American air force. Military and industrial targets were heavily damaged. Finally, in August, 1945, Japan surrendered.

As mentioned before, during the colonial period, the Japanese brought about fundamental changes in the Taiwanese society, which were conducive to Taiwan's subsequent development. Taiwan's economy was skewed to depend on Japan, but the Japanese legacy differed from the more typical dependent structure in important ways. The infrastructure and factories built by the Japanese were dispersed throughout the island, thus avoiding the phenomenon of "dual economy" or "internal dependency," i.e., a tiny modern channel in a sea of traditional society. Such distortion was further prevented by the pervasive primary education system and farmers' associations. These institutions brought at least a minimal level of literacy and appreciation of modern productive skills to the majority of the population. Taiwanese peasants were not driven off their land and onto plantations, the general rule in other colonies. Rather, they retained their private holdings and applied scientific inputs to improve productivity. The standard of living was markedly improved. Basically, the colonial administration did not make Taiwan "underdeveloped" (Gold, 1986: 45-46).

The Building of the KMT State on Taiwan

There had been a chaotic interregnum between the departure of the colonial administration in 1945 and the arrival of the KMT central government in 1949. Taiwan was formally returned to China on October, 25, 1945. General Ch'en Yi, a former Fukien warlord, was appointed administrator-general and garrison commander to take charge of the retrocession and governance. Originally, the Taiwanese had eagerly welcomed the Nationalists and looked forward to participating as full citizens of the Republic of China. But Ch'en Yi's administration treated them arrogantly, as colonized people. Ch'en staffed his government with other mainlanders and token Taiwanese who had spent the war years in China. Other Taiwanese were relegated to the lowliest positions. In addition, preoccupied with its struggle against the Communists, the Nationalists could provide little assistance or attention to the economic development of the new territory. In fact, Taiwan had to supply materials to the mainland to support the Nationalists against the Communists. This extra burden devastated Taiwan's economic base and caused soaring inflation. Along with political and economic retrogression, the Ch'en authorities created an environment of disorder filled with lawlessness and corruption (Myers, 1973: 42-43; Gold, 1986: 45-50).

The incapacity and arrogance of Ch'en's administration deteriorated the relationship between Taiwanese and mainlanders and eventually resulted in the bloody riot of February 28, 1947. Thousands of Taiwanese and mainlanders were killed. After the riot was put down, Ch'en Yi was transferred to the position of governor of Chekiang procince and Wei Tao-ming, a civilian who had served as the ROC ambassador in Washington, replaced him. The Nationalists also upgraded Taiwan from a military territory to a province and called for immediate local elections. The "2-28 Incident" had a profound effect on Taiwan's social character and subsequent development. On the one hand, it triggered the antagonism of Taiwanese against mainlanders and the Nationalist regime. This had been a potential danger for Taiwan's social stability for quite a while, but it has ebbed gradually during the course of Taiwan's development. On the other hand, it liquidated the stratum of the Taiwanese intelligentsia and weakened the force of the island's social elites. Many Taiwanese killed in the riot were lawyers, newspaper editors, teachers, and students since they were suspected to be critical of the government (Kerr, 1965). Their death impressed upon the Taiwanese that politics is dangerous and should be kept at arm's length. Thus, when the KMT state moved its capital to Taipei on December 9, 1949, it faced an angry populace, nevertheless, the society as a whole was leaderless, atomized, quiescent, and apolitical (Gold, 1986: 51-52). This situation gave the KMT state an advantage to resettle its organization and to consolidate its control over Taiwanese society.

The Nationalists brought their formal national-level party and government structures onto Taiwan. There are parallel party and state structures at all levels–national, provincial, county, municipal, and district–to ensure party control over the state and society. The party's supreme organ is the National Congress, or during recess, the Central Committee. But the real power center is the Central Standing Committee (CSC) that handles the work when the Central Committee is not in session. The National Congress convenes every four or more years. The Central Committee holds annual plenary sessions. Power organs at the other levels are respective congresses and committees. Major vocational groups–such as journalists, seamen, railroad and highway transportation workers–have their own branches. Commissions have been formed for women and overseas Chinese. Party cells, each having from three to twenty-nine members, are the basic units for training, publicity, investigation, and service activities, existing in schools, the military, enterprises, social organizations, and residential communities (there were about 2.2 million members on the island by 1985 and most of them were Taiwanese). Four hundred service centers around the island provide a variety of social services as well as a means of keeping informed of local affairs. At the local level, party cadres are also charged with selecting candidates for elections (Winckler, 1981a and 1981b; Republic of China 1986, 1986: 146; Gold, 1986: 59-60). Although the party system plays an important role in policy coordination and major state policies have to get approval by relevant party organizations, the main responsibility and functions of public policymaking are retained in the state system.

The organization of the state at central government level is shown in figure 2.1. It was devised by Sun Yat-sen, the founding father of the Republic of China. The chief of state is the President. He is elected

Figure 2.1
Organization Chart of the Central Government of the Republic of China

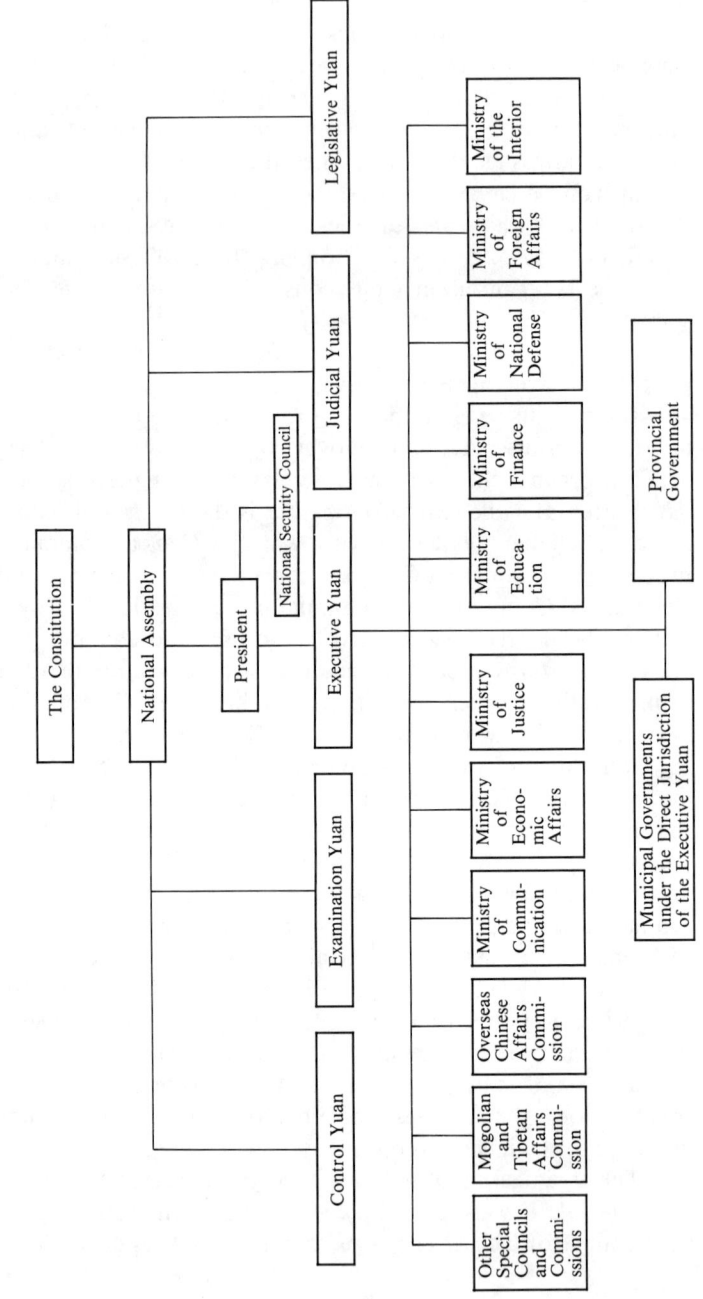

by the National Assembly for a six-year term. Originally a president could only serve twice, but this rule was amended by the Temporary Provisions Effective During the Period of Communist Rebellion in the constitution. The provisions were enacted by the National Assembly in 1948 to grant the President a wide range of emergency powers for dealing with the communist rebellion. The first session of the National Assembly convened in March, 1948 in Nanking. Chiang Kai-shek was elected President. Under the President, there are five branches of national government: (1) the Executive Yuan (or Cabinet), with a range of ministries and commissions, whose members are appointed by the President and headed by the Premier. (2) The Legislative Yuan, elected by the people based on region and profession. It is responssible for legislation, approving the budget, interpellation of government officials, etc. (3) The Judicial Yuan, whose justices are appointed by the President. (4) The Examination Yuan for examinations for the civil service and professional licenses, whose members are appointed by the President. (5) The Control Yuan, the chief agency for censoring government officials, whose members are elected by the provincial assembly and municipal councils. The KMT has dominated the two electoral bodies, i.e., the Legislative and Control Yuans, overwhelmingly since they were established (Wei, 1973; Gold, 1986: 60-61).

The KMT has also continuously kept its dominance of government at all local levels. Beneath the national level is the Taiwan Provincial Government. Except for a few offshore islands, it governed actually the same territory controlled by the KMT before Taipei was elevated to the status of special municipality under the direct jurisdiction of the Executive Yuan in 1966 (Kaohsiung was elevated to the same status in 1978). The governor of Taiwan is appointed by the President but the members of the Provincial Assembly are elected. The Executive Yuan granted Taiwan self-government or home rule in 1950. A fifty-five-person Provisional Provincial Assembly was elected by county and municipal assemblies at the end of 1951. Subsequent assemblies were elected by direct vote of the electorate. The main duties of the Provincial Assembly are approval of the provincial budget, interpellation of provincial officials, and an assortment of advisory powers. Beneath the provincial level are *Hsien* governments and councils, and then *Hsiang* and *Chen* offices and representative conferences. All the administrative heads and councilmen of these levels are elected. There are members of two other parties and independents occupying some seats in the state system through election or appointment. But they are a small minority (Republic of China 1986, 1986: 141-142; Gold, 1986:

61).

The organizational pattern of the KMT state on Taiwan therefore resembles the so-called one-dominant-party system or *party-state bureaucracy* (Fainsod, 1963: 235). In parallel with the dominance in administrative and representative systems, the KMT also retains control of the military and security agencies. Chiang Kai-shek and several other leaders of the KMT had military backgrounds. Although they established a civilian government on Taiwan, they still controlled the military. At the same time, most military officers were the party members. An extensive network of overt and covert quasi-military security agencies further ensured the KMT's rule. The KMT state thus displayed a strong capacity to penetrate the society on the island.

The KMT state also enjoyed a great degree of *state autonomy* from the Taiwanese society. This was mainly due to the KMT state's "exogenous" status on Taiwan. From 1945 to 1949, most people from the mainland were either servicemen or civil servants. They naturally occupied positions in various state bureaucracies and the military. The relocation of the central government made the feature even more remarkable. Most state and party cadres and military officers were the mainlanders and had no property or connections in Taiwan. As a result, the split between the state elites and local elites made the KMT state highly autonomous from Taiwanese society. In addition, the absence of a strong dominant class also accounted for the state's autonomy. The Japanese did not create a Taiwanese bourgeoisie during the colonial period. The "2-28 Incident" eliminated the intelligentsia and dampened the motivation to organize social forces. And as we will discuss later, the land reform that took place between the years 1949 and 1953 led to the disappearance of the landlord class. All of these factors weakened the ties between society and the state. Moreover, the party's ideology, Sun Yat-senism (The Three Principles of the People), made the KMT state somehow self-conscious about maintaining its autonomy. According to Sun's doctrine, the state should acquire a strong capacity for administration and play an active role in promoting economic development but preventing the concentration of economic power in the hands of a few. He sees the implementation of land reform and the state control of key industries as the major means of state intervention. The state, asserts Sun, should pursue the general interests of the people as a whole rather than of any particular social group or class (Sun, 1924; Linebarger, 1937: 107-109 and 122-156).

Aside from an extensive party-state bureaucracy and a great degree of state autonomy, the following factors also contributed to defining the KMT state's capacities in governing Taiwan. The first was an influx of experienced professionals and administrators who followed the KMT state move to the island. As Rueschemeyer and Evans (1986: 51) argue, the construction of an extensive, internally coherent bureaucratic machinery should not be taken as a simple instrumental project requiring only the creation of a set of formal organizational ties joined with a corresponding structure of incentives. Instead, it is a delicate, long-term process of institution building. It requires a lot of time and effort to institutionalize the division of labor, to accumulate expertise, to cultivate *esprit de corps,* and to implant organization into a society. While the mainlanders overstaffed the state bureaucracy and blocked Taiwanese's way to higher positions in the state apparatus, they took care to include an abundance of well-trained and committed officials. Their arrival filled the vacancies left by the Japanese technicians, managers, administrators, and experts. Due to the discriminating policy operative during the colonial period, the Taiwanese did not have the required training and experience to take over these positions.

The second contributing factor was a change of personnel due to the relocation of the state apparatus. Those who came with Chiang Kai-shek to an uncertain future on Taiwan were for the most part loyal and willing to make sacrifices. A reform program of the KMT during the period of 1950-52 expelled those whose allegiance seemed doubtful thus broke the factions that had hampered the KMT state's rule on the mainland. In the reform program, the KMT admitted past errors, purged its ranks, recruited new members (including Taiwanese), and strengthened discipline and indoctrination to reinvigorate the party. Many younger members were upgraded to replace older members in both the party and state systems. The state apparatus became organizationally much more cohesive after the reform (Riggs, 1952: 36-42; Hsu, 1984; Gold, 1986: 59).

The colonial legacy and U.S. aid were advantageous factor as well. The KMT state inherited from the colonial administration a well-established bureaucratic system and a number of powerful policy instruments, such as the revenue system, the banking system, the big enterprises, the farmers' associations, and the record of agricultural holdings, etc (Ho, 1975: 433-439). U.S. aid extended the KMT state's financial resources and made up for the insufficient tax revenue the state managed to extract. The American advisors also helped the KMT officials to improve their administrative skills (Jacoby, 1966).

Finally, the role of Sun Yat-senism ought to be taken into account. When the CCP took Marxian-Leninism as the governing principle in

China, the KMT upheld Sun Yat-senism as its guideline for the management of Taiwan's development. In contrast to the Chinese Communist regime, which suffers from the struggle between opposing lines of interpretations on Marxism, there has been no severe ideological clash within the KMT state. The main reason for this difference is the relatively practical, tolerant, and flexible character of Sun's doctrine (Pang, 1980), which provides the KMT state with systematic ideological underpinnings (Gold, 1986: 124).

In sum, owing to a particular historical conjuncture, the KMT state on Taiwan acquired relatively favorable conditions with regards to both *state autonomy* and *state capacities*. This relatively autonomous and capable state has actively intervened in Taiwan's economic transformation since its retreat from Mainland China in 1949.

CHAPTER 3

CONSTITUTIONAL STRUCTURE OF ECONOMIC POLICY-MAKING

In this chapter, we are going to present an overall picture of the decision-making process of economic policy in a relatively generalized way. The purpose is to present a succinct exposition of the economic policy-making structure drawing out its essential features so as to pave the way for the analyses developed in the following chapters.

A very straightforward way of plotting this picture is to follow the constitutional flow chart of economic policy-making which can be drawn as figure 3.1. Three organizations at different levels-the economic bureaucracy, the Executive Yuan Council, and the Central Standing Committee (CSC) of the Kuomintang-are directly related to the task of formulating economic policy. In addition, the Legislative Yuan is responsible for deciding the statutory bills concerning national economic activities. Among these organizations, the economic bureaucracy is the one in charge of drafting economic policies. These drafts will then be sent to the Executive Yuan Council who will see that they agree with the policies proposed by other ministries or commissions and decide whether they should be submitted to the CSC, or dropped, or revised. If the drafts are approved by the Council and seen as important national policies, they will then be submitted to the Policy Coordination Commission of the Central Committee of the KMT (one of the department of the KMT at the central level which carries out policy coordination between government units especially the Executive Yuan and the Legislative Yuan) to be put into the agenda of the CSC. After obtaining the approval of the CSC, the policies will be returned to the Executive Yuan to be either executed directly or enacted as a bill. The policies enacted as bills will further be submitted to the Legislative Yuan. The structures and functions of these organizations will be now presented in more detail.

The Economic Bureaucracy

The economic bureaucracy refers to the organization or organizations that are in charge of triggering economic policy-making. One distinctive feature of making economic policy in Taiwan is that in order to cope with the extraordinary situation in the early stage of Taiwan's postwar development, to utilize U.S. aid efficiently, and to handle the subsequent development of Taiwan's economy, the Kuomintang

50 THE STATE AND ECONOMIC TRANSFORMATION

Figure 3.1
The Constitutional Structure of Economic Policy-making

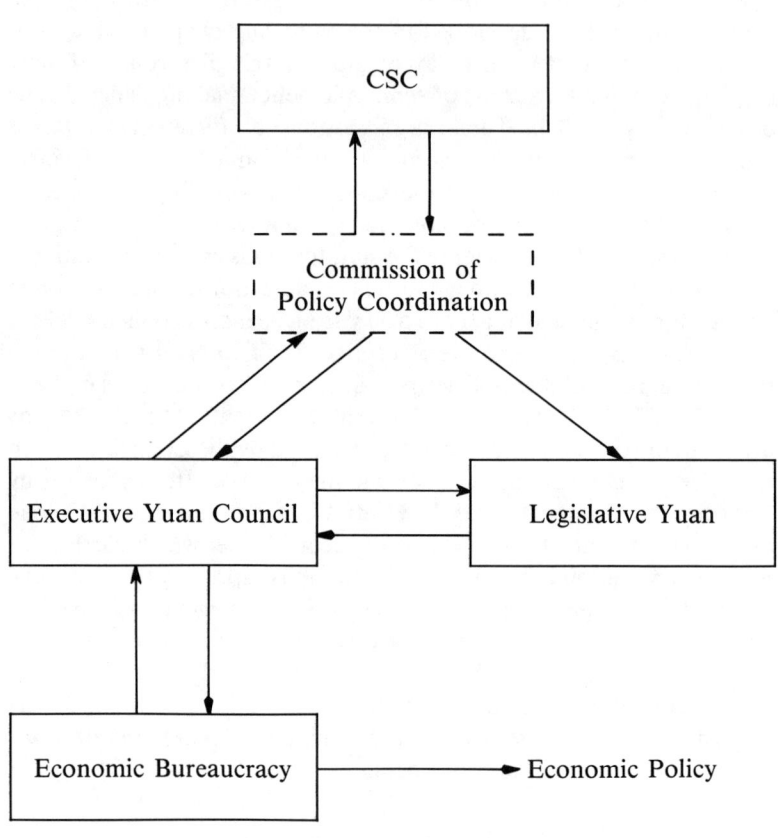

government created in 1949 a number of supra-ministry and relatively independent organs for economic transsformation. These ad hoc organs gave a considerable number of economic officials a base and the machinery need to operate amid the confusion created by the preservation of duplicated ministries and departments at both central and provincial levels (Lin, 1973: 40). These organs can be classified into four kinds.

First there was *the agency for administering U.S. aid.* This is the Council for United States Aid (CUSA). It was established in 1948 when U.S. Congress passed the China Aid Act under which 500 million U.S. dollars was granted for the reconstruction of China. With the loss of the mainland to the Communists in 1949, this aid was suspended. Funds were diverted to other areas in East Asia; however, the Council was still retained and moved to Taiwan with the Kuomintang government. When the outbreak of the Korean War in June, 1950, led to a resumption of aid, the Council also resumed its work (Jacoby, 1966: 29-30). The basic official functions of the CUSA were: (1) to select the aid project, to procure and allocate aid-financed commodity imports, (2) to utilize the sales proceeds of such imports in the Local Currency Program (it allowed the Kuomintang state to "pay for" the imports by depositing New Taiwanese dollars in segregated accounts which were controlled by either the U.S. government, the KMT state, or had a joint control), (3) to supervise the execution of the aid projects, and (4) to maintain a liasion with the U.S. AID Mission to China. The CUSA, which was reorganized into the Council for International Economic Cooperation and Development in 1963, reflected the new objectives of terminating aid and drawing on broader sources of external investment (Jacoby, 1966: 61).

The second kind of organ created was *the agency for controlling foreign exchange and foreign trade.* The shortage of foreign exchange was a serious problem in the early stage of Taiwan's postwar development. To balance foreign trade and payment, an Industrial Financing Committee was set up in June, 1949, under the jurisdiction of the Taiwan Production Board–the top agency for economic activities at that time. This committee was reorganized into the Foreign Exchange and Foreign Trade Committee in 1953 when the Taiwan Production Board was merged into the Economic Stablization Board. The new committee was attached to the Taiwan provincial government and supervised by the Ministry of Economic Affairs and the Ministry of Finance. Later, in February, 1955, the Foreign Exchange and Trade Control Commission (FETCC) was established, which took over the functions of the Foreign Exchange and Foreign Trade Committee as well as some other business concerning foreign exchange and foreign trade originally handled by other departments at the level of central government (Liu, 1980: 9-10). The Commission undertook to decide foreign exchange rates, determine import requirements, assist export expansion, screen applications for foreign exchange, coordinate with U.S. aid, and keep in communication with competent authorities in connection with foreign exchange and foreign trade (China Yearbook, 1957-58: 96-97). It was dismissed in 1969 when Taiwan's foreign trade reached a new phase and the KMT state decided to bring the functions of controlling foreign exchange and trade back to the ordinary departmental structure of government. Thus, its functions were merged into the Ministry of Economic Affairs, the Ministry of Finance, and the Central Bank of China (Li and Ch'en, 1984b: 271).

The third kind was *the agency for agricultural development*. Taiwan's agricultural and rural development was undertaken by the Joint Commission on Rural Reconstruction (JCRR). Like the Council for United States Aid, the Joint Commission originated on Mainland China in October, 1948, as an organ to implement the China Aid Act. Unlike the CUSA, which was a purely Chinese institution, the JCRR was jointly run–originally, by three Chinese and two American commissioners appointed by the respective presidents of the two countries and, later, by two Chinese and one American. The Joint Commission had virtual plenary powers with respect to the rural development of Taiwan. It reviewed, approved, and supervised the execution of rural projects; It advised and monitored the land reform in Taiwan; It streamlined and democratized the farmers' associations; It also provided money and human power to improve rural health conditions and the technology for water resources, agricultural crops, livestock, forestry, and fishing. Although it had to submit its programs through the CUSA to the U.S. AID Mission, CUSA rarely disapproved of any its proposals (Jacoby, 1966: 62). When U.S. aid was ceased in 1965, the JCRR was retained to promote Taiwan's agricultural development. It was reorganized as the Council for Agricultural Planning and Development in 1979 due to the termination of official relations between the United States and the Republic of China. In 1984, the Council for Agricultural Planning and Development was replaced by the Council of Agriculture. The latter had more money and power for agricultural development.

The forth and last kind of organ was *the agency for economic planning*. There were a series of bureaucracies that performed similar functions yet held different hierarchical positions and power during different periods. As early as June, 1949, before the central government moved to Taiwan, in order to direct and supervise the state enterprises which had already relocated in Taiwan, the central government delegated authority to the Taiwan provincial government to create the Taiwan Production Board (TPB). In addition to monitoring all of the public enterprises in Taiwan, the Board also worked as an organ for the coordination of financial and economic affairs between the central government and the provincial government. It was in charge of the planning of production and supply, as well as the financing of the project, the export arrangements, and the disposal of Japanese indemnities. The TPB was nominally chaired by the governor of Taiwan (Ch'en Ch'eng for June to December in 1949, Wu Kuo-cheng for December, 1949 to April, 1953, and O. K. Yui for April to July, 1953) but actually directed by the vice chairman of the board, i.e., K. Y. Yin. It had no power in economic policy execution, but it had very substantial functions in economic policy formulation (Yin, 1973a: 8). A Four-Year Self-sustaining Economic Plan was mapped out by the Taiwan provincial government in 1952, which was then revised to be Taiwan's first Four-Year Economic Development Plan.

The Taiwan Production Board was absorbed into the Economic Stabilization Board (ESB) in July, 1953. Before the merger, a special committee on economic and financial affairs composed of senior officials and led by the minister of Finance and the governor of Taiwan was established in March, 1951, to review and coordinate trade, payments, and monetary and fiscal policies, in the interests of stabilizing the price level. The ESB was the enlargement of the committee. The Board consisted of five divisions. The first division was responsible for industrial development planning; the second division was in charge of utilizing U.S. aid; the third division assumed the responsibility to control government budget, taxes, as well as revenue and expenditure of state enterprises; the fourth division undertook the economic planning for agriculture, forestry, and fishing; the final division was in charge of making policies for controlling the price level. An Industrial Development Commission (IDC), which combined the TPB and the Joint Commission on Industrial Development of the CUSA, was established as a subsidiary of the first division to implement the industrial parts of the first Four-Year Economic Development Plan (Li and Ch'en, 1984a: 169; Jacoby, 1966: 59-60). The first and second Four-Year Economic Development Plans covering the periods of 1953-56 and 1957-60 were drawn up by ESB.

In September, 1958, the ESB was dissolved. On the one hand, inflation had been curbed and the objective of economic development had gradually come to the fore (Jacoby, 1966: 60); on the other hand, the ESB was considered by an ad hoc Administrative Reform Committee as a redundant organization since its functions overlapped with those of other ministries (Li and Yeh, 1982: 104). The functions of sectoral economic planning in agriculture, industry, and transportation and communications were decentralized into the Ministry of Economic Affairs and the Ministry of Communications, while the functions of devising a macro economic plan and utilizing U.S. aid as well as the IDC were shifted into the CUSA. Consequently, the CUSA became the chief organ for overall economic development. The third Four-Year Economic Development Plan was introduced in by the CUSA.

As mentioned earlier, the CUSA was reorganized into the Council for International Cooperation and Development (CIECD) in September, 1963. This reorganization was due to both the aniticipation of the ceasing of U.S. aid and the recognition of the inefficiency of decentralizing economic planning. In addition to searching for broader sources of capital formation beyond U.S. aid and the opportunities for bilateral or multi-lateral cooperation in technology, the Council regained the functions of sectorial economic planning that had been handled by different agencies before. As a result, the central planning agency was once again restored. Besides plan formulation, it was also charged with the responsibility for the coordination, follow up, and evaluation of plan implementation (Li and Yeh, 1982: 104). During 1969, the CIECD was partly reorganized under the leadership of the newly appointed Vice Premier Chiang Ching-kuo. Some of its officials and functions were transferred to the Industrial Development Bureau, which had been recently created within the Ministry of Economic Affairs. In the meantime, a coordinating agency–the Financial, Economic, and Monetary Conference–was irregular held and presided over by Vice Premier Chiang. Under the supervision of the CIECD, the fourth and fifth Four-Year Economic Development Plans covering the periods of 1965-68 and 1969-72 were implemented and the sixth Plan covering the time span of 1973-76 was mapped out (Li and Ch'en, 1984a: 172-175).

In July, 1973, one year after Chiang Ching-kuo became Premier, the CIECD was replaced by the Economic Planning Council (EPC). The status of the EPC was degraded to that of a mere staff organ. Many experienced CIECD cadres went to other ministries, and the EPC's members no longer included any ministers but rather officials concerned directly with the economy. The EPC thus lost its significance and power as a supra-ministry agency; its functions were reduced to only economic planning and research. The real policy-making power shifted to a new, five-man Finance and Economic Group of the Executive Yuan. Headed by the governor of the Central Bank of China, the other members of the Group were the minister of Economic Affairs, the minister of Finance, the secretary-general of Executive Yuan, and the director of Directorate-General of Budget, Accounting and Statistics. The Group reported directly to Premier Chiang (Wen, 1984: 23). For coping with the oil crisis and the turmoil of international economy, the EPC introduced a Six Year Plan for Economic Development (1976 to 1981).

Since the mid-seventies, Taiwan began to feel pressured by competition from South Korea. Many criticisms of Taiwan's economic policy-making structure asserted that the EPC was too feeble to undertake the responsibility of economic development and that Taiwan needed a more capable and powerful economic bureaucracy like that of the Economic Planning Board in the Republic of Korea. The KMT state sent an investigation team to Korea in August, 1977. Based on this team's report, the EPC was enlarged and upgraded to become the Council for Economic Planning and Development (CEPD) through the combination of the EPC and the five-man Group in December, 1977. The CEPD was therefore in charge of reviewing important economic policies, making macro and sectorial planning (except agriculture), researching economic conditions in Taiwan and major markets, approving large public investment projects over 500 million N.T. dollars, and advising on the economic issues the Executive Yuan Council refered to it. In 1981, when the Six-Year Plan expired, the CEPD decided to have the economic development plan revert to a four-year term (Li and Ch'en, 1984: 177-178). Another two Four-Year Economic Development Plan were carried out during the period 1982-1985 and 1986-89. To make the organizational evolution of the agency for economic planning easier to follow, we chart figure 3.2.

Even though the organs noted above were organizationally outside the ordinary departmental structure of government, they nevertheless played a major role in drafting economic policies and performed the functions of the economic general staff. In contrast, the state units concerning economic activities within the ordinary departmental structure of government, such as the Ministry of Economic Affairs, the Ministry of Finance, and the Central Bank of China, had policy execution as their main function. The relationships among these agen-

56 THE STATE AND ECONOMIC TRANSFORMATION

Figure 3.2
Evolution of the Agency for Economic Planning

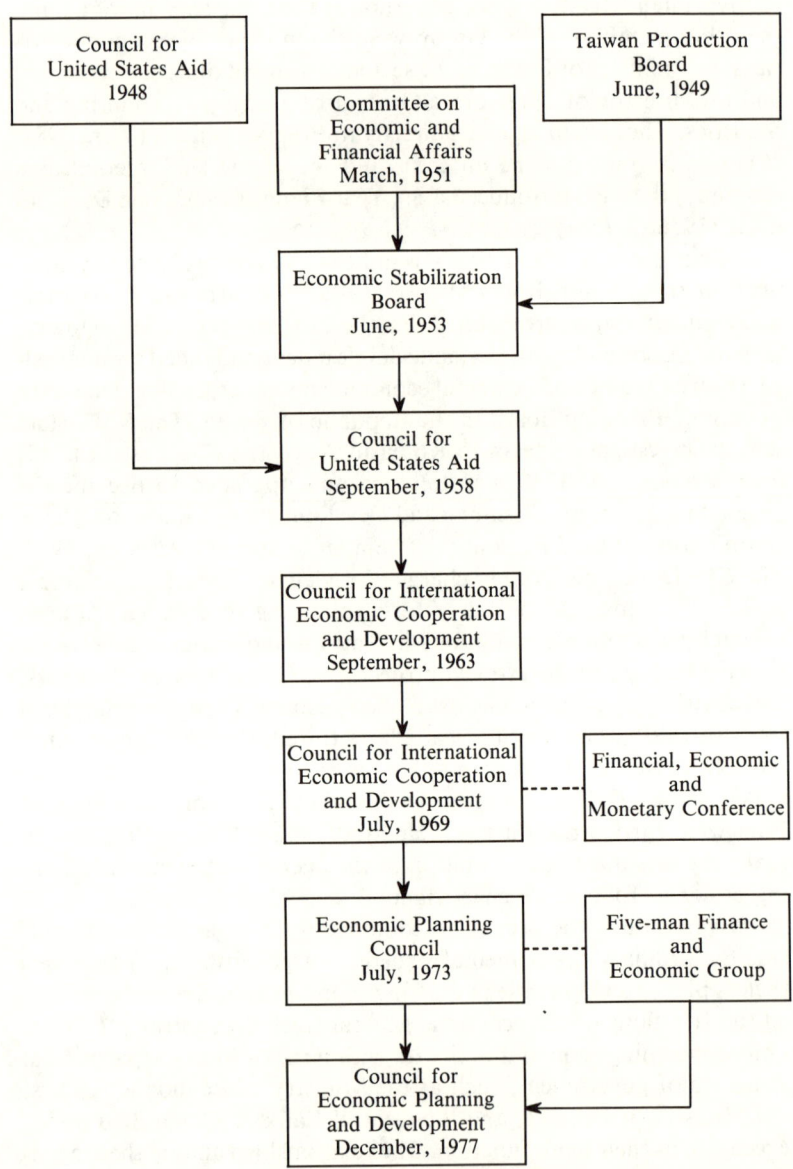

cies can be sketched as figure 3.3. Generally speaking, while every unit in the figure bore its own function and weight on economic policy-making, the agency for economic planning was the confluence of opinions from various units and the main trigger of formulating economic policy. Therefore, the term "economic bureaucracy" carries three distinct meanings: in its narrowest sense, it means the agency for economic planning; second, it refers to the organs outside the ordinary departmental structure of government; and in its broadest sense, it includes the Ministry of Economic Affairs, the Ministry of Finance, and the Central Bank of China.

Several organizational features can be extracted from the concept of "economic burearcracy" in its broadest sense. First, we find that the economic bureaucracy underwent constant change. The CUSA and the FETCC were disbanded. The agencies for agricultural development and economic planning lost influence while the Ministry of Economic Affairs, the Ministry of Finance, and the Central Bank of China gained more weight in economic policy-making. What were the causes and implications of this loss of power? Three factors could be discerned: (1) the change of environment, (2) the pressure to "normalize" organizational structure, and (3) the change of personnel. The interaction of the three factors contributed to the rise and fall of the various economic agencies.

Fristly, it is quite clear that those agencies which separated from the common administrative system, such as the CUSA, the FETCC, and the TPB, were reflecting the demands of the external environment. That is, they utilized U.S. aid, controlled foreign exchange and trade, and monitored state enterprises with local government status. Therefore, when the external environment changed, for instance, U.S. aid ceased, foreign exchange reserve became ample, and the central government established itself on Taiwan, the agencies were either dissolved or reorganized. In the same way, when Sino-U.S. diplomatic relations were broken off, the JCRR had to be reorganized into the Council for Agricultural Planning and Development; And when the competition with other developing countries in the international market was getting tough, the EPC was upgraded to the CEPD.

With respect to the pressure to normalize organizational structure, we discover that contradictions and tensions existed between the agencies inside and outside the ordinary departmental structure of government. This was due to the fact that their functions and powers were somewhat overlapping and could not all previal at the same time. The expansion of the agencies outside the ordinary structure was seen as

Figure 3.3
Organizational Chart of the Economic Bureaucracy

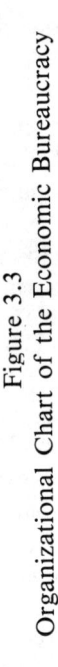

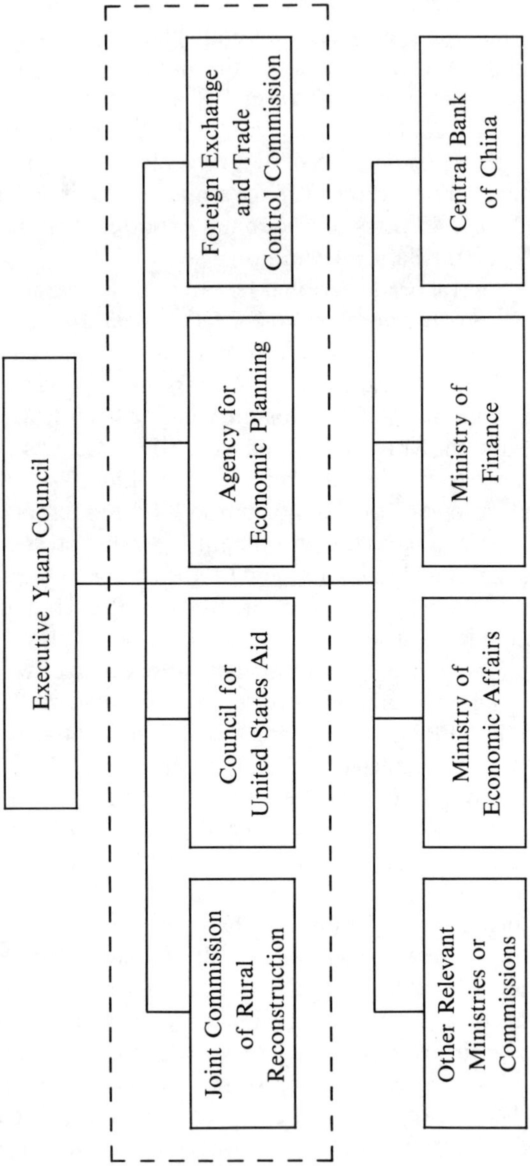

overstepping boundaries. At the same time, the independent budget and high pay of these agencies also caused complaints of discrimination and institutional distortion from other state units. Hence, there always has been the pressure to bring the relatively independent agencies back into the common administrative system. The dissolution of the ESB and the FETCC, the down-gradaing of the CIECD, and the strengthening of the Ministry of Economic Affairs, the Ministry of Finance, and the Central Bank of China represented such cases.

Finally, we observe that in the KMT state a leader's prestige and authority often determines the power of the agency he leads. For example, when Chiang Ching-kuo took charge of CIECD in 1969, although the agency's functions had been relatively reduced, its weight in formulating economic policy and evaluating policy execution was kept the same or even increased. But when Chiang became Premier and no longer headed the CIECD, the latter was soon transformed into the EPC and the power center of making economic policy was shifted to the Executive Yuan.

Given the change of power and the contradictions among the agencies, other organizational features aided the coherence and efficacy of the economic bureaucracy. Firstly, there was an overlap of officers at the top echelons of the economic bureaucracy in the medium sense. For example, in 1955 the members of the ESB included the governor of Taiwan (as chairman), the ministers of Finance, Economic Affairs, Communications, and National Defense, the chief of the General Staff of National Defense, the chairman of the JCRR, the secretary-general of the CUSA, the commissioner of Finance of Taiwan provincial government, the chairman of the board of the Bank of Taiwan (standed proxy for the Central Bank of China at that time), the executive secretary of the ESB, and the chairman of the IDC, etc (Li and Ch'en, 1983: 169). The CUSA was composed of the Premier (as chairman), the governor of Taiwan, the ministers of Finance, Economic Affairs, Communications, National Defense, and Foreign Affairs, the chairman of the board of the Bank of Taiwan, the executive secretary of the ESB, and so on (China Handbook, 1956-57: 100). And the FETCC was consisted of the minister of Finance, the minister of Economic Affairs, the secretary-general of the CUSA, the executive secretary of the ESB, the chairman of the board of the Bank of Taiwan, the president of the Central Trust of China, and the representatives from the Central Bank of China as well as the Taiwan provincial government, etc (FETCC, 1969: 59-60). The overlap of personnel removed the boundaries that separated these organizations. It reduced the conflicts between the various agencies and made the economic bureaucracy as a whole relatively cohesive.

Moreover, with their budgets supported by U.S. aid, the organs covered by the economic bureaucracy in the medium sense (except the FETCC) enjoyed a degree of financial independence. Being free of the need to obtain legislative approval for its expenditures, these agencies were able to get rid of bureaucratic redundancy and act speedily on development projects. When U.S. aid ceased in 1965, a Sino-American Fund for Economic and Social Development was established to keep the agency for economic planning and the agency for agricultural development out of government budget. The source of the fund was the savings of a counterpart fund generated by the Local Currency Program. Continuously maintaining its principal in the amount of about 400 million U.S. dollars, the fund provided an outlay that shared 11.3% of the central government expenditure in the budget year of 1966. Owing to the progress of the economy, it offered only 0.6% of the central government expenditure in 1982 (CEPD, 1982: 19-22). The contributions of the Sino-American Fund to the independence and efficacy of the two agencies after the termination of U.S. aid should not be underestimated.

Finally, enjoying the advantage of financial independence and not being subject to civil service regulations, the agencies were able to pay higher salaries. This enabled them to recruit and retain a highly competent staff. The staff members of the agencies were payed 5 times higher than other government officials in equivalent positions in the early 1950s, although the gap has been gradually narrowed and reduced considerably today. These agencies were thus able to attract talented people and cultivate *esprit de corps* among their staff members. The turnover rate in these agencies was relatively low. The continuity of personnel in turn enabled the staff members to build a consensus on managing Taiwan's economic transformation and to switch the policies for development without organizational disruption. Along with the growth and increasing complexity of the economy, the organization of the economic general staff was also enlarged. For example, the professional staff of the ESB in the 1950s was less than fifty whereas the CEPD has a professional staff of more than 250 today. The expansion of the organization implied the increase of state capacity in managing economic activities.

In sum, the core agencies in the economic bureaucracy of the Kuomintang state were characterized by plentiful financial resources and a group of loyal and skilled officials. Although the various departments concerning economic development somehow conflicted with each other, this did not prevent the economic bureaucracy from acting as a corporate actor capable of triggering economic policy-making coherently. The concept of *unevenness of state capacities* points out that the state possesses different kinds of state capacities and these are not likely to be equal (for instance, a state may be strong in building military strength but weak in encouraging economic production or extracting taxes) (Skocpol, 1985: 17-18; Evans, Rueschemeyer, and Skocpol, 1975: 351-352). According to this concept, then, the KMT state undoubtedly showed a relatively strong capacity for intervening in economic transformation.

The Executive Yuan Council

The Executive Yuan is the highest administrative organ of the KMT state. Its function is equivalent to that of a cabinet in a cabinet system. There are three categories of subordinate organizations under the Executive Yuan: policy-making organization–the Executive Yuan Council; executive organization–the ministries and commissions; and subordinate organization–the Secretariat, Directorate-General of Budget, Accounting and Statistics, the government Information Office, and other special commissions. What should us concern here, of course, is the Executive Yuan Council.

The Executive Yuan Council is composed of the Premier and Vice Premier of the Executive Yuan, heads of the ministries and commissions, and ministers of state (without portfolio), with the Premier as chairman. The council meets once a week. It is responsible for the discussion and finalization of the statutory or budgetary bills and of bills concerning martial law, general amnesty, declaration of war, conclusion of peace or treaties, and other important matters to be submitted to the Legislative Yuan, as well as matters that are of concern to more than one ministry and commission (Republic of China 1986, 1986: 126). As a matter of course, all of the economic policies proposed by the economic bureaucracy have to be submitted to the Council to agree with those policies proposed by other ministries and commissions.

What was the status of the economic bureaucracy in the Executive Yuan Council? How much weight could the economic bureaucracy exert on the decision-making of the Council? As noted above, the core agencies in the economic bureaucracy were supra-ministry organizations that normally invited several ministers of the economy into their decision-making bodies. In addition, these organizations also included ministers heading the other strategic state units which might compete with the economic bureaucracy in the allocation of resources (i.e., the minister of National Defence and the minister of Communications). On the one hand, the economic bureaucracy occupied several seats in the Executive Yuan Council; on the other hand, the policies proposed by the economic bureaucracy had been consented to by the various competitors before they were submitted to the Council. Therefore, it seems quite plausible to argue that the policies submitted by the ecomonic bureaucracy would be seriously considered in the Council.

More importantly, in many cases, the economic bureaucracy was dominated by real power-holders. For instance, Ch'en Ch'eng, the strong man second only to Chiang Kai-shek in the 1950s and early 1960s, had served as the chairman of TPB from 1949 to 1953 and the chairman of the CUSA during 1950-54 and 1958-63; Chiang Ching-kuo, the new leader of the state since the late 1960s, headed the CIECD for the period of 1969 to 1973. As a matter of fact, for the last thirty-seven years, all of the Premiers, namely, Ch'en Ch'eng (from March, 1950 to June, 1954 and from July, 1958 to December, 1963), Yui Hung-chun (known as O. K. Yui, from July, 1954 to July, 1958), Yen Chia-kan (known as C. K. Yen, from December, 1963 to June, 1972), Chiang Ching-kuo (from June, 1972 to May, 1978), Sun Yun-suan (from May, 1978 to May, 1984), and Yu Kuo-hwa (since May, 1984), either had a professional background in managing the economy or had certain experience in directing the economic bureaucracy before holding the post. It is not inappropriate to call the Executive Yuan of the Kuomintang state an "economic-development-oriented cabinet." That is to say, the Executive Yuan Council rarely dropped or significantly revised the policy proposals submitted by the economic bureaucracy. And through most of Taiwan's postwar development period, the economic bureaucracy acted as a superministerial shadow cabinet.

The Central Standing Committee of the KMT (CSC)

The Central Standing Committee of the KMT is the supreme judge in the constitutional structure of making economic policy. As being the ruling party, the Kuomintang is supposed to guide the state by its ideals, its platform, and its policies. The CSC, the power center of the party, is the organ responsible for carrying out this task including that of national economic policy-making.

Nominations for the members of CSC are made by the chairperson of the party and they double the number of openings. The Central Committee holds a plenary session every year. The chairperson and the members of the Central Committee are elected by the National Congress of the party which holds its plenary session once every four years. Since the KMT state retreated to Taiwan, the two chairpersons of the party have been Chiang Kai-shek (who was *Tsungtsai* of the party until his death in 1975), and Chiang Ching-kuo who has been Chairman of the party since 1976. With the chairperson presiding over the CSC, the number of its members has been constantly on the rise. In 1952, there were 10 members (without counting Chiang Kai-shek as *Tsungtsai*); by 1984 the number had become thirty-one (without counting Chiang Ching-kuo as Chairman).

In the fifties and sixties, the CSC met with twice a week; since the seventies it meets only once. According to the meeting rules, the quorum of a regular meeting should be no less than one-half of the entire members. The resolution of proposal follows the rule of simple majority vote by raising hands. But, in reality, the CSC did not adopt the method of vote as a conventional way for any decision-making except personnel appointment. The decision-making process in CSC usually followes a pattern of mixing what James March and Herbert Simon (1958: 129-131) define as "problem-solving" and "persuasion." In normal situations, if a proposal involves technical or professional knowledge that highly relies on information collecting and fact judgement, the resolution is likely to be decided by the way of "problem-solving" which stresses the principle of respecting expertise. For those policies involving value judgement and arousing controversy between members, the resolutions tend to be obtained by "persuasion" in order to attain a certain degree of consensus among members (Ger, 1980: 101-102). Bitter debate and lasting bargaining rarely happen. Basically, the CSC is quite a cohesive organization. This is also a crucial reason for the persistent stability and coherence of the Kuomintang state.

Regarding the procedure of deciding national policy, proposals usually are sent to the Policy Coordination Commission first before they are submitted to the CSC. To coordinate relations between the party and the state, the Policy Coordination Commission of the Central Committee operates as a policy-formulating, coordinating, and liaison organ. There are several committees under the Commission to review the proposals. Among them, the Committees on Economic Affairs, Finance, the Budget, and Communications are the most relevant to economic policy-making. The comments by these committes on the proposals will be offered to the CSC also. In case of an emergency, however, the Executive Yuan can send the proposals to the CSC directly without going through the Commission.

What role did the CSC play the development of Taiwan's economy? What functions did it perform in making economic policy? To answer these questions, we need to put the CSC in a more comprehensive historical framework concerning the shift of the state's priorities and the switch of development strategies in Taiwan's economic transformation.

As Amsden (1985: 78) argues, a main challenge in understanding the role of the state in Taiwan's economic development is the fact that the state's initial aims were so clearly military and geopolitical rather than economic. When the Kuomintang government retreated to Taiwan in 1949, Amsden says, "the Guomindang was obsessed with one objective: military buildup in order to retake the Mainland." If this is true, then how can we explain the shift of the state's priorities of development from strengthening military power to promoting economic transformation which was particularly dramatic in the late fifties and early sixties?

In addition, the shift of the state's priorities during the period was accompanied by a switch of Taiwan's development strategies from import-substitution industrialization to export-led industrialization. This switch transformed Taiwan from a relatively closed economy to a highly open system. It influenced not only the economic aspect, but also the socio-political aspect of the society. While it remarkably improved Taiwan's socioeconomic situation as a whole, it also intruded upon the vested interests of many individuals or groups within or outside the state apparatus. Again, how can we explain this tremendous but smooth change?

According to the constitutional structure in making economic policy, the CSC seems to be the clue to the puzzle. The CSC, formally at least, is not only the power center of the Kuomintang, but also the center of state policy determination. It is an aggregation of power elites who hold the helm of Taiwan's postwar development. During the last thirty-seven years, all important policies that influenced Taiwan's economic transformation were undertaken only with the approval of the CSC. While promoting economic development and strengthening military might were conflicting objectives in the context of scarce resources in the Taiwan of the fifties and sixties, it was likely to be the top authority who gave the final judgment.

To a certain degree, we might assume that the CSC is a miniature of the Kuomintang state which reflects the nature of the state both in its internal structure and in its relation to the surrounding social structure. If the assumption is acceptable, then it is quite reasonable to analyze the relevance of the CSC and the policy-making for national development by studying the composition of its personnel, its evolution, as well as its operational practices.

There are two clues that can be followed in determining the composition of the CSC staff: their ethnic background and their professional background. With respect to the ethnic background (which implies the state's relation to Taiwan's society), we have already mentioned that due to the events of 1949, there had been a split between the state elits and the local dominant classes which brought about a separation the state from the society. We can assume that to extend its legitimacy and power base, the KMT began during the late fifties and early sixties to absorb more Taiwanese into the CSC. Insofar as this is the case, we can further hypothesize that since the Taiwanese members of the CSC would prefer promoting economic development to strengthening military power, the state's priorities were rearranged.

In regard to the professional background, which implies the state internal structuring, it is plausible to assume that the decision-making of the CSC should be strongly influenced by its members' career background and professional knowledge. Thus, if the CSC had been continuously dominated by the military rather than the economic officials, then the dramatic shift of the state's priorities would have been impossible. Meanwhile, in contrast to import-substitution industrialization, export-led industrialization requires more economic expertise and a freer socio-political environment with less military control. Moreover, export-led industrialization may imply less self-sufficiency with regard to security-relevant production. We hence assume that the military preferred import-substitution industrialization whereas the economic technocrats prefered export-led industrialization. Again, if the military had persistently occupied more seats than the economic technocrats in the CSC, the switch from import-substitution industrialization to export-led industrialization would have been unlikely.

In sum, we may hypothesize that, during the late fifties and sixties, the CSC had more Taiwanese staff members as well as people with economic professional background and less Mainlanders and military officers. Was this true?

Table 3.1 shows us the evolution of personnel composition in the CSC in terms of their ethnic background from 1952 to 1984. We discover that although the CSC did recruit more Taiwanese members

Table 3.1
Ethnic Background of the Members of the CSC, 1952-1984

	Total*	Taiwanese	Mainlander
1952	11	0	11
1953	11	0	11
1954	11	0	11
1955	11	0	11
1956	11	0	11
1957	17	1	16
1959	17	2	15
1960	17	2	15
1961	17	2	15
1962	17	2	15
1963	17	2	15
1964	19	2	17
1966	20	2	18
1967	20	2	18
1969	22	2	20
1970	22	2	20
1972	22	3	19
1973	22	3	19
1976	23	5	18
1978	23	5	18
1979	28	9	19
1981	28	9	19
1984	32	12	20

* These total numbers include Chiang Kai-shek as *Tsungtsai* from 1952 to 1973, Chen Cheng as Vice *Tsungtsai* from 1957 to 1964, and Chiang Ching-kuo as Chairman since 1976. These positions are elected by the National Congress which is convened in principle once every four years.

during the period of late 1950s and early 1960s, from none to one and then to two, the increase of Taiwanese members in the CSC was not significant. Furthermore, if we look at the background of these Taiwanese members in more depth, we find that they actually had resided in the mainland before Taiwan was retroceded to the ROC in 1945 and had no close relationships with Taiwanese local capitalists. Their presence in the CSC was meant to increase the foundation of the state rather than a signal of cutting down the autonomy of the state from the society. The first real native Taiwanese who resided in Taiwan before 1945 was recruited into the CSC in 1969. He was the owner of a manufacturing corporation (Liu, 1986: 64). But even in this case, he was nominated not because he represented the force of local capitalists but because he became the speaker of the Taipei City Council and his interest in developing national industry was appreciated by Chiang Kai-shek (Szuma, 1986b: 260-263). Moreover, according to relevant sources, he has not taken any initiative since his entrance into the highest elite circle of the KMT.

The situation remained in effect until Chiang Ching-kuo became Chairman of the party and of the CSC in 1976. In that year, 2 more native Taiwanese were absorbed into the CSC. This raised the number of Taiwanese members in the CSC to 5 and the proportion to 22%. Among these 5 members, 2 of them were local capitalists. But, again, they were nominated because they served as the speakers of Taipei City Council and Taiwan Provincial Assembly that represent, formally at least, the whole people of Taipei City and Taiwan Province rather than any specific class. Since that time on, the tendency towards "Taiwanization" became clearer. In 1979, of twenty-eight members, there were nine Taiwanese which constituted 32% of the total members. By 1984, the Taiwanese were increased to 12 thus constituting 38% of the entire 32 members. Most significantly, a Taiwanese member was recruited in 1981 who had not held any official post before but rather had served as the chairman of the Chinese National Association of Industry and Commerce–a non-official organization. The force of local capitalists was eventually invited into the power center of the party and the state approximately 20 years later than the time span that the hypothesis predicted. As a matter of fact, it was not the increase of Taiwanese members in the CSC that led to the policy shift of the KMT state, but the policy decision of "Taiwanization" by the party leaders that resulted in the increase of Taiwanese members.

In short, to augment its legitimacy and power base of ruling, the Kuomintang did absorb more Taiwanese into the CSC. But this movement was far behind the rearrangement of the state's priorities and did not become significant until the policy of "Taiwanization" had already been on the way. Most Taiwanese members had nothing to do with the interests of local capitalists or dominant classes. The force of local capitalists was recognized by the CSC only after the late seventies. Before that time, the local capitalists were recruited not owing to their economic influence but owing to their political influence of serving as people's representatives. The hypothesis concerning ethnic background therefore is not congruent with the findings. The shift of the state's priorities and the switch of the state's development strategies during late 1950s and early 1960s were irrelevant to the personnel evolution of the CSC regarding to their ethnic background. In other words, the concept of "pact of domination" which is determined by "the interrelations between the various parts of the state apparatus, on the one hand, and the most powerful classes or class fractions, on the other" (Rueschemeyer and Evans, 1985: 47), cannot be fitted in the facts we find.

Then, is the hypothesis concerned with professional background well-grounded? Table 3.2 demontrates the personnel evolution of the CSC in terms of professional background. We divide the professional background into four categories: military, economic, political, and cultural. The "military" category includes those members coming from the military. They either still serve in the military or have transferred to a civilian post but holding the military status concurrently. The "economic" category refers to work in economic planning, technical development, or enterprises (private or public). The political profession refers to the person whose regular work is people's representative or general administration in the party or the state other than the economic bureaucracy and the educational system. It includes the members of the five Yuans, governor of Taiwan, mayors of Taipei and Kaohsiung, speakers of Taiwan provincial assembly and Taipei and Kaohsiung city councils, and heads of the departments of the Central Committee of the KMT. And finally the cultural category refers to work in educational administration, university teaching, or mass media (Liu, 1986: 63).

From what we can deduce from table 3.2, it becomes clear that the hypothesis concerned with professional background should also be rejected. The personnel composition of the CSC regarding professional background remained virtually unchanged from 1952 to 1967. The percentage of CSC's members with military profession during late fifties and early sixties increased slightly from 29% (5 out of 17) to 35%

Table 3.2
Professional Background of the Members of the CSC, 1952-1984

	Total	Military*	Economic	Political**	Cultural
1952	11	3	0	6	2
1953	11	3	0	6	2
1954	11	3	0	6	2
1955	11	3	1	5	2
1956	11	3	1	5	2
1957	17	5	1	9	2
1959	17	5	1	9	2
1960	17	6	0	9	2
1962	17	5	0	10	2
1963	17	6	0	9	2
1964	19	6	1	11	1
1966	20	6	1	11	2
1967	20	6	1	11	2
1969	22	6	5	8	3
1970	22	6	5	8	3
1972	22	6	6	8	2
1973	22	5	6	9	2
1976	23	4	7	9	3
1978	23	4	7	9	3
1979	28	5	7	12	4
1981	28	4	7	11	6
1984	32	5	7	14	6

* Chiang Kai-shek (1952-73) and Chen Cheng (1952-64) are put in this category.
** Chiang Ching-kuo (1952-88) is put in this category.

(6 out of 17). At the same time, the proportion of the members with economic profession decreased from 6% (1 out of 17) to zero. The significant change had not happed until 1969. In that year, the number of the members with economic profession jumped from 1 to 5, whereas the number of the members with military profession remained at 6. That is to say, before 1969, economic officials basically did not enter the power center. They were excluded from the decision-making process in the CSC and did not outnumber the members in the military category.

From 1969 onward, the influence of the members with economic background evidently extended. In contrast, the number of military officers decreased steadily while there has been an increase of cultural elites and professional politicians from elective offices. The implications of these changes will be discussed later. What should concern us here is the connection between the CSC and the policy-making for Taiwan's economic development given these contradictory findings. It is obvious that no matter how rapidly the state's priorities and strategies for economic development changed during late 1950s and 1960s, the composition of the staff in the CSC basically remained the same with regard to both ethnic background and professional background. How can we explain this discrepancy between the personnel evolution of the CSC and the change of national development policies?

The answer, we believe, is that while the CSC nominally has the function of making economic policy and deciding the state's priorities for national development, in reality, it performs a passive rather than an active role in determining national policies. The substantive functions of the CSC are restricted for three reasons: (1) The power is not evenly shared by all of its members but highly concentrated in the hands of its chairperson, namely Chiang Kai-shek, Ch'en Ch'eng (he had been Vice *Tsungtsai* from 1957 to 1964), and Chiang Ching-kuo. If a policy has been decided by them before being submitted to the CSC, the other members rarely challenge the decision. It is the top political leadership's decisions rather than the votes of the members that give the final resolutions to the policy proposals submitted to CSC. (2) As we mentioned above, the style of decision-making in the CSC is a mixture of "problem-solving" and "persuasion" instead of bargaining and vote. Under the principle of respecting expertise, most policy proposals, especially those concerning economic activities, will be passed in original form without a great deal of change. (3) Due to the division of labor between the state and the party, the staff of CSC, such as the Policy

Coordination Commission, can only execute regular work in policy coordination rather than policy formulation. The main task of formulating policy is left to the elites in the state.

This argument can be confirmed by reviewing the minutes of the CSC during the period of late fifties and early sixties. We learn that although the change of policies for national development was so dramatic for this period, there were no heated debates on these policy proposals at the meetings of the CSC. In addition, we discover that these policy proposals had all been reported to and approved by Chiang Kai-shek and Ch'en Ch'eng before they were submitted to the CSC. With the support of Chiang Kai-shek and Ch'en Ch'eng, these policies were passed by the CSC almost unanimously. In other words, the decisive steps of making these policies were determined outside the jurisdiction of the CSC. Since the CSC was not a crucial component in the KMT state's economic policy-making process, our analysis of the economic policy-making structure will leave out this organization and focus on the economic bureaucracy.

In sum, the CSC was a cohesive and autonomous organization. Its decisions on economic policy and national development in principle reflected the top political leadership's will rather than the interests of social dominant classes or the compromise among different factions of state managers. It acted much more as a corporate unit representing what the top political leadership believed or claimed to be universal interests for the country than as an expression of pacts of domination or an arena of social conflict.

The Legislative Yuan

The Legislative Yuan is the highest lawmaking organ of the state. Its functions and powers are similar to that of the parliaments in Western nations. According to the Constitution of the Republic of China, the Legislative Yuan exercises the powers of legislation, consent, initiation of constitutional amendments, decisions on statutes, government budget, martial law, general amnesty, declaration of war, conclusion of peace, and making of treaties, and other constitutional powers and functions (Hoh, 1971: 13-16). The Executive Yuan is required to keep the Legislative Yuan informed of its administrative policies and acts. The Legislative Yuan has the right of interpellation, refusal to concur, and of altering by resolution any important policy. Confronted with the Legislative Yuan's resolution, the Executive Yuan may, with the approval of the President of the Republic, request the Legislative Yuan's reconsideration. If, after reconsideration, two-thirds of the attending members of the Legislative Yuan uphold the original ressolution, the Premier must either accede to the Legislative Yuan's view or tender his resignation.

The members of the Legislative Yuan are elected by the people. A member serves a term of three years and is eligible for re-election. But since Mainland China was lost to the Chinese Communists in 1949, no national election has been held on the mainland. With the nation confronted with a serious situation, Chiang Kai-shek sent request to the Legislative Yuan for members of the first constitutional Legislative Yuan elected in 1948 to continue excercising the right of legislation. With the concurrence of the Yuan, the practice was further conformed when the Council of Grand Justices ruled that, "When elections of new members cannot be conducted according to law, it is necessary that members of the Legislative Yuan of the first convention continue to perform their functions," on January 29, 1954 (Republic of China 1986, 1986: 129).

The members of the first convention of the Legislative Yuan were elected in 1948. While the total membership under the pertinent regulations was set at 773, 760 were actually elected. When the central government was relocated in Taipei, 539 of them followed the Kuomintang state moving to Taiwan (China Handbook, 1956-57: 117). By continuously holding their posts without re-election, consequently, the overwhelming majority of the members in the Legislative Yuan are those who were elected by the people on the mainland more than three decades ago. To fill the membership of the central elective offices which have become vacant by the death of those "old" members and the increase of population on Taiwan, as well as to broaden fundation to the Kuomintang state, elections have been held since 1969. As a result, in the 1983 election, 98 new members entered the legislative Yuan. By May 31, 1985, the number of the members of the Legislative Yuan totaled 348. In other words, about 250 among them were the "old" members (Republic of China 1986, 1986: 130).

No less than 90% of the old members are party members of the KMT. In the fifties and sixties, before the new members joined the Yuan, the old Kuomintang members split roughly into two factions. The minor faction often allied themselves with other old non-Kuomintang members to play a role of opposition, whereas the dominant faction with absolute majority always supported the bills submitted by the Executive Yuan. Nevertheless, the new, non-Kuomintang, radical members elected after 1969 have gradually substituted the role of opposition originally played by the minor factions of the old members. Confronted with the challenge and radical assertions from the new non-Kuomintang members, the minor faction of the old Kuomintang members have changed their attitude to cooperate with the major faction. Meanwhile, among the new members, more than 80% are the KMT's members. Therefore, the Kuomintang can control the Legislative Yuan easily (Ch'en, 1985: 133-172; Peng, 1985: 284-287).

The Policy Coordination Commission of the KMT is responssible for coordinating the Executive Yuan and the Legislative Yuan. For an important policy already decided by the CSC, the Policy Coordination Commission will help the Executive Yuan to get passage for the bill by calling on the KMT's members in the Legislative Yuan. That is to say, CSC can guarantee that the bills submitted by the Executive Yuan will be passed in the Legislative Yuan.

In a normal case, the Legislative Yuan is most likely to be an instrument of domination or an arena of social conflict. However, due to the prolongation of tenure of the old members, the Yuan became quite autonomous from society. Even though there were a few factions among the members and the opposition continually produced dissensions, the Yuan in effect operated coherently in cooperating with the Executive Yuan.

Therefore, in spite of its role and functions as the representative of the people, the Legislative Yuan of the Kuomintang government was relatively insulated from the society on Taiwan. It operated more like a part of an autonomous state than a confluence or a battlefield of social forces. The whole constitutional structure of making economic policy of the Kuomintang state thus operated rather coherently. Of course, due to the increment of the new members in recent years, the situation has somewhat changed.

A Remark on the Constitutional Structure of Economic Policy-making

In the preceding analysis, we tried to figure out the characteristics of the Kuomintang state in making economic policy by tracing the formal bureaucratic mechanisms. We discovered that the constitutional structure of making economic policy was mainly composed of four organizations at different hierarchical positions and with diverse legal authorities: the economic bureaucracy was responsible for drafting policy proposal and triggering policy formulation; the Executive Yuan

Council was in charge of according proposed economic policy with other national policies; the CSC represented the ruling party and held the supremacy of making final decisions; and the Legislative Yuan representing the people bore the responsibilities of deciding on the statutory bills submitted by the Executive Yuan.

The configuration of these components showed some distinctive organizational features conducive to the ability of the Kuomintang state to regulate economic transformation. In regard to the aspect of *state capacities,* we observed that all of the organizations individually enjoyed a certain degree of internal cohesiveness that brought their official functions easier into play. Combined as a whole, these organizations were integrated into a quite coherent network with the extremely dominant ruling party as the pivot. At the same time, the core agencies of the economic bureaucracy were characterized by plentiful financial resources and competent officials. In respect to the aspect of *state autonomy,* we observed that the CSC, the power center of both the state and the party, was highly autonomous from society, the same as the Legislative Yuan, which normally tends to be an instrument of domination or an arena of social conflict. In a certain sense, we may contend that the analysis of the constitutional structure of making economic policy is strikingly corresponding with our argument that the Kuomintang state plays a capable and autonomous role in managing Taiwan's economic transformation.

However, we also learned that there are some important features of the state do not become apparent when only examining the constitutional structure of economic policy-making. For example, when we pointed out that the CSC formally was the supreme judge in economic policy-making, we at the same time realized that instead of contributing substantive functions, the CSC in practice did not play an active role. It was the real power-holders' decisions rather than the votes by the members of the CSC that gave the final resolutions to the policy proposals. The decisive steps of making many important economic policies were determined by the top political leadership and some economic policy makers outside the jurisdiction of the CSC. In fact, the policy-making in the KMT state, especially in the earlier stages of Taiwan's postwar development, was somewhat colored by the characteristic rule of certain men rather than law or bureaucratic regulations. Many important economic policies were fomented and decided in the interactions among certain state elites that did not wholly correspond with the constitutional structure of making economic policy. Then, what happened there?

It has been argued that Taiwan's economic transformation was propelled by a group of officials whose viewpoints of managing Taiwan's economy were tolerated and respected by the leadership of the KMT (King, 1981: 10). If this is true, the continuous control of government by the KMT should enable us to identify the personnel who formulated economic policy and probe into their ideas about managing Taiwan's economy. It could also answer the following questions: What were the relationships between these officials and the top political leadership? How did they handle conflicts between the proposed economic policies and policies proposed by other competitory state units? And how did their opinions prevail in regulating Taiwan's development?

As Johnson (1982: ix) puts it, we should not treat bureaucracies and state policies as disembodied abstractions having little reference to the way things actually happened. Development policy-making cannot be abstracted from the state elites' assessments of development situation, their preferences of development objectives, their personal interests and those of their constituencies. To understand the implications of state policies concering economic transformation on Taiwan, we ought not simply accept the approach of examining functions and authorities of constitutional organizations; we should further step in the practice underneath the constitutional process of policy-making.

Moreover, by viewing the state as a decision-making arena, we could imagine that no matter how autonomous the state is, the decision-making in the state apparatus cannot be absolutely impervious to the demands or opinions from the external environment at intra-national level or even international level. The KMT state received a great amount of U.S. aid and invited many Americans to be its advisors in the 1950s and early 1960s. Further, the KMT state was originally an "exogenous" state which needed to consolidate its legitimacy and extend its foundation in the Taiwan society. Finally, the state shifted the strategies for development from import-substitution industrialization to export-led industrialization since the early 1960s which required more cooperations from both the local and multinational capitalists. Given all these three factors, there probably existed certain kinds of mechanisms that brought the opinions and demands from the external environment into the decision-making process in the state apparatus. What were these mechanisms? Since the constitutional structure of economic policy-making did not cover these issues, an operational structure combining all of the strategically important components within and outside the state apparatus might offer us a more comprehensive picture of the actual operational process of formulating economic policy in Taiwan's postwar development. We will discuss this constitutional structure of economic policy-making in the next chapter.

CHAPTER 4

POLICY MAKERS AND THE OPERATIONAL ECONOMIC POLICY-MAKING STRUCTURE

An Introduction to the Operational Economic Policy-making Structure

The operational structure of making economic policy in Taiwan's postwar development may be drawn as figure 4.1. There were several groups at different levels involved in the policy-making. Within the state apparatus, three groups could be distinguished: the top political leadership, the economic policy makers, and the economic bureaucrats. With respect to the social structure surrounding the state apparatus, there were a group of consulting economists and a group of local capitalists at intra-national level accompanied by a group of American advisors and a group of transnational capitalists at international level, contributing to the formulation of economic policy.

In comparison with the constitutional structure of making economic policy, the operational structure displays some important special features. Firstly, it presents a better portrait of the real power structure of making economic policy in the KMT state. To a certain extent, the KMT state was characterized by an authoritarian style of leadership, in which the top political leadership was the real powerholder. All important national policies had to obtain the approval of the top political leadership before they were formally formulated and executed. At the same time, if a policy had already got the support from the top political leadership, it usually could get the passage in the relevant legal authorities, such as the CSC and the Legislative Yuan, without much resistance. Therefore, it was the interactions between the top political leadership and a group of economic policy makers rather than the votes by the members of the CSC and the Legislative Yuan that decided the economic policies. In this sense, the operational structure can offer us a more fruitful clue to understand the practice of making economic policy in the KMT state.

Secondly, it demonstrates a more comprehensive and penetrating picture of the formulation of economic policy in Taiwan's economic transformation. We believe that a better exposition of national policy-making should bring all of the strategically important components within and outside the state apparatus into the discussion. It should examine the organization and interests of the state, specify the organization and interests of socioeconomic groups, and inquire into the com-

Figure 4.1
The Operational Structure of Economic Policy-making

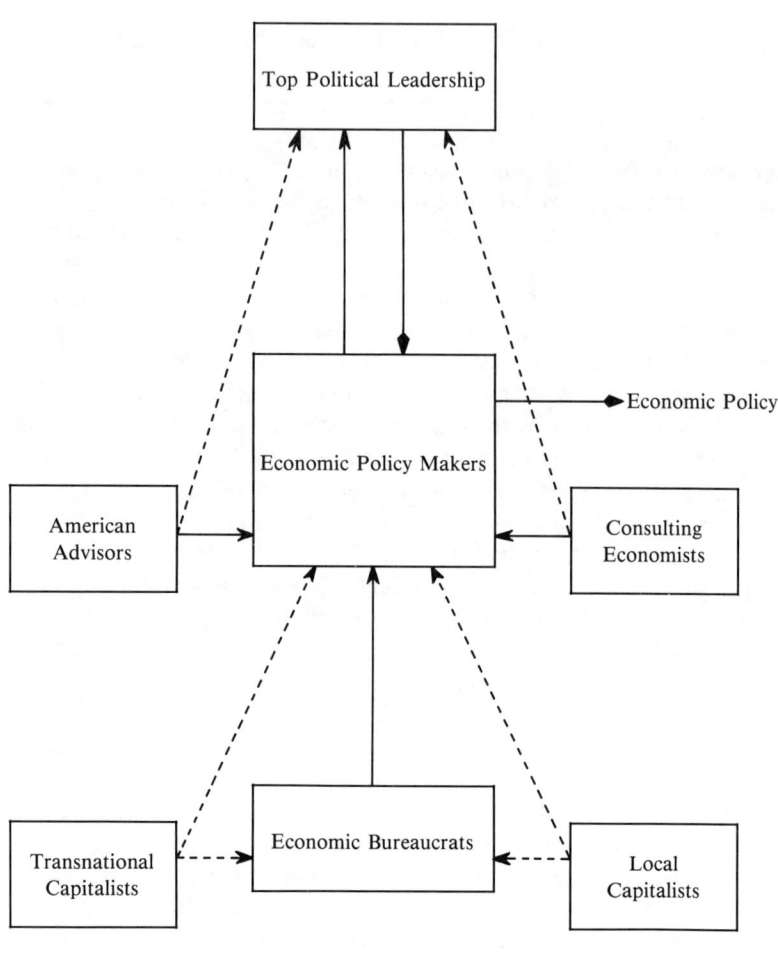

```
*    ----→  Indirect input
**   ―――→  Direct input
***  ―――►  Policy decision
```

plementary as well as conflicting relationship of state and societal actors (Skocpol, 1985: 20). Although the KMT state was highly autonomous from the Taiwan society, it was not impervious to the influence from the external environment both at intra-national and international levels. In the meantime, although the internal organization of the KMT state was quite coherent, it could not totally avoid the conflicts derived from different factions. The operational structure will enable us to cover these issues. It tries to combine all the major interest groups and political action groups into a policy network that embodies the internal structure of the KMT state and the relationship between the state and its surrounding social structure.

Lastly, the operational structure of making economic policy allows us to probe into the thinking or ideology that directed Taiwan's economic transformation. As regard the relevance of ideology to making national economic policy, we are of the opinion that aside from the interests of the individuals and groups within and outside the state apparatus, economic policy-making cannot be abstracted from policy makers' knowledge about the essence of economic activity, from their preferences for certain development goals, and from their assessments toward development situation. As Keynes (1964: 383-384) wrote in the concluding paragraph of the *General Theory*, "...the ideas of economists and political philosophers, both when they are right and when they are wrong, are more powerful than is commonly understood. Indeed the world is ruled by little else....I am sure that the power of vested interests is vastly exaggerated compared with the gradual encroachment of ideas....soon or late, it is ideas, not vested interests, which are dangerous for good or evil." This argument is particularly applicable to the case of Taiwan. We will find out later that since the Kuomintang state was highly autonomous from and extraordinary dominant over the society on the island, the formulation of economic policy in Taiwan's postwar development, especially for the earlier stage, to certain degree should be attributed to the thinking of some leading state managers. In addition, we will discover that along with the transformation of Taiwan's economy, there came a change of the state's attitude toward the role and functions of the state in managing economic development, which should be somehow related to the gradual encroachment of certain ideas and could not be explained entirely by the interplay of interests. Indeed, the persistence or change in the thinking of some key figures of the KMT state constitutes a crucial clue to grasp the evolution of Taiwan's development strategies. It undoubtedly deserves a study in more detail.

The Top Political Leadership

Let us start with the supreme power center of economic policy-making in the operational structure–the top political leadership. It mainly refers to Chiang Kai-shek (1887-1975) and Ch'en Ch'eng (1898-1965) for the 1950s and 1960s as well as Chiang Ching-kuo (1910-1988) since the 1970s. For the last thirty-seven years, these three persons have been the real power-holders and final decision-makers as far as the priorities for national development and the regulation of Taiwan's economic transformation is concerned. All of the important economic policies that influenced the economy were formulated and executed under their supervision. Without their approval and support, the various reform programs contributing to Taiwan's economic progress would have been impossible.

Aside from economic policy-making, the role and functions of the top political leadership were actually more political than economic. As Gold (1986: 5) points out, in order to explain Taiwan's miraculous development we need to ask, first, how Taiwan attained and sustained the high economic growth rates, second, how it maintained political and social stability in the course of its economic takeoff. Or, put another way, we may ask how the KMT state managed to maintain the stable socio-political circumstance that allowed Taiwan to bring about such an economic miracle. Among the many possible reasons, a strong and stable top political leadership was an unquestionable one.

The state on Taiwan was characterized by a paternalistic style of leadership. Within the state apparatus, the leadership meant rule by a dominant figure who held ultimate authority on all problems (Pye, 1985: 7). Residing at the apex of the power pyramid, the top political leadership was immune from the power or ideological struggle among its subordinates. Under its control, the conflict among the subordinate state managers would not be permitted to hurt the cohesiveness of the state orginazation and the coherence of the state action too much–it thus constituted the main source of the cohesiveness and coherence of the Kuomintang state. Meanwhile, regarding the relationship between the state and the society, the paternalistic style of leadership implied that the ruler had an obligation to look after his subjects, while they owed loyalty to the ruler so long as he did not depart from the expected norms of right conduct (Clough, 1978: 48-49). One of the main tasks of the state in this system was to nurture a spirit of national consensus and to encourage cooperation among all elements of the society. The people were taught to conform to state policies and the state felt it should have the right to limit real dissent (Pye, 1985: 6). Of course, as we will see in the later discussion, the situation has changed a lot. Accompanied with the rapid transformation of the economy, today's Taiwan in many aspects has left behind those features noted above. But, roughly speaking, the preceding description is applicable to most of Taiwan's postwar development.

In this paternalistic system, the top political leadership's attitude toward national development and its ability to lead the state as well as rule the society should undoubtedly be seen as crucil to understand Taiwan's economic miracle. Accordingly, it is necessary to examine the thinking and doing of the top political leadership in more depth. We will start with our discussion on Chiang Kai-shek, followed by Ch'en Ch'eng, and then Chiang Ching-kuo.

Born in a middle-income family in a small town of Chekiang province (a coastal province near the estuary of the Yangtze River) in 1887, Chiang Kai-shek received a traditional Chinese primary education in Confucian classics. He then spent his adolescence in military schools, first in China and then in Japan. According to a study by Allen P. L. Liu (1986: 42-52), the early socialization of Chiang-his memory of rural society, his attitude toward traditional culture, and his experience of adolescence-formed the foundation of his ideology concerning the social and economic rescnstruction of China. Roughly speaking, Chiang's memory of Chinese rural community led him to believe that land reform should be implemented in a mild and peaceful way; the education in his childhood made him a fervent believer in the fundamental worth of Confucian ethics; and his adolescent life in military schools molded him into an "administrator" type of politician who identified himself with less remote objects and attached himself to specific individuals, such as Sun Yat-sen.*

Chiang joined *T'ung-meng-hui,* the forerunner of the Kuomintang, in 1907 when he studied in Japan at the age of 20. Once out of military school, Chiang had quickly taken part in the revolution that overthrew the Manchu dynasty led by Sun Yat-sen. He was appointed the commander of Whampoa Military Academy in Kwangtung province by Sun Yat-sen in 1923 at age 36. He thereafter started his career as a leader

---

* Harold Lasswell (1960: 125-126 and 151-152) distinguishes two types of politicians: agitators and administrators. Agitators tend to identify themselves with remote objects such as abstract doctrines or ideals. A dministrators, nevertheless, tend to identify themselves with less remote objects and attach themselves more or less to some specific individuals. Liu identifys Mao Tse-tung as the agitator in contrast to Chiang Kai-shek as the administrator.

first in the military and then in politics. In 1926, he was appointed the commander-in-chief of the National Revolutionary Army to lead the Northern Expedition, which resulted in the unification of China in 1928 though did not really eradicate the entrenched warlords. From 1928 to 1931, he was elected President of the Nationalist government and held at different periods the posts of Premier and minister of Education. He had been the chairman of the National Military Council for 1932 to 1946. At certain periods between 1932 and 1937, he was concurrently the chief of general staff, chairman of National Economic Council, Premier, and state councilor. During World War II, he was the supreme commander of the Allied Forces in the China Theater. He was reelected President of the Nationalist government in 1943 and then elected the President of the Republic of China by the first constitutional National Assembly in April, 1948. When the Kuomintang was defeated by the Chinese Communist Party on the mainland, Chiang Kai-shek temporarily retired from the presidency on January 21, 1949. He resumed it on Taiwan on March 1, 1950. He then had been reelected President for 5 terms (6 years for a term) until his death on April 5, 1975. In addition, Chiang had been a member of the Central Executive Committee–the forerunner of the CSC–between 1926 and 1950. He was elected *Tsungtsai* (Director-General) of the Kuomintang in 1938 and held the post for the rest of his life (China Handbook, 1956-57: 712; Tung, 1967)

Due to his training background, Chiang considered himself a layman at economic and financial affairs. He admitted that much in a talk in 1966 when he explained why he nominated C. K. Yen as the candidate for Vice President of the Republic of China after the death of former Vice President Ch'en Ch'eng. Trying to persuade the senior and important members of the KMT to support this nomination, Chiang Kai-shen frankly stated that "My specialties are in military and party affairs whereas comrade C. K. Yen's specialties are in foreign, financial, and economic affairs. His merits are just my weak points..." (Yang, 1986: 160). Indeed, since he assumed the total command of the KMT state in the late 1920s, Chiang rarely intervened in economic policy-making directly. Before retreating to Taiwan, he relied on T. V. Soong and H. H. Kung in dealing with financial and economic affairs. After withdrawing from Mainland China, he trusted the economy to Ch'en Ch'eng and a new cohort of economic officials. However, this by no means implies that Chiang had no idea about the way the economic transformation of China or Taiwan should go. Also, it is not true that Chiang had no preference as to the often-conflicting goals of economic development. On the contrary, he did express his views on Chinese economy in lectures and writings.

Since Chiang Kai-shek joined the Nationalist Revolution, he had attached himself to the pioneer of the revolution–Sun Yat-sen. Thereafter, and during all of his life, Chiang had always been a true believer in Sun Yat-sen's ideology. His views on Chinese economy were basically an elucidation of Sun's doctrine–the *Min-sheng* Principle (or the Principle of People's Livelihood). To demonstrate his adovocacy to Sun Yat-senism, Chiang had added two supplementary chapters to Sun's lectures on the Min-sheng Principle, unfinished due to the demise of Sun in 1925 (Chiang, 1954). A more systematic exposition of Chiang's thinking on China's economic development was displayed in his work, *Chung-kuo ching-chi hsueh-shuo* (The Theory of the Chinese Economy), written in 1943 (Chiang, 1963). In this work, Chiang stressed the principle of *Chung-yung* (Golden Mean), traditional Chinese ethos, conciliation of interests of various social groups, planned development, equal emphasis on public and private enterprises, mutual respect between workers and professionals, and peaceful land reform so as to attain the general goals of *yang-min* (caring for the people) and *pao-min* (maintaining the livelihood of the people) (Liu, 1986: 54).

Unfortunately, troubles within and without China prevented Chiang from carrying out those ideas. He had to devote most of his attention and skill to military campaigns against the remnaning warlords, the Communists, and the Japanese as well as to the delicate process of keeping competing political cliques and restless military subordinates under control. Even worse was the measures that he resorted to extract resources for military campaigns, such as unlimited increase of money supply and budget deficit, which resulted in uncontrollable inflation. The inflation bankrupted China's economy and also the KMT state in the late fourties. As a result, the Communists defeated the KMT and took over the mainland.

The defeat that Chiang suffered in the mainland forced him to examine the course of his action. After moving to Taiwan, in various talks in the 1950s, Chiang (1958) stated that the KMT had hitherto spent its energy more in the political and national revolution than in the economic and social reform, and that the party was too factionalized in itself and too exclusive from society (Liu, 1986: 54). From July, 1950 to June, 1952, he established the Central Reform Committee (an ad hoc organization to substitute for the Central Executive Committee and the forerunner of the CSC) to eliminate the "unauthorized factors" in the party (Riggs, 1952: 37-38). In the reform plan, Chiang told his

followers:
> Almost every one of our comrades knows that our failure in the anti-communist struggle is due to our neglect of the *Ming-sheng* Principle in the mainland. Every comrades also knows that henceforth in our anti-Communist struggle we must rely on the Principle. However, let me ask: During the past four years in the mainland, did any of our party branches in the villages ever carry out land survey? Did any city party office conduct any labor survey? Did any provincial party office submit any report based on systematic social and economic investigation? We should realize the *Min-sheng* Principle through practical action, not theoretical discussion (Chung-hua min-kuo nien-chien 1950, 1951: 123).

At the same time, the impact of economic chaos on postwar China improved his knowledge about economic activity and reshaped his preference towards the objectives of economic development. Economic stability became his major concern which in turn formed the fundamental line of Taiwan's development. In contrast to the previous policies adopted in Mainland China, the KMT state tried to do its best to check inflation and balance government budget on Taiwan even at the expense of economic growth. Accordingly, Taiwan's economic policymaking was featured by paying much attention to economic stability. However, Chiang's most important contribution to the economy was the reorganization of the KMT state into a coherent organization and his service as an impregnable leader.

As Ralph Clough (1978: 47-48) argues, from the time that Chiang Kai-shek assumed control of the Nationalist government on Taiwan, the general acceptance of his legitimacy as the national leader was an important stabilizing factor. Before moving his force to Taiwan, Chiang Kai-shek had been elected *Tsungtasi* of the KMT and President of the Republic of China in 1948. He was also commander-in-chief of the armed forces. Despite the blow of losing the mainland to the Communists, when he arrived in Taiwan in 1949 as head of the state, party, and army, no one was in a position to challenge his authority. Retaining in his hands broad powers to appoint, dismiss, or transfer officials, both military and civilian, Chiang Kai-shek employed a system of checks and balances in his assignment of personnel to prevent any individual or agency from becoming too powerful. By controlling the chains of command in state, party, military, and security, he placed himself in an impregnable position. Undoubtedly, the orientation and priorities of Taiwan's development were firmly guided in accordance with his thinking and will.

Chiang Kai-shek's decisive role in determining Taiwan's development can be portrayed by his disposition of the contradiction between the return-to-the-mainland ideologues and the pro-development pragmatists in the state and the party. For many years, there was a continual tension between those who placed prime emphasis on the goal of recovering Mainland China, consisting mainly of old party figures and high-ranking military officers, and those who favored concentrating on the development of Taiwan, consisting mainly of economic and technical officials. The distinction between them should not be exagerated, for both groups were staunch Chinese nationalists who strongly opposed accepting domination by Peking on the one hand, and separating Taiwan from China permanently on the other. The conflict was on the priorities and allocation of resources. The ideologues did not oppose the development of Taiwan, but were against allowing it to detract from the struggle with the Communists. The pragmatists did not reject the goal of recovering the mainland, but they argued that the best hope of achieving this goal was to develop and modernize Taiwan as rapidly as possible in order to improve its capacity to serve as a base for the future recovery of the mainland, rather than to divert attention and resources to quixotic attempts to act before the time was ripe.

According to Clough (1978: 45), Chiang Kai-shek himself headed the ideologues by insisting on a greater diversion of resources to military and security purpose than the pragmatists would have preferred. But Clough also recognized that Chiang was not impervious to the arguments of the pragmatists. On the contrary, Chiang decided time and direction for permitting the rapid economic development to go forward. As the final authority in Taiwan, he determined how the balance should be struck between ideologues and pragmatists, and with the passage of time and the fading of prospects for recovering the mainland by arm force, the balance tilted increasingly in favor of the pragmatists.

In fact, contrary to the view that Chiang Kai-shek had mortgaged Taiwan's development to his desire of recovering Mainland China, as early as the Kuomintang government was driven out of the mainland, Chiang had attributed the debacle in large part to the callapse of the economy and given great scope over Taiwan's economy to Western-trained experts and avoided to hurt economic development by military building-up. Despite his dedication to the goal of mainland recovery, Chiang Kai-shek had given priority to economic development soon after he resumed the leadership on Taiwan. Thus, the Kuomintang communique on party reform in 1950 stated, "We must start from Taiwan. We must not only defend but also build Taiwan." And Chiang declared in 1951, "What we should be concerned with is *not* that we are unable to take the mainland back but that we are incapable of building Taiwan up" (emphasis added) (Ch'in, 1966: 317; Liu, 1986: 87).

Chiang Kai-shek's authority as leader derived not only from his skill at political maneuver but also from his selection of able officials for key positions. Although he was criticized for valuing loyalty above ability on the mainland, many of his military and civilian officials in Taiwan were competent. Among them, Ch'en Ch'eng was a key figure.

Ch'en Ch'eng was born also in Chekiang province in 1897. Younger than Chiang Kai-shek by 10 years, Ch'en Ch'eng joined the Kuomintang in 1920 and graduated from Paoting Military Academy in 1922, the same school that Chiang Kai-shek had graduated from in 1906. When Chiang set up Whampoa Military Academy in 1924, Ch'en served as a member of the faculty with the rank of captain. Thereafter, he followed Chiang to almost every important military campaign and became one of Chiang's most important assistants. During the war against Japan's invasion, Ch'en had been the governor of Hupeh province from 1938 to 1944 and the minister of War for 1944 to 1945. After the war, he was promoted chief of general staff and concurrently commander-in-chief of the Chinese Navy for the period 1946-48. When the situation on Mainland China began to deteriorate in 1949, Ch'en was appointed by Chiang governor of Taiwan in order to handle the mission of relocating the central government in Taiwan. Soon after the central government moved to Taipei, he was made Premier in 1950. Four years later, he became the Vice President of the Republic of China. He was also elected Vice *Tsungtsai* of the Kuomintang in 1957. In 1958, when Premier O. K. Yui resigned and crisis of the Taiwan Strait had started, Ch'en resumed the post of Premier and reorganized the cabinet. He had held the posts of Vice President and Premier concurrently for 5 years. In December, 1963, he resigned as Premier because of health problems. He died on March 5, 1965 (China Yearbook, 1963-64: 722; Yang, 1986: 146-159).

Ch'en Ch'eng's training and career background was similar to Chiang Kai-shek's. As a serviceman, his specialty was not in economic and financial affairs; however, the experience of serving as the governor of Hupeh province in the period of 1938-44 seem to have improved his ability in managing administrative and economic affairs to a certain degree. He had already tries during that period to carry out some policies for land reform, such as the reduction of farm rents. This device was then applied on Taiwan as the first step of the well-known land reform. Indeed, Ch'en was the most important figure in putting forward and carrying out the task. More importantly, while Chiang Kai-shek held away over Taiwan's entire development in the fifties and sixties, he delegated full authority concerning the managing of the economy on Ch'en Ch'eng until Ch'en's death. For this period, in addition to the posts of Premier and Vice President, Ch'en also took charge of some core agencies for economic development; he became chairman of the TPB (June, 1949 to December, 1949), and chairman of the CUSA (March, 1950 to June, 1954 and July, 1958 to December, 1963).

Holding the authority delegated by Chiang Kai-shek, Ch'en Ch'eng became the most powerful man in determining economic and financial affairs. Although he had no professional knowledge in economic development, he enthusiastically backed a group of brilliant economic officials who shaped Taiwan's economic transformation (Clough, 1978: 48; Liao, 1986: 52-61). The relationship between Ch'en and these economic officials is defined in his famous phrase: "I am not a learned man myself, but I can accept and execute opinions from learned people." Sincerely trusted by Chiang Kai-shek, Ch'en Ch'eng also fully delegated authority and gave complete support to his subordinates that in turn brought state capacities into play (Chou, 1982a: 8). Ch'en Ch'eng's untimely death somewhat slowed down the vigorous dynamics of reforming Taiwan's economy; it was Chiang Ching-kuo, Chiang Kai-shek's son, who opened a new era of Taiwan's development.

Chiang Ching-kuo was born in Chiang Kai-shek's hometown in 1910. Like his father, he received Chinese traditional education in his childhood. But he went to Shanghai in 1922 and received Western education there. Probably influenced by the atmosphere against Western imperialism in Shanghai and the first alliance of the Kuomintang and the Chinese Communist Party (CCP) at that time, Chiang Ching-kuo decided to study abroad at Sun Yat-sen University, a college newly set up in Moscow in memory of Sun Yat-sen, in October, 1925 at age 15. He then entered Central Tolmatchef Military & Political Institute in Leningrad in 1927. Due to the breaking off of the KMT-CCP alliance, Chiang was forced to stay in the Soviet Union for 12 years until March, 1937, after the second united front of the KMT and the CCP was established. During this period, Chiang had worked as a teaching assistant at Lenin University, had been an apprentice in an electric manufactory, a farmer, a mining worker, an engineer of a heavy machinery plant, and an associated manager of the plant (Chiang, 1984: 11-75). The experience of living in the Soviet Union gave him the keenest eyes on the practice of communism and revised the radical socialist inclination in his adolescence while molding his popular style of leadership.

From 1939 to 1945, Chiang Ching-kuo had been the administrative commissioner for the southern region of Kiangsi province. His performance won him the nickname of *Chiang Ch'ing-t'ien,* an honorable appellation for the upright official in old China. After the victory over Japan, he was appointed special foreign affairs commissioner for Northeast China to deal with Russia about taking over Munchuria. Then, in August, 1948, when the economic situation was quickly getting worse, Chiang accepted a special appointment as deputy economic control supervisor for Shanghai to try to order the economic activities of that financial and monetary center of China. Those two special missions were not successful (Chiang, 1984: 76-146); the experience, nonetheless, improved his understanding of foreign and economic affairs.

When Ch'en Ch'eng was appointed governor of Taiwan province to handle the relocation of the state in 1949, Chiang Ching-kuo was appointed chairman of the KMT Taiwan Provincial Headquarters with orders to rebuild the party. From 1950 to 1952, he was a member of the Central Reform Committee and, since 1952, he has been a member of the CSC. He was elected Chairman of the KMT in 1975 to succeed Chiang Kai-shek. In the state system, he started his career as director of the Political Department of Ministry of National Defense during the period of 1950-54. From 1954 to 1967, he had been deputy secretary-general of National Defense Council. He concurrently held the posts of chairman of Vocational Assistance Commission for Retired Serviceman (1957-64), vice minister of National Defense (1964-65), and minister of National Defense (1965-69). After affirming his influence within the military and security spheres, he moved upward through the state hierarchy. He first took charge of supervising economic transformation in 1969 when he was appointed Vice Premier and director of the chief organ for economic development–the CIECD. He then became Premier and began to handle the entire national development in 1972. When Chiang Kai-shek died in 1975, he had already taken over his father's position as Taiwan's principal active leader. He was elected the President of the Republic of China in 1978 and has been reelected to continue his second term since 1984.

Chiang Ching-kuo's ideology of managing economic development can be discribed through his doings in southern Kiangsi. For instance, he tried to implement a land reform whose contents were similar to the land reform in Taiwan; he set up a cooperative system to save necessary consumer goods from the hands of speculative businessmen and save the people from severe inflation; and he improved the primary and secondary education system to develop human capital. In addition, when he was carrying out the special mission of controlling Shanghai's economy, he adopted some ruthless measures to punish the profiteers within and outside the state apparatus. Of course, what we should keep in mind is that these measures were undertaken during extraordinary periods and should not be considered as Chiang's fundamental viewpoints. In effect, his contribution to the economic transformation of Taiwan has been political rather than economic, just like Chiang Kai-shek's and Ch'en Ch'eng's.

Chiang Ching-kuo has been widely accepted as a successful leader by demonstrating the skill of combining willingness to take decisive action, ability to select and use competent subordinates, and receptivity to advice from a variety of sources (Clough, 1978: 67). His popular style of leadership won support from the people on the island. He also showed a strong will to make economic development the state's first priority. As we can see, the proportion of the members with economic profession in the CSC has quickly increased since he assumed the post of Vice Premier in 1969. In addition, the two Premiers after his term, namely Sun Yun-suan and Yu Kuo-hwa, were both in charge of economic and financial affairs before the promotion. The achievement of Taiwan's economic development under his leadership has been so remarkable that even his critics are forced to give him full credit (Chiang, 1984: 326-329).

Accordingly, for the last thirty-seven years, Taiwan's development has been directed by a strong and stable leadership; it has payed much attention to economic development, selected and used competent subordinates, showed tolerance and respect for expertise, controlled the state apparatus firmly, and won the support from the people. With its backing, a group of brilliant economic policy makers were able to display their competence to manage Taiwan's economic transformation.

The Economic Policy Makers

While the top political leadership had the supremacy of determining the state's priorities and policy orientation for national development in principle, Taiwan's economic transformation in practice was propelled by a group of economic officials who headed the economic bureaucracy in the broadest sense. The personnel evolution of these

economic policy makers is presented in table 4.1. Among these people several names are worth identifying here. There are Yui Hung-chun (known as O. K. Yui) (1897-1960), Hsu Peh-yuan (1902-1980), Yin Chung-jung (known as K. Y. Yin, 1903-1963), Yen Chia-kan (known as C.K. Yen) (1905-), Yang Chi-tseng (1989-), Li Kwoh-ting (known as K. T. Li, 1910-), Sun Yun-suan (1913-), and Yu Kuohwa (1914-) for industry and finance as well as Chiang Monlin (1886-1964) and Shen Tsung-han (known as T. H. Shen, 1895-1984) for agriculture (Chou, 1982a: 7). As pointed out earlier, to understand the functions and weights
of the economic policy makers upon Taiwan's economic development, we need to explore the ways of thinking and doing of them. In addition, we must answer the following questions: What were the relationships between these economic policy makers and the top political leadership? What were the relationships among these people themselves? And what were the relationships between these people and other relevant groups in economic policy-making?

As far as the ways of thinking and doing of the economic policy makers are concerned, there are some significant findings. First of all, a study which compares birthplace, education, and experience abroad of the economic planners during the fifties and sixties (including 44 economic policy makers and bureaucrats in the TPB, the ESB, the CUSA, and the CIECD) and the 1957 members of the CSC discovers that the economic planners were more exposed to Western influence in terms of birthplace, had higher education degree, and higher proportion in the experience of studying abroad, especially in the United States. The finding is presented in table 4.2. Regarding birthplace, about 75% of the economic planners came from the coastal areas of China, especially the three main centers of Western influence, i.e., Kwangtung, Chekiang, and Kiangsu provinces whereas 47% of the CSC members were born in China's coastal areas. With respect to education degree, the proportion of those with university education among the economic planners was nearly 98% whereas the proportion was about 70% for the party elites. With regard to the experience of studying abroad, 52% of the economic planners received advanced education in the United States and 9% in the Western Europe whereas 28% of the CSC members received advanced education in the United States, 13% in the Western Europe, 7% in Japan, and 7% in the Soviet Union. The implication of the finding is that the economic policies in Taiwan were formulated by a group of people who have a more cosmopolitan and liberal mentality (Liu, 1986: 89-91).

Table 4.1
Personnel Evolution of the Economic Policy Makers, 1949-1985

Agency for Economic Planning

	Chairman	Vice Chairman	Secretary-General
06/49	Ch'en Ch'eng	K. Y. Yin	
12/49	Wu Kuo-cheng	K. Y. Yin	
04/53	O. K. Yui		
06/54	C. K. Yen		
09/58	Ch'en Ch'eng	K. Y. Yin	K. T. Li
01/63	Ch'en Ch'eng	C. K. Yen	K. T. Li
12/63	C. K. Yen	K. T. Li	Chang Chi-cheng
01/65	C. K. Yen	K. T. Li	T'ao Sheng-yang
08/69	Chiang Ching-kuo	K. T. Li	Chang Chi-cheng
10/69	Chiang Ching-kuo	Fei Hwa	Fei Hwa
07/73	Chiang Ching-kuo	Chang Chi-cheng	Chang Chi-cheng
08/73	Chang Chi-cheng	Shirley W. Y. Kuo Sun Chen	Tsui Tsu-k'an
06/76	Yang Chia-lin	Shirley W. Y. Kuo Sun Chen	Tsui Tsu-k'an
12/77	Yu Kuo-hwa	Wang Chang-ch'ing Sun Chen Shieh Shen-chung	Tsui Tsu-k'an
05/84	Chao Yao-tung	Wang Chou-ming Yeh Wan-an Tsui Tsu-k'an	

Agency for Agricultural Development		Agency for U. S. Aid	
	Chairman		Chairman
10/48	Chiang Monlin	03/50	Ch'en Ch'eng
06/64	T. H. Shen	06/54	O. K. Yui
05/73	Lee Ch'ung-tao	08/57	C. K. Yen
07/81	Chang Hsien-ch'iu	07/58	Ch'en Ch'eng
05/84	Wang You-tsao		

Table 4.1 (continue)
Personnel Evolution of the Economic Policy Makers, 1949-1985

Agency for Foreign Exchange

Chairman

02/55 Hsu Peh-yuan
03/58 K. Y. Yin
01/63 Hsu Peh-yuan

Ministry of Economic Affairs		Ministry of Finance	
Minister		*Minister*	
02/50	C. K. Yen	03/50	C. K. Yen
03/50	Cheng Tao-ju	06/54	Hsu Peh-yuan
05/52	Chang Tse-k'ai	03/58	C. K. Yen
06/54	K. Y. Yin	12/63	Ch'en Ch'ing-yu
12/55	Chiang Piao	12/67	Yu Kuo-hwa
03/58	Yang Chi-tseng	07/69	K. T. Li
01/65	K. T. Li	06/76	Fei Hwa
07/69	T'ao Sheng-yang	06/78	Chang Chi-cheng
10/69	Sun Yun-suan	12/81	Hsu Li-teh
06/78	Chang Kwang-shih	05/84	Lu Jun-k'ang
12/81	Chao Yao-tung	03/85	Ch'ien Ch'un
05/84	Hsu Li-teh		
03/85	Lee Ta-hai		

Table 4.1 (continue)
Personnel Evolution of the Economic Policy Makers, 1949-1985

Bank of Taiwan *		Central Bank of China *	
Chairman of Board		*Governor*	
1951	Hsu Peh-yuan	07/60	Hsu Peh-yuan
1952	O. K. Yui	06/69	Yu Kuo-hwa
1953	Chang Tse-k'ai	05/84	Chang Chi-cheng
1960	K. Y. Yin		

* The functions of the Central Bank of China had been suspended and not reactivated until July 1, 1961. In the interim, the Bank of Taiwan performed most of the function of a central bank.

In addition, we discover that most of the economic policy makers came from middle class families: civil servants, small businessmen, or owner-cultivators. As compared with the economic policy makers before 1949, notably, T. V. Soong and H. H. Kung, their connections with the bourgeoisie have been far remote. Both T. V. Soong and H. H. Kung were born in very wealthy families. They had extensive connections with the capitalists in the mainland and their economic policy-making were criticized strongly for benefiting their own business. In contrast, no any economic policy maker in the KMT state after 1949 has had his own business on Taiwan. Their economic policy-making therefore is relatively autonomous from the influence of local capitalists.

Moreover, a distinctive feature of these economic policy makers is that most of them had their training background not in economics or business but in engineering or science (Hofheinz and Calder, 1982: 57; Yang, 1984: 160-163). For example, among the 13 ministers of Economic Affairs from 1950 to 1985, 10 were trained in engineering and science. This is partly due to the fact that many economic policy makers started their careers from working in state enterprises and partly due to the reason that many projects in the economic development were concerned with engineering construction. Therefore, they managed Taiwan's economic transformation in a way of learning by doing rather than following any specific school of economics.

The particular training background allowed the economic policy makers to adopt a relatively practical and flexible attitude toward economic development. They saw economic transformation as a sort of scientific experiment and adjusted their policies along with the progress of their knowledge about economic development. This can be well illustrated by the lives and deeds of the two most influential architects of Taiwan's economic development: K. Y. Yin for the 1950s and early 1960s as well as K. T. Li since the mid-1960s.

In Taiwan's economic circle, there is a consensus that K. Y. Yin was "the pilot of Taiwan's economic development." He laid the foundation for Taiwan's industrialization and cleared the way for Taiwan's economic takeoff. Born in Hunan porvince in 1903, Yin came from a scholar's family of moderate income. At age 22, Yin graduated from Nanyang University (renamed Chiao T'ung University later) in Shanghai, earning a degree in electrical engineering. After graduation from the university, he got his first job in the Ministry of Communications in Peking and then moved to a number of other positions in various parts of China. In 1936 he was assigned the assistant manager

Table 4.2
A Comparison of the Birthplace and the Educational Background of the Economic Planners and the 1957 Members of the CSC

	The Economic planner	The 1957 members of the CSC
Birthplace in the coastal areas	75%	47%
University degree	98%	70%
Education abroad		
United States	52%	28%
Western Europe	9%	13%
Japan	0	7%
Soviet Union	0	7%

Source: Liu, 1986: 89 and 92.

of the China Development Finance Corporation, a semi-official organization founded by T. V. Soong. He was recruited to the ad hoc National Resources Commission in the winter of 1939, which pooled the best technical specialists of China together during war years. From 1941 to 1945, he had been the director of Chinese Foreign Trade Office in New York. He came back to China at the end of 1945 and served as the secretary of T. V. Soong who was the Premier at that time. He then became the executive director of the Hwainan Mining and Railway Company, a branch of the China Development Finance Corporation, in the spring of 1947. When the situation on Mainland China turned to the worse and the KMT state began to move some state enterprises to Taiwan, Yin was appointed vice chairman of the TPB in the summer of 1949 and was actually in charge of the agency. When the TPB was absorbed into the ESB in July, 1953, Yin took the chair of the IDC, a division of the ESB responsible for industrial development. He became minister of Economic Affairs in June, 1954. Meanwhile, he still held the chair of the IDC and the post of president of the Central Trust of China. In the fall of 1955, Yin resigned from all of his posts because he was suspected by the Legislative Yuan of being involved in a collusion. The investigation cleared him of any blame in the fall of 1956. He returned to the state in August, 1957 as the secretary-general of the ESB. He became the chairman of the FETCC in March, 1958 and also held the posts of vice chairman of the CUSA since September, 1958 and chairman of the board of the Bank of Taiwan since July, 1960 until his death in January, 1963 (Shen, 1972; Liu, 1986: 95-96; China Yearbook, 1960-61: 871).

The policies that Yin adopted to develop the economy will be elaborated in chapters V and VI. Our major concern here is his thinking of Taiwan's economic development that was recorded in his 4-volumes work, *Wo-tui Taiwan ching-chi ti k'an-fa* (My Views on Taiwan's Economy) (1973a; 1973b; 973c; 1973d). To put it briefly, Yin's attitude toward economic development and relevant theories was critical, synthetic, and practical (Liu, 1986: 96). This attitude was sufficiently demonstrated in the preface of the volume II of his work, when he explains the different policies he employed to promote economic development. He states, "In the past, some people criticized me as an extreme interventionist; then, some people said that I had changed my mind and become an advocator of free economy. As a matter of fact, my fundamental viewpoint is just 'how to solve problem efficiently and thoroughly in the practical circumstance.' It does not adhere to any specific theory but aims at seeking greatest economic interests for our country. The problems in actual situation are ever-changing and definitely cannot be solved by adhering to a certain theory or a certain assertion only" (Yin, 1973b: i-ii). Hence, his basic view on economic policy-making was that "Regarding the controversy on liberalization and protection, I have no preconception about these out-of-date theories. If liberalization has more advantages, we should prefer liberalization; if protection can yield more advantages, we must chose protection. Policies are made for solving problems therefore should be adapted to time, place, and issue. Economic policy-making must not be inflexible" (Yin, 1973b: 3). And of all the rules in economic planning, said Yin, the most precious one is the rule of Golden Mean (Yin, 1973a: 27).

Being a man of "Golden Mean", Yin upheld a mixed economic system. He stressed the importance of a free economy as the fundamental principle, combined with variable degrees and types of state intervention. According to Yin (1973d: 29), in a developing country, when the society lacks entrepreneurs, the state should play a leading role to accelerate economic development: the state must create conditions conducive to private investment such as the construction of infrastructure and the provision of fiscal incentives; the state must lay down the general direction of development by overall planning; the state must take initiatives to establish those enterprises which local capitalists are not yet able or unwilling to invest in; and the state must also take the lead in opening up foreign trade, renovating old facilities of production, and educating and diffusing technical and professional knowledge. "Once enough people with leadership qualities have been fostered, the leadership in economic development will naturally be transferred from the state to the society."

While stressing flexible and pratical applications of economic theory and foreign experience, Yin paid special attention to Japanese economic development (Liu, 1986: 98). Examining the experience of the Meiji Reform, he derived the following insights: (1) To develop a backward economy, the state must take the lead, at least in the beginning. Relying entirely on a free economy is not enough. (2) There must be a leading industrial and commercial stratum, whether it is composed of individuals or corporations. The state and the society must tolerate the existence of such a group so it could fully perform its functions. (3) The requisite capital and manpower for economic development should mainly come from internal sources. The state must take necessary measures to regulate capital accumulation and cultivate human resources. (4) Economic development must be coordinated with reforms in culture, social structure, and politics. Regarding the economy itself, the attention should be paid to the establishment of basic institutions. (5) The people must be made to rely on themselves to improve their lives. The state should focus its effort on creating employment opportunity rather than relieving the poor (Yin, 1973b: 173). In 1950 and 1951, Yin made two trips to Japan (3 months for the first time and a couple of weeks for the second time) and observed carefully how Japan recovered from the war. The Japanese model of development greatly influenced his participation in Taiwan's economic transformation.

K. Y. Yin dominated and forged the broad lines of Taiwan's economy in the 1950s and early 1960s; his tireless efforts prepared the ground for its "take off". He became a model of engineers, not professional economists, running the key economic planning agencies. After Yin's death, nobody seemed ready to control the economy like he did. In a certain sense, however, K. T. Li has followed in Yin's steps since the mid-sixties.

K. T. Li was born in the city of Nanking in 1910. He graduated from National Central University in Nanking in 1930 and earned a degree in physics. After graduation, Li spent three years as a college teacher in the sciences. In 1934, he was awarded a scholarship to study physics at Cambridge University in England. Due to the outbreak of the Sino-Japanese War in July, 1937, he decided to give up his study and offer his services to his country. Li returned to China in October, 1937, and taught at the National Wuhan University from 1937 to 1940. He then was recruited into the National Resources Commission and concentrated in iron and steel work. After arriving in Taiwan, Li went to work in industry first as vice president and later as president of the Taiwan Shipbuilding Corp., a state enterprise. In 1953, when the ESB was set up, Li was invited to serve as a full-time member of the IDC which was chaired by K. Y. Yin. Thereafter, he had worked with Yin until the latter's death. He became the secretary-general of the CUSA in 1958 after the ESB was abolished. When the CUSA was reorganized into the CIECD in 1963, Li was promoted the vice chairman of the agency. He became minister of Economic Affairs from January, 1965 to July, 1969 while still holding his post with the CIECD. He then became minister of Finance for 7 years. At present, his is minister of state (without portfolio) and in charge of promoting high technology industrialization in Taiwan (Li, 1980: 9; Republic of China, 986: 427; Liu, 1986: 102-104).

In contrast to Yin who had the flair of a theorist, Li's style of learning has always been empirical and practical. Li's motto is "learn from practical experience and use scientific methods" (Liu, 1986: 104). But from Li's various lectures and writings (1976; 1980; 1985), we can still somehow figure out his thinking on Taiwan's economic development. Basically, Li's viewpoint was not much different from Yin's. He believed that in a developing country, like Taiwan in the fifties and sixties, the state must assume the leadership and take the initiative in promoting economic development since the society lacks the farsighted entrepreneur and the imaginative banker (Li, 1976: 41). As K. Y. Yin, he held that economic development should be accompanied with reforms in culture and politics. In his opinion, the society and cultural tradition of Taiwan were not very advantageous to the development of industry because many traditional traits tended to constrain the spirits of cooperation and risk-taking. Further, tradition often limited modern economic practices, such as the circulation of cheques, delivery on time, and uniform quality; in addition, it encouraged consumption for social prestige, such as extravagant festivals and construction of pompous ancestral shrines, temples, villas, and tombs (Li, 1976: 314-315). He criticized the Chinese preference for and family-centered enterprises while insisting that the efficiency of scale is a requisite for Taiwan to survive in the world economy in the future. According to Li, many people both in the state and society tend to have animosity toward private enterprises and not to make a distinction between legitimate profit and profiteering. This shortsightedness makes the cooperation between the state and local capitalists more difficult (Liu, 1986: 107-108). He also complained about the obstructions of economic transformation derived from bureaucracy, anachronistic laws and regulations, backward ideas, incoherence, and officialism in the state apparatus (Li, 1976: 12-19; 1986a; 1986b).

Another economic policy maker worth being introduced here is C. K. Yen. Yen was born in Kiangsu province in 1905. He earned a BS degree in chemistry from the St. John's University in Shanghai in 1926. Having never studied abroad, Yen nevertheless is famous for his fluent english; earning a degree in chemistry, Yen nonetheless shows his talent in finance. His competence in handling financial affairs was first displayed in his performance as the commissioner of finance of the Fukien provincial government for the period 1939-45. When Taiwan was receded to China, he was appointed the first commissioner of communications of the Taiwan provincial government in 1945. Later, he became the commissioner of finance of the provincial government and concurrently the chairman of board of the Bank of Taiwan from 1946 to 1949. In June, 1949, when the economic situation in Mainland China became chaotic, Yen took charge of issuing a new currency (new Taiwan dollars) to cut the destructive impact from the mainland and stabilize Taiwan's economy. He once again demonstrated his ability in carrying out this task. He then had been the minister of Finance and concurrently the vice chairman of CUSA for 1950-54, the governor of Taiwan province and concurrently the chairman of ESB for 1954-57, the minister of state (without portfolio) and concurrently the chairman of CUSA for 1957-58, the minister of Finance (second time) for 1958-63, and concurrently the vice chairman of CUSA in 1963. He succeeded Ch'en Ch'eng as the Premier in December, 1963 for 9 years. Concurrently, he was the chairman of CIECD between 1963 and 1969. In 1966, he was elected the Vice President of the Republic of China. When Chiang Kai-shek died in April, 1975, C. K. Yen succeeded the rest term of the President of the ROC in Taiwan. He retired from the presidency in 1978 (Szuma, 1986a: 20-31; Republic of China, 1986: 450).

In contrast to K. Y. Yin and K. T. Li, both of whom are outspoken and quick-tempered, C. K. Yen is known to be tactful and gentle. Among the economic policy makers he is not outstanding in pushing reform or opening up new situations, but he is an excellent mediator in resolving strifes between conflicting opinions and a good partner easy to cooperate with. Accordingly, his contribution to Taiwan's economic transformation consists in his having given support and assistance to other economic policy makers, such as Yin and Li, rather than in originating new policies.

In a certain sense, however, Yen's contribution is beyond the economic policy-making *per se*. To put it clearly, Yen deserves credit for having bridged the discontinuity of power succession due to the death of Ch'en Ch'eng and the immaturity of Chiang Ching-kuo. Younger than Chiang Kai-shek by 10 years, Ch'en Ch'eng was expected to be Chiang Kai-shek's successor when he concurrently held the posts of Vice President and Premier of the state and Vice *Tsungtsai* of the party in the late 1950s and early 1960s. His death in 1965 thus caused to a problem of power succession because on the one hand Chiang Kai-shek was already 78 years old and on the other hand Chiang Ching-kuo had not yet consolidated his authority and prestige at that time (Chiang Kai-shek seemed to begin to consider Chiang Ching-kuo as his successor when Ch'en Ch'eng resigned the Premier in December, 1963 due to the deterioration of his health). It is C. K. Yen, who made the transition to the top political leadership smoothly. While skillful in financial and administrative affairs, Yen has no ambition of power.

He clearly understands his role as a transmitter and sincerely identifies himself with it. With Yen's assistance and cooperation, Chiang Chingkuo is able to accede to power smoothly and thus open a new era for Taiwan's development (Yang, 1986: 157-163; Szuma, 1986a: 20-31).

To understand the thinking and doing of the economic policy makers further, we need to do some comparisons of their similarities and differences. Of course, it is reasonable to start with the most influential figures, namely, K. Y. Yin and K. T. Li. A difference between K. Y. Yin and K. T. Li seems to be their attitudes toward the operation of opportunity costs and comparative advantages. Although both of them agree on the thesis of making the prices right, Yin tends to be more aggressive and more likely to "create" comparative advantage for and jump to advanced industries by adopting certain types of state intervention. In contrast, Li tends to be more moderate and more likely to "follow" comparative advantage step by step without rushing into higher level. In this sense, Yin's stance is relatively close to structuralism in development economics whereas Li's position is relatively close to the neoclassical economic theory. But this is only a matter of degree and may well be a reflection of the different stages of Taiwan's development. Yin's opinion is mainly concerned with the period of the fifties and early sixties before Taiwan's takeoff while Li's viewpoint mainly deals with the period after Yin's death. At the same time, Yin changed his opinion on state intervention during the late 1950s and early 1960s from stressing state control to emphasizing free economy in at least certain aspects. In spite of their differences, it is quite clear that they have a common belief in the importance of the state in regulating economic transformation. And this is also a common feature of all the economic policy makers.

However, just like K. Y. Yin and K. T. Li differ in their attitudes toward the degree and ways of state intervention, the opinions of the economic policy makers on the strategies for economic development are not uniform. In the first half of the fifties, all the economic policy makers were inclined to control the economy by strict state intervention. In the late fifties, notwithstanding, a split between the economic policy makers who favored continued state dominance of the economy and those who advocated more range for the private sector took place. Their disagreement about development strategies caused much debate on economic policies and much power struggle; as a result, the more free-market-oriented officials prevailed over the more state-intervention-oriented cadres. Since the mid-1960s, a line of argument for further liberalization of the economy has gradually coming to the fore, though some dissent still exists.

Of course, this by no means implies that the economic policy makers have totally given up the ideas or intention of intervening in the transformation of the economy. Actually, in the eyes of neoclassical economists, the action toward economic liberalization in Taiwan has been too slack. According to Hsing Mo-huan (1986: 154), an economist who has-since the early fifties-consistently advised the KMT state to loosen up its control over the economy, most economic policy makers, especially those trained as engineers or scientists, are the believers of "technocracy", i.e., all of the social problems can be and must be solved by scientific technology and the society should be put in the hands of scientists. These economic policy makers see economic development as an engineering system that requires elaborate planning and tend to think little of market mechanism. While there was a trend of moving the state to loosen up the overall economic system for the last three decades, the trend moved slowly for most of the time. While these officials advocated the reduction of the role of public enterprises and state domination of industry, they still intended to guide the direction of industrial development by operating direct instruments such as selective tariff rates, designated priority sectors, incentive packages, and credit allocation, etc. While these policy makers had gradually left aside the thinking and doing of the "technocrat" due to the accumulation of experience and recognition of market mechanism, for a neoclassical economist, most of them were still too involved with economic planning to give up state intervention.

Since the thinking and doing of the economic policy makers were not uniform and there had been conflicts between different lines of development, a question not to be overlooked is why and how some economic policy makers were able to overtake others. The answer is that it was decided by the top political leadership. Similar to the case of the return-to-the-mainland ideologues and the pro-development pragmatists, the top political leadership became the final judge of the conflicts between the economic policy makers. Therefore, the results depended on which development line or economic policy could get the approval and support of the top political leadership. Roughly speaking, the decisions of the top political leadership were based on their assessment of situational imperatives, such as the necessity to consolidate the state's legitimacy, the intention of the Chinese Communist regime, and the stance of the U.S. government; as well as to their experience of defeat in Mainland China which deeply influenced their preference in arranging the state's priorities for development and balancing the trade-offs between socioeconomic growth, equality, and stability, etc. Of course, the influence of the economic policy makers on the thinking of the top political leadership should also be taken into account. The economic policy makers' report on economic situation was an important reference to the judgement of the top political leadership. At the same time, the economic policy makers usually took initiative to persuade the top political leadership to adopt certain development policy.

The economic policy makers usually got full support from the top political leadership. This was shown in the fact that except Ch'en Ch'eng and Chiang Ching-kuo, all the Premiers, namely, O. K. Yui, C. K. Yen, Sun Yun-suan, and Yu Kuo-hwa, were originally economic policy makers. With the buttress of the top political leadership, the problem of the clashes between the policies proposed by the economic policy makers and other government departments, e.g., the military or the Ministry of National Defense, became less critical.

As we have mentioned, the military has been controlled tightly by the top political leadership since the retreat. Both Chiang Kai-shek and Ch'en Ch'eng are servicemen themselves. All of the military officers were either their subordinates or their students of the Whampoa Military Academy. Although Chiang Ching-kuo is not a serviceman himself, he consolidated his influence in the military through his service as director of the Political Department of Ministry of National Defense, chairman of Vocational Assistance Commission for Retired Serviceman, vice minister and then minister of National Defense. They retained in their hands broad powers to appoint, dismiss, or transfer high-ranking military officers. Therefore, the military could not form a strong interest group independent from the top political leadership.

In addition, U.S. aid had the function to insulate the military from economic policy-making. The military assistance from the U.S. alleviated the tension between the military and non-military sectors for resource competition. Controlling the crucial resource for the KMT state, the American advisors usually gave the economic policy makers full support and discouraged the interference from the military. Moreover, the military had its own production facilities. Military arsenals produced much of the equipment and less sophisticated weaponary and ammunition needed by the armed forces. And the Vocational Assistance Commission for Retired Servicemen owned a complex of more than forty firms. The military thus had their own business to take care of and became less concerned with the civilian sector (Amsden, 1985: 99). Consequently, the military was largely insulated from economic policy-making.

To put it briefly, the economic policy makers played a pivotal role in the operational structure of making economic policy. They received the different opinions and demands concerning economic activities from the people and social groups outside the state apparatus. They were the leading actors in shaping Taiwan's economic development program. They took the initiative to persuade the top political leadership to put more attention on the economic development. And they also played the major role in supervising and evaluating the execution of economic policy.

The Economic Bureaucrats

The economic policy makers would not have been able to adopt proper economic policies if they did not have a competent staff. In fact, since most of the economic policy makers have their training background in science and technology rather than economics and business, they need economists and other experts as their assistants to offer them ideas and information and to draw up policy proposal for them. In this sense, the function of a group of secondary and middle level officials in the economic bureaucracy, particularly the core agencies, should not be neglected. These economic bureaucrats have no power to decide what policies should be adopted to develop Taiwan's economy, but their expertise in economic and technical development, their research reports on the economic situation, and their suggestions to resolve economic problems have substantive impact on the economic policy makers' decisions.

As noted above, enjoying the advantage of paying higher salaries and not being subject to civil service regulations, the core agencies of the economic bureaucracy were staffed with a group of loyal and skilled officials. They cultivated a strong *esprit de corps* among themselves and were proud of their own effectiveness in cooperating with Taiwan's economic transformation. According to relevant interviewees, these people were relatively hard-working and clean-handed They were remarkably diligent in discharging their official duties, especially in the earlier stage of Taiwan's postwar development when the state had the power to control the economy.

Like the economic policy makers, many of the economic bureaucrats have their training background in engineering. In regard to the nature of Taiwan's economic development, Barrett (1983: 38) maintains that the economic development "brain trust" in Taiwan was made up of a coalition of bureaucrats, many of whom were young, American-trained economists and that these people took American capitalist social and economic institutions as models for Taiwan's development. His argument is not totally wrong in a certain sense but can only be applied to a part of the fact for recent years. For example, as early as in the beginning of the 1950s, the agency for economic planning had already recruited some distinguished economists into its staff. However, they were a minority when compared with the engineers in the agency and the situation had remained in effect until the mid-1970s. In this sense, the creators of the Taiwan miracle were primarily engineers by training, though today economists make up 40% (engineers only 20%) of the agency's staff (Wade, 1985a:14).

In addition, even though some of those responsible for making economic planning and drafting policy proposal are American-trained economists, they do not appreciate the American capitalist system very much. This was especially clear in the earlier stage of Taiwan's postwar development. For instance, Wang Tso-jung (or Wang Tzouh-rong, 1919-), a chief architect of the Four-Year Economic Development Plans in the 1950s and early 1960s as well as the leading economisst in K. Y. Yin's staff, who earned his B.A. degree in economics from National Central University in 1943 and M.A. degrees first from the University of Washington (Seattle) in 1949 and then from Vanderbilt University (Nashville, Tennessee) in 1958, made the utmost effort to advocate the Japanese model. According to Wang (1981: 1-54; 299-319; 1984), the Japanese way for economic development which combines important state planning and the mechanism of free market is the solution for Taiwan. In his opinion, Taiwan should learn from Japanese to establish a strong leadership, set up an efficient and high-quality state bureaucracy, use fiscal and monetary instruments energetically, increase capital accumulation by forced measures such as inflation policy, develop heavy industry, encourage large-scale enterprises, open up export, loosen up import, and strengthen education and research. To a certain degree, K. Y. Yin's thinking of Taiwan's development was influenced by Wang. Wang's viewpoint of developing the economy was somewhat weighted toward the "interventionist" end as compared with the mainstream of the economic policy makers and bureaucrats after the mid-1960s (Liu, forthcoming: 111). Regarding himself as a dissenter in the community of the economic planners, Wang left the economic bureaucracy temporarily during 1967 to 1970 and served as the director of the Industry Studies Section of U.N. Economic Commission for

Asia and the Far East. He resigned from the CIECD permanently in 1973. Thereafter, he has been teaching economics at National Taiwan University and serving as the chief economic columnist for *Chung-kuo shih-pao* (Chou, 1982b).

Just like K. Y. Yin's aggressiveness and expansiveness was complemented and succeeded by K. T. Li's moderation and empiricism at the level of economic policy maker, among the economic bureaucrats Wang Tso-yung's mode was complemented and succeeded by a more moderate fashion after the mid-1960s. A representative of this new fashion is Yeh Wan-an (1924-) (Liu, 1986: 112). Earning a B.A. degree in banking from National Shanghai College of Commerce in 1947, Yeh was first recruited by the National Resource Commission and then dispatched to Taiwan in 1948 to manage the Taiwan Sugar Corporation. He entered the ESB in 1953 as a low level official subordinate to Wang Tso-jung. Like Wang, Yeh had been sent abroad to study modern economic system. He was a research fellow at the International Monetary Fund in 1964 and at the Economic Development Institute of the World Bank in 1967-70. Currently, he is the vice chairman of the CEPD. Since the mid-sixties, Yeh's relationship with K. T. Li has been similar to Wang's relationship with K. Y. Yin. As compared with Wang, Yeh's thinking of economic development is more inclined to "follow" rather than "create" comparative advantage through state action and more inclined to enlarge the scope of free economy. Therefore, a trend toward economic liberalization has started not only among the economic policy makers but also among the economic bureaucrats.

A similar tendency toward economic liberalization was also reflected in the opinion of another staff leader and policy maker, Sun Chen (1934-). After Sun earned a M.A. degree in economics from National Taiwan University in 1959, he became a staff member of the CUSA and subordinate of Wang Tso-jung. In 1970, he got a Ph. D. degree from Oklahoma University. He was again invited into the economic bureaucracy in 1973, serving as vice chairman of the EPC for 1973-77 and vice chairman of the CEPD for 1977-84. In 1984, he was appointed the president of National Taiwan University. Reviewing Taiwan's industrial development, Sun (1984: 19-46) argues that although industrial development cannot totally follow the principle of comparative advantage in a static sense, an important secret of Taiwan's success is that the state guided and helped industrial development mainly in accordance with comparative advantage and market mechanism rather than against them. He further believes that Taiwan's economy can still be prosperous in the future by maintaining the secret of success in the past.

Along with the personnel evolution of the economic policy makers, there has been a replacement of the old with the new in the economic bureaucrats. Some of the senior members have been promoted step by step from a low rank position in the staff to the rank of policy maker, such as Wang Chou-ming and Yeh Wan-an. Some of the members moved from the economic bureaucracy to the positions in banking system and state enterprises. Some of them retired. And some other people left the economic bureaucracy ealier and developed their careers at universities, research institutes, and newspapers as professors, researchers, or economic columnists, such as Wang Tso-jung and Sun Chen. In contrast to the previous patterns, the economic bureaucrats seeking their careers in private enterprises were strikingly few. This particular phenomenon was an important factor in explaining the relatively remote relationship between the state and businessmen on Taiwan, which is to be discussed in a little more detail in the section concerned with the local capitalists. As Barrett observes, many new-comers to the group are young, American-trained economists. As compared with the seniors, they seem to be more inclined to a free market system. However, in comparison with a group of consulting economists outside the state apparatus, they are still not very "liberal."

The Consulting Economists

In Chinese cultural and political tradition, intellectuals and the state are closely connected with each other. Intellectuals are expected to contribute their wisdom and capabilities to the state and the state is supposed to respect intellectuals and listen to their advice. Partly due to this tradition and partly due to the personalities of the top political leaders and some key economic policy makers, such as K. Y. Yin and K. T. Li, economic policy-making in the Kuomintang state has consistently been influenced by many non-government economists. Among these people, a small group of prominent scholars who are members of the Academia Sinica (the highest academic institution in the Republic of China), namely, Liu Ta-chung (1914-1975), Tsiang Sho-chieh (1918-), Hsing Mo-huan, Koo Ying-ch'ang (Anthony Y. C. Koo, 1918-) Fei Ching-han (John C. H. Fei, 1923-), Chow Chi-chong (Gregory C. C. Chow, 1930-), are most influential.

Stricktly speaking, these scholars initially did not have close relationship with Taiwan. Most of them finished their undergraduate studies in Mainland China and then went to the United States or England to do advanced studies in economics. When the Communists took over the mainland, most of them either fled to the United States or were still doing their studies abroad; only Hsing Mo-huan followed the Kuomintang state to move to Taiwan. Therefore, except Hsing Mo-huan who has lived in Taiwan for most of the time and Tsiang Sho-chieh who has returned to Taiwan to set up the Chung-hua Institute for Economic Research–a semi-official organization–a few years ago, the other people are still living in the United States and teaching at American universities, such as Yale (John Fei), Princeton (Gregory Chow), and Michigan State University (Anthony Koo) (Liu Ta-chung died in 1975 when he was a professor at Cornell University). In this sense, they might be seen as foreigners rather than natives to the Taiwan society. Their Chinese origin, however, makes them cencerned with Taiwan's economic development and leads them to offer their advices to the Kuomintang state enthusiastically, though Taiwan is not the place where they were born and grew up.

All of these scholars can be roughly classified as neoclassical economists. Compared with most of the economic policy makers and bureaucrats, they are much more in favor of the mechanisms of free market. They do not trust the functions of the state in regulating economic transformation except for maintaining a stable and competitive free-enterprise environment. They oppose state intervention in the market by the measures of state-managed enterprises, official set interest rates, guaranteed prices for certain commodities, customs duties, import restrictions, or control of foreign exchange (Hou, 1985). They believe that Taiwan's economic miracle is a consequence of following or at least gradually embodying the neoclassical ideals (Tsiang, 1984 and 1985; Hsing, 1986; Fei, 1984). For the last three decades, they constituted a trend of appealing to the KMT state for liberalizing the economy.

The influence of these neoclassicalists is not limited to serving as consultants of the economic authorities. As Wade (1985a: 13) observes, since the mid-seventies, "Taiwan's large establishment of universities, research institutes and consulting firms is heavily involved in policy formulation, though in an *ad hoc* rather than institutionalised way." Many people in these organizations are these scholars' friends, students, or subordinates. Their ideas thus also entered the economic policy-making through other channels.

In addition to these neoclassicalists and their adherentss, there nevertheless are some other voices in the Taiwan society which mainly come from a number of professors in economics and a handful of economic columnists. Among them, the most famous person and also an opponent to those neoclassicalists is Wang Tso-jung, a former economic bureaucrat and currently a professor and columnist. As mentioned above, Wang was an advocate of the Japanese style developmental state. He upheld state intervention in the market with various direct or indirect policy instruments to reach its economic and political goals. Although he considered himself a pragmatist free from any economic school, to a certain extent his stance for developing Taiwan's economy was close to the "structuralism" in development economics–the view related to P. N. Rosenstein-Rodan (1943), Raul Prebisch (1950), Ragnar Nurkse (1953), Hans Singer (1954), W. Arthur Lewis (1955), Gunnar Myrdal (1957), and Albert Hirschman (1958). His preference for a strong, interventionist state clearly dissented from the neoclassical scholars' stance (Wang, 1981 and 1983; Fei, 1982). After leaving the economic bureaucracy, Wang's assertions might not have direct impact on the economic policy-making. Spread through newspapers and journals, however, his viewpoint has certain influence on public opinionss that in turn might influence the economic policy-making. But in recent years, Wang's stance has changed dramatically. As the society has grown and the economy is facing "graduation" to a new and higher technological stage, Wang now is one of the most active advocators for reducing state protection and regulation (Wang, 1984).

There are still some other scholars and columnists who contribute their opinions directly or indirectly to the economic policy making. Like the economic policy makers, most of them are located somewhere between the neoclassicalists and Wang Tso-jung in the past. Actually, an interesting feature of the relationship between the economic officials and the intellectuals in Taiwan is that many economic officials concurrently also serve as economic commentators for newspapers or journals and teach at universities. The exchange between scholars and officials is quite common in Taiwan.

Generally speaking, the consulting economists have had little role in the formulation of Taiwan's industrial policies or in the day-to-day decisions about its application to particular cases; their contribution has been mainly on fiscal and monetary policies (Wade, 1985a: 14). For economic officials, the decision-making for economic development involves many facets while economic issues *per se* are only one of them. In addition to the pure economic aspect, an economic policy maker has to take care of some other issues, such as the political, social, and cultural reality. Non-government economists sometimes are likely to neglect those aspects. Consequently, the consulting economists usually tend to be more "idealistic" than the economic policy makers and bureaucrats.

The American Advisors

It may be debatable whether some of the influential consulting economists should be foreigners; nevertheless, a group of them exerted influence upon the economic policy-making in the KMT state. These people were the American officials and experts of the Agency for International Development (AID). When Washington resumed its aid to Taipei, the economic aid program within Taiwan was administered by the U.S. AID Mission to China, whose director was selected by the administrator of AID. During the period of aid, the total personnel of the Mission averaged 350 people, including consultants, contractors, and Chinese personnel. In addition, the J. G. White Engineering Corporation of New york was financed by U.S. funds to make technical and economic studies of projects proposed by the Koumintang state for U.S. assistance. Its technical staff numbered 32 Americans in 1957 (Jacoby, 1966: 57-58).

In contrast to the situation on Mainland China when the United States failed to urge the Kuomintang state to utilize U.S. aid efficiently and to reform itself, the U.S. AID Mission had a strong and persistent influence upon the formation of economic policy in the KMT state on Taiwan. One main reason for this change surely is that U.S. aid was very crucial for the KMT state's survival in the period of the 1950s. On the other hand, the defeat on the mainland also gave the KMT state a good lesson and made it more prudent. The primary instruments of influence used by AID were written analysis and oral presentations made to the KMT state by its staff members. Another technique, often utilized to define problems, resolve disagreements, or deter the projects that American advisors thought to be economically unsuitable, was to retain independent experts to study and report on the subjects. American authorities in such fields as central banking, taxation, foreign exchange rates, or housing were sent on missions to Taiwan to give advice to the Chinese government (Jacoby, 1966: 133). Moreover, Americans sat in the meetings of ESB, CUSA, JCRR, FETCC to coordinate the use of the aid, and Chinese officials had to hold their meetings in English for the benefit of American advisors (FETCC, 1969: 7; Gold, 1986: 68-69). With their control over the funds, the Americans had *de facto* power to the policies involving U.S. aid and therefore played a decisive role.

A major thrust of the American advisors' influence was directed to elevating economic development as the first priority for Taiwan. In the continual tension between the return-to-the-mainland ideologues and the pro-development pragmatists, the American advisors completely supported the latter. While committed to the defense of Taiwan against Communist aggression, the U.S. government was unwilling to support or to participate in an armed attack to Mainland China. AID consistently pressed the view that economic development was important in itself, and would concurrently serve the basic political purpose of the KMT state in terms of creating a strong base for military defense and demonstrating to the world the ability of the Chinese people to improve their livelihood rapidly under free economic institutions. In many cases. The American advisors played the role of "whipping boy" for the development-minded officials. These officials could argue for economic reforms within the KMT state on the ground that they were under pressure by the U.S. government (Jacoby, 1966: 135-137).

The second important influence that the American advisors exerted upon the economic policy-making was to promote the private sector rather than the public one. In the early postwar years, the state dominated most industry and some officials were inclined to expand state enterprises further. Partly under U.S. pressure the KMT state sold four state enterprises in cement, paper, forestry, and mining in 1953 to compensate landlords for compulsorily purchased land and devised various measures to improve the climate for private investment (Jacoby, 1966: 138-140; Gold, 1986: 70). In addition, the Americans also encouraged the state to liberalize the economy and to set up supra-ministry organs for economic planning.

In contrast to the contribution of the consulting economists, the American advisors' influence was limited in the field of fiscal and monetary policy. There were two basic reasons for this. On the one hand, some of the policy advice would have required alteration of the military and political objectives deeply held by the Kuomintang state; on the other hand, the effect of these suggestions was questionable (Jacoby, 1966: 144-146). According to some Chinese officials and consulting economists who had experience of working with the people of AID, most of the American advisors were enthusiastic and helpful. Their advice was basically correct in its direction though sometimes impractical in its execution. The Chinese officials' attitude toward the policy advice from the American advisors was "adopting those which were able to be carried out but declining gently those which were difficult to implement and explaining why" (Li and Ch'en, 1984a: 179-180). Several names of the American advisors were frequently mentioned by Chinese economic officials, such as Joseph L. Brent, Wesley C. Haraldson, Howard L. Parsons, H. B. Killough, etc (Hsu, 1969: 4-5; Chao, 1985: 17).

In summary, the American advisors' advice to the economic policy-making was accepted by the Kuomintang state in its direction. Trusted on by the top political leadership and backed up by the American advisors, the free-market-oriented developmentalists were able to begin gradually exerting influence; this, in turn shaped the economic transformation on Taiwan. After the termination of U.S. aid and the withdrawal of the U.S. AID Mission, the Kuomintang state occasionally still asked for advice from American consulting firms, e.g., Arthur D. Little, Inc. (Gold, 1986: 94).

The Local Capitalists

When Taiwan was under Japanese occupation, the more important industries on the island were all controlled by a few large Japanese corporations. With the encouragement and protection of the colonial government, these corporations supplied the key technicians and capital required by Taiwan's industries. After World War II, the supply of Japanese technicians and capital was cut off and those Japanese entrepreneurs and technicians originally working in Taiwan were repatriated to Japan. This change accompanied with war devastation and inflation caused private industry to suffer a setback during the early postwar years. Since there were few Taiwanese entrepreneurs and technicians able to operate the Japanese corporations, the KMT state took over these Japanese corporations in order to hasten their rehabilitation and strengthen the control over the economy. Local capitalists were few and weak in this period (Li, 1981: 302; Chang, 1980: 254-255; Pan, 1983: 12).

The situation changed dramatically after the central government moved its seat to Taiwan. First, there was an influx of capital and industrial personnel following the government from the mainland to Taiwan. Most of these mainlander entrepreneurs were from Shanghai as well as Shantung province and had the experience in running the business of textiles or food processing. They applied to the government for an allotment of AID-financial imported cotton or wheat. Under the encouragement and protection of the state, they developed rapidly and then expanded into other industries. Second, a few Taiwanese also benefited from the government and U.S. assistance. They started their careers in textiles or plastics and developed the business into diversified or integrated conglomerates. Third, some Taiwanese landlords profitted from the land reform. They accumulated shares in the four state enterprises and shifted their business to the industrial sector. Fourth, since the mid-sixties, based on a variety of technical and equity linkage with transnational corporations, a new cohort of entrepreneurs mainly in the electronics industry has emerged. Most of them are Taiwanese with petty bourgeois backgrounds. And lastly, a large number of small- and medium-size local firms in various industries emerged with the boom of export (Pan, 1983: 16-28; Gold, 1986: 70-85). Thus, although the private sector accounted for only 27.5% of the total production value in 1949, the preponderance of state enterprise over private enterprise was reversed in 1958 (Li, 1981: 236). By 1985, the production of private enterprise further reached 83.9% of the total (CEPD, 1986: 87).

However, as Wade (1985a: 13) and Barrett (1983) observe, Taiwan's government-business relations were relatively "distant" and "cool." Local capitalists and government officials in Taiwan existed in a relationship of "commensualism" (i.e., they lived together but acted as two separate parts) rather than the "symbiosis" (i.e., they not only lived together but also acted as an integral unit) of the Japanese or Korean elites. The cleavage between the state and local capitalists could be illustrated by the personnel composition of the three organizations in the constitutional structure of making economic policy. The counsellors of the core agencies of the economic bureaucracy were all government officials with no business representatives. The Executive Yuan Council has never included any local capitalist. And by 1984, among 32 members of the CSC, only two were local capitalists. Since the early seventies, because of the enlargement of election to the level of central government, many local capitalists entered the Legislative Yuan. Nevertheless, they were still a minority as compared with the old members. Industrial associations and trade unions were plentiful, but they were controlled from above and were not very effective in expressing the opinions of their members.

The distant relationship between government officials and local capitalists is somehow related to cultural tradition. In contrast to the case of intellectuals, the state in Chinese cultural tradition is not supposed to connect with businessman too closely. For Chinese, the mentality of businessman, which is interested only in material gains, is in compatible with the requirement of a state elite, who should value justice above material gains. At the same time, traditional Chinese culture tends not to make a distinction between legitimate profit and profiteering. Therefore, in Taiwan an intimate interaction between government officials and local capitalists is likely to be suspected as a collusion. As a matter of fact, both K. Y. Yin and K. T. Li had been censored by the Legislative Yuan and the Control Yuan. In both cases, they were trying to foster new enterprises in private sector and were thus easily accused of having colluded with local capitalists (Liu, 1986: 108). In addition, Barrett (1983) argues that the divergence of the state and the bourgeoisie was initially explicable in ethnic terms, and then was due to differences in class outlook, self-definition, and mobility strategies between members of the two sectors. There were two different roads to social mobility and two different logics of thinking for being either a government official or a businessman. Exchange between these two groups was infrequent. Indeed, unlike Japanese economic bureaucrats who move from government to powerful positions in private enterprise upon their retirement in their early fifties (Johnson, 1982: 21), few Chinese officials did. In Taiwan, it is not easy to find many retired economic bureaucrats in private enterprise.

We are not arguing that there was little interaction between government officials and local capitalists. In order to carry out economic policy or state intervention, some economic policy makers took it upon themselves to contact local capitalists. For instance, when K. Y. Yin was presiding over the IDC in the early 1950s, a number of the local capitalists were invited in the commission as advisors. But basically they had no right to say anything about the decision-making aside from offering the information that the economic policy makers needed and obeying the policy that the economic policy makers decided. The economic policy makers also encouraged local capitalists to set up organizations to communicate with the government. For example, the Chinese National Association of Industry and Commerce was set up by a group of leading businessmen as an umbrella organization in 1951. Economic policy makers maintained close links with it. However, unlike Japan's *Keidanren* which is an association for the private sector to represent its interests to the state, it functioned more like a channel by which state policies were relayed to businessmen (Gold, 1986: 71). The relationship between the state and local capitalists in economic policy-making was thus closer to the style of making decisions from above than from below.

The Transnational Capitalists

Since the retreat of the KMT state, Taiwan had been insulated from the world system by two factors. On the one hand, a great amount of U.S. aid in materials, finance, and military cocooned Taiwan within American hegemony and lessened the necessity for Taiwan to rush into the world system (Cumings, 1984: 22-26). On the other hand, the uncertainty of the political situation, the scarcity of natural resources, and the small size of the domestic market in Taiwan deterred foreign capital. Contrary to Amsden's (1979: 368) argument that foreign firms did not arrive in Taiwan in significant numbers mainly because the state did not abandon its traditionally conservative attitude toward foreign investment until the export boom of the late sixties had got underway, the KMT did try to attract foreign capital by promulgating Statute for Investment of Foreigners in 1954 and Statute for Investment of Overseas Chinese in 1955. Both of the statutes offered certain incentives to foreign direct investment (Wu et al., 1980: 23-28). But the noted two factors caused to the hesitance of foreign investment in the 1950s and early 1960s.

Meanwhile, during the 1950s and early 1960s, the KMT state dominated the heights of the economy and accounted for a sizable and crucial portion of industrial production. A few cases of foreign investments were basically linked to the public sector. Under various measures of encouragement and protection for import subsitution, local capital supplied most of the needs of the small and poor domestic market. Extensive import restrictions, especially on nonessential consumer goods, severely curtailed the presence of transnational capitalists. Given American cooperation and assistance, the state had more range to determine its relation with the outside world because it had avoided both foreign interests domestically and economic pressures externally (Gold, 1986: 75). The result was that when the U.S. aid stopped and Taiwan had to incorporated itself into the world capitalist system, it had already developed a strong capacity of capital accumulation from domestic savings, a prospering private enterprise owned by local capitalists, and a relatively autonomous and capable state which played the most important role among the three partners of the "triple alliance".

In contrast with most Latin American countries, where the state was in a weak position *vis-a-vis* its own societies and transnational corporations, the state on Taiwan was cohesive internally and dominant both economically and politically. Where the states in Latin America played a minor direct role in the economy and had to consider the wishes and global strategies of the transnational capitalists in their policies to resolve economic problems, the KMT state had the capacities to lay down the rules for transnational capitalsts to follow. Taiwan's economy did not have an enclave entrenched by transnational capitalists and foreign-oriented local elites. Therefore, similar to the case of local capitalists, when the state might accept the demands of transnational capitalists, the economic policy-making was mainly determined by government officials.

Moreover, we should notice that transnational capitalists did not all come to Taiwan with the same purpose, nor did they act on the island uniformly. Roughly speaking, the transnational capitalists in Taiwan can be classified into three groups: Americans, Japanese, and overseas Chinese. Their behaviors and strategies of making profit should not be generalized. As Gold (1981: 208) observes, the Americans come to Taiwan with the overriding objective of cutting costs in certain stages of a global production process intended to manufacture items for the U.S. market. The Japanese invest in Taiwan as a means of transplanting obsolete parts of their domestic industrial structure as well as a means of continuing to import from Japan and sell in the local and international markets. In contrast, concentrating their investment on light industry in which Taiwan's local capitalists were active and on those investments of a speculative or service nature, the overseas Chinese do not see Taiwan as part of a global strategy or production process, but rather as a preferred place for investment as compared with the countries they reside in. They are closer to the KMT state than the Americans and Japanese. For the KMT state, overseas Chinese are not foreigners and they fulfilled a propaganda function–they identify the Republic of China rather than the People's Republic of China. In this sense, overseas Chinese's contribution to Taiwan's development is very similar to that of local capitalists, for they are also quite well integrated into society.

Some Remarks on the Operational Structure of Economic Policy-making

To trace out the interrelations among various kinds of state autonomy and state capacities, we must pay attention to the operational networks and shared norms that intertwining with the formal organizations compose the structure of the state apparatus. Likewise, as we avoid global characterizations of state strength which confounds the matter of state autonomy with issues of state capacities, we have to conceptualize specific dimensions of state capacities and a range of possible relationships between state actors and other social groups (Evans, Rueschemeyer, and Skocpol, 1985: 355-356). In the preceeding sections, we tried to figure out the operational networks and respective norms and ideas concerned with economic policy-making in the Kuomintang state and between the state and other relevant social groups.

We discover that there are several groups at different levels involved in the process of making economic policy. Within the state apparatus, we discern a strong and stable leadership who recruits competent subordinates devoted to economic development and supports them; a group of honest, and capable economic policy makers who play a pivotal role in synthesizing various opinions and demands from different groups within or outside the state apparatus; and a company of skilled and loyal economic bureaucracts who works quite hard. Outside the state apparatus, we distinguish a group of consulting economists who work with intellectual enthusiasm; a group of American advisors who are willing to give well-meaning advice and back up the free-market-oriented developmentalists; a cluster of local capitalists who are relatively remote from the center of making economic policy but respond sensitively to the improvement of the business climate provided by the state; and a cluster of transnational capitalists who have little leverage on the economic policy-making and are not able to retrench an enclave in Taiwanese society. To be brief, the Kuomintang state enjoys a high degree of *state capacities* and a high degree of *state autonomy* in terms of operational structure of economic policy-making.

Two issues are worth discussing here. The first issue is what influence does the KMT's political doctrine–Sun Yat-senism–exert upon the economic policy making? In theory, of course, Sun Yat-senism is supposed to be the guideline for the KMT state to manage Taiwan's development. In practice, however, there are some different observations on this issue. Some scholars (King, 1981: 10; Barrett, 1980: 3-4) contend that for the last three decades Sun Yat-senism had little impact on economic decision-making in the KMT state and that the economic officials' ideas of managing the economy were basically immune from ideological constraints. Some other scholars (Gregor, Chang, and Zimmerman, 1981; Myers, 1986: 44) assert that Sun Yat-senism has served as a beacon for the economic policy makers. In addition, the economic officials of the KMT state have reiterated that achievements on Taiwan are the result of following Sun Yat-senism. The ideology has been upheld as being more suitable for national development than capitalism and communism (Yin, 1973b: 60-62; Wang, 1981: 202-215; Sun, 1981; Yen, 1982; 7; Li, 1985: 189-202). Which point of view is correct then?

The key point here is the essence of Sun Yat-senism. Briefly, Sun Yat-sen's idea of managing a national economy–the *Min-sheng* Principle–is akin to socialism in its advocacy of regulation of capital and equalization of land tenure, but it is also parallel with capitalism because it retains a major role of free enterprise and opposing class struggle (Gold, 1986: 48). For those people who stress the socialist ingredients of the *Min-sheng* Principle, the ideology will be socialistic in nature, especially in its prescription for state control of basic industries. Then, the trend of liberalization and the expansion of private enterprise in Taiwan's economic transformation is likely to be seen as a deviation of Sun's doctrine. But for those who emphasize the capitalist ingredients of the *Min-sheng* Principle, the story will be totally different. As a matter of fact, the more free-market-oriented economic officials have repeatedly insisted that the policy-making for managing Taiwan's economic transformation has followed Sun Yat-senism faithfully.

For example, some people argued that Sun's lecture on the *Min-sheng* Principle advocated that "China must not only regulate capital, but she must also develop state capital and promote industry" (Sun, 1924: 180); accordingly, the KMT state should develop state enterprise and curb private enterprise. The answer of the economic officials was that to understand the real meaning of the quotation, we have to grasp the distinction Sun made between private enterprise and state enterprise. As Sun said in his book *The International Development of China* (1922: 9):

> The industrial development of China should be carried out along two lines: (1) by private enterprise and (2) by national undertaking. All matters that can be and are better carried out by private enterprise should be left to private hands which should be encouraged and fully protected by liberal laws. And in order to facilitate the industrial development by private enterprise in China, the hitherto suicidal internal taxes must be abolished, the cumbersome currency must be reformed, the various kinds of official obstacles must be removed, and transportation facilities must be provided. All matters that cannot be taken up by private concerns and those that possess monopolistic character should be taken up as national undertakings.

Therefore, state enterprises under Sun's principle are confined to the following: (1) enterprises that are monopolistic in nature; (2) enterprises that private individuals are unable to establish; and (3) public utilities of the nature of (1) and (2). However, economic officials in the KMT state further argue that even public utilities and other monopolistic enterprises can also be entrusted to the private sector. The point is whether the private sector has the financial capability as needed, and whether private operation would adversely affect the well-being of the general public (Li, 1985: 193-194). Since many state enterprises are inherited from the Japanese as historical accidents and inertia that have no ideological or economic reason should be retained in the public sector (Little, 1979: 468), the transfer of non-crucial state enterprises to local capitalists' hands and the expansion of private enterprise by no means divert from Sun's principle (Yin, 1973b: 61).

The question of which argument corresponds with Sun's principle better, actually, is not our major concern here. What we want to point out is the ability of the economic officials to interpret Sun Yat-senism as non-dogmatic pragmatism (Fei, 1982: 94). There were some debates among intellectuals about the essence of the *Min-sheng* Principle (Fu, 1976: 231-251), but it never significantly influenced the economic policy-making in the state. Neither do we find within the state apparatus any serious ideological disagreement on the economic policy-making due to the different understanding of Sun's doctrine. Surely, as indicated earlier, most credit must go to Sun Yat-senism *per se*. Sun's eclectic attitude toward capitalism and socialism may be responsible for some vagueness in his doctrine, but it also makes the ideology fairly balanced, comprehensive, and flexible (Pang, 1980: 155-168). Thus, when the ideology serves as a beacon of national development for the state and society, it offers the KMT's elites a wide range to manage the economy from a pragmatic way.

The second issue is concerned with the evolution of the internal structure of the KMT state in the operational structure of making economic policy and its relationship with the constitutional structure. In regard to the top political leadership, we point out that for the last thirty-seven years Taiwan's development was supervised by a paternalistic style leadership. While out of tune in some respects with the modernizing trends on the island, the leadership served to manage a society at Taiwan's stage of development (Clough, 1978: 48). But a potential crisis entailed with the paternalistic leadership, which means rule by a dominant figure on all problems, is the question of succession (Pye, 1985: 48). As a matter of fact, the KMT state had somehow encountered the crisis in the second half of the 1960s. It was the predicament resulting from the death of Ch'en Ch'eng and the immaturity of Chiang Ching-kuo. The crisis was finally resolved by entrusting the mission to C. K. Yen.

In recent years, the problem of power succession emerges again. Chiang Ching-kuo has been getting old and his health has deteriorated. Differing from his father's doing, however, Chiang Ching-kuo has not groomed or appointed any successor. Instead, he has tried to break through the predicament by accelerating democratization and enhancing the principle of rule by law rather of man. In 1985, he announced that he had never considered naming a member of his family to the presidency and that there should never have a military government on Taiwan. Consequently, there has not been any person who is able to succeed Chiang's entire power. The leadership of the KMT state in the future is thus likely to be a collective leadership controlled by a group of people rather than one strong man. It is hard to predict the impact of this new style of leadership on the KMT state's organizational coherence. What we do know is that a strong and stable top political leadership has continued from 1949 to the present.

Similar to the situation of the top political leadership, the personnel evolution of the economic policy makers has shown a stable continuity and smooth transition. From K. Y. Yin to K. T. Li and then to Sun Yun-suan (B.S. in electrical engineering, had been chief engineer of the Taiwan Power Company for 1950-53, vice president and then president of the company for 1953-62 and 1962-64, general manager of the Electricity Corporation of Nigeria for 1964-67, minister of Communications for 1967-69, minister of Economic Affairs for 1969-78, and Premier for 1978-84) and Yu Kuo-hwa (B.A. in political science, advanced study in finance and economics at the Graduate School of Harvard University and the Lodon School of Politics and Economics, had been alternate executive director of the International Money Fund for 1951-55, president of the Central Trust of China for 1955-61, chairman of the board of the Bank of China for 1961-67, minister of Finance for 1967-69, minister of state (without portfolio) and concurrently governor of the Central Bank of China for 1969-84, chairman of the CEDP for 1977-84, and Premier since 1984), the succession moves smoothly. Again like the situation of the top political leadership, most leading economic policy makers are getting old and facing the problemof handing over the duty. In recent years, more and more people in the society are worried about the potential loss of the energy and aggressiveness of the economic leadership. They expect the emergence of a new cast of economic policy makers with K. Y. Yin's mode in order to lead Taiwan's economy to overcome new challenges (Kau, 1982: 34-39).

Due to the growth and differentiation of the economy, the economic bureaucrats have progressively shared more responsibility and power in managing Taiwan's economic transformation. As Eric Wright's interpretation on Max Weber's work on bureaucracy argues (Wright, 1978: 183-194; Weber, 1968: 956-1005), with the development of capitalism and the increasing complexity of society, the needs for rational administration, such as precision, speed, unambiguity, knowledge of the files, continuity, discretion, unity, strict subordination, reduction of friction and of material and personal costs, tend to make the state apparatus more and more bureaucratized. When bureaucratization increases, the power of bureaucrats in turn tends to expand because the bureaucrats control the expert technical knowledge, the "administrative secrets", and the effectiveness of the organization. This is also true in the Kuomintang state, especially with the economic bureaucracy since the economic and financial affairs are relatively more professional. Consequently, the phenomenon of "domination of staff" has crept into the economic bureaucracy. As Weber points out, if the top administration of a state apparatus is in the hands of bureaucrats, then there will be a tendency for the political direction of the bureaucracy to be irresponsible and ineffective, especially in times of crisis, and for the behind-the-scenes influence of big capitalists in the running of the state bureaucracy to be maximized. Recent events in Taiwan seem to evidence this tendency in the KMT state. Fortunately, it has not been so advanced as to be past remedy. A more detailed analysis will also be presented later.

Finally, in parallel with the bureaucratization in the Kuomintang state and the proliferation of interest groups in the Taiwan society, a tendency of convergence between the constitutional and operational structures of economic policy-making has been noticed in recent years. The tendency moves on along two lines. Along the first line, the function of the Executive Yuan Council in formulating economic policy has increased while the dominance of the economic policy makers has somewhat ebbed. One reason for this transformation is the changing attitude of the people toward socioeconomic development. Owing to the improvement of living standards, more and more people on Taiwan readjust their preferences; economic growth is no longer the predominantly sole objective. Some other social goals, such as environment protection and labor rights, have attracted people's attention. As a result, the trade-off between economic development and social development becomes an increasingly important issue. The weight of the other government departments on the policy-making has thus augmented and the function of the Executive Yuan Council in coordinating state policies has to be enhanced.

Along the second line, there have been more and more interest groups in society exerting pressure on economic policy-making through the Legislative Yuan. Due to the expansion of democracy in recent years, the power of the Legislative Yuan has extended to a certain degree. At the same time, the increment of the new members, who have to go through the election, brings more constituency-oriented politics into the Yuan. Consequently, in addition to the direct and indirect linkages with the economic policy makers and economic bureaucrats, the social groups outside the state apparatus, especially the local capitalists, have also opened up the channels via the Legislative Yuan to exert their weight upon economic policy-making. In the following chapters, we will try to depict this evolution.

CHAPTER 5

FORMULATION AND EXECUTION OF ECONOMIC POLICY BEFORE THE LATE 1950S

Situation Imperatives

International Situation

During the fifties, Taiwan had been cocooned within American hegemony both geo-politically and economically. When World War II ended in 1945, only the United States remained powerful, rich, and unscathed among the great powers. The other victors along with the defeated were in ruins or near exhaustion. Under the leadership of President Franklin D. Roosevelt, America attemped to remake the entire world in their own image so as to bring about world peace and prosperity experienced and defined by the Americans. Although the grand vision of unifying the entire world under a dominion centered on America began to crumble more or less after Roosevelt's death, it would be wrong to say that the vision passed away with him. In effect, the vision spawned policies that eventually led to the formation of the "free world," a collection of nations big and small led and dominated by the U.S. and tied together by growing military, economic, and political bonds.

What died with Roosevelt was the hope that Russia could be woven into the new order and China could be kept out of the hands of the Communists. Consequently, a policy of containment directed against Russia and its allies was adopted. The contents of the policy included: American military power strategically placed throughout the world, a new monetary system based on the U.S. dollar, economic assistance to the destroyed countries, political linkages realized through the United Nations and other international agencies. By the end of the 1940s, an American hegemony had clearly emerged. The United States "lost" Russia and China, but it gained the remainder of the world, which it proceeded to energize, organize, and dominate in a most active way (Schurmann, 1974: 3-5). The Republic of China on Taiwan was an outpost of these efforts in the anti-Communist free world.

The Kuomintang state on Taiwan was incorporated into the American state's containment plan mainly due to the outbreak of the Korean war. When the Nationalist government withdrew to Taiwan, the United States government basically adopted an attitude of noninvolvement toward the rivalry between the KMT and the CCP. Although there was general agreement that it would be highly desirable for Taiwan to remain under a friendly, non-Communist regime, the U.S. government was unwilling to keep Taiwan out of Communist hands through direct military intervention. By the end of 1949, the continuation of a modest economic aid program was approved while massive economic aid was rejected. President Harry S. Truman also decided against reinstituting a military aid program in Taiwan, despite the recommendation of the Joint Chiefs of Staff and demands of some prominent Republican members of Congress. In January, 1950, Truman clearly announced that the United States would neither establish military bases in nor provid military aid or advice to Taiwan. Then the surprise attack by North Korean forces against South Korea in June, 1950 brought about a reversal of the hands-off policy. The Korean War and the resulting confrontation of American and Chinese Communist forces led to the resumption of large-scale military and economic aid to the Republic of China on Taiwan and convinced the United States that a prime purpose of its East Asian policy should be the military and political containment of the Communist regime on the mainland. This containment concept dominated U.S. policy in the region for the next twenty years, until President Richard M. Nixon set it on a new course in 1972 by opening relations with Peking (Clough, 1978: 1; 7-8).

Not only did American military power shield the island from Communist invasion, but it prevented the KMT from going to war on the mainland, too. This was reflected in the Defense Treaty between the United States and the Republic of China signed on December 2, 1954. In the exchange of notes, the U.S. government asked the Chinese government to recognize, "In view of the obligations of the two Parties under the said Treaty and of the fact that the use of force from either of these areas by either of the Parties affects the other, it is agreed that such use of force will be a matter of joint agreement." The Chinese government replied it by confirming this "understanding" (Chiu, 1973: 250-253). Thus, although the Kuomintang state benefitted from U.S. military assistance, at the same time it lost its autonomy since its military action was also subject to the approval of U.S. government. The reluctance of the U.S. government to support an armed attack on Mainland China blocked the way for the Kuomintang state to recover the mainland by virtue of its military strength. More efforts consequently were put into economic development.

Meanwhile, American financial and commodity assistance isolated the island's economy; substantial input of resources into a relatively small area alleviated the necessity for Taiwan to rush into the capitalist world system. Afforded security and breathing space by American aid, the KMT state undertook various reforms–American aid was tied to reforms as an added incentive. Through a control of the resources for the Nationalists, Americans had great influence on the direction of change; however, the fact that the Republic of China on Taiwan was a sovereign state in the United Nations and an important ally in the global anti-Communist crusade which did face an implacable threat limited the leverage the United States exerted upon the regime. After all, reform had to be deviced and carried out by the KMT itself. Much of the KMT's reform was in fact accomplished by self-selection (Gold, 1986: 58-59).

The Sino-American alliance was surely not free from disagreement on certain issues, especially on the importance of some offshore islands near to the mainland and the future of Taiwan. The fundamental objective of the KMT state was to overthrow the CCP regime and regain authority over Mainland China. It clung to the offshore islands as a political symbol of its dedication to this goal. Those islands also served psychologically as a symbol of Taiwan's defense against Communist invasion. But the American government did not wish to be committed to assist in such an enterprise. The United States just wanted Taiwan to stay as an integral part of the U.S.-backed security system with the least probability of provoking war in the Taiwan Strait thus forcing direct U.S. intervention. As a matter of fact, the U.S. government had continuously tried to moderate its relationship with the Communist regime. Hoping to reduce the risk of conflict with the PRC and to obtain the release of eleven pilots shot down during the Korean War as well as some forty American civilians imprisoned in China, a direct communication through a series of bilateral meetings at the ambassadorial level began in Geneva in August, 1955. Due to their widely opposing stances, however, the talks failed and were eventually suspended in December 1957. Less than 9 months later, a severe crisis provoked by the Communists' massive bombardment of the offshore islands made the conflict among the three parties even graver (Clough, 1978: 12-15).

Intra-national Situation

When the KMT state retreated from Mainland China to Taiwan, the island's economic and political situation was disastrous. Allied bombing and general neglect during the war left much of Taiwan's economy in ruin. Preoccupied with its struggle against the Communists, the Nationalists could provide little assistance or attention to the new province during the initial postwar period. In fact, Taiwan had to supply materials to the mainland to support the Nationalists against the Communists. This extra burden accelerate the decline of Taiwan's economy by inflation. The repatriation of the Japanese, including numerous technicians, managers, entrepreneurs, and administrators, caused confusion in the economic system. From 1946 to 1950, more than 1 million mainland refugees, mainly servicemen and civil servants, arrived in Taiwan (it had about 6 million population in 1946). This sudden increase in population worsened the problems of food, necessary consumer goods, and employment. In addition, the 2-28 Incident led to a deterioration in the relationship between Taiwanese and Mainlanders. This, in turn, made mutual trust and cooperation between the state and society very difficult. As a result, by the end of the forties and the beginning of the fifties, the KMT state found itself dealing with a bankrupt economy, an angry populace, and an unstable political future (Myers, 1973: 42-43).

To bring order and progress to the economy, however, Taiwan could count on a number of vital assets. Notwithstanding wartime destruction, the island's infrastructure was still sufficiently extensive. Its agriculture, although rathe disrupted as a result of the war, was still the most advanced in the Far East, second only to Japan. The colonial education system left Taiwan with one of the most literate populations in Asia. Institutions favorable to development created during the colonial period, such as the farmers' association, credit cooperative, agricultural experiment station, and various banking facilities, could be quickly revived to prove their usefulness. Most significantly, because of the stability during the colonial period, Taiwan at the time of World War II, unlike other parts of China, had an extremely well-ordered society. This enabled it to survive the war in relatively better shape. Even though the 2-28 Incident brought about severe distrust between the state and the society, Taiwan did not fall into anomie.

Besides the favorable inheritance from its colonial past, some other factors also made postwar recovery and development less difficult. First, among the last wave of Mainlander refugees that reached Taiwan in 1949-50, there was a group of technicians, managers, and entrepreneurs. Their arrival bridged to a certain extent the human resource gap produced by the departure of the Japanese in 1946. Second, the resumption of U.S. aid and the patrol of the U.S. Navy's Seventh Fleet in the Taiwan Strait after the outbreak of the Korean War gave the Taiwan people a significant and more-needed psychological lift (Ho, 1978: 104-105). Third and most important, as we have mentioned, the retreat of the Kuomintang elites brought a capable and autonomous state, which took over the active and dominant role of the state in developing the economy during the colonial period, into the Taiwan society.

During the fifties, the KMT state had operated under a power structure with Chiang Kai-shek and Ch'en Ch'eng as the top political leadership. At the time that Chiang Kai-shek's resumed the presidency on March 1, 1950 (Vice President Li Tsung-jen, who had been acting President during Chiang's temporary resignation from January 21, 1949 to February 28, 1950, flew to the United States and refused to go to Taipei with the Nationalist government), a new cabinet was inaugurated (March 15) with Ch'en Ch'eng as Premier. Backed by Chiang Kai-shek, he held substantial power as the head of the administrative system. The formal power structure of the KMT state, according to the Constitution promulgated in 1947, is a mixture of cabinet system and presidential system. Under normal circumstances, this power structure should be closer to a cabinet system. That is to say, the Premier rather than the President is the major power-holder. However, since May, 1948, with the enactment of the Temporary Provisions Effective During the Period of Communist Rebellion, the President has been granted a wide range of emergency powers. This shifts the outward structure of the central government of the ROC toward the presidential system. Consequently, the delineation between President and Premier becomes vague, and either one has the possibility of becoming the effective ruler (Liu, 1960: 136-137; Sah, 1974: 216; Wei, 1973: 89). The subtle relationship between President and Premier carries a potential crisis for power struggle that can only be avoided through cooperation with each other. Fortunately, the Chiang-Ch'en leadership became an example (Yang, 1986: 144-145).

Showing loyalty to Chiang Kai-shek and trusted, in turn, by Chiang, Ch'en Ch'eng had substantial power in determining the personnel of the cabinet, especially in the ministries or commissions concerning financial and economic affairs. A number of brilliant people were recruited to take charge of economic development, notably, C. K. Yen (minister of Finance), K. Y. Yin (vice chairman of TPB and then member of the ESB and convener of the IDC), and Chang Tse-k'ai (minister of Economic Affairs, he earned a M.B.A. degree from New York University in 1932, and had been general manager of the China Petroleum Corporation for 1947-49, vice minister of Finance for 1950-51, minister of Economic affairs for 1952-54, and chairman of board of the Bank of Taiwan for 1953-60 and retired from the position) (Liao, 1986c: 86-95). He also presided over the CUSA. Under the strong leadership of Chiang and Ch'en, the KMT state operated quite coherently. In March, 1954, when Chiang was reelected President for the second term, Ch'en was elected Vice President. Ch'en thus resigned as Premier and the Executive Yuan needed a new head. O. K. Yui was appointed to assume the position (B.A. in foreign language and literature from St. John's University in Shanghai, secretary-general of Shanghai municipal government 1930-37, mayor of Shanghai 1937, president of the Central Trust of China 1938-40, vice minister of Finance 1941-44, minister of Finance 1944-48, governor of the Central Bank of China 1948-49 and 1950-60, chairman of board of the Bank of Taiwan 1952, governor of Taiwan 1953-54, Premier 1954-58, and died in 1960) (China Yearbook, 1957-58: 684).

In Yui's cabinet, Hsu Peh-yuan, Yui's top aide, was minister of Finance and concurrently chairman of the FETCC (B.A. in commerce and advanced study in finance in the U.S., vice minister of Finance 1946-48, deputy governor of the Central Bank of China 1948, chairman of board of the Bank of Taiwan 1951-52, commissioner of Finance of Taiwan provincial government 1952-54, minister of Finance 1954-58, chairman of FETCC 1955-58 and 1963-69, and governor of the Central Bank of China 1960-69) (Liao, 1986a: 32-39); K. Y. Yin was minister of Economic Affairs and concurrently convener of the IDC; and C. K. Yen became governor of Taiwan and concurrently chairman of the ESB. O. K. Yui himself chaired the CUSA and the Central Bank of China simultaneously. The new cabinet lay a heavy emphasis on economic development. Although trusted by Chiang Kai-shek, O. K. Yui's prestige and power could not compare with Ch'en Ch'eng's. In his term as Premier, there were some frictions both within the cabinet and between the Executive Yuan and other state branches. For example, K. Y. Yin resigned in 1955 partly due to the increasingly tense relationship with Yui. And Yui himself resigned from the position of Premier in June, 1958 because the Control Yuan accused him of holding too many posts concurrently and living in a luxurious style (Ch'en, 1985: 155-156; Yang, 1986: 153-154). At the same time, the crisis of the offshore islands was intensifying and Taiwan needed a strong cabinet to withstand the difficulty. Hence, Vice President Ch'en Ch'eng, who had been also elected Vice *Tsungtsai* of the KMT in November, 1957, resumed the position of Premier and reorganized the cabinet. With his support, K. Y. Yin was given some important assignments and started a series of reforms in the late fifties and early sixties. These reforms reshaped both Taiwan's economy and society in the following years. Their formulation and execution will be discussed in the next chapter.

In this chapter, we are going to focus on the economic policy-making that took place on Taiwan before 1958. Given the favorable and unfavorable factors noted above, the most urgent economic problems that the KMT state faced in the fifties were (1) how to increase food products to feed the abruptly increased population; (2) how to increase the production of necessary consumer goods to meet the basic needs of the people; (3) how to curb inflation; and (4) how to solve the problem of foreign exchange shortage. The policies for resolving these problems and the conjuncture that influenced their making are to be presented in the following sections.

Agricultural Policy

As mentioned above, more than 1 million mainland refugees, most of them servicemen and civil servants, accompanied by scholars and entrepreneurs, arrived in Taiwan during the period from 1946 to 1950. The population on the island was increased by one sixth. With this sudden increase in population, the need for rapid agricultural development became obvious and urgent. The end of the colonial rule and the loss of the protected Japanese market meant that the previous pattern of resource use, based on exporting agricultural products to and importing industrial goods from Japan, required modification–a different approach was needed. In addition to feeding a much enlarged population, agriculture also had to supply much of the labor, foreign exchange, and savings required for industrialization. To meet these demands, the KMT state, having suffered from its neglect of agriculture in the mainland, adopted a set of measure to develop and extract agricultural resources (Ho, 1978: 105).

Reorganization of the Institutional Infrastructure

The institutional infrastructure of Taiwan's agriculture was extensively reorganized and improved during the 1950s. Two organizations were most important, namely, the JCRR at central government level and the farmers' associations at local levels. As noted in chapter II, the JCRR was initially set up as a bilateral agency for the postwar rural reconstruction of China. After the fall of the mainland in the hands of the Communists and the reactivation of the U.S. aid to the ROC, the JCRR was relocated in Taiwan and served as the agricultural branch of the U.S. AID Mission to China. Whereas the U.S. AID Mission, a purely American organization, devoted its attention mainly to industrial development projects, the JCRR worked on rural and agricultural development. In addition to allocating U.S. aid, the JCRR was concerned with both technological improvements and institutional adjustments in the agricultural sector. The former included the research and introduction of better farming techniques, new crops, improved varieties, etc. The latter had to do with the implementation of the land reform, the reorganization of the farmers' associations, the irrigation associations, and the fishermen's associations, as well as the improvement of marketing procedures and facilities (Shen, 1970: 2).

The governing body of the JCRR was originally composed of five commissioners, three Chinese and two American. They made all the policy decisions and exercised general supervision over the implementation of the JCRR supported projects with the assistance of technical and administrative staff. In September, 1964, effected by an exchange of notes between the Chinese and American governments, the number of commissioners was reduced to two Chinese and one American (Shen, 1970: 20-21). The reduction in a certain sense signified the decline of the importance of agricultural sector in Taiwan's economy. However, through the fifties, agricultural development had been the main thrust of Taiwan's economic transformation and the JCRR had contributed a lot to this energetic development. The success of the JCRR could be attributed to both its personnel and organization.

Since the governing body of the JCRR was consisted of both Chinese and American from different cultural backgrounds, communication seemed to be a considerable problem. Fortunately, all Chinese commissioners, notably, Chiang Monlin (Ph. D. of Columbia University in 1917, minister of Education for 1928-30, chancellor of National Peking University for 1930-45, secretary-general of the Executive Yuan for 1945-47, chairman of JCRR for 1948-64, and died in 1964), T. H. Shen (Ph. D. of Cornell University in 1928, vice director and later director of the National Agricultural Research Bureau for 1938-50, commissioner of the JCRR for 1948-73, chairman of the JCRR for 1964-73, retired in 1973), Chien T'ien-ho (M.S. of Cornell University in 1918, vice director of the National Agricultural Research Bureau for 1932-37, director of Agricultural and Forestry Department of Ministry of Economic Affairs for 1933-40, vice minister of

Agriculture and Forestry for 1940-47, chief of the Agricultural Improvement Division of the JCRR for 1948-51, commissioner of the JCRR for 1951-61, and retired in 1961), and later Tsiang Yien-si (Ph. D. of the University of Minnesota in 1942, executive officer of the JCRR for 1948-52, secretary-general of the JCRR for 1952-61, commissioner of the JCRR for 1961-78, secretary-general of the Executive Yuan for 1967-72, minister of Education for 1972-77, secretary-general of the Office of the President for 1978, minister of Foreign Affairs for 1978-79, secretary-general of KMT for 1979-84, and currently vice chairman of the Committee for Science Development of the National Science Council as well as national policy advisor to the President), had all studied at American universities and come to understand the American way of approaching problems. With such cooperation among the commissioners, the joint structure ran smoothly (Shen, 1970: 14-15; 20-21). The two chairman of the JCRR, Chiang Monlin for 1948-64 and T. H. Shen for 1964-73, were acknowledged for their outstanding performance. Chiang Monlin was also known as a leader of Chinese intellectuals and a friend of Chiang Kai-shek's. His prestige made the cooperation between American advisors and Chinese officials quite cohesive (Chou, 1982a: 25-27).

Furthermore, several organizational feature of the JCRR are considered innovative and imaginative. First, it was established as a semipublic institution which provided it some independence from the government. Since its budget was almost totally financed by U.S. aid, the JCRR could take a long-range view of the agricultural development process without the daily political and bureaucratic pressures of an ordinary agricultural ministry. Second, it combined the planning function with the actual implementation of research, extension, and irrigation. The responsibility for carrying out these activities was concentrated in only one agency which allowed the activities to be implemented in an integrated fashion. And third, it operated at local levels in a decentralized fashion, thereby circumventing what might otherwise have been a cumbersome bureaucracy and bringing its effectiveness into full play (Thorbecke, 1979: 22). At local levels, the functions of the JCRR were brought into effect through the revitalization and strengthening of the farmers' associations, the irrigation associations, and the fishermen's associations. Among them, the farmers' associations played the key role in translating the plan of the JCRR and other economic agencies at the central government level into specific local actions. One of the JCRR's great contributions to Taiwan's agricultural and rural development was the reorganization of the farmers' associations.

The farmers' associations and credit cooperatives set up by the Japanese to facilitate agricultural extension programs and rice procurement, were hierarchical institutions originally dominated by landlords and the local gentry. As a result, they became an instrument for landlords and the local gentry to engage in usury and commission earning. In September, 1949, based on a suggestion of the JCRR, the KMT state carried out the reorganization in three steps: (1) it merged the farmers' associations with credit cooperatives, which were the main formal banking units in rural areas taking charge of the farmers' savings and loans, in order to generate financial resources for the associations; (2) it purified the membership of the associations by denying subsidy to those associations not truly representing the farmers; and (3) it developed a more tenant-and-owner-cultivator-based farmers' association system by prescribing that every farm household have only one person as a member of the associations, more member representatives be elected from the member assembly, and no less than two-thirds of the member representatives in the boards be tenants or owner-cultivators. Consequently, the landlords were deprived of their leadership and dominance in the associations (Shiau, 1985: 6-7).

In September, 1950, W. A. Anderson, a professor of rural sociology at Cornell University, was invited to Taiwan by the U.S. AID Mission and the JCRR jointly to review the existing laws, regulations, and organization of the associations. After leading a visiting group of JCRR to Japan to observe the actual situation of the Japanese agricultural organizations and institutions, which had been intentionally reformed by the Supreme Command of Allied Powers, Anderson made a number of recommendations for their revision. Following the previous the JCRR approach to upgrade staff quality, to increase financial resources, and to emphasize the function of agricultural extension, Anderson further suggested that the associations participate in the agricultural policy-making and emphasized that the political manipulation should be excluded out from the associations. A reform plan was proposed in early 1951, but it was turned down by the KMT state because the state could not completely accept the recommendation about political control over the associations. Then, after a series of prolonged discussions during which the original draft was modified to reconcile conflicting interests, the revised law and supplementary regulations were eventually promulgated in August, 1953 (Anderson, 1950; Shen, 1970: 72-73).

In accordance with the new law, three more steps were taken to reform the associations: (1) membership review; (2) reelection of the directors, the supervisors, and the member representatives; and (3) installment of the director-general. In the membership review, a household earning at least half of its income from farming is entitled to have one of its men enrolled in the local farmers' association as an active member. Active members have the right to vote, to hold office in the associations, and to use all its facilities. Otherwise, he can only be an associate member, who can neither vote nor be elected member representative. After the review, associate members increased from 28.9% to 32.9% of the total members. In the reelection (in early 1954), tenants and owner-cultivators together took up 97.7% of the member representatives and 98.1% of the directors, contrasting to the earlier 84.8% and 76.0%. All absentee landlords and most part-time farmers were expelled from the organization. This result was surely facilitated by the 1949-53 land reform which changed land tenure and ownership system. Finally, the installment of the director-general (elected by the board of the directors as a device for improving division of labor in name) strengthened the political control of the state over the organization in effect. After all, controlling one person is easier than controlling a group of directors. Hence, after the reorganization, the functions of the associations included provision of agricultural extension services, cooperative economic and credit services, and internal training and education services; there was to be no more usury and commission-earning. Thus, their roles changed from that of an instrument manipulated by landlords and the local gentry to an agency controlled by the state (Shiau, 1985: 8-9).

The alternation of the roles and functions of the farmer's associations was a process involving the collusion and collision among related groups in the reform. The related groups were the KMT state, the American advisors, the landlords, and the small farmers (tenants and owner-cultivators). While they did receive profits in the reorganization, the small farmers had actually no major participation. The primary pattern of the collusion and collision was featured by the coalition of the KMT state and the U.S. AID Mission against the landlords. This interaction pattern underlied the whole reorganization process and resulted in the gradual exclusion of the landlords from the associations The new functions of the associations were basically defined by a compromise between the KMT state and the U.S. AID Mission. Although both Chinese officials and American advisors agreed about the necessity of the reorganization as a measure of securing the loyalty of the peasants and containing the infiltration of Communism, they had different viewpoints with respect to the operation of the associations. The American advisors intended to organize self-governed farmers' associations enpowered with sufficient autonomy and the right to take part in the agricultural policy-making, whereas the KMT state sought to consolidate its dominance over and extract more resources through the associations. As a result, the announced functions of the associations showed an ecletic feature of the two groups' respective objectives (Shaiu, 1985: 10-11).

Among the newly announced functions of the farmers' associations (such as the agricultural extension services, the cooperative farm credit services, the internal training and education services, and the cooperative supply and marketing business in the cooperative economic services), most of them were designed exclusively to serve the farmers. But the state entrusted business in the cooperative economic services was mainly a device for the state to control and extract agricultural resources. The entrusted business required the associations to take charge of the rice-fertilizer barter system; to collect rice for land tax and land price repayment from the farmers who got land through the land reform; to buy peanuts, wheat, and other crops; to sell salt, flour, and other commodities; as well as to send rationed commodities to the military and civilian families for the state. Through the entrusted business, the farmers' associations acted as the local branches of the state's agricultural and food bureau (Shaiu, 1985: 12-13). Thus, with the JCRR at central government level and the farmers' associations at local levels, the KMT state effectively carried out its agricultural policies. Among those policies, the land reform and the agricultural pricing policy were most crucial.

Land Reform

During the course of colonialism, although the Japanese had developed a substantial agricultural infrastructure in Taiwan, they had paid relatively little attention to the distribution of land. As Myers and Ching (1964: 555) discover, the strategy used by the colonial state to increase Taiwan's agricultural production was to repeat the institutional and organizational devices, tested during the early Meiji period, of working through the landlord and wealthy farmer classes rather than the rural masses to encourage the introduction of innovations. The colonial administration was not interested in altering the existing unequal land ownership but taking advantage of it. Moreover, the fruit of the agricultural growth was hardly shared by the rural people who offered the most contribution to the growth. The surplus was transferred to Japan at the expense of the Taiwan's farmers. In short, Taiwan's agriculture under Japanese colonialism was charaterized by "growth with inequality and exploitation" (Hsiao, 1981: 44-45).

The unequal land tenure structure had become even worse in the colonial period due to the increase of population. When Taiwan retroceded to China in 1945, the number of tenant farmers reached about 70% of the whole agricultural population. Among them, 39% were full tenant farmers and 31% were part-owners (Koo, 1968: 27). Given the large class of tenants, competition for the scarce land was so fierce that the average lease was less than one year. As a result, rents were often equal to 50% of the anticipated harvest. In the more fertile areas, the rent could run as high as 70% (Koo, 1968: 31). Contracts were frequently oral and subjected to landlords' arbitrary decision to change; rent payments had to be given in advance; and no adjustments could be made for crop failures. These conditions and practices left the typical tenants helpless in any dispute with their landlord (Yang, 1970: 9-11; Kuo, Ranis and Fei, 1981: 49).

From 1949 to 1953, the KMT state instituted a successful land reform. The reason for the land reform was basically political. Although the ideal of "equalization of land rights", conceived by Sun Yat-sen in his *Min-sheng* Principle, had always been an essential part of the ideology of the KMT, it was neglected by Sun's successors before moving to Taiwan. This was partly due to the continuous troubles within and without China that drained the attention and energy of the KMT elites and also partly due to the relatively close ties between the KMT state and the landlord class on the mainland. The occupation of Mainland China by the Communists who announced they were land reformers and the perception of the KMT of the potential danger of the land-tenure and farm-tenancy system in Taiwan made the redistsribution of land and wealth a particular important issue for the state. The land reform was an effort to secure the loyalty of the peasants and to combat the Chinese Communists' intrigue of using the weaknesses of the tenancy structure to instigate agrarian uprisings (Ch'en, 1961: x; Yang, 1970: 12-13; Hsiao, 1981: 102-108).

The land reform consisted of three phases: (1) the program to reduce farm rents, (2) the sale of public lands, and (3) the land-to-the-tiller program. In the first phase, the emphasis was placed on "reduction of rent" and "security of tenancy" (Hsiao, 1981: 47). This program had five basic provisions: first, farm rents were set at no more than 37.5% of the annual yield of the main crops; second, if crops failed because of natural forces, tenants could apply to local farm-tenancy committees for further reduction; third, tenants, no longer had to pay their rent in advance; fourth, written contracts and fixed leases of three to six years had to be registered; and fifth, tenants had the first option to purchase land from its owners. Soon, the reform had cut the prices of farmland drastically. It also enabled tenants to benefit from their own increased efforts. This incentive increased Taiwan's agricultural productivity during the early fifties. With higher yields and lower rents, the average income of tenant farmers rose by 81% between 1949 and 1952. These rising incomes enabled tenants to purchase land for themselves (Kuo, Ranis and Fei, 1981: 50).

The second phase started in 1951. Given the success of the program to reduce farm rents, the KMT state decided to sell public land to tenant farmers. These lands (which amounted to approximately 170,000 hectares) were taken over from the Japanese The aims of this program were to promote owner-farmers; to set an example to the landlords concerning the sale of land to the tiller; and to increase land use. The sale price was fixed at 2.5 times the value of the annual yield of the main crops; payments in kind were set to coincide with the harvest season over a ten-year period without interest. From 1951 to 1964, six sales were conducted and 110,935 hectares of public lands were transferred to the private ownership of 243,023 tenant families (Hsiao, 1970: 333).

The third and last phase, known as the land-to-the-tiller program, was initiated in 1953, involving the compulsory sale of land by landlords. This program stipulated that privately owned land in excess of specified amounts per landowner had to be sold to the state and for it to be resold to the incumbent tillers. The price was also set at 2.5 times the annual yield of the main crops. The landlords were paid 70% of the purchase price in land bonds denominated in kind and 30% in industrial stock of four public enterprises previously owned by the Japanese. The selling prices and conditions of repayment were the same as for the sale of public lands (Kuo, Ranis and Fei, 1981: 51). These arrangements had two important effects on Taiwan's economy: first, they avoided the possibility of stirring inflation by a sudden increase of currency in circulation; and second, they forced the landlords to shift their investment from land to industry (Hsiao, 1981: 48-49). Between May and December of 1953, tenant household acquired 244,000 hectares of farmland, which shared 16.4% of the total arable land in Taiwan during the early fifties.

The land reform had dramatically transformed Taiwan's agrarian structure. Tables 5.1, 5.2 and 5.3 summarize the effects of the land reform on the redistribution of wealth in rural Taiwan. Because of the reform, the proportion of tenant farmers in farm families and the proportion of land cultivated by tenants fell. The ratio of owner-cultivators to total farm families increased. The families owning small and medium-sized plots of land increased. And the families owning large-sized plots of land much decreased. Many tenant farmers became owner-cultivators and improved their income significantly. Due to land ownership, higher income, and greater security in lease, the farmers raised their social status and developed an optimistic and hopeful outlook. The better socioeconomic conditions enabled the farmers to participate in rural organizations, such as the farmers' associations and the farm-tenancy committees; this gave them more leverage in controlling and improving their own life. Needless to say, the land reform pleased the majority in the rural area and contributed to social and political stability in Taiwan (Yang, 1970; Kuo, Ranis and Fei, 1981: 51-52).

There is a debate on the effect of the land reform on agricultural productivity. While most people tend to conform the contribution, some scholars suspect that the increase of agricultural productivity in this period should largely be attributed to the improvement of agricultural technology (Wang, 1978: 36). Nevertheless, there is no doubt that the incentive to maximize the efforts at cultivation was greater after the land reform. The rent reduction allowed the tenant not only that benefit but also any increase in production beyond the standard one. At the same time, owner-cultivators had a freer choice of crops because they no longer had to produce rice for rental payment. The share of other more suitable and profitable crops thus increased. Moreover, along with the technological change in agriculture which largely centered on the intensive use of land with more labor input, more labor and capital were invested in the fields. Therefore, the land reform encouraged more efficient utilization of agricultural crops, labor force, and capital (Ho, 1978: 165).

Landlords were the losers in the land reform. Economically speaking, the effect of the land reform on landlords involved a substantial reduction in the size of their wealth and therefore a reduction in their future income. Although the state compensated landlords for the land they were forced to give up, the compensation was only 2.5 times the standard annual yield. The actual market value of the land ranged between 4.5 and 8 times the annual yield at the time. Furthermore, the bonds used to reimburse the landowners paid an interest rate of 4%, substantially less than the real current market rates (Ho, 1978: 166-167). Because of the lack of experience in running nonagricultural business, most landlords did not place much value on the 30% of their compensation received as industrial stocks. They sold the stocks immediately at prices far below value and turned to either consumption or investment in small business. The majority of the landlords thus ended up being not much better off than the new owner-cultivators (Yang, 1970: 230-260). Socially and politically, the social status of landlords dwindled as a result of the wealth redistribution, The reorganization of the farmers' assiciations deprived landlords of their dominance in rural society; besides, their leadership was taken over by the newly rising small farmers. Consequently, the landlord class almost totally disappeared after the land reform (Yang, 1970: 419-506).

In contrast to the previous situation on the mainland, the KMT state finally turned its long-promised land reform into action in Taiwan. The key of the success was obviously the particular conjuncture of the relationship between the state and the society. In Taiwan, political and military powers had been concentrated in the hands of the Kuomintang since the end of World War II. Coming from the mainland, the KMT state was an "outsider" with no tie or commitment to the local landed gentry. Thus, when the KMT elites decided to carry out land reform, they enjoyed a great state autonomy. The firm determination of Chiang Kai-shek and Ch'en Ch'eng to get the work done prevented any attempt to weaken the program (Hsiao, 1981: 114-115). Great state autonomy and coherent state action guaranteed its success.

The U.S. aid, of course, also enhanced the capaicty of the KMT state to implement the reform. In fact, carrying out the land reform was an essential ingredient of the U.S. aid program and foreign policy in postwar Asia. The Japanese land reform executed by the Supreme Command of Allied Powers convinced American officials that land reform is a powerful weapon to meet the challenge of peasant redicalism and contain the expansion of Communism (McCoy, 1971: 1). While the KMT state still held the reign over the mainland, American officials had tried to push the KMT elites to carry out land reform. After the KMT state moved to Taiwan, the pressure persisted. The JCRR permitted Americans to express their viewpoints effectively and provided an excellent base for the progressive Chinese commissioners to be more influential. U.S. advisors and technicians had been deeply involved in all aspects of the land reform since September, 1951. The determination of the KMT state to fulfill the land reform in Taiwan was undoubtedly strong, yet the U.S.-backed JCRR and its financial and

Table 5.1
Area and Households Affected by Land Reform (by Type of Reform)

	Type of Reform			
Item	Reduction of Farm Rents	Sale of Public Land	Land-to-the-tiller Program	Total Redistribution[a]
Area affected (chia)[b]	256,948	71,663	143,568	215,231
Number of farm households affected	302,277	139,688	194,823	334,511
Ratio of cultivated area affected to total area[c]	29.2%	8.1%	16.4%	24.6%
Ratio of farm households affected to total farm households[d]	43.3%	20.0%	27.9%	47.9%

a Comprises land distributed under the sale of public and the land-to-the-tiler program.
b 1 chia = 0.9699 hectare.
c Total cultivated area used in this caculation is the average of 1951-55.
d Total number of farm households used in this calculation is the average of 1951-55.

Sources: Ho, 1978: 163.

Table 5.2
Types of Farm Families Before and After the Land Reform

Item	Before Land Reform (1949)		After Land Reform (1957)	
	Number of families	%	Number of families	%
Owner	224,378	36	455,357	60
Tenant	239,938	39	125,635	17
Part-owner	156,558	25	178,224	23
Total	620,875	100	759,234	100

Source: Kuo, Ranis and Fei, 1981: 53.

Table 5.3
Changes in the Number of Landowner Families Before and After the Implementation of the Land-to-the-tiller Program (by Size of Holding)

Holding Size (hectare)	Before Implementation (1952)		After Implementation (1955)	
	Number of families	%	Number of families	%
Below 0.5	288,955	47.3	378,923	48.0
0.5-1.0	142,659	23.4	204,128	25.9
1.0-3.0	138,178	22.6	176,669	22.4
3.0-10.0	36,350	5.9	28,193	3.5
Over 10.0	5,051	0.8	1,516	0.2
Total	611,193	100.0	789,429	100.0

Source: Tang and Hsieh, 1961: 125.

political support unquestionably made the action more effective (Hsiao, 1981: 209-220).

Another favorable condition for the carrying out of the reform was the relative weakness of the landlord class in Taiwan. Before the land reform, although the land ownership was unequal, very few Taiwanese had great land holdings. In the eve of implementing the land-to-the-tiller program, only 66 landlords on the whole island, or 0.01% of all landowners, had farms of more than 100 chia (97 hectares) of land. The large holders who had more than 10 hectares accounted for only 0.8% of all landowners and possessed merely 16% of the entire farm land (Tang and Hsieh, 1961: 124-125). It is obvious that there was no way for them to form a strong force to resist the state action. Some observers surmise that the decision of the KMT on land reform was aimed at removing the landed gentry as a potential opposition (Kerr, 1965: 420; Israel, 1964: 59). As Michael Hsiao (1981: 113) points out, these arguments are not tenable. Given the traditional linkage between the KMT state and the landlord class, the landlord would have become an ally rather than a potential opponent. As a matter of fact, knowing how the Communists purged the landlords on the mainland and remembering the ruthlessness of the KMT in suppressing the 2-28 Incident, the Taiwan's landlords conformed themselves with the reform program quite submissively. They were afraid that the same thing might happen to them if they did not obey the state and make timely concessions without compulsion (Hsiao, 1981: 115). Therefore, the KMT state faced very little opposition from the landlord class during the course of the reform. A bloodless land reform was hence smoothly carried out.

Agricultural Pricing Policy

Land reform was undoubtedly the most dramatic agrarian program implemented by the KMT state in the postwar Taiwan. But other aspects of its agricultural policy also had profound effects on agriculture, or even on the whole economy. As mentioned earlier, the KMT's agricultural policy in the 1950s was both developmental and extractive. Aside from its active participation in the reconstruction of Taiwan's agriculture, the KMT state also took several measures to extract agricultural surplus for other economic and political objectives. For the Taiwan of the fifties, the extractive part of the agricultural policy seemed to be inevitable, considering that the state had to feed more than 1 million mainland refugees, to support a huge military establishment, and to propell industrial development (Ho, 1978: 175). Agriculture was expected to meet the demands of not only domestic consumption but also the exports in order to earn the foreign exchange that would allow them to buy capital goods and the raw materials for industrialization (Hsiao, 1981: 56).

The extractive ingredient of agricultural policy was carried out mainly through various agricultural pricing programs. The programs included collection of land tax in kind, the compulsory purchase of rice, and the rice-fertilizer barter system. The land tax, composed of the land tax proper and various surtaxes, was the most important one in the agricultural taxes. After World War II, landowners were required to pay to the state a specified amount of paddy rice for every dollar of land tax. To increase the yield of the tax, the cash/rice conversion ratio was raised periodically. In the meantime, the cultivators of paddy fields had to sell to the state certain amount of rice at an official purchase price to pay for their agricultural taxes. Although the official purchase price had increased steadily in the fifties, it nevertheless remained consistently 25 to 30% below the wholesale market price. Hence, through the collection of land tax in kind and the compulsory purchase of rice at prices substantially below the wholesale market price, the state imposed hidden taxes on the landowners and the cultivators (Ho, 1978: 180).

Moreover, the rice-fertilizer barter system provided the KMT state with a most powerful extractive instrument. During the fifties and sixties, the KMT state had been the sole source of chemical fertilizer in Taiwan. It controlled all fertilizer production and imports and distributed the supply according to the crops: those for sugar cane were distributed by the state-owned Taiwan Sugar Corporation and those for other crops were distributed by the farmers' associations. About 70 to 80% of the fertilizer was allocated to rice and was distributed to rice farmers through the rice-fertilizer barter system. At the time, the rice collected through this barter system accounted for over one-half of the rice collected by the state. Producers of crops other than rice and sugar cane could purchase fertilizer from the state's Food Bureau at an official price closely tied to the rice/fertilizer barter ratio. The price of fertilizer in the barter system was substantially higher than that in many neighboring countries, such as Japan, Thailand, Sri Lanka and Pakistan, the differences ranged from 50% to twice. Through the bartering of fertilizers for rice, the state made huge profits (Ho, 1978: 180-182). At the same time, by various methods of compulsory rice collection, the state controlled the supply of rice and kept a large part of rice consumption from going through the market mechanism. From 1950 to 1960 the state collected more than 50% of the rice sold and more than 30% of the total rice produced (Lee, 1971: 80-81). Table 5.4 shows the amount of rice collected through various state programs. The state thus firmly controlled the supply and price of rice.

In addition to the obvious economic and financial purposes (subsidizing the industrial sector and increasing revenue), the reason why the KMT state was very concerned with rice collection is also a political one (consideration of controlling the supply and price of rice). As Robert Bates (1981) argues, in Third World nations, agricultural "policies are designed to secure advantages for particular interests, to appease powerful political forces, and to enhance the capacity of political regimes to remain in power" (Bates, 1981: 5-6). The resources expropriated from agriculture are usually diverted to other sectors, such as the state, the urban-based industrial enterprises, and the bureaucrats who administer the publicly structured markets for farm products. The policy of keeping food prices low is usually used to appease the urban workers and their employers, who constitute the dominant social forces. In the case of Taiwan, rather, the strongest support for the state came from the Mainlander refugees–servicemen and civil servants. It is mainly to appease these people that the KMT state had to assure sufficient supply and low price of rice. Through the farmers' associations and the military ration network, the state was able to distribute cheap rice to every family of the servicemen and civil servants. This is turn enabled the KMT state to maintain a large military establishment and a massive bureaucracy by paying lower salaries. It thus solved the problems of food, employment, salary, and inflation resulted from the sudden increase of the Mainlanders at the expense of the farmers.

However, in contrast to many developing countries where state intervention in agricultural markets often leads to the decline of the agricultural sector and bring about harmful consequences for society (Bates, 1981), both the developmental and extractive aspects of the KMT's agricultural policy were reasonably successful in Taiwan, despite some inherently conflicting elements between the two objectives (Ho, 1978: 175). One important factor contributing to this achievement was surely the land reform, which equalized the wealth in the rural area and enriched the farmers' production incentive. In addition, certain extractive measures seemed to have some positive effects on the agricultural production. For example, while the rice-fertilizer barter system often required farmers to purchase fertilizers they did not need (Ho, 1978: 183), the system also permitted that they obtain the key

Table 5.4
Government Collection of Rice, 1950-1960
(unit = 1,000 metric tons of brown rice)

Period	Land tax and compulsory purchase	Barter exchange	Other collection through loan	Land price repayment	Total
1950	155	228	4		388
1951	157	194	43		393
1952	144	260	25		429
1953	141	279	50	26	496
1954	140	287	115	12	554
1955	128	310	34	65	519
1956	132	323	37	28	520
1957	143	349	21	22	535
1958	145	339	19	41	505
1959	113	326	23	51	543
1960	134	293	23	16	466

Source: Lee, 1971: 81.

modern input without being worried about its supply (Amsden, 1985: 86). This is very different from the situation in many Third World nations where the unavailability of fertilizer often results in the failure of small-scale farmers to improve their cultivation (Bates, 1981: 55). In addition to extracting agricultural resources, the KMT state also made a significant effort to improve rural irrigation facilities, rural organizations, and agricultural research and experiment institutions. With the help of the JCRR and the farmers' associations, the state effectively perserved an agrarian structure of small farmers by stabilizing prices and by making credit more widely available. The result was "a self-exploitative peasantry, working long hours to maximize production per hectare, and a superexploitative state, ticking along effectively to extract the fruits of the peasantry's labor, operated hand in hand in Taiwan to great advantage until the late 1960s" (Amsden, 1985: 87).

There are different interpretations of the phenomenon of "growth with squeeze" in Taiwan's agricultural development during the 1950s and 1960s. For some scholars (Hsiao, 1981), the relations between the agricultural and nonagricultural sectors during this period should be seen as an "unbalanced" strategy of development with the terms of trade unfavorable for agriculture. They claim that the unbalanced strategy damaged Taiwan's agriculture through the squeeze which led to agricultural slowdown and the income disparity between the rural-agricultural and nonagricultural households since the late 1960s. For some other observers and the state officials (Ho, 1978; Fei, Ranis and Kuo, 1979; Li and Yeh, 1982), the KMT state adopted a strikingly "balanced" strategy between agriculture and industry which not only brought prosperity to Taiwan's rural areas but also freed the economy of food-shortage problems. As a result, industrialization on Taiwan proceeded smoothly from the very beginning and a firm fundation was laid for the subsequent growth of the economy. This approach can be described by the state's own slogan: "Fostering industry by virtue of agriculture and development agriculture by virtue of industry." We are not interested in judging which argument is more tenable but rather wish to point out that the key to fulfilling the double goals of development and extraction in Taiwan's agriculture was the presence of a relatively capable and autonomous state. This is the same state that had created the import-substitution industries on Taiwan during the fifties.

Industrial Policy

In the 1950s, under the encouragement and protection of the KMT state, a group of industrial capitalists emerged. As we have mentioned, under Japanese colonialism, the Taiwanese were excluded from the more important industries. Clearly, industry in colonial Taiwan included a traditional sector and a modern enclave. The enclave (modern transportation and the corporate industrial sector) was owned, managed, and operated by Japanese. The Taiwanese participation in the enclave was limited to the contribution of their labor. The domain of the Taiwanese was the traditional sector, which was made up of small manufacturing establishments and handicraft shops. In sharp contrast to the Japanese enclave, it was undercapitalized and used traditional or slightly modified traditional production techniques (Ho, 1978: 89). Accordingly, after Japanese entrepreneurs and technicians were repatriated to Japan with the end of the colonialism, there were almost no local capitalists on the island. The Mainlander capitalists who followed Chiang Kai-shek were also few–most leading Mainlander capitalists went to more secure climates, such as Hong Kong or the United States. The few businessmen who did go refrained from investing due to the instability and inflation. It therefore became the state's responsibility to foster the emergence of a bourgeoisie (Gold, 1986: 70). But what kinds of industry should be encouraged?

Not unlike most newly independent developing economies, the KMT state initiated Taiwan's industry from primary import substitution. This approach seemed the natural response to Taiwan's situation. Given the small population and low per capita income, Taiwan could not rely on the domestic market alone as a source of sustained growth. In this respect, Taiwan had to adopt an outward-oriented approach stressing export in accordance with comparative advantage. The changes in the circumstances nevertheless had made it difficult for Taiwan to depend upon the export of primary products. Ready markets for such products as rice, sugar, bananas, canned pineapple, and tea were much shrunk due to the loss of protected or preferential markets in Japan and Mainland China. The surplus of rice was substantially reduced by the influx of Mainlanders. On the other hand, the separation of Taiwan from Japan created many opportunities for the domestic production of manufactured goods hitherto imported from Japan. Therefore, the situation prescribed a more inward-oriented appraoch, i.e., an import-substitution approach (Lin, 1973: 40-41; Ranis, 1979: 211-212). Of course, the desire of the KMT state to establish a national industry also gave the approach more weight.

The import-substitution industries were mainly run by local capitalists, including both Taiwanese and Mainlanders. During the early fifties, and not unlike the industrial scene in the colonial period, there was a relatively modern, large-scale public sector and a relatively traditional, small-scale private sector. This pattern was largely a consequence of the KMT state's takeover of Japanese assets. In addition, before the move of the central government, the KMT state had shipped some state enterprises to Taiwan (Kuo, Ranis and Fei, 1981: 61). Consequently, the larger enterprises producing sugar and important intermediate products, such as electric power, petroleum products, chemical fertilizers, aluminum and copper, alkali products, cement, and paper, were kept in the hands of the state. Their rehabilitation was facilitated by the extention of low-cost loans from public banks and U.S. aid. In contrast, the numerous smaller private enterprises producing consumer goods and other simple manufactured goods did not enjoy the same kind or magnitude of public assistance in the initial postwar years. Being a newcomer in the field with poor product quality and higher production costs, many of these enterprises encountered great difficulties in marketing during the period 1949-50. The state adopted several measures to salvage these incipient industries from extinction (Lin, 1973: 41-43). Among the measures adopted, the expanded use of a system of import controls beginning in June, 1949, together with the imposition of foreign exchange controls were most important; these we will discuss later. In this section, we are going to examine some policies directly related to "inventing the bourgeoisie.".

In his capacity as the vice chairman of the TPB and the president of the largest trading agency, the Central Trust of China, and then member of the ESB and convener of the IDC, K. Y. Yin forged the broad lines of fostering private enterprises. He first employed an "entrustment" scheme in the textile sector. When the TPB was set up in June, 1949, the economic policy-makers decided to give priority to the development of electric power, chemical fertilizers, and textiles because electric power was the basic energy for all industries; chemical fertilizers were the necessary input for rice production; and textile goods were Taiwan's main imports at the time (Wang, 1978: 23-26). The first two items were managed by the state while textiles were largely left to local capitalists. Owing to the alleged dumpings of fabrics from Japan, cotton fabrics could be imported more cheaply than produced domestically (using imported cotton yarn) at that time. Some academic economists therefore advocated the importation of fabrics rather than yarn or raw cotton on the grounds of guarding consumer welfare and following comparative advantage. This argument was rejected by Yin, who believed in Taiwan's long-term comparative advantage in importing "yarn rather than fabrics" and "cotton rather than yarn." He organized a joint textile group comprised of representatives from concerned government agencies. The group worked to give full support to the expansion of cotton yarn facilities by providing the necessary raw materials to the manufacturing firms through U.S. aid imports, by purchasing the yarn or final products, and by precluding foreign competition through outright import restrictions (Lin, 1973: 60-63).

Under the production of the entrustment scheme whereby the state supplied raw materials and purchased the products, the "entrepreneur" had no risk and stood to make a fortune in a market where demand far outstripped supply. As a result, the prices of textiles shot up during 1951 and 1952, despite rationing and police interventions. At the same time, the overpriced and poor quality goods stirred resentment against these state-backed manufacturers among consumers. But the domestic production of cotton textiles also expanded quickly in response to the profit incentive and the prices of cotton fabrics started to decline since 1953. A number of major textile corporations in today's Taiwan developed in this environment. Enjoying the assistance of the state and the high profit obtained, they expanded into man-made fibers and other industries later in the decade. Their expansion constituted one of the major dynamics in Taiwan's subsequent economic development (Wang, 1978: 25-26; Gold, 1986: 70).

Most of the capitalists who benefited from the entrustment scheme were Mainlanders though officially anyone could apply for an allotment of AID-financed imported cotton. This was partly due to the fact that most entrepreneurs who had experience and facilities in textile business were Mainlanders from Shanghai and partly because Mainlanders had better connections with the KMT state, being familiar with procedures and having friends or relatives in the bureaucracy. Relatively few Taiwanese benefited. American advisors had complained about this to Chinese officials (Gold, 1986: 70-71). But via other programs for fostering local industries in plastics, glass, cement, rubber products, wood products, paper and pulp, pharmaceuticals, chemical products, bicycles, sewing machines, and household electrical appliances, etc, many Taiwanese became capitalists in the mid-1950s. In these programs, the state took the responsibilities of searching for investment opportunities, making investment plans, analyzing the feasibility, providing technical support, foreign exchange, and low-interest loans, and then looking for local capitalists to take over the enterprises. Although the conditions were so favorable, sometimes it was still hard to find the "entrepreneur." A number of enterprises created by these programs have now become big conglomerates (Wang, 1978: 41-42).

Some other Taiwanese got their start from the land reform. Partly due to the persuasion of American advisors and partly due to the suggestion of economic policy makers, during the early 1950s the state began transferring to private ownership the four public enterprises under its control: Taiwan Cement Corporation, Taiwan Pulp and Paper Corporation, Taiwan Industrial and Mining Corporation, and Taiwan Agriculture and Forestry Development Corporation. Owing to the lack of accumulated private wealth and entrepreneurial expertise and the poor track records of these enterprises, the state had difficulty in finding buyers. In 1953 these enterprises were, nevertheless, transferred as partial payment to landlords under the land-to-the-tiller program (Kuo, Ranis and Fei, 1981: 62). The main beneficiaries were the biggest landlords. Accumulating shares in the four enterprises and enjoying state protection and contracts, those landlords had varying performance in playing the role of the capitalist. Among them the shareholders of the Taiwan Cement Corporation stood out as the most successful (Gold, 1986: 71).

The U.S. AID Mission also supported the growth of the private sector through its Small Industry Loan Fund and Model Factory Program. Initiated in 1954, the Small Industry Loan Fund had operated through the entire aid period; its purpose was to make medium-term loans available at below-market interest rates to small private industrial firms, to enable them to expand their output, improve their quality, and raise their productivity. For the whole period, AID made grants and loans to the Fund totaling nearly 10 million U.S. dollars plus more than 401 million Taiwan dollars. Up until the end of 1964, some 896 firms had received loans from the program (Jacoby, 1966: 191).

Under the various measures of protection and encouragement, the import-substitution industries developed very fast. Their dramatic transformation is shown in Table 5.5, which demonstrates the changes in ratios of domestic production to total supply. From this transformation, there emerged a group of industrial capitalists. Evans'study (1982), which examines the attempts of the Brazilian state to promote the expansion of the role of local capital in the capital goods and petrochemical industries during the period 1974-79, points out that without a reliable market structure as a base, the state's efforts to

Table 5.5
Changes in Ratios of Domestic Production to Total Supply
(by Major Subsectors of Manufacturing in 1937, 1954, and 1961)

Manufacturing Subsector	Domestic Production as Percent of Total Supply		
	1937	1954	1961
Textile and wearing apparel	35.9	94.4	91.7
Wood products and furniture	42.9	92.7	100.0
Paper and pulp	33.8	85.8	91.5
Leather and its manufactures	37.4	73.3	95.3
Rubber manufactures	37.4	70.4	61.1
Chemical fertilizers	37.4	59.0	80.8
Pharmaceuticals	37.4	59.0	48.6
Plastics and products	37.4	59.0	80.2
Other chemicals and chemical products	37.4	59.0	63.0
Petroleum products	52.0	87.9	89.9
Cement and its products	52.0	87.9	100.0
Other nonmetallic mineral products	52.0	87.9	94.3
Iron and steel products	66.1	63.9	70.6
Aluminum and its products	66.1	63.9	99.1
Other metals and metal products	66.1	63.9	49.9
Machinery	66.1	32.9	28.2
Household and electrical appliances	66.1	41.8	42.5
Communications equipment	66.1	41.8	42.5
Other electrical apparatus and equipment	66.1	41.8	42.5
Transportation equipment	66.1	55.7	68.0
Printing	62.5	96.4	74.6
Miscellaneous manufacturing	26.9	66.4	—
Total	40.4	77.0	75.7

Source: Lin, 1973: 66.

strengthen the national bourgeoisie are likely to be fruitless. In a Third World country, if the entry of transnational corporations cannot be effectively regulated or if the market in question requires the bourgeoisie to grapple with a situation of atomistic competition, "reinventing the bourgeoisie" from existing bases tends to become a quixotic endeavor (Evans, 1982: S240). When there are no existing bases, "inventing the bourgeoisie" from a low development level can prove an impossible task. Fortunately, during the 1950s, there was no any entrenched TNC in Taiwan; dominating the society, the KMT state was able to offer the local capitalists a "regulated" market with stable oligopoly. As a result, the effort of "inventing the bourgeoisie" in Taiwan turned out to be reasonably successful.

K. Y. Yin's endeavor of inventing the bourgeoisie did not fail to arouse criticism. For neoclassical economists, the state intervention distorted market forces and caused the inefficiency of the resource use (Hsing, 1986: 170-174). For the local capitalists who were not qualified to receive state assistance or lacked an inside track to get state subsidy, the programs appeared fraught with partiality and collusions. Yin's political opponents saw oversights or unexpectedly negative outcomes in the execution of the policy that could be used to attack him. Yin's enthusiasm for fostering entrepreneurs thus made many enemies both in the state and the society. These enemies converged as a force against Yin and expelled him from the state for two years in the mid-1950s. We will talk about this event in a little more detail in the next chapter.

Fiscal and Monetary Policies

Curtailing inflation and stablizing the economy had been the overriding economic consideration of the KMT state during the fifties (Li, 1980: 10). This orientation was a consequence of historical experience and socio-political context. Based on the belief that the downfall of the Nationalist regime on the mainland had been related to hyperinflation (as well as to unequal land ownership), the KMT elites were possessed with a genuine anti-inflationary attitude. This anti-inflationary attitude was further strengthened by Taiwan's own inflationary experience during the years 1946-49 (Lundberg, 1979: 266). Naturally, price stabilization became the most urgent need for an overall economic development, a need which appeared reflected in the title of the leading economic agency for the period–the Economic Stabilization Board.

Stabilization policies were implemented through various measures of which the monetary reform was the essential one. To cut off the destructive impact from the mainland and make Taiwan an independent economy, the New Taiwan Dollar Reform was put into effect on June 15, 1949, amid rampant hyperinflation. The old currency was devalued; the most conservative full reserve system was adopted; and the limitation on issuance was strictly enforced. The state banned the speculation in gold and sold gold periodically in order to stabilize the price of gold and absorb money supply. Soon after the monetary reform, the inflation rate slowed down. In contrast to the 3,000% increase in the first half of 1949, prices only tripled in 1950. Inflation was further controlled after 1951. The annual increase rate in prices became 8.8% during 1952-60 before it decreased to 3% in 1961 and afterwards (Kuo, Ranis and Fei, 1981: 64).

Another important measure for stabilization was the introduction in March, 1950, of the preferential interest savings deposits with their high interest rate. It meant that even during the high rate of inflation of 1950 and 1951 people could still earn a positive real interest on their savings. In 1951 the rate of inflation was about 50% per year, but a nominal interest rate of 4% per month, if compounded, would amount to 60% per year. As the inflation rate was reduced after 1951, these preferential rates were subsequently lowered from 4% per month to about 20% per year at the end of 1953. But still the real rate could be kept high and positive. The real yield of one-year deposit in 1958 was as high as 17% (Lundberg, 1979: 290).

The essence of the anti-inflationary monetary policy was the absorption of excess liquidity and idle capital from the market. Under this policy, the commercial banks received more money in preferential deposits than they could lend to their customers under the prevailing conservative credit standards. The rising excess deposits were increasingly redeposited with the Bank of Taiwan, which permitted the latter to succeed in bringing credit expansion of the commercial banks under its control. It is worth noting that Taiwan had no formal central bank during 1949-61. The functions of the old Central Bank of China had been suspended and not reactivated until July 1, 1961. In the interim, the Bank of Taiwan, the largest state-owned commercial bank, performed most of the functions of a central bank. Thus, extensions of loans to business were carefully coordinated with the overall policy (Kuo, Ranis and Fei, 1981: 66), and excess liquidity was thus absorbed and put into less liquid form.

To what extent the high-interest policy contributed to the dampening of inflation is an open question. For its supporters (Tsiang, 1984: 313; 1985: 65-95), the policy effectively increased voluntary savings and reduced money supply which greatly contributed to curtail inflation and stabilize the economy. For some other observers (Wang, 1983: 81-112), the main factors conducive to economic stabilization during the fifties were actually the promotion of productivity and the increase of material supply, such as the reconstructing of production facilities destroyed in the war, the carrying out of land reform, the encouraging of private investment, the selling of U.S.-aid materials, and the balancing of government budget, rather than simply the control of money supply. Without going to either extreme, it seems fair to say that both the decrease of money supply and the increase of material supply were contributing to the economic stabilization in the 1950s. It would be one-sided to maintain that the high-interest policy was the only significant measure in stabilizing Taiwan's economy, but it probably is correct to argue that Taiwan was the first among the developing countries to abandon boldly the almost universally approved low-interest policy by raising the interest rate on saving deposits to approximately the prevailing rate of price inflation (Tsiang, 1984: 314).

Under the prevailing influence of Keynesian economics, in the 1950s and 1960s, most states in developing countries believed that interest rates should be kept low even in the face of considerable inflation so as to insure a cheap supply of credit to the new industries at home. This policy was supposed to stimulate real investment and growth as well as to prevent the cost-puch inflation from higher interest rates. Although such a policy in fact might fuel domestic inflation by creating an enormous excess demand for bank credits for nonproductive use while retarding real capital formation and genuine savings, state managers in developing countries tend to overemphaisze by the expectation of growth while ignoring stability. In this respect the KMT elites were admiralbly bold and unorthodox in their policy-making (Lundberg, 1979: 290; Tsiang, 1984: 314).

That the KMT state could manage to break through the conventional apporach to the adoption of realistic interest rates should largely be attributed to the preference of the KMT elites for stability in the course of economic transformation. The extraordinary concern of the KMT elites, including the top political leadership and the economic policy makers, with economic stability delineated Taiwan's economic development with the control of inflation as an overriding objective. In the meantime, with the banking system in its hands, the KMT state had full capacity to execute the anti-inflationary monetary policy. Combining the institutional assets inherited from the colonial administration and the human capital coming from the mainland, Taiwan's banking system was relatively advanced as compared with most developing countries during the 1950s. The rapid response to the change of prices aided the anti-inflationary policy in coping with the problem.

The emphasis on economic stability was also reflected in the state's fiscal policy, especially the management of the government budget. A great effort was made to achieve a balanced budget. While the tremendous rise of public expenditures (around 60% for defense in the fifties) was not and could not be matched by increased taxes, a part of U.S. aid was utilized to supplement the government deficit up until 1961. The government budget, including transfer receipts, actually had a surplus every year, even before 1961. This provided an important financial source of investment in infrastructure (Kuo, Ranis and Fei, 1981: 66). Table 5.6 presents the contribution of U.S. aid to the balance of the government budget. The state also issued high-interest government and corporation bonds as a means to increase revenue and curtail inflation. In sum, even though monetary and fiscal policies usually have a complex aim reference basis as well as conflicts of targets, the overriding objective of the KMT's fiscal and monetary policies in the fifties was to curb inflation and stabilize the economy.

In studying the variation in national responses of Sweden, Britain, and the United States to the Great Depression in the 1930s, Weir and Skocpol (1985) argue that the different national reactions of these countries to the economic crisis can be better explained by a distinctive approach which highlights the structural features of states and the preexisting legacies of public policies. They believe that to understand government policies better, we should give significant weight to states as sites of potentially autonomous official action or as complexes of preexisting policies and institutional arrangements. The explanation for policy responses to cope with economic crisis should focus on how state structures and policy legacies affect the formulation of new economic ideas and innovative government policies. At the same time, we must pay attention to how state structure and policy legacies influence the political orientations and capacities of conflicting parties and coalitions of social groups.

This explanatory approach is particularly applicable to the making of fiscal and monetary policies in Taiwan during the 1950s. Without entrenched foreign banks and strong dominant classes or oppositions in the society, the KMT state enjoyed sufficient automony and capacities in formulating and executing its fiscal and monetary policies;

Table 5.6
Foreign Transfers and Government Current Surplus

	Foreign Transfers to the Government Sector in Percent of Government Expenditure	Government Current Surplus Net of Foreign Transfers in Percent of Government Expenditure	Government Current Surplus Inclusive of Foreign Transfers in Percent of Government Expenditure	Government Expenditure in Percent of GNP
1951	32.5	−11.3	21.2	17.6
1956	20.8	−5.2	15.6	20.1
1961	25.2	−7.2	18.0	19.1
1963	7.6	−0.2	7.4	18.7
1964	1.8	6.5	8.3	17.5
1965	3.7	10.5	14.2	17.0

Source: Kuo, Ranis and Fei, 1981: 67.

its advantages were a relatively advanced banking system and a great amount of U.S. aid for budget deficits. The policy legacies–the lesson of the failure in controlling inflation on the mainland–stimulated new ideas and strengthened the determination of the KMT state to adopt extraordinary measures to cope with the problem of economic stabilization. The American advisors to a certain degree also had an impact on policy attitude during this period. Although their influence on actual measures to curb inflation may have been limited, their strong support to the anti-inflationary attitude of the Chinese officials helped carry through the policy innovations.

Foreign Trade Policy

Taiwan's foreign trade policy during the 1950s aimed at promoting import-substitution industries and regulating foreign exchange. To attain these goals, the KMT state employed the usual policy package of tariffs, import controls, and multiple exchange rates. The tariff structure in Taiwan was originally transplanted from the mainland. For an economy that was largely an exporter of raw materials and importer of manufactures, the tariff table enacted on Mainland China in August, 1948 tended to emphasize more protection for the production of raw materials than of finished goods. Similar considerations appeared in the negotiation of concession rates between the KMT state and other members of the General Agreement on Tariffs and Trade (GATT). As a result, rates for raw materials were often set at the same levels as, or even above, those for processed goods. This tariff structure was obviously incompatible with the protective purposes for import-substitution industries. But probably because the state itself needed to import the goods for its own use, the lower GATT agreement rates for a total of 275 items of processed or manufactured goods remained in effect for several years, even though the KMT state had withdrawn from GATT membership in May, 1950. It was not until January, 1955 that the KMT state eliminated the GATT agreement rates by setting up a revised tariff table. The average nominal tariff rate for all imports was raised from around 20% to nearly 45%. Since the rates governing important intermediate or capital goods and raw materials stood largely unchanged, this step had the effect of raising the effective tariff rates for many nondurable consumer goods (Lin, 1973: 47-49).

While the tariff rates of many manufactured goods related to the import-substitution industries were kept relatively low before the mid-1950s, the KMT state had nevertheless adopted import restrictions to protect infant industries and save foreign exchange since as early as June, 1949. After 1951 imports were classified into four categories: permissible, controlled, suspended, and prohibited. The permissible category included essential capital equipment, raw materials, and essential consumer goods, all of which were importable within the prescribed quotas. The controlled and suspended lists included commodities that were either altogether banned or could be imported only under special conditions, usually by government agencies. The prohibited category comprised goods considered dangerous or luxury items. Of the approximately 500 groups of commodities classified during the early fifties, 55% were in the permissible category, 40% in the suspended and controlled categories, and 5% in the prohibited category. In the mid-1950s, controls became even tighter as many commodities, such as cotton yarn and fabrics, woolen yarn and fabrics, man-made fibers and yarn, ammonium sulfate and other chemical fertilizers, wheat flour, monosodium glutamate, plywood, leather and leather products, cement, paper, rubber products, aluminum ingots and products thereof, sewing machines, bicycles and bicycle parts, and soap and cleaning compounds, etc, were switched from the permissible to the suspended and controlled categories (Ho, 1978: 91).

Moreover, the state kept the new Taiwan dollar overvalued and employed a multiple exchange rate system to regulate imports and exports. Initially, when the monetary reform was put into effect, a simple exchange rate was adopted. Those exchanging foreign for domestic currency were given part in cash, at the rate of 5 new Taiwan dollars to 1 U.S. dollar, and the other part in exchange settlement certificates (ESCs) of equivalent value. These ESCs were freely negotiable in the market or could be sold to the Bank of Taiwan at the official rate. For importers, foreign exchange was approved rather liberally; the ESCs were sold for importation of permissible items at the official rate. Owing to the great deficit of trade balance and continued inflation, however, applications for foreign exchange soon outgrew the available supply. The official supply price of ESCs was forced to be devalued repeatedly (Kuo, Ranis and Fei, 1981: 67).

In 1951, along with the substantial devaluation, a multiple exchange rate system was introduced. This system applied lower rates to exports than to imports. The export earnings of sugar, rice, and salt were further given a lower ESC rate than other private export earnings. The exchange system thus offered the state one more instrument to extract resource from the export of agricultural products. Regarding imports, goods imported by the public sector as well as of capital equipment and raw materials for import-substitution activities by the private sector were given a lower official rate, whereas imports of other goods were given a higher ESC rate. Due to continuous inflation, the exchange rate was kept overvalued in order to avoid the impact of imports on production costs. At the same time, the price ratio of import substitutes to export goods went up appreciably in the early 1950s. For instance, the relative prices of cotton textiles, the major imports, and rice, the main exports, increased from 2:1 during 1949-50 to nearly 5:1 in 1951-52. This gave full official blessing to the import substitution of textile goods. The exchange rate system, therefore, encouraged imports and import substitution but hampered exports (Kuo, Ranis and Fei, 1981: 67-68).

The state also adopted some measures to promote exports. In 1954 a system of rebates of import duties on raw materials for export use was introduced. Another system of utilizing a certain portion of foreign exchange earnings for importing raw materials was initiated in 1956. But the overvaluation of the new Taiwan dollar and the multiple exchange rate structure still favored import substitution (Kuo, Ranis and Fei, 1981: 69).

These exchange and trade controls effectively promoted the growth of import-substitution industries on Taiwan. They shielded many of Taiwan's consumer goods markets from foreign competition and conserved foreign exchange for capital and raw material imports. The prohibition of the importation of luxury goods not only saved foreign exchange from conspicuous consumption but also prevented the widening of disparity in consumption patterns among the people (Gold, 1985: 78). According to Giddens (1973: 108-109), in addition to the division of labor and the authority relationships within the enterprise, the third source of the proximate structuration of class relationships is that originating in the sphere of consumption rather than production—"distributive groupings" based on consumption patterns. In this sense, consumption patterns may be regarded as major influence upon class structuration and class conciousness. The prohibition to import luxury goods, which was loosened up only after the balance-of-payments problem was overcome completely by the boom of exports in the 1970s, somehow blurred the demarcation of classes in Taiwanese society and lessened the potentiality of class confrontation even before the "growth with equity" really got underway.

The prohibition to import luxury goods was effectively enforced in part because of the frugal life style of the top political leadership and leading economic policy makers. Both Chiang Kai-shek and Ch'en Ch'eng advocated a diligent and frugal style of life and set an example by their own action. Their behavior undoubtedly had demonstration and warning effects to other state officials. At the same time, as we have mentioned, most economic policy makers were known to be clean-handed. K. Y. Yin was praised by many people for never taking anything not rightfully and maintaining a life style far below his status. Consequently, the economic policies of the KMT state during the 1950s seemed to be permeated with a spirit of autark.

The introduction of various measures for exchange and trade controls had gradually intensified the restraints of state intervention on the economy. To execute the increasingly complicated measures for regulating foreign exchange and trade, the agency concerned was enlarged continually. As mentioned in chapter III, initially the agency was set up within the TPB; it was reorganized into the Taiwan provincial government when the TPB was merged into the ESB; then it was upgraded to the FETCC in February, 1955. Presided over by Hsu Peh-yuan, the organization and power of the FETCC expanded quickly. Under the control of this agency, the efforts to protect domestic infant industries and conserve foreign exchange for capital and raw material imports were largely successful. But some negative effects of the intensification of state control on the economy had also appeared. A dramatic reform of the foreign exchange and trade system was eventually put into practice in 1958. This reform not only involved a change of policy attitude and actual measures but also the reorganization of power relationships both among the economic policy makers and between the state and the society. We will discuss this reform in the next chapter.

The 1950s as a Starting Point

During the 1950s Taiwan's economy underwent a fundamental reorientation. From a classic dependent economy it transformered itself into a quasi-dependent economy, which was largely insulated from the world capitalist system but heavily dependent upon the United States. Excluding the importation of U.S.-aid commodities, the volume of trade declined dramatically when Taiwan shifted from the typical colonial-style orientation of primary products trade for manufactured goods with Japan and then China to the development strategy of import-substitution industrialization. A main reason for this change was the loss of those traditional markets; besides, the population, suddenly increased, consumed now more products for export than before. Under the various measures for protecting and encouraging domestic incipient industries, import-substitution industrialization developed very fast. By the end of the fifties the industrial production had more than doubled. Its contribution to net domestic product increased from 18.0% in 1952 to 23.9% in 1958 while that of the agriculture declined from 35.9% to 31.0%. A shift in employment out of the primary sector into the secondary sector could also be discerned. In 1952 the primary sector absorbed 56.1% of the labor force as compared with 16.9% of the secondary sector; the proportions changed to 51.1% and 19.7% in 1958. A further trend was the faster growth of the private sector than state enterprises. When the private sector accounted for merely 27.5% of the total value of industrial production in 1949, the ratio had increased to about 50.0% in 1958 (Li, 1981: 326; Commwealth, 1986: 72; CEPD, 1986: 16, 39, and 87).

The transformation of the economy was definitely a consequence of the state policies which were formulated and executed in a particular historical conjuncture of economic and political circumstances. As far as the international situation is concerned, the Nationalist government was incorporated into American hegemony to play a political rather than economic role in the crusade against communism. With the assistance of the United States, the KMT regime institutionalized a socio-political structure within which Taiwan's economy evolved. Totally controlling the military force, the overstaffed KMT state faced few obstacles to consilidate its position and rule the society on the island. Because the Taiwanese had never experienced democratic governance during the colonial period; because the social elites had suffered great losses in the 2-28 Incident; because no enclaves of disobedient foreigners were entrenched; and because the pressure of democratization from the United States were constrained by its need for a stable ally, the KMT state found a favorable environment to rule the society and manage the economy through an authoritarian one-dominant-party system (Gold, 1986: 72-73).

The internal structuring of the KMT state for economic policy-making was composed by an impregnable top political leadership and a group of competent economic policy makers assisted by a company of hardworking bureaucrats. Facilitated by the physical and institutional legacies inherited from the colonial era as well as the material and technical aids of the United States, the KMT state adopted a set of policies to reorient Taiwan's economy. It carried out a "revolution from above" to equalize land ownership and remove the landlord class. It stimulated agricultural production while ensuring its own control of the surplus. It invented a bourgeiosie while controlling the capitalists by regulating loans, foreign exchange, capital goods, raw materials, and energy. It adopted "unorthodox" monetary and fiscal policies to curtail inflation and stabilize the economy. And it employed a variety of measures concerning foreign exchange and trade to extract agricultural surplus, to guide consumption patterns, to conserve foreign exchange, and to protect domestic firms so as to promote import substitution in light industry.

The state was dominant over and autonomous from the society. Holding political and military powers, the KMT elites had no intimate ties with the dominant social classes. The full-blown state bureaucracy penetrated society to the residential neighborhood, village, school, and larger work unit. There were no native or foreigner forces in the society which were strong enough to manipulate the formulation or resist the execution of state policies. The only force outside the state apparatus that could exert significant weight upon the policy-making was that of the American advisers. Keeping control over U.S. aid, the Americans urged the KMT state to retrench somewhat from production and promote private enterprises more actively. They also helped the more development-minded Chinese officials become influential in formulating development strategy.

The state, however, could neither consolidate its rule nor augment its social foundation by insulating itself from the society. It needed the allegiance of the Taiwanese to fill the ranks of the armed forces and to improve the production the would increase supplies. The KMT state facilitated this by granting home rule at the local level and opening the opportunity for upward mobility through economic activities. These sufficed to motivate the Taiwanese to devote their talents and energy along the desired lines (Gold, 1986: 73).

As a result, agricultural production increased remarkably and import-substitution industrialization proceeded quickly. But by the midfifties, import-subsitution industrialization had encountered some severe difficulties; a new road was needed for Taiwan's further development. Through a process of backing and filling, a series of economic reforms were eventually brought to effect during the period 1958-61.

CHAPTER 6

THE TURNING POINT OF TAIWAN'S ECONOMIC
DEVELOPMENT: 1958-61

The years 1958 to 1961 marked a critical turning point for the economic transformation on Taiwan. The domestic market for import substitution was by this time saturated, and a decision was made to shift the emphasis of economic policy to export. The Kuomintang state adopted a series of policies to promote this transformation: (1) a reform of foreign exchange and trade, (2) a Nineteen-Point Program of Economic and Financial Reform, and (3) a Statute for Encouragement of Investment. The results of these policies were impressive. They reshaped the character of Taiwan's economy from import-substitution industrialization to export-led industrialization and from a relatively closed system to a highly open system. They influenced not only the economic aspect, but also the socio-political aspect of the society. While they improved remarkably Taiwan's socioeconomic situation as a whole, they obviously also intruded upon the vested interests of many individuals or groups within or outside the state apparatus. How did the state elites handle this dramatic change?

Situation Imperatives

International Situation

Although saft within American hegemony, Taiwan's economic development could not overcome the Communist threat. For instance, the annual volume of Taiwan's private investment did not rise smoothly throughout the 1950s as was expected, given the constant support of U.S. aid. The private investment expanded from 1951 through 1954; thereafter, fell off and stabilized through 1958; and, then, expanded rapidly again. According to Jacoby (1966: 89), the disappointing decline between 1954 and 1958 could be attributed to the 1954 Communist attack on Tachen, an offshore island serving as one of the outstations for Taiwan's defense but given up in 1955. This attack frightened the investors by raising the fear of insecurity and the suspicion of investment opportunities. Indeed, it is hard to imagine that the KMT state would have dared switch the orientation of the economic development and the society would have responded to it positively if the state and the society had no confidence on Taiwan's security and the viability of its economy. In this sense, the 1958 successful resistance to attacks of the Communists on Quemoy, a small island located a few miles off the shore of Fukien province in southeastern China and serving as the most important outpost in the defense of Taiwan, strenthened the political confidence of economic reform (Lundberg, 1979: 269).

On August 23, 1958, the Communists' heavy artillery began a massive bombarment of Quemoy. It was less than nine months after the talks between the United States and Red China had been suspended in Geneva. The Chinese Communists, having made no progress in the Geneva talks toward diplomatic recognition by the United States and having failed to weaken the U.S. commitment to Taiwan, decided to engage in another test of strength over the offshore islands. Mao Tse-tung apparently believed that conditions were unusually favorable. The orbiting of satellite Sputnik by the Soviet Union ahead of the United States and other developments led Mao to declare on his visit to Moscow in 1957 that "the East wind was prevaling over the West wind." To the leaders of the Chinese Communist Party, the balance of forces seemed to be shifting and the time was ripe for probing the strength of the U.S. determination to assist the Kuomintang (Clough, 1978: 16-17).

Responding to the Communist blockade of Quemoy, the United States quickly deployed naval and air forces nearby and sharply warned Peking that it would not hesitate to use armed forces in defense of Taiwan, stressing that the defense of Quemoy and Matsu, another offshore island and important defense outpost north of Quemoy, had become increasingly related to the defense of Taiwan. To assist the Nationalists in breaking the blockade, the United States began to escort Nationalist supply vessels, though the U.S. destroyers cautiously turned back at the three-mile limit off the island to avoid direct involvement in the war. In the end, confronted with the brave performance of the Nationalists assisted by the United States, the blockade did not succeed. By the end of September, 1958, bombardment gradually diminished while Quemoy and Matsu still stood firmly in the hands of the Nationalists (Clough, 1978: 17).

Most importantly, the Republic of China (ROC) showed her strength in resisting the attack from the People's Republic of China (PRC) and emerged from the crisis appreciably stronger. It acquired new military equipment from the United States, notably the 8-inch howitzers located on Quemoy, the Sidewinder missiles for the jet fighters, and landing craft to facilitate the supply of the offshore islands. Morale was boosted by the outstanding performance of the airforce-which consistently defeated the enemy's air force-and by the success of the resupply of Quemoy by sea and air. On October 6, the United States stationed a Nike-Hercules missile unit to strengthen Taiwan's air defense. Al of these events increased the confidence of the state and the society in Taiwan's security (Clough, 1978: 18).

The crisis, however, highlighted the conflict of interests between Washington and Taipei over the importance of the offshore islands and the future of Taiwan. For the KMT, the offshore islands not only served as the outposts of the defense of Taiwan but also as a stepping-stone for the recovery of the mainland. Throughout the crisis, although the KMT did obtain the U.S. statements and decisive action necessary to frustrate the Communist attempted blockade, it failed to obtain the outright U.S. commitment to defend the offshore islands. In the United States, many Americans who approved of the U.S. commitment to help defend Taiwan strongly opposed U.S. military intervention in defense of the offshore islands. In the United Nations, most members supported the withdrawal of ROC forces from the offshore islands and favored placing Taiwan under a trusteeship as well as admitting the PRC to the United Nations. Seeking to counter the criticism of the U.S. policy at home and abroad, Secretary of State John F. Dulles expressed at a press conference that the United States would favor a reduction of ROC forces on the offshore islands and that the United States had no commitment to help the ROC return to the mainland (Clough, 1978: 18-20).

Chiang Kai-sheh reacted to Dulles' talk by rejecting any reduction of the forces on the offshore islands. To soften the impact of the divergent opinions, Dulles visited Taipei on October 21. As a result, Dulles obtained Chiang's agreement to reduce the forces on the islands by 15,000 in exchange for an increase in firepower there. More significantly, in a joint communique issued on October 23, the two governments recalled that the Mutual Defense Treaty signed on December 2, 1954, was defensive in character, and the KMT state declare that "the restoration of freedom to its people on the mainland is its sacred mission. It believes that the fundation of this mission resides in the minds and the hearts of the Chinese people and that the principal means of successfully achieving its mission is the implementation of Dr. Sun Yat-sen's principles (nationalism, democracy and social well-being) and not the use of force" (Chiu, 1973: 288). Therefore, while Chiang Kai-shek refused to abandon the offshore islands and the right to return to the mainland, he agreed to shift the focus from strengthening military might to accelerating socioeconomic development.

The offshore island crisis hit the Communist camp too. While the United States proved its determination to assist the ROC, the PRC found that its action did not call for enough support from the Soviet Union. The disappointment of the PRC with its ally resulted in growing disputes that would eventually caused the alliance to collapse. In addition, the crisis discouraged the PRC from trying to reconquer the offshore islands. Both the United States' readiness to intervene and the world's reaction to the crisis had shown the PRC that seizing the offshore islands from Taiwan would heighten support for "two Chinas." Many countries, including the United States, clearly favored cutting the link between Taiwan and the mainland. From Peking's viewpoint, leaving the KMT in possession of the islands was a means of perpetuating the commitment of both sides to "one China." The year 1958 proved the high point of tension in the Taiwan Strait. Thereafter, the PRC has never again attempted to seize the offshore islands (Clough, 1978: 20-21).

In the meantime, the turmoil on the mainland prevented the Communists from coveting the interests in the Taiwan Strait. Before the bombardment of Quemoy, the Great Leap Forward (1958 to 1960) had been launched; a series of radical policies were carried out to reshaped society and economy. The results were serious economic dislocations, a horrible famine, and widespread social disorder. Mao Tse-tung's authority was quickly declining after the failures of the bombardment and the Great Leap Forward. The power struggle between Mao and Liu Shao-ch'i and Teng Hsiao-p'ing was worsening. The Chinese Communists, preccupied with the chaos on the mainland, were not able to attempt anything else in the Taiwan Strait. As soon as the threat was alleviated, the KMT state gained more confidence to undertake its economic reform.

Moreover, there was a change of the objectives of the U.S. aid to Taiwan in the late fifties. It shift the purpose of the aid from improving Taiwan's military strength and monetary stability to promoting Taiwan's economic development. Along with this change, there was also a switch of American foreign aid policy. This switch decided to provide more money with those aid recipients which had better performance in utilizing U.S. aid. These changes influenced directly the formulation of the 19-Point Reform Program. We will discuss the changes in more detail later.

Intra-national Situation

Under the encouragement and protection of the state, Taiwan's primary import substitution boomed fast. By 1954, domestic production had increased to supply 77% of apparent domestic consumption. Imports of consumer goods as a percentage of total domestic supply of consumer goods were further cut down to nearly 7% by the late 1950s. Attainment of a high rate of import substitution means that growth of domestic output would have to depend mainly upon the net increase in the domestic demand. But partly due to the 1954 Communist attack on Tachen and partly due to the gradual exhaustion of the protected domestic market, the growth of investment and output in several light-manufacturing subsectors, particularly textiles, wood products, and rubber goods, had decreased since the mid-1950s. In the late fifties, industrial surveys indicated increasing excess capacity in textiles, paper, rubber goods, and soap. Consequently, competition among firms for domestic sales increased and prices fell. The situation had become so acute by the end of 1957 that the Provincial Association of Industries appealed to the Ministry of Economic Affairs to permit firms to organize sectoral industrial cartels in order to restrict domestic sales competition and price cutting. Some other local capitalists asked that the FETCC grant export subsidies via tax rebates and the like so as to promote industrial exports or at least partially redress the discrimination against exports (Lin, 1973: 68-70). Pressure for change mounted. It was time for the state to plunge into the transformation of the economy.

The state action for breaking through this bottleneck of economic development over a longer term can take one of two forms: first, it can be directed toward the maintenance of growth in the more labor-intensive nondurable consumer goods industries, to open the door to the shift from domestic to export markets; or it can be directed toward a further expansion of the more capital- and technology-intensive durable consumer and capital goods industries, to make way for secondary import substitution in other sectors of the domestic market. As Ranis (1979: 218-219) argues, most observers have tended to characterize the transition path of Taiwan as one of a relatively smooth progression from primary import substitution in the 1950s to export expansion in the 1960s. However, the period between 1954 and 1958 was in fact colored by a great deal of backing and filling.

Undoubtedly, some economic policy makers clearly recognized that protectionist policies not only reduced economic efficiency but also hampered exports of manufactured goods made from import materials. Yet, during the mid-fifties, few could imagine that Taiwan's exports of manufactures would ever grow as fast as they did. Most people thought of Taiwan only as an exporter of traditional products, such as sugar, rice, and the like. When K. T. Li was arguing the case for rebating taxes on materials used in the manufacture of exports in 1954, there was much skepticism about the effects this would have. As a matter of fact, K. T. Li was asked, ironically, "Do you want to turn Taiwan into another Lancashire?" (Scott, 1979: 379-380). In the meantime, there started an increasingly frantic search for new (and the expansion of old) secondary import-substituting industries, including chemicals, rayon fiber, urea fertilizer, prevulcanized plastics, and compact cars. Not until about 1958 did the small size of the market, the continuing pressure of surplus labor, and the obviously steeply rising costs associated with the expansion of these more capital- and technology-intensive industries shift the balance of the private and the public opinion in favor of the outward-oriented path (Ranis, 1979: 219).

Another important factor that delayed the change in economic policy were the power struggles and personnel change in the state apparatus. Being the vice chairman of the TPB from 1949 to 1953, the president of the Central Trust of China from 1950 to 1955, member of the ESB and convener of the IDC since 1953, and minister of Economic Affairs from 1954, K. Y. Yin was the key figure in the promotion of import substitution. He has been widely credited with supporting the plastic, artificial fiber, glass, cement, fertilizer, plywood, and above all, textile, and other industries in this period. As mentioned in the last chapter, apart from the restriction of imports, other measures he took included making loans on favorable terms, allocating imported materials directly to manufacturers, and imposing penalties on producers of poor-quality products to encourage the improvement of quality. However, as early as 1954, he himself pointed out the adverse effects of the import substitution, such as the proliferation of profiteers due to the disparity of exchange rates between the market price and the actual cost of imported commodities; the inefficiency of certain manufacturers survived under protection; and local firms attempted to form monopolistic agreements to keep up prices rather than improving quality, cutting costs, or driving out inefficient firms (Yin, 1973b: 27-28).

To remedy these adverse effects, Yin proposed the following measures: (1) Restrictions on the establishment of new factories should be lifted, but some minimum standards with regard to size and quality should be enforced. Those existing but unqualified factories should be deprived of the privilege to apply for raw materials, U.S. aid, and loans on favorable terms. (2) Imported raw materials should be auctioned or, should this prove impractical, allocation should be made preferentially to factories producing high-quality products and selling at low prices. (3) The period of protection by import restriction for any industry should be specified, although subsequent protection by tariffs should be allowed. (4) An antitrust law should be promulgated and, until this was done, liberalization of imports should be used to counteract local monopolistic arrangements (Yin, 1973b: 29-30; Scott, 1979: 316). But these measures can only diminish the problem of inefficiency; the plight of exhausting the domestic market was still unsolved. Thus, in a lecture about the way of Taiwan's economic development in June, 1954, Yin emphasized that the only way to develop Taiwan's economy was to promote production and expand the exports. He also stressed that in addition to agricultural products, the share of manufactured goods in the exports should be increased and the state should adopt all possible methods to help local capitalists to exploit foreign markets (Yin, 1973b: 32-35).

Although Yin put forward these remedies in 1954, the remedies were not adopted until some years later. In July, 1955, Yin resigned from all of his posts because of a court case involving a local firm that had been lent money by the Central Trust of China and then defaulted on the loan. The case was triggered by a member of the Legislative Yuan who questioned Premier O. K. Yui in a session about the suspicion of a collusion in the loan. Yin found himself involved since he was heading the Central Trust of China. The measures that O. K. Yui could employ to deal with the problem were somewhat elastic. Nevertheless, because K. Y. Yin was too active in managing the economy and often went beyond his duties to intrude upon O. K. Yui's jurisdiction, their relationship had become quite strained at that time. Meanwhile many of Yin's enemies within or outside the state apparatus took advantage of this opportunity to launch a pile of merciless attacks on him. As a result, Yui did not really try to defend for Yin in reponse to the question by the Legislative Yuan and eventually sent the case to the court (Shen, 1972: 264; Hu, 1964: 398-400). The pace of economic reform accordingly slowed down.

In September, 1956, the court cleared Yin of any blame. He returned to the state in August, 1957 as the Secretary-General and member of the ESB. Shortly afterwards, he was promoted to other high posts in economic affairs: chairman of the FETCC in March, 1958, vice chairman of the CUSA in September, 1958 (Ch'en Ch'eng was the chairman but Yin was actually in charge), and chairman of the board of the Bank of Taiwan in July, 1960. He was thus in charge of U.S. aid, foreign exchange and trade, monetary policy, and economic planning (the CUSA became the chief organ for economic planning and overall economic development when the ESB was dissolved in September, 1958). By holding all of these positions, Yin was able to implement a series of reforms designed to promote private investment and exports of manufactured goods effectively during the late fifties and early sixties.

Of course the various policies for economic reform initiated by the KMT state were formulated and executed not without conflict and compromise as well as domination and subordination. We now turn to a more detailed exploration of why, when, and how these distinctive policies were fashioned by the KMT state.

Formulation and Execution of the Foreign Exchange and Trade Reform

Plight of the Economy

Together with the gradual exhaustion of the domestic market and the slowing down of the growth in import substitution industries, another serious problem of Taiwan's economic development in the second half of the 1950s was the persistence of foreign exchange deficits. While imports of raw materials, capital equipment, and intermediate goods climbed up quickly with the development of import substitution industries, exports as a fraction of gross domestic product (GDP) rose only slightly between 1952 and 1957, from 8.1% to 9.6% (Ranis, 1979: 211; CEPD, 1986: 41). As a matter of course, the imports exceeded the exports by more than 60% in the 1950s (Ho, 1978: 115). During this period, the inflow of private capital and loans from international financial institutions was trivial, and the large payments were fulfilled almost solely by the receipt of U.S. aid, ranging from 67% to 128% of the annual trade deficit. It is very true that the huge trade deficits would not have been maintained for so long if U.S. aid had not been available. Suppose U.S. aid had been absent, then the elimination of trae deficits through such methods as floating exchange rates and the cutback of import demand would have caused severe adverse effects on the stabilization and growth of the economy (Lin, 1973: 70). But Taiwan could not and should not depend on U.S. aid forever. K. Y. Yin wrote to Chiang Monlin in May, 1952, "At present, Taiwan has not been able to balance the international payment yet, and it is the arrival of U.S. aid that can compensate for the trade deficits. However, we should not rely on U.S. aid for a long time. U.S. aid can merely offer us a breathing space temporarily. We should use it only as a catalyst to revive our economy" (Shen, 1972: 152). How could Taiwan overcome these payment difficulties?

The best strategy, as Yin emphasized in 1954, was promoting production internally and expanding exports externally. Since Taiwan is a small economic entity constrained by limited resources and a tiny domestic market, it cannot constitute by itself a self-sustained economy. It had to import many goods either for direct consumption or for import substitution. In order to obtain these goods, it needed foreign exchange, and the only way to generate foreign exchange apart from relying on U.S. aid was extending the exports. In fact, Taiwan did tried to earn more foreign exchange by exporting sugar and rice and other agricultural products in the 1950s. But just as the peripheral countries, according to dependency theory, suffer disadvantages in international trade, so did Taiwan suffer from slow growth and sharp fluctuations. Despite the reopening of trade relations with Japan in the fifties, exports to Japan at that time never exceeded the range of 45-80 million U.S. dollars, which was at most only one-third of the prewar record. This was partly due to the need for exchane rationing and for agricultural protection in Japan after World War II. Although some alternative markets were found in the United States, the Middel East, and other areas for Taiwan's sugar and tea, exports of primary goods from Taiwan were not able to recover their prewar volume (Lin, 1973: 71-71). Therefore, the prospects of generating foreign exchange through exporting the primary goods seemed dim. Actually, given its small area and extraordinary high population density, it was not viable for Taiwan to develop its economy merely via exporting agricultural products. Then, how about the industrial products?

In addition to the agricultural products, there were a few manufactured articles on the export list during the fifties. These products, including plywood, bagasse pulp, DDT, caustic soda, aluminum wares, and cotton cloth, were basically the results of the restoration of the Japanese-built industrial facilities and the progress of import substitution. However, the export of these industrial products was handicapped not only by their poor quality and high costs but also by the system of controlling foreign exchange and trade that favored the import-substituting activities. The authorities first reacted rather passively to these industrial and trade difficulties by briefly operating a subsidy system for a number of traditional exports in excess supply; by enlarging the coverage of export products receiving preferential exchange rates; by reluctantly yet periodically devaluating the exchange rate; and by introducing a system of tax rebates for the export of industrial products. These piecemeal actions reduced to some extent the disadvantages suffered by the exporters. The continuation of overvaluation of the exchange rate and the multiple exchange rates system favoring certain imports, nevertheless, still worked to prolong the profitability of inward-oriented activity (Lin, 1973: 72-75).

Thus, as mentioned above, the sales competition between the producers of light manufactured goods became acute by 1957. In January, 1958, the "Topic of the Month" in *Inudstry of Free China,* the organ of the agency for economic planning, was an article on "Competition at Home." It drew attention to an appeal by the Taiwan Provincial Association of Industries to the Ministry of Economic Affairs "to take preventive measures against the runaway competition in the home market" (Scott, 1979: 320). At the same time, the shortage of foreign exchange peristed while there were ominous predictions about the export markets and about the reduction of U.S. aid. By the beginning of 1958, there was a growing realization in the state and in the society that more fundamental changes in the system of policy incentives had to be made to improve Taiwan's balance of payments and industrial structure (Lin, 1973: 75). A major foreign exchange and trade reform toward devaluation and trade liberalization was announced by the authorities on April 12, 1958. It was less than a month after K. Y. Yin was inaugurated as the chairman of the FETCC on March 26 (Shen, 1972: 452). Indeed, Yin was the leading figure in this reform; the decision-making process, however, soon became filled with conflicts and obstructions ideologically and structurally.

The Policy-making Structure and Policy Formulation

The conflicts and obstructions came from two fronts: popular ideas and vested interests. With respect to the issue of ideas, a prevailing viewpoint in development policy during the 1950s held that the world demand for the exportables of the developing countries was likely to be inelastic. Hence, devaluation, coupled with the removal of protective tariff barriers or quantitative restrictions on imports, might lead to a deterioration of the terms of trade that the welfare of the country may actually suffer in spite of some increase in exports. Sugar and rice were Taiwan's main export goods at the time. They accounted for nearly 80% of the value of exports for the first half of the 1950s. Taiwan's sugar exports were practically fixed for her by the international sugar arrangement that allotted world market share annually for each participating sugar-producing country. Its rice export went exclusively to Japan. The quantity and price were fixed each year by direct negotiation between the two governments. These two major export goods were thus confronted with literally zero demand elasticity with respect to the exchange rate. In this sense, Taiwan appeared to be a typical case of producing only a few traditional export products and facing an extremely inelastic world demand. Devaluation and trade liberalization, according to the popular ideas, would only worsen the terms of trade, drive up the domestic prices of imported goods, and thus add fuel to domestic inflation (Tsiang, 1984: 304-306).

The consulting economists played an important role in reversing the ideas. When Liu Ta-chung and Tsiang Sho-chieh were called upon by the Kuomintang state to advice on economic policy in the summer of 1954, they immediately sought to persuade the government to devalue the exchange rate of domestic currency to a realistic level, to loosen import restrictions, and to lower protective tariffs. They persisted in arguing that even if the traditional major exports were confronted with foreign demands of little elasticity, there has to be many new products that could be produced with cheap labor supply and readily sold in the world market, provided that the relative abundance and cheapness of labor in Taiwan was not artificially covered by the overvaluation of her currency. Therefore, devaluation could establish a more realistic set of relative factor prices, enhance efficiency, and promote exports. The increase of exports would in turn allow more imports without deteriorating foreign exchange payment. Since domestic market prices of imported goods tend to be determined by the strength of domestic effective demand and the quantities allowed to enter rather than by their landed costs when their supplies are quantitatively restricted, the prices of imported goods need not rise if devaluation is coupled with trade liberalization (Tsiang, 1984: 306-307). In addition, Hsing Mo-huan wrote an article in October, 1954 on *Inudstry of Free China* advocating the liberalization of foreign exchange and trade in accordance with comparative advantages, which aroused K. Y. Yin's attention. Moreover, some economic bureaucrats also realized the defects of the existing system and proposed a reform program, such as Liu Feng-wen's *Kai-shan wai-hui chih-tu ch'u-i* (My Humble View for the Improvement of the Foreign Exchange System) (1957). There was also a growing interest among the business sector and the press to improve the system.

The argument of devaluation and trade liberalization gradually won the approval of some economic policy makers, notably K. Y. Yin and C. K. Yen (Little, 1979: 475). Thus, soon after returning to the state in August, 1957, K. Y. Yin started the plan for foreign exchange and trade reform. However, there were some obstructions, derived from vested interests, entrenching to block the reform. In the society, those profiteers who made money by manipulating the disparity of exchange rates or by illegally transfering foreign exchange quotas or business licenses as well as those businessmen who searched for secondary import-substituting industries formed a resistant force. But given the high autonomy of the state from the society and the feebleness of this force *vis-a-vis* the capacities of the state, their influence on the policy-making was relatively insignificant. The stubborn resistance that should be overcome in fact resided within the state apparatus.

As noted before, to balance international payment, an agency for controlling foreign exchange and foreign trade was set up in the state. Its organization and power had been continually enlarged in order to control foreign exchange and trade more thoroughly. The measures for controlling foreign exchange and trade had also become more and more complicated. Unfortunately, the more thorough and complicated the control resulted in more speculation in the foreign exchange and trade system and that in turn needed even more thorough and complicated controlling measures. Thus, from the Industrial Financing Committee in the TPB (June, 1949) to the FETCC (February, 1955), the administrative burden of the agency had been increasing again. Consequently, a lot of harmful practices emerged under the complicated multiple exchange rate system and import restrictions: excessive regulations and red tape, inappropriate allocation of foreign exchange, improper profits, and above all, administrative corruption (Yin, 1973b: 131-132; Wang, 1978: 52) As Skocpol (1985: 47) argues, "autonomous state actions will regularly take forms that attempt to reinforce the authority, political longevity, and social control of the state organizations whose incumbents generated the relevant policies or policy ideas." When K. Y. Yin initiated the plan for improving the foreign exchang esystem, partly due to the organizational inertia of retaining existent official functions and partly due to the private motive of maintaining vested interests, many officials in FETCC opposed the reform (Liu, 1980: 51).

One feature of the state is that, "Despite their obvious interest in unified action, state managers are likely to be divided on substantive goals" (Rueschemeyer and Evans, 1985: 47). The process of formulating the foreign exchange reform program was characterized by the conflict of the substantive goals among the state managers. The resolution was a change of personnel. At the end of 1957, when the problem of foreign exchange and trade was becoming worse, a nine-man group was nominated by Chiang Kai-shek to deal with the problem. Headed by Ch'en Ch'eng, the group was composed of O. K. Yui (Premier), Hsu Peh-yuan (chairman of FETCC and minister of Finance), Chiang Piao (minister of Economic Affairs), K. Y. Yin (secretary-general of ESB), and C. K. Yen (chairman of CUSA), etc. In a series of meetings, the opinions went in two directions: a conservative-interventionist line, represented by Hsu Peh-yuan, maintained that the existing system had a great deal to contribute to the stability of Taiwan's economy and that overemphasis on market mechanism would hurt the growth of Taiwan's infant industries; therefore, the existing system should not be changed too much or too dramatically; a liberal-reformist line, represented by K. Y. Yin, contended that the existing system had triggered too many corrupt practices and too much inefficiency which could only be remedied by a comprehensive and radical change. The liberal-reformist line finally won the support of the top political leadership. As a result, Hsu Peh-yuan resigned from his posts in March, 1958 while K. Y. Yin became the chairman of the FETCC and C. K. Yen, the minister of Finance. K. Y. Yin submitted his proposal of foreign exchange and trade reform soon after that. It was quickly passed in a meeting of the CSC on April 9, and promulgated by the Executive Yuan on April 12.

The Execution of the Reform

The reform aimed at (1) simplifying the exchange system, (2) loosening import restrictions, and (3) encouraging exports. The unification of exchange rates was executed in several steps. In April, 1958, the multiple exchange rates were first consolidated into two buying rates in parallel with two selling rates. Further simplifications were then made during the following years. By October, 1963, a foreign exchange system with single exchange rate was constituted and the unification of exchange rates was completed. A more significant change which accompanied the simplification of exchange rate of New Taiwanese dollar to U.S. dollar was about 25 for 1. In November, 1958, the ratio was adjusted to around 36 for 1 which was already quite close to the realistic exchange rate. And then, in July, 1960, the ratio was further adjusted to about 40 for 1. At this time, the difference between the official exchange rate and the market price of exchange rate was actually eliminated. In the meantime, the import restrictions were loosened step by step. The budgeting and allocation of foreign exchange was made more flexible; the list of non-importable goods was made shorter. Moreover, the policy incentives for encouraging exports were strengthened, such as fully supplying foreign exchange to exports, offering favorable exchange rate to the import materials for export use, reducing export controls, simplifying the formalities for export and tax rebate, and enlarging export loan, etc (Lin, 1973: 74-78; Wang, 1978: 53-54; Liu, 1980: 57-60).

The announcement of the reform won instant acclaim from the majority of the society. According to a report in *Industry of Free China,* "The programs...met the expectations of the industrial and commercial leaders. The general reaction has been heartening. Even our foreign friends have rallied heartily to their support..." (Lin, 1973: 75). Most the local capitalists and the press were positive toward the reform. For those who had vested interests in the old system, the new system was surely unwelcome. But they did not dare to object the reform openly in the face of the public opinion. Only some overseas Chinese and their domestic representatives as well as the state officials in charge of overseas Chinese affairs expressed their disagreements because one of the reform programs was the cancellation of the import restrictions on the goods that were produced or imported by overseas Chinese. They argued that to attract the capital and political identity of overseas Chinese, the protective measure should be retained. But K. Y. Yin insisted that overseas Chinese should earn their money through proper management rather than unsuitable and unfair protection (Liu, 1980: 51). In other words, economic efficiency ought not to be sacrificed for political interest. Generally speaking, the execution of the foreign exchange and trade reform received the cooperation of the majority of the society.

Within the state apparatus, aside from the officials who were responsible for overseas Chinese affairs, some administrators in the FETCC continually expressed their anxiety about the possibility of running out of foreign exchange reserve and the crisis of inflation. In response to the complains from his subordinates, K. Y. Yin consistently expressed his confidence and determination in carrying out the reform. He also spreaded his ideas through the mass media to gain the support of society and to overcome the resistance within and outside the state apparatus (Shen, 1972: 454-464; Liu, 1980: 51). Since the reform curtailed the power that the administrators could abuse, they were not able to obstruct or distort the execution of the reform programs.

The effects of the foreign exchange and trade reform were impressive. It revived the market mechanism and promoted economic efficiency; it increased production and expanded exports. Meanwhile, it did not produce inflation and shortage of foreign exchange as the opponents argued (Liu, 1980: 61-68). After the devaluation and trade liberalization, the expansion of exports took off. The value of exports in U.S. dollars expanded at the average rate of 24.5% per annum for the 1960s, so that over the decade it increased 9 times. Consequently, the economic structure was thoroughly reoriented toward exports. The transition can be shown by the following figures: In 1952, as mentioned above, the total exports of goods and services constituted 8.1% of the GDP of Taiwan; in 1957, this ratio increased only slightly to 9.6%; in 1961, it climbed to 13.8%; in 1970, it reached 29.7%; and in 1978, it jumped to 52.4% and has never fallen below 50% since that time (Tsiang, Chen, and Hsieh, 1985: 6; CEPD, 1986: 41). The rapid development of export industries alleviated the difficulties in foreign exchange payment, though the trade deficits had pesisted till the end of the 1970s. As soon as the loosening of import restrictions took place, imports flooded the market. But the contents shifted to the goods for production and export. With regard to the issue of inflation, the wholesale prices had increased only slightly after the reform. And the mild inflation in fact might be attributed largely to the offshore island crisis of August, 1958 and a bad typhoon in August, 1959 that resulted in a great among of increase in government expenditure and money supply, and a serious disruption in rice and other foodstuff supply (Lin, 1973: 78; Liu, 1980: 61-64). In sum, the reform was quite successful.

Formulation and Execution of the Nineteen-Point Program of Economic and Financial Reform

The Context of the 19-Point Reform Program

The changes of the AID's policy and the KMT state's view on Taiwan's development were the main factors contributing to the formulation of the Nineteen-Point Program of Economic and Financial

Reform. Since Taiwan was incorporated into American hegemony to play the political (rather than economic) role of containing communism, the U.S. aid program for Taiwan originally did not emphasize economic development. Military strength and monetary stabilization instead were the major objectives of the U.S. aid to Taiwan. By 1956, Taiwan regained the prewar level of per capita GNP. In a sense, postwar recovery was complete. The AID Mission to China felt that Taiwan could embark on a path of sustained, rapid development and the next logical goal of U.S. aid should give more weight to this development. In early 1955, AID's presentation of the aid program for Taiwan to the U.S. Congress for 1956 proposed to refine and improve the program to help the island achieve a self-supporting economy (Jacoby, 1966: 33).

The U.S. Congress, however, still supported the purpose of aid with military defense against the Communists. Despite a gradual shift in *de facto* objectives from military strength and monetary stabilization to economic development, the shift was not explicit. There was no marked change in the statuory instruments of assistance. Defense support, direct forces support, and surplus agricultural commodities continued to be the dominant instruments. AID had to rationalize assistance for economic development within the loose statutory definition of "defense support." Only in 1958, with the inauguration of the Development Loan Fund, did Congress started to provide aid for the goal of stimulating economic development *per se*. In the same year, AID established an Office of Private Enterprise. The stance of AID's policy for Taiwan to foster private investment, to expand exports, and to look toward the phasing-out of U.S. aid became clear (Jacoby, 1966: 33-35).

In parallel with the shift in AID's policy, there was also a change in the view of the KMT state about national development. For the first half of the 1950s, the KMT elites sought U.S. aid mainly to bring monetary and social stability to Taiwan and to offset the deficit of government budget resulted from the large burden of military expenditure. An outsized military establishment was maintained to defend the island against communist attack and to launch an offensive under propitious circumstances. While economic development was by no means neglected, military considerations determined the bottom line of resource allocation. The dominant aim of the state was to build a socially and politically stable (as well as economically capable) base for the recovery of the mainland (Jacoby, 1966: 36). Therefore, military rather than economic considerations defined the orientation of the national development

The KMT state began to shift its attention around 1956. By that time, the state had successfully diminished inflation, relieved distress, and recovered prewar living standards. Restrained by the Mutual Defense Treaty, the possibility of launching an overall military action to recover the mainland was much reduced. Consistently held by the American advisors and the development-minded Chinese officials, the view of developing Taiwan into a "showcase" of Chinese development under free economic institutions became increasingly appealing to Chiang Kai-shek. The KMT elites gradually realized that economic development ont only promised greater welfare for the people of Taiwan and could augment the legitimacy of the Nationalist regime on the island, but also had powerful propaganda values in both the ideological battle with the Chinese Communists and in the attempt to vindicate the Nationalist regime in the eyes of the world. Sun Yat-sen's principle of improving the people's livelihood was now more frequently voiced as a primary purpose of the state's policy. The emerging aim of economic development was, however, not weakening the determination to "return to the mainland." As Neil Jacoby (1966: 36-37) points out, it was actually seen by the KMT elites as a means of increasing the probability of success in attaining this ultimate goal.

A few state actions signaled the change in the view of the KMT state on national development. In February, 1958, Chiang Kai-shek ordered Vice Premier Wang Yun-wu to organize an *ad hoc* Administrative Reform Committee to carry out a comprehensive study of the issues of organization, power, personnel, budget, and regulations for the state organizations at all levels. The committee was set up after the example of the U.S. Hoover Committee. After a half-a-year research and discussion, it presented 88 reform suggestions. Among them, many were concerned with the management of the economy. Regarding to the issue of finance, the committee suggested to improve tax structure and administration by diminishing bad taxes and increasing income tax as well as to improve the financial situation of local governments by increasing tax dividends and subsidies.

Regarding the monetary system, the committee suggested to establish modern credit system by reactivating the Central Bank of China and some other public banks, setting up a stock market, and opening the life insurance business; to control foreign exchange effectively by enhancing the execution of import restrictions, prescribing state organizations to procure domestic products, and acutioning rather than rationing imported raw materials; and to encourage savings and capital formation by raising interest rates, simplifying saving formalities, promoting insurance business, shortening depreciation period, reducing extra tax burden, and lowering tariffs for importing capital goods. With respect to economic affairs, the committee suggested to improve the management of state enterprises by revising concerned laws and regulations to stengthen the evaluation of their performance; to foster private enterprises by revising and enacting concerned laws and abolishing unnecessary controlling measures; and to improve the utilization of U.S. aid by enhancing the coordination between the authorities concerned, including private sector into economic planning, and increasing the amount of loans for private enterprises. With regard to government budget, the committee suggested to reform it by revising the procedure of compilation, unifying treasury system, and improving accounting system (Li and Ch'en, 1984a: 182-188). In sum, the main purpose of these suggestions were aimed at loosening unneccessary economic controls, revising inappropriate laws, and improving investment climate.

The comments on the contribution of this committee are not unanimous. For some observers (Li and Ch'en, 1984a: 188), the suggestions of the committee had profound impact on Taiwan's development strategy and subsequent economic transformation. For other commentators (Wang, 1978: 56-57), the committee did not bring about any significant achievement for the administration. It failed in carrying out a thorough reform for strengthening state capacities which would enable the state to play a more active role in propelling socioeconomic transformation. On the contrary, some suggestions of the committee, such as the dissolution of the ESB, tended to reduce the capacities of the state in managing the economy. Nevertheless, there was a consensus that this reform implied an effort of the Kuomintang to establish a more capable state in order to cope with the new socio-political situation and promote economic development. Together with the administrative reform, the reform of foreign exchange and trade was also put into effect. Moreover, soon after securing the offshore islands, an overall economic reform plan, the Nineteen-Point Program of Economic and Financial Reform, was mapped out.

The Policy-making Structure and Policy Formulation

The 19-Point Program was an collaboration of the American advisors and the economic policy makers. In 1959, Under Secretary of State C. Douglas Dillon and deputy director of AID Leonard Saccio visited Taiwan in October and December respectively. Both of them indicated to Chinese officials that, in their opinion, Taiwan possessed the potential to accelerate her economic growth to such an extent that she could stand out as an example, for other Asian countries to follow, of what could be accomplished by a people determined to work their problems of economic development. Saccio particularly stated to Ch'en Ch'eng that AID would consider rendering effective assistance in an accelerated economic growth program provided that the KMT state would make the maximum possible contribution to such a program by mobilizing all the available domestic resources (Liu and Tso, 1983: 6). This was a dramatic change of American foreign aid policy. AID had so far adopted a policy which gradually decreased the aid to the countries with better performance in utilizing U.S. aid and promoting economic growth while increasing the aid to the recipients whose situation still remained problematic. It thus failed in bringing the effects of U.S. aid to light. The new policy decided to enlarge the aid to those countries with better performance in order to make them as the models for other recipients.

On December 20, 1959, director Wesley C. Haraldson of the AID Mission sent an outline of an Accelerated Economic Development Program to the CUSA. In the outline, Haraldson first stated the reasons for proposing the program: (1) "It is necessary to speed up the economic expansion in order to feed and provide jobs for a rapidly growing population and to create in this part of the world a 'show case' of the achievements of a free society"; and (2) "The prerequisites for rapid economic expansion-leadership, skills, energy, and resources-already exist on Taiwan and can be readily utilized." And the objectives of the program was "aimed at maximizing sound economic growth for the next four or five yers, thereby attaining a condition where the needed future growth will be self-generated, and thus eliminating the need for foreign aid except for heavy items of military equipment and some surplus agricultural commodities. It is expected that in this process Taiwan will prove to be increasingly attractive to foreign investors and will also be able to establish an enviable international credit rating."

To accomplish these objectives. Haraldson proposed an 8-point program of action by the KMT state: (1) A "firm decision" to reduce the amount of resources for military purposes; (2) Non-inflationary fiscal and credit policy to achieve price stablization; (3) Tax reform to abolish all possible existing tax deterrents to business; (4) Uniform and realistic exchange rate to avoid uneconomic use of resources, encouragement of consumption, discouragement of exports, and discriminates against certain types of business; (5) Liberalized exchange controls to revive market mechanism; (6) Establishment of a utilities commission to give public utility management the freedom necessary to operate efficiently its enterprises; (7) Establishment of investment banking machinery with simplified investing formalities to attract capital from the general public; and (8) Sale of state enterprises to private owners.

Ten days later, a meeting concerning the outline was held in Ch'en Ch'eng's official residence. In addition to Ch'en and Haraldson, the other attendants were C. K. Yen, K. Y. Yin, and K. T. Li, and the *charge d'affaires* of American embassy. At the meeting, Haraldson and the *charge* explained the background and purpose of the outline to Ch'en. According to them, when American foreign aid to the world was decreasing in general (due to the slowdown of economic growth in the United States), the U.S. government decided to give more support to a few countries with better utilization of U.S. aid. The purpose was to accelerate the development of these countries and make them the models for other recipients. In addition, the progress of these countries could prove the superiority of a free economy and deal a blow to the Communist camp. This should be a common goal shared by the ROC and the U.S. Taiwan was on the list because of her previous outstanding performance. But in order to reach the goal and thus convince the U.S. Congress to appropriate more money for Taiwan, a concrete reform program was needed. They expected to obtain the agreement of the Chinese government on the reform program as soon as possible in order to include it into the U.S. foreign aid program for 1961.

Ch'en Ch'eng's response was very positive. He indicated that the KMT state agreed with the AID Mission on the necessity of adopting various measures to facilitate economic development and added that the state had already been carrying out various reforms; that in regard to the improvement of investment climate the state had recently set up an Industrial Development and Investment Center in the CUSA to revise the corresponding statutes and simplify administrative formalities; and that the KMT state had a consensus with the U.S. government on recovering the mainland through a political approach-they sought to improve people's living standards. This was confirmed by Chiang Kai-shek and John Dulles in the joint communique of October 23, 1958. Ch'en believed that the reform program should be able to win the applause of the business sector and that of the general public. Although he expected divergent opinions from the Legislative Yuan, he was confident he would get the approval for the reform. He anticipated that some items in the 8-point program, such as the establishment of a utilities commission to determine reasonable prices for public utilities would encounter some difficulties. This referred especially to an upward adjustment of electricity rates urged by the American advisors. But he showed determination in overcoming these problems. At the conclusion of the meeting, Ch'en Ch'eng again expressed the attitude of accepting the 8-point program in principle and promised to draw out a formal response of the Chinese government as soon as possible.

On January 4, five days after the meeting, a memorandum together with the minutes and the 8-point program were submitted to Chiang Kai-shek. Another meeting was quickly convened in Chiang Kai-shek's official residence on January 7. Besides Chiang Kai-shek and Ch'en Ch'eng, the other attentands were secretary-general to the President Chang Chun, C. K. Yen, K. Y. Yin, and K. T. Li. Reports on the background, purpose, and conclusion of the last meeting as well as the socioeconomic situation of Taiwan were presented to Chiang. Ch'en emphasized that all items on the 8-point program were actually required measures for promoting Taiwan's economic development even in the case that the program did not warrant an increase of U.S. AID. Among the 8 points, the reduction of military expenditures and the raise of electricity rates were underscored. As far as reducing military expenditures, the American advisors hoped to cut down expenditures drastically. But the economic policy makers doubted this suggestion would get Chiang's permission. Based on C. K. Yen's suggestion, they adopted an eclectic proposal which suggested that the expenditures for the national defense during the fiscal year 1961 would be fixed at the constant prices of 1960 (Li and Ch'en, 1984a: 195). The implications was that while the amount of military expenditure needed not to be cut down, the proportion of military expenditure in the national product would decline given that the economy would continue to develop. Chiang accepted the suggestion without hesitation. As far as raising the electricity rates was concerned, the meeting decided to establish a public utility commission outside the Legislative Yuan. The commission would be attached to the Executive Yuan and in charge of drafting a formula for calculating electricity rates. The Legislative Yuan would only discuss and determine the formula rather than the prices *per se*. Once the formula was determined, the commission had the privilege to adjust the prices automatically in accordance with the variations of the components in the formula. This decision was expected to save time to the official authorities. The reform program thus obtained the support of the top political leadership and K. Y. Yin was charged with the duty of pushing it forward.

When K. Y. Yin was taking charge of drafting a formal response of the KMT state to the 8-point program, some economic policy makers and bureaucrats felt that the 8-point program was not comprehensive enough. Several important issues which needed to be remedied were not included. Yin therefore decided to enlarge the scope of the reform. Following the existent reform programs, namely the Administrative Reform and the Foreign Exchange and Trade Reform, and based on the needs of the current situation, the 8-point program was finally extended into a 19-Point Program of Economic and Financial Reform (Wang, 1978: 58-59). In essence, the 19-point program aimed at liberalizing the economic controls, promoting exports, improving banking and tax systems, creating a business climate to stimulate private local and foreign investment, and balancing government budget. It added actions to encourage saving, establish central banking system, liberalize trade regulations, fully utilize government production facilities, adjust salary payments and diminish hidden subsidies to government employees, raise public utility rates, and hold the military expenditures to the real 1960 level.

On January 14, a formal document-the Accelerated Economic Growth Program, the Republic of China-was sent to Wesley Haraldson from K. Y. Yin. The document summarized the goals of the third Four-Year Economic Plan covering the period 1961-64 and the estimated amount of investment required. It also listed the 19-Point Program of Economic and Financial Reform with indications of the length of time required for the implementation of each item. In a letter attached with the document, Yin informed Haraldson that the 19-point program had been approved in principle by Chiang Kai-shek personally and Yin was authorized to assure the AID Mission of the Chinese government's determination to carry out the reform with all resources at its command and regardless of difficulties that might be encountered in the course of the implementation. On the same day, the Accelerated Economic Growth Program was approved by the Executive Yuan Council. Eight days later, Yin received a letter from Haraldson notifying that the document had been forwarded to Washington. In the letter, Haraldson also tried to clarify that statement relating to defense expenditure in the document by interpreting it as: "on the assumption that there is no change in the over-all situation, the military budget of the Government of the Republic of China would be fixed at the present level, and that it would be increased only to compensate price rises and to cover payments for goods and services that are presently being obtained by the military but are either not paid for or are paid for at unrealistic prices; also, that the United States military local currency programs would be increased only to cover any increase in local currency costs caused by military modernization." The KMT state accepted this interpretation. Then after some stylistic modifications, the Accelerated Economic Growth Program (including the 19-Point Program of Economic and Financial Reform as the major part) was passed by the CSC on March 23.

The Execution of the Program

The 19-point program was mapped out as an internal document for the administration rather than as a law. It therefore did not have to be sent to the Legislative Yuan or promulgated to the society. But the Policy Coordination Commission of the KMT had convened the KMT members in the Legislative Yuan to hear their responses. In the Executive Yuan, a committee headed by the Vice Premier was set up to monitor the implementation of the Program. The committee come together about once a month to review the progress of the reform. A formal report about the implementation of the program was prepared made in June, 1961. According to the report, every item in the reform program had been carried out to a certain degree. An Industrial Development and Investment Center headed by K. T. Li has been established in the CUSA. A China Development Corporation with KMT capital in it had been set up. A Statute or Encouragement of Investment, which we will discuss in the next section, had been promulgated. A stock exchange had been established. Foreign exchange controls had been liberalized. Efforts were being made to raise the level of personal savings. The salary payments to government employees had been adjusted. While most items were ultimately implemented, actions on several of them were not taken on schedule. In particular, the reduction of military expenditures and the raise of electricity rates (Jacoby, 1966: 135).

Probably influenced by the disastrous outcome of the Great Leap Forward, which brought the economy on the mailand to the brink of a total collapse and seemed to offer an opportunity for the KMT to launch a certain kind of military action, the military expenditures of the fiscal year 1961 was not kept at to the 1960 level. Its amount raised from 7,371 million N.T. dollars in 1960 to 8,563 million N.T. dollars in 1961. The ratio in total government budget raised from 60.5% to 60.8% (CEPD, 1986: 164-165). The increment exceeded the raise of prices. With regard to the adjustment of electricity rates, as Ch'en Ch'eng anticipated, the formula of calculating electricity rates and the proposal of raising the rates roused different opinions in the Legislative Yuan. Partly due to the objection of the Legislative Yuan and partly due to the fear of stirring inflation, the action of raising electricity rates was behind schedule.

The American advisors played an important role in stimulating these actions. Originally AID promised to offer an additional program loan of 20-30 million U.S. dollars to encourage the KMT state to implement the program promptly. The amount of the promised program loan was reduced to 20 million as a penalty for incompletely of reducing military expenditures. As a result, the effort of holding military expenditures was effectively carried out in the following years. For the issue of adjusting electricity rates, a million threatening to withhold aid was ued to obtain the desired action. With the promise to approve the proposed aid to construct new power plants, AID finally obtained the raise of the electricity rates in 1962 (Jacoby, 1966: 135)

The dramatic reforms undoubtedly posed a potential danger to the KMT state. The reduction of the economic controls could wreck the price stability and stir inflation. Already scarce foreign exchange could become less or even vanish. An expansion in trade would increase the vulnerability of Taiwan's economy to the world system. Foreign investment could bring back the bitter memory of foreign invasions in Chinese modern history, which resulted in the hated treaty port system and extraterritoriality on Chinese land allowing foreigners to run freely through the economy and society. Many officials still disliked businessmen, and the reforms would further the state's retrenchment from the economy and grant ever greater rein to local and foreign capitalists. This would probably entail concentration of capital into the hands of few, a move which contradicted Sun Yat-sen's *Min-sheng* Principle (Gold 1986: 77).

K. Y. Yin pushed the reforms very hard, backed by the top political leadership and the American advisors. According to K. T. Li, Chiang Kai-shek supported the reforms because they would enable Taiwan to give up U.S. aid and become self-reliant. In other words, the KMT perceived their dependency on aid negatively and viewed the establishment of an open economy positively, as a means to open Taiwan's own way in the world (Li and Ch'en 1984a: 189; Gold, 1986: 77).

As a follow-up to the 19-point program, a high-level economic and financial conference was held in 1961. Major business leaders were invited to attend the conference, where they were encouraged to speak out their opinions about economic matters. This conference was of considerable significance because, deprived of opportunities for participation in policy-making through the elections at the central government level, local capitalists finally could make their voices heard. We are not arguing that local capitalists were totally excluded from economic policy-making. At the lower level, they did have an established channel for expressing their grievances through the periodic group consultations with officials of the development agency on the occasion of preparing the four-year development plans. Also, a few business leaders were invited by the IDC as advisors. But the opportunities to exchange opinions with the economic policy makers face to face were rare (Lin, 1973: 84).

The execution of the 19-point program had significant influence on Taiwan's subsequent development. For Wang Tso-jung, however, the 19-point program was in effect the KMT's first attempt to establish a self-sustained modern economy but did not succeed. He attributes its relative lack of success to the following reasons: (1) The 19-point program was only an internal document for administration-rather than a law-which could not be compulsorily executed; (2) Many authorities concerned and state officials did not really fully comprehend the essence of the reforms and did not sincerely support them since they were initiated by the CUSA, a privileged department; and (3) Economic policy makers did not push the reforms hard enough after Yin's death in January, 1963. Nevertheless, the enactment of the Statute for Encouragement of Investment, a corollary of the 19-point program, was acknowledged as a successful state action (Wang, 1978: 61-62).

Formulation and Execution of the Statute for Encouragement of Investment

The Investment Climate Before the Enactment of the Statute

In the 1950s, when Taiwan's economy was still suffering from inflation and the shortage of foreign exchange, incentives for private investment were provided by the KMT state mainly through the preferential allocation of foreign exchange, the availability of U.S. aid and bank loans at interest rates much lower than in the market, as well as the price advantage of domestic producers vis-a-vis their foreign competitors created by various protection measures. While these actions quickly invented a bourgeiosie in primary import-subsitution industries, they also distorted the market mechanism, and caused inefficient resource use, low-quality products, and the unhealthy psychology of local capitalits of relying on state protection. At the same time, when inflation was under control and the rate differentials of foreign exchange between official and black markets were substantially narrowed in the late fifties, these policy incentives gradually lost their attractiveness (Lin, 1973: 84). To meet the new situation, a new package of incentives was needed.

Before the enactment of the Statute for Encouragement of Investment, the KMT state had enacted two investment laws. Promulgated in July, 1954 and November, 1955, the Statute for Investment of Foreigners and the Statute for Investment of Overseas Chinese were aimed at facilitating the inflow of foreign and overseas Chinese capital. Both statutes allowed investors to use freely the foreign exchange to import plant equipment, raw materials, and other goods that were needed to implement the investment projects concerned. The rather dim market prospects and investment climate, however, did not attract a significant inflow of overseas Chinese and foreign capital into Taiwan (Lin, 1973: 85). Meanwhile, with the assistance of U.S. aid, the KMT state did not feel an urgent pressure to search for resources of capital formation outside the island. But expecting the termination of U.S. aid in the mid sixties, the economic policy makers realized that the KMT state had to adopt measures promptly to make up for the loss of U.S. aid.

Three problems deterred local and foreign investments at that time. First, the tax burden was unbearable. Second, the formalities of investment were terribly complicated and time-consuming. Some administrators took advantage of this to extort money from investors. And third, the acquisition of plant sites was troublesome. To prevent the system of land-to-the-tiller from being eroded, the state laid down strict regulations to limit the transfer of land ownership. A by-product of this policy was the difficulty to acquire plant sites. The KMT state had theretofore adopted some fragmented measures to improve the situation. For example, tax exemptions and deductions for export products had already been implemented. These piecemeal actions, nevertheless, did not change the situation too much. In the meantime, some actions were administrative orders rather than laws, whose effects were limited. Since it would take a very long time and cost enormous human power to revise the laws and regulations concerned case by case, the economic policy makers decided to enact a special law, based on the principle that a special law is superior to an ordinary law, that would include all of the measures to handle the three problems from one statute. Therefore, a Statute for Encouragement of Investment was drawn up (Wang, 1978: 62-63).

The Policy-making Structure and Policy Formulation

Under Ch'en Ch'eng's order, the CUSA was in charge of drafting the Statute for Encouragement of Investment. In addition to the authorities concerned, a number of scholars and lawyers were also invited to join the team for drafting of the statute. Some business leaders were also consulted. After a series of discussions, a draft was submitted to the Executive Yuan Council on May 19, 1960. With some small revisions, the draft was approved by the Executive Yuan Council on June 2.

Ch'en Ch'eng assigned the CUSA the major role in the making of the statute because he wished to avoid the interference of conflicting goals and the vested interests of the authorities concerned. Likewise, the Industrial Development and Investment Center was set up in the CUSA rather than at other state agencies under Ch'en's order. Since the improvement of the investment climate covered many related issues, such as plant sites, tax, labor, public utilities, foreign exchange and trade, entering and leaving Taiwan, various administrative formalities, and socioeconomic stability, etc., many state departments were involved in the policy making. Conflicts derived from the attempts to preserve existing official authorities and vested interests were foreseeable. With its special status in the state apparatus, the CUSA was relatively free from these organizational restraints and more likely to take an unbiased stance. In addition, K. Y. Yin's enthusiasm to improve the investment climate and his selfless but very aggressive way of doing things won the support of the top political leadership to entrust him with the mission. Moreover, because the CUSA was headed by Ch'en Ch'eng, its status and powers were superior to other ministries and commissions in the Executive Yuan. This gave the CUSA more leaverage to coordinate the different opinions held by the various authorities concerned.

A most controversial issue in the process of making the statute was the measures for tax incentives. Tax exemptions and deductions directly influence the revenue and the authority of the Ministry of Finance. It is predictable that the Ministry of Finance would take a conservative attitude toward the measures for tax incentives. As a matter of fact, debates did happen in the policy-making process. The officials in the Ministry of Finance naturally attempted to reduce the scope and range of the tax exemptions and deductions. Fortunately, C. K. Yen, the minister of Finance at the time, unlike his subordinates, supported the action for improving investment climate (Chou, 1982a: 15). A number of significant devices for providing tax incentives were finally put in the statute.

Soon after the draft of the Statute for Encouragement of Investment was passed by the Executive Yuan Council, it was sent to the Legislative Yuan to be enacted. At the same time, it was sent to the Policy Coordination Commission of the KMT and further submitted to CSC. In a meeting of July 6, the CSC decided to enact the statute as soon as possible. Through the coordination of the Policy Coordination Commission, the KMT members in the Committees on Economic Affairs, Finance, the Budget, and Communications in the Legislative Yuan convened to exchange opinions on the bill. Twenty-five joint meetings of the four committees and four panels were held to review the draft. It was passed almost intact by the Legislative Yuan at the end of August. The statute was formally promulgated on September 10, 1960 (Liu and Tso, 1983: 94).

The Execution of the Statute

The salient points of the statute may be given as follows: (1) Income tax holiday. The strongest production incentive is the "five-year tax holiday" set forth in Article 5 of the statute, whereby a productive enterprise conforming to the statute's criteria is exempt from income tax for five consecutive years. (2) Preferential business income tax rate for productive enterprises. The maximum rate of income tax for a productive enterprise, including all forms of surtax, is not to exceed 18% of its total annual income as compared with 32.5% for ordinary profit-seeking enterprises. (3) Tax exemption for undistributed profit. The amount reinvested for productive purposes is deductible from taxable income. (4) Tax deduction of exports. Within certain limits a deduction from taxable income of 2% of annual export proceeds is permissible. (5) Exemption or reduction of stamp tax. This tax is either waived or reduced in a large number of cases. (6) Tax exemption of foreign currency debt. productive enterprises are allowed to set aside 7% of their profits before taxation of the unpaid balance of foreign currency debt, calculated in local currency, as a reserve against possible loss caused by exchange rate revision (kuo, Ranis and Fei, 1981: 75). In addition, the articles concerned with the acquisition of plant sites and the cooperation between public and private enterprises are also put in the statute (Yu, 1976: 113-121).

As a result of the statute, a large proportion of the taxes were reduced. This is shown in Table 6.1. We can find that there was a sudden increase of tax reduction and refunds from fiscal years 1958 to 1960 which reflected the effect of tax exemptions and deductions for exportation before the execution of the statute. After the promulgation of the statute, another jump of tax reduction and refunds happened between fiscal years 1961 and 1962. The change was quite significant. The response of local and foreign capitalists to the statute in the early 1960s was still hesitant. But when the development strategy was entirely shifted to export-oriented in 1965 by adding more export and investment incentives into the statute as well as establishing the Kaohsiung Export Processing Zone, the situation changed significantly. This change will be dicussed in the next chapter.

A Review on the Economic Reforms

Today Taiwan is taken for granted as a single-minded exporter of manufctured commodities whose goods flood the world market, expecially the United States, and earn a huge surplus of foreign exchange. But Taiwan's adoption of an export-oriented development strategy was not inherent to its earlier import-substitution approach. Rather, the shift from import subsitution to export orientation as a strategy for industrialization, as we have demonstrated, derived from the political debates within the state apparatus, influenced by the American advisors and the consulting economists. As a matter of course, the various economic reforms, which reshaped the character of Taiwan's economy, were formulated and executed not without conflict and compromise as well as domination and subordination. They were outputs of a specific conjuncture of policy-making.

K. Y. Yin was unquestionably the key figure in these reforms; his success would have been questionable, however, if there had been no advantageous conditions both in the state apparatus and in the social environment. In fact, his success can be better explained in terms of the internal structure of the KMT state and its relation to the surrounding social structure, or in more succinct terms, *state capacities* and

Table 6.1
Tax Reduction and Refunds from 1955 to 1979
(as Percentage of the Corresonding Tax)

Fiscal Year	Income Tax	Stamp Tax	Customs Duties	Commodity Tax	Total Refund in the Four Taxes
1955	—	—	2.3	0.2	1.5
1956	—	—	4.2	0.3	2.6
1957	—	—	2.9	3.0	2.9
1958 *	—	—	6.6	2.8	5.1
1960 *	—	—	13.5	8.5	11.5
1961	2.4	25.3	14.5	12.5	11.9
1962	21.5	37.6	20.3	24.3	23.2
1963	25.2	16.5	21.6	13.0	19.0
1964	17.3	20.3	38.8	18.0	26.4
1965	17.2	20.3	31.0	21.2	24.5

1966	21.4	51.1	32.6	20.1	28.1
1967	23.4	49.7	40.5	22.0	32.2
1968	19.0	48.2	39.2	23.0	31.1
1969	14.6	45.2	36.4	18.7	26.6
1970	15.1	52.2	49.2	25.1	34.1
1971	13.5	73.5	77.3	34.3	47.5
1972	14.9	60.0	86.1	37.3	52.4
1973	15.9	57.0	72.3	37.6	48.0
1974	22.0	50.9	46.2	31.7	36.9
1975	12.2	51.8	54.6	37.7	38.2
1976	15.3	48.7	42.2	37.3	34.3
1977	12.7	50.5	57.2	40.6	40.0
1978	14.9	34.2	40.5	36.0	31.8
1979	13.2	12.8	40.3	35.2	29.9

* Fiscal year 1958 runs from July, 1958 to June, 1959 while fiscal year 1960 runs from July, 1959 to June, 1960 due to the change in fiscal year system.

Source: Kuo, Ranis and Fei, 1981: 76.

state autonomy. As we have reiterated, to undertake effective interventions, the state must constitute a bureaucratic apparatus with sufficient corporate coherence and hold a certain degree of autonomy from society, especially the dominant social forces or classes (Rueschemeyer and Evans, 1985: 68). Generally speaking, the reforms coupled nicely with these two propositions

Within the state apparatus, Yin enjoyed ample support. On the top level, he won the trust of Chiang Kai-shek and Ch'en Ch'eng. By the late fifties, confined by the international political situation and the U.S. global policy, the top political leadership had demonstrated its inclination than ever to view Taiwan's economic development as a means of counterattacking the Chinese Communist regime. Besies, it probably also saw economic development as psychological compensation for the defeat on the mainland, which to a large extent could be attributed to a collapse in the economy (Wang, 1978: 69). Yin's main opponent, Premier O. K. Yui, resigned in June, 1958 due to an impeachment by the Control Yuan. The impeachment, accusing him of holding too many posts concurrently and violating the regulation of frugality, was actually originated in the factional struggle within the KMT (Ch'en, 1985: 155-156; Yang, 1986: 153-154). Ch'en Ch'eng, Vice President of the Republic of China at the time, was again appointed by Chiang Kai-shek to take charge of the Executive Yuan. After delegating sufficient authority to handle economic matters by Chiang, Ch'en gave his full support to Yin's reform programs. Backed by the top political leadership, Yin was able to push forward his projects.

In the middle level, Yin obtained the cooperating of his colleagues, notably C. K. Yen (minister of Finance from 1958 to 1963) and Yang Chi-tseng (minister of Economic Affairs from 1958 to 1965, had his educational background in mechanical engineering, had been vice minister of National Defense, vice minister of Economic Affairs, and president of Taiwan Sugar Corporation). They constituted an excellent partnership in propelling the reforms. When detabes arose between Yin and Yang, Yen acted as mediator; the "Yin-Yen-Yang" cast had a firm commitment to accelerate Taiwan's economic development and showed admirable coherence in their corporate actions.

At the lower level, Yin gained a competent staff and several brilliant aides, notably K. T. Li (secretary-general of the CUSA, 1959-63) and Wang Tso-jung (counselor and director of the Economic Research Center of the CUSA, 1959-63). Li was Yin's most capable associate in administrative affairs, and Wang's knowledge in economic theories offered Yin many innovative ideas. In addition, enjoying financial independence and not being subject to civil service regulations, the CUSA retained a group of competent and hardworking bureaucrats by paying much higher salaries. Solidified by a particular *esprit de corps,* they made the CUSA the vehicle of economic reforms. Moreover, presiding over CUSA, FETCC, and the Bank of Taiwan simultaneously, Yin was able to combine the policy instruments in resource allocations, foreign exchange and trade, as well as monetary system into a set of powerful reform measures. These favorable conditions brought *state capacities* into full play and facilitated K. Y. Yin's reform programs.

State capacities were also enhanced by assistance from outside the state apparatus. As we have presented, Yin's reform programs received considerable help from the consulting economists and the American advisors. The foreign exchange and trade reform was initiated by the consulting economists. The 19-point program was a collaboration based on the 8-point program originated from the American advisors. The American advisors also used the level of aid to stimulate state actions for economic reforms and augment the capacities to implement them.

In regard to the external environment, there were no vested interests in the society that were strong enough to challenge or distort the reforms. The former landlords were turned into either industrialists relying on the state's assistance or protection, or small businessmen having limited influence, or small farmers. The local capitalists emerging from the development of import-substitution industries were still weak *vis-a-via* the state and most of them welcomed the reforms which in effect benefited most of them. Transnational capitalists, no matter whether foreigners or overseas Chinese, were small in both numbers and amount of capital, and the reforms hardly intruded upon their interests. Therefore, the social structure surrounding the state apparatus, both at intra-national and international levels, were conducive for the KMT state to reshape the economy.

In other words, the economic reforms were carried out in a conjuncture of favorable conditions– *state capacities* and *state autonomy* – allowed the KMT to launch distinctive new state policies. On the one hand, there existed a constellation of organizationally coherent collectivities of state elites; on the other hand, the collectivities of state elites faced a relatively docile people and were relatively insulated from currently dominant socioeconomic interests in society. The conjuncture of social and polical circumstances was in favor of the state pursuing transformative strategies. We can take the Foreign Exchange and Trade Reform as an example to present the argument in more detail.

The KMT state corresponded in its power structure and organizational structure with the conditions needed for coherent corporate action. With respect to the power structure, the KMT state was free from disjoined action was because although there were inevitably certain conflicts among the economic policy makers, the top political leadership was immune to rivalry and played the role of final decision maker. Under the supervision of the top political leadership, the conflicts among the economic policy makers were not allowed to hinder the state from implementing coherent action. Thus, when the liberal-reformists group won the support of the top political leadership, no opposition remained in the state apparatus to obstruct the reform.

With regard to the organizational structure, the organization of the agency for controlling foreign exchange and trade, the FETCC, was conducive to coherent state action. As already mentioned, the decision-making body of the FETCC was composed of the minister of Finance, the minister of Economic Affairs, the secretary-general of the CUSA, the secretary-general of the ESB, the governor of the Bank of Taiwan, the president of the Central Trust of China, and the representatives from the Central Bank of China and the Taiwan provincial government. Since all of the leading officials in economic and financial affairs were invited to join the policy-making, it was easier for various state bureaucracies to cooperate with each other. The coherence was further enhanced when K. Y. Yin was promoted to take charge of the CUSA and the Bank of Taiwan concurrently (Liu, 1980: 69-70).

For the proposition of the autonomy from society, the fact that the KMT state faced a weak opposition from certain factions within the still incipient dominant class contributed to its autonomy from society. As Amsden (1985: 98) observes, a foreign exchange and trade reform, as what Taiwan carried out, may stir class conflict through devaluation and deflation. It is harmful to the profiteers sucking money from exchange rate disparity and certain import-substituting firms and the banks that are financing them. If these social actors are foreign, they may bring extraeconomic power to resist new policy directives. Fortunately, all of these factors were absent in the case of Taiwan.

This situation was different from that in Latin America. When the KMT state decided to put the reform into effect, Taiwan's economy was both far less industrialized and far less inflationary than those Latin American countries whose economies fell after the saturation of primary import substitution, so that fewer entrenched interests were upset. Actually, the reform benefited the local capitalists who were able to reorient their import-substituting firms to exploit new foreign markets. They had already become the majority in the business sector at the time. In order words, the "division within the dominant class" favored the implementation of the reform. Besides, the state controlled many sectors that would otherwise have been hurt, such as the banking system and the more capital- and technology-intensive enterprises. This yielded the state powerful policy instruments to regulate the economy. That is to say, Taiwan was able to carry out the foreign exchange and trade reform rather effectively and smoothly because the balance of power between the state and society was weighted far more to the state's advantage.

Following the logic, we might argue that K. Y. Yin's success was mainly due to his ability to take advantage of the right time and the right circumstances. Just the Wang Tso-jung's comments on the success of the foreign exchange and trade reform, "By 1957 and 1958, the whole economic situation was evolving to a point conducive to a reform in foreign exchange and trade on the one hand, and showing a urgent demand for the reform on the other. The time and circumstances were ripe. Anybody who could make use of this conjuncture would be the hero of time and circumstances. Since Mr. Yin had the wisdom to grasp this opportunity and the courage to adopt determinate action, he succeeded. His success was due to the above reason and not to magic" (Wang, 1972: 9-10).

The 19-Point Program of Economic and Financial Reform as well as the Statute for Encouragement of Investment were formulated and executed in the same conjuncture. Of course the policy-making structures of these three reforms were somewhat different with one another; the objects of the reforms were also not the same. These differences in turn influenced the effects of the reforms. For example, the relatively limitd achievement of the 19-point program can be explained in terms of its scope and objectives. Different from the other two reforms, which mainly dealt with social objectives, the 19-point program involved groups within the state apparatus or under the state system, such as the military, the civil servants, and the state enterprises. The favorable conditions of *state autonomy* were not entirely applicable in this case. At the same time, *state capacities* were restrained by more conflicts and compromises between the various state departments in the state apparatus. Accordingly, the effects were not so remarkable.

CHAPTER 7

FORMULATION AND EXECUTION
OF ECONOMIC POLICY AFTER THE EARLY 1960S

Situational Imperatives

International Situation

When the KMT state made great efforts to reorient Taiwan's economy from import substitution to export expansion, a timely international economic situation emerged. Under the leadership and with the assistance of the United States, the economy of the advanced capitalist world was quickly restored from the destruction of the World War II. Accompanying the evolution of the capitalist world system and as a consequence of transnational corporations, international flows of resources and goods had been much thriving and were still growing. Stimulated by the increasing interaction with the advanced societies and driven by nationalism, the less developed countries also devoted themselves to economic development. The innovations in technology and management for the war had been transferred to civil productive activities, which increased the productivity of private enterprises and helped a great deal of new products appear in the market. The discovery of new oil fields kept the supply of energy abundant and cheap. All of these factors contributed to a prosperous world economy and to the growth of foreign trade. An international market in favor of the supplier of consumer goods was continuously expanding (Wang, 1978: 70-71).

Coincidently Taiwan's interest in fostering an investment climate meshed the unfolding of the world capitalist system, especially the operation of product cycle in Japan and the United States. After World War II, due to the progress of technology and the rise of wage rates, many advanced capitalist societies had to shift gradually their industrial structures to more technology- and capital-intensive industries and give up the more labor-intensive industries to the LDCs. By the early 1960s, both Japan and the United States had encountered the problem of losing competitiveness in certain labor-intensive manufactured goods. Transferring the whole or a part of the production of the goods to the places with cheaper wages seemed to be the best way to salvage these industries. The switch of Taiwan's development strategy and the efforts to improve her investment climate coupled with cheap and abundant labor that was virtually free of disputes and strikes, good levels of health and education, adequate transportation, and cheap electric power, attracted the attention of Japanese and Americans (Ranis, 1979: 246). Thus when the economic aid on concessional terms from the U.S. was phased out in 1965, Taiwan was able to lure considerable amount of foreign private capital to make up for that loss (Gold, 1981: 173-207).

By 1970, the favorable international economic situation had lasted for about a decade. During this period, facilitated by the prosperous world economy, Taiwan's foreign trade and light industries of consumer goods had enjoyed a fast and steady growth. The average growth rates of GNP and industrial production from 1963 to 1972 were as high as 10.8% and 18.5%, while the average inflation rate of consumer prices was as low as 2.9%.

The situation turned gloomy in the early 1970s, however, due to the decline of the economy of the United States and the sudden rise of the oil price. By the late 1960s, the U.S. dollar had already felt the pressure of devaluation. In August, 1971, President Richard M. Nixon finally announced a new economic policy and devaluated the U.S. dollar from 35 dollars for 1 ounce of gold, which had been fixed since 1934, to 38 dollars for 1 ounce of gold. The ratio was further changed to 42.2 dollars for 1 ounce of gold soon after that. The devaluation of the U.S. dollar caused a turmoil in the international market (Wang, 1978: 93-95).

The thing was aggravated by the spiraling of oil price. The outbreak of the Middle East War in October, 1973 brought about the oil crisis; the oil price soared for 4 times within 3 months. It not only increased the cost of production and transportation of almost all products but it also resulted in an extra burden in international payments for the oil-importing countries, such as Taiwan. At the same time, the international food price rose owing to the drought in many major food exporting and consuming countries. World shortages of primary products and essential supplies plus the oil crisis led to a worldwide slumpflation (Wang, 1978: 95-96).

These dramatic changes had grave impact on Taiwan's economy. Since Taiwan's economic development is founded mainly upon an "import-labor added-export" process, any fluctuation in world prices will influence the production costs and living expenses immediately. Moreover, Taiwan's economy is highly dependent on foreign trade. Any stagnation in export will result in an economic setback and unemployment. The international economic turmoil thus taxed Taiwan's economy heavily. Taiwan began to suffer the effects of the recession in the latter half of 1974 as its export trade and industrial production dropped sharply. The growth rate of GNP for the year fell to 1.1%, the lowest in the last 20 years. Wholesale prices jumped 40.6% and consumer prices rose 47.5%. The exports of 1975 shrank 5.7%. This was the most serious disaster of Taiwan's economy since 1949 (EPC, 1976: 3).

The world economy began to revive during the latter half of 1975, but progress was rather slow. As a matter of fact, many countries found themselves suffering from a very unusual combination of macroeconomic circumstances–"stagflation." At one and the same time, they confronted with not inconsiderable inflation and not inconsiderable unemployment, a phenomenon quite strange to economists and hard to be explained by existing economic theories (Robbins, 1982).

In contrast to these countries, Taiwan quickly broke out of that predicament. The economy began to recover in the second quarter of 1975 as export trade and industrial production rose again. The second oil crisis of 1979, which again raised oil prices about 3 times, somewhat frustrating the growth of the economy for the period 1980-82; but it regained its momentum in 1983. Thus for 1973 to 1985, the average growth rate of GNP achieved 7.9%; the average growth rates of industrial production and exports attained 9.2% and 19.6%; while the average growth rate of consumer prices was 9% (CEPD, 1986: 2). The entire process was not comparable to the proceeding decade but it was still outstanding.

The speedy expansion of Taiwan's foreign trade and export-oriented industries propelled the island to prosperity no one would have believed in 30 years ago but it also deepened the vulnerability of Taiwan's economy, i.e., the extreme trade dependence upon a couple of countries, notably the United States and Japan. Since the early 1950s, the share of Taiwan's commodity trade with these two trading partners has never been less than a half of the total amount of the foreign trade. Although Taiwan has tried to divert its market from these two countries, the effort has not been very successful. In recent years the United States has become the biggest buyer of Taiwan's export goods whereas its exports to Taiwan have not increased proportionally. The surplus in favor of Taiwan in the bilateral trade started growing rapidly since 1980, increasing from 2.1 billion U.S. dollars to 15.6 billion in 1986. The continuously enlarged trade deficit provoked protectionism against Taiwan in the U.S. Various pressures asking for opening markets and lowering import duties were pressed on Taiwan (Hsu, 1985: 8-9). A request to raise the exchange rate of the New Taiwan dollar for U.S. currency was further raised recently. How to deal with the pressure from the U.S. has become a major issue in Taiwan's economic policy-making.

In addition to the pressure from the U.S., another threat to Taiwan's economic development in the international market has been the intensified competition from other LDCs. Accompanying the development of "growth with equity," the living standard and wage rates in Taiwan rose quickly. As a result, Taiwan no longer enjoys the factor of cheap labor as compared with most LDCs. Many of its products have lost competitiveness in the international market. The product cycle bringing the labor-intensive industries from Japan and the U.S. to Taiwan is now removing some of them from the island. Accordingly, how to upgrade the industrial structure, improve the kinds and quality of export products, and exploit new foreign markets have been Taiwan's other unavoidable challenge.

The influence of the evolution of the international economic situation affected Taiwan; however, the island has also felt the impact of the change in the international political situation. Roughly speaking, during the sixties Taiwan still enjoyed a steady external political environment supported by the U.S. Following the example of France, which established diplomatic relations with the PRC in 1964, some nations shifted their diplomatic missions from Taipei to Peking and the American view of Taiwan as a strategic position essential to the containment of communism gradually began to change due to the increasingly severe breakdown of the Sino-Soviet alliance; nonetheless, economic and military assistance from the U.S. to the ROC continued. The U.S. government sent out tentative feelers to the PRC in the mid-1960s. But before anything could be developed from this mission, the Cultural Revolution broke out, sealing Mainland China off from the world and strenthening Taiwan's supporters abroad (Clough, 1978: 22; Gold, 1986: 86).

The Vietnam War demonstrated the value of Taiwan for supporting U.S. military operations in Southeast Asia and brought large amounts of dollars to the island. As the Korean War had contributed to Japan's economic growth, the Vietnam War nourished Taiwan's economy. The U.S. purchased a lot of agricultural and industrial commodities from Taiwan as supplies for the war. The soldiers went to the island for vacation. American aircrafts stationed on Taiwan's air bases because Taiwan provided the best overhaul and repair facilities in East Asia outside of Japan. Taiwan also undertook many contract works for and in Vietnam (Clough, 1978: 23; Gold, 1986: 87). These businesses to a certain degree made up for the loss of U.S. aid.

After Richard Nixon was elected President in 1968, however, the strong role of the U.S. in Taiwan's security entered a phase of uncertainty. In the light of the decline of U.S. military strength and the worsening of the Sino-Soviet dispute, President Nixon began to reexamine Washington's policy toward Peking. Recognizing that public backing for the war in Vietnam was crumbling, President Nixon and his national security adviser, Henry Kissinger, Perceived that an easing of the rigid hostility between the U.S. and the PRC might contribute to the disengagement of U.S. forces from the fighting. Moreover, they seemed to believe that a more constructive relationship between Washington and Peking would reduce the risk of war and increase international stability in East Asia. In July, 1971, Kissinger made a secret visit to China. In the fall of the same year, the ROC withdrew from the United Nations before a vote by the General Assembly to give the China seat to the PRC. President Nixon went to the mainland and issued the Shanghai Communique with Chou En-lai in February, 1972, opening the door for "normalizing" the relationship between Peking and Washington. In the same year Japan recognized the Communist regime as the only legal government of China. Since then more and more nations began to establish diplomatic relations with Peking, which, by the rule of "one China" agreed upon by both the KMT and CCP, necessitated breaking relations with Taipei (Clough, 1978: 24-25; Kau, 1984: 3-4; Gold, 1986: 93).

On January 1, 1979, the ROC broke its diplomatic relations with the U.S. The American embassy in Taipei was substituted by the nongovernmental American Institute in Taiwan, staffed by "retired" State Department officials, while the ROC changed its embassy in Washington into the Coordination Council for North American Affairs. The Mutual Defense Treaty expired on January 1, 1980. The Taiwan Relations Act, however, passed by Congress in March, 1979 and signed by President Jimmy Carter on April 10, served as the basis for relations between the peoples of the United States and Taiwan. The people in Taiwan were cheered up by the election of Ronald Reagon in 1980, who used to be a good friend of the Nationalists. But they soon found out that he also intended to improve the relations with the PRC. The so-called Second Shanghai Communique of August, 1982 gave another shock to the KMT state by setting out an agenda for winding down U.S.-Taiwan military ties (especially weapons sales) (Gold, 1986: 99).

Amid the diplomatic frustration, various political and military threats came from across the Taiwan Strait. Under the radical "Gang of Four," the Communists clamored to "liberate" Taiwan. After the fall of the Gang in 1976, Peking changed its approach by emphasizing "reunification" instead of "liberation" and offering a number of concessions to entice Taipei to "peace talk." But the Communists never renounced the right to use force or deploy a blockade. Moreover, they insisted that the KMT state on Taiwan could only be a local government subordinate to Peking after the reunification. In 1984, the PRC signed an agreement with Great Britan to turn Hong Kong over to PRC's sovereignty in 1997, with a promise not to change its existing capitalist system for 50 years. The Communists clamied that a similar model could be applied on Taiwan (Gold, 1986: 98-100). In addition to the political and military threats, the Communists also launched a series of economic challenges against the Nationalists. Following the example of Taiwan's Export Processing Zones, they set up Special Economic Zones in the coastal areas. They aggressively solicited foreign capital, especially from overseas Chinese. They drove their exports into Taiwan's market by selling similar goods. They joined various international economic organizations, such as the IMF, the World Bank, and the Asian Development Bank. Due to the principle of "one China," Taiwan had to withdraw from or limited its activities in these economic arenas.

The unfavorable international political situation shook the confidence of many people about the security prospects of Taiwan and deterred their willingness to invest. The state faced the problems of strengthening the morale of the people and maintaining capital accumulation. At the same time, the alternational of the external political environment gave rise to some new tasks for the state's economic policy. It urged the state to provide an enlarged role for the nation's foreign economic activities, substituting international economic presence for conventional diplomatic relations, on the one hand (Wu, 1985: 5-6), and pushed the KMT state to be more aggressive in soliciting foreign capital to the island, substituting TNC offices for embassies, on the other (Gold, 1981: 303). In sum, the state was expected to adopt effective measures to cope with the various external impacts.

Intra-national Situation

The economic reforms during 1958-61 laid down the fundamental lines for Taiwan's subsequent development and prepared the ground for Taiwan's economic take off. But K. Y. Yin, the leading architect of these reforms, did not witness the completion of his plans for he died in January, 1963. His death ended the extraordinary concentration of power in economic policy-making. Since his death, no body has wielded so much power over the economy. C. K. Yen succeeded the post and mission in economic planning left by Yin while K. T. Li gradually assumed more duties. Hsu Peh-yuan regained powers within the monetary system (as governor of the Central Bank of China) and foreign exchange and trade (as chairman of FETCC). The CUSA was reorganized into the CIECD in September, 1963, with Ch'en Ch'eng as chairman, C. K. Yen as vice chairman, and K. T. Li as secretary-general. Three months later, Ch'en Ch'eng resigned as Premier and chairman of the CIECD. C. K. Yen was appointed to take over the posts left by Ch'en Ch'eng and K. T. Li was promoted to succeed C. K. Yen. In January, 1965, K. T. Li took charge of the Ministry of Economic Affairs concurrently. C. K. Yen and K. T. Li thus became the main architects of Taiwan's economic development for the latter three quarters of the 1960s.

The CIECD turned to be less aggressive in regulating Taiwan's economic transformation as compared with the CUSA during the turning-point period. An important reason for that was the change in personnel. In contrast to K. Y. Yin, who was bold and uncompromising in carrying out his ideas, C. K. Yen tended to avoid direct clash with people of different opinions. In addition, the decentralization of power in economic policy-making naturally made the formulation and execution of economic policy less coherent. Moreover, Ch'en Ch'eng's death in March, 1965, made the economic policy makers lose a strong dependable man. Consequently the energetic dynamics of reform so alive during the late fifties and early sixties seemed gone. At the same time, the rapid and smooth development of Taiwan's economy alleviated the pressure on the state to adopt drastic transformative policies.

Chiang Ching-kuo's inauguration as Vice Premier and chairman of the CIECD in 1969 opened a new era of Taiwan's development. Many state actions were adopted in the following years to upgrade Taiwan's economic structure and meet the challenges from the turmoil of the world economy. There were also some changes in the personnel composition of the economic policy makers. Since C. K. Yen fully delegated his authority to Chiang Ching-kuo, Chiang not only took over Yen's position as the head of the economic bureaucracy but also gained much power in other spheres. Hsu Peh-yuan resigned as governor of the Central Bank of China due to a scandal concerning a bribe. His post as chairman of the FETCC had vanished since the FETCC had been dissolved earlier. Yu Kuo-hwa succeeded him as governor of the Central Bank of China. K. T. Li was shifted to preside over the Ministry of Finance with the goal to improve the financial administration and raise more money for a series of construction projects. T'ao Sheng-yang, Li's top aide and former general-secretary of the CIECD, was appointed minister of Economic Affairs; however, he died of cancer three months later. Sun Yun-suan was appointed to take over the post left by T'ao. Under Chiang Ching-kuo's leadership, a new cast of economic policy makers consisted of K. T. Li, Sun Yun-suan, and Yu Kuo-hwa emerged. These mainlander officials forged the broad lines of Taiwan's economic development since the end of the 1960s.

Chiang Ching-kuo was appointed Premier in June, 1972 when the external political situation began to deteriorate. The impact was aggravated by the worldwide economic recession that would become grave a year later. Chiang's cabinet thus encountered serious external challenges. In Chiang's cabinet, the leading economic posts remained unchanged: K. T. Li was in charge of finance; Sun Yun-suan was in charge of economic affairs; while Yu Kuo-hwa was in charge of the monetary system. The CIECD was downgraded to the EPC with Chang Chi-cheng (Ph. D., Civil Engineering, Cornell University; chief of general affairs division, CUSA, 1958-63; secretary-general, CIECD, 1963-65 & 1969; vice minister of Economic Affairs, 1965-69; minister of Communications, 1969-72; vice chairman and secretary-general, CIECD, 1972-73; chairman, EPC, 1973-76; secretary-general, Executive Yuan, 1976-78; minister of Finance, 1978-81; chairman of the board, Central Trust of China, 1981-84; governor, Central Bank of China, 1984-) as chairman. The power of economic policy-making was shifted to the Five-man Finance and Economic Group while the final decision depended on Chiang Ching-kuo. Facing the external troubles, Chiang displayed a strong ability in leading the state and society. The economy quickly revived from the depression of 1974.

In May, 1978, Chiang Ching-kuo was inaugurated as President of the Republic of China and Sun Yun-suan became Premier. Originally K. T. Li was considered the best candidate for the post of Premier. But he declined the offer due to his health. As a matter of fact, Li had already resigned as minister of Finance in June, 1976 because of a heart condition. He then became a minister of state (without portfolio) and took charge of the promotion of high-tech industries. His influence on general economic and financial policies was therefore somewhat reduced. At the same time, Yu Kuo-hwa's power was rising. The EPC was upgraded to the CEPD in December, 1977. Governor Yu was appointed to take charge of the CEPD concurrently. Therefore, while Li, Sun, and Yu were still the main architects of Taiwan's economic development during the late 1970s and early 1980s, the power structure changed from a configuration headed by Li and assisted by Sun and Yu to one headed by Sun and assisted by Li and Yu. In addition, the minister of finance Chang Chi-cheng and the minster of Economic Affairs Chang Kwang-shih (had been engineer and manager of the China Petroleum Corporation and vice minister of Economic Affairs) also had a certain degree of influence.

Sun's cabinet was partly reorganized in December, 1981. Yu's *protege,* Hsu Li-teh (master in political science, had been commissioner of Finance of Taiwan provincial government and vice minister of Finance), was promoted as minister of Finance while Chao Yao-tung (master in engineering from MIT in 1945, had been engineer and manager of various state enterprises, project manager of various textile companies in Vietnam and Singapore, he was invited back to Taiwan in 1969 to establish the state-owned China Steel Corporation which became one of the world's most profitable steel companies) was appointed minister of Economic Affairs. Chao's style of thinking and doing was very similar to K. Y. Yin's. Under his leadership, the Ministry of Economic Affairs suddenly became quite energetic. Backed by Sun Yun-suan, he put forth several ambitious projects of economic development. But before these projects could be really carried out, the cabinet was wholly reorganized because Sun suffered a stroke. During his six years as Premier, Sun had shown talent in leading the Executive Yuan and managing Taiwan's economy. Under his leadership, Taiwan safely overcame the strike of the second oil crisis.

Yu Kuo-hwa was appointed to succeed Sun Yun-suan in May, 1984. Hsu Li-teh became minister of Economic Affairs and vice minister of Finance. Lu Jun-k'ang (master in law, had been secretary of Ministries of Finance and Economic Affairs, director of the Taxation Bureau of Taipei City, and president of the Central Trust of China) was promoted as minister of Finance. Chang Chi-cheng succeeded Yu Kuo-hwa as governor of the Central Bank of China while Chao Yao-tung was transferred to the chairmanship of the CEPD. Since Chao's aggressive style was not so compatible with Yu's view of leadership, his new post as chairman of the CEPD was seen as a promotion but was in fact a demotion. As a result, the power structure of economic policy-making was changed to a configuration with Yu Kuo-hwa as the head, K. T. Li and Hsu Li-teh at the second echelon, and Chao Yao-tung, Chang Chi-cheng, as well as Lu Jun-k'ang at the third echelon (Sun, 1984: 57). The cabinet, however, was partly reorganized ten months later. Hsu Li-teh and Lu Jun-k'ang were ousted from the cabinet due to the bankruptcy of Cathay Plastics (a once high-flying local enterprise having good connections with many high ranking state officials), which will be discussed in more detail later. Hsu and Lu were accused of delinquency in their duties. Yu's top aide, Ch'ien Ch'un (master in economics from the University of Minnesota in 1957, had been director of secretariat, general manager of banking department, and deputy governor of the Central Bank of China) became minister of Finance and Lee Ta-hai (B.S. in chemistry, had been engineer, general manager, president, and chairman of the board of Chinese Petroleum Corporation) assumed the post of minister of Economic Affairs. The current power structure of economic policy-making is still headed by Yu Kuo-hwa and assisted by K. T. Li, Chao Yao-tung, Chang Chi-cheng, Ch'ien Ch'un, and Li Ta-hai.

Yu's cabinet was not so popular as Sun's. In contrast to Sun, who was open-minded and determined, Yu appeared relatively conservative and indecisive. His cabinet also gave the public the same image. Under the increasing pressure from the external political and economic circumstances, most people in Taiwan, nevertheless, expected a cabinet showing a high-key appearance and composed of more aggressive state managers. Yu's leadership and cabinet did not fulfill those expectations too well. State actions in regulating the economy appeared hesitant and less coherent. The response of society to the incompetent performance of the state produced a setback of capital accumulation in recent years.

Apart from the change of internal structuring of the state apparatus, the decline of *state capacities* in recentyears to a certain extent should be attributed to the falling of *state autonomy*. In parallel with the development of the economy and the expansion of the private sector, a variety of social forces have risen on the island and changed the relationship between the state and society. At first, the local capitalists had much leverage to influence the formulation and execution of economic policy. Many small local firms emerging in the 1950s or 1960s have now become big companies. Although the relationship between the economic officials and the local capitalists was relatively distant when compared to that of Japan's and South Korea's, the businessmen in Taiwan never gave up any opportunity to influence the economic policy-making of the state. Through the enlargement of electoral process to central government level, and the establishment of various pressure groups, the local capitalists have increasingly shown their weight. Meanwhile, a number of leading entrepreneurs, enjoying their close relationship with the high-ranking economic officials, have been able to express their opinions and demands directly to the economic policy makers (Ch'en, 1982: 20; Lung, 1982: 55-56; Fu, 1982: 8-13). Some local capitalists even believe that business interest groups have already had more weight than the state officials in economic policy-making for quite a period (Ho, 1986: 16-18). A more detailed description will be given in the final section of this chapter.

Apart from the local businessmen, the force of transnational capitalists has also become stronger. Taiwan had originally been relatively free from the influence of TNCs. In contrast to the Latin American economies which had for a long time been penetrated by transnational corporations, there was basically no transnational capitalism influencing Taiwan before the mid-1960s. Although a significant amount of foreign capital has flowed into Taiwan since the mid-1960s, the TNCs did not occupy a dominant status in Taiwan's economy. On the contrary, the KMT state was strong enough to regulate the transnational capitalists. However, due to the increasing diplomatic isolation, the presence of foreign capital on Taiwan was laden with the function of breaking through the diplomatic predicament. Moreover, the KMT state also expected TNCs to help Taiwan upgrade her industrial structure through technological cooperation or transfer. The transnational capitalists thus enjoyed more leverage in economic policy-making.

Moreover, the influence of consulting economists has augmented due to the rapid development of mass media. In addition to the influential senior scholars and columnists mentioned in chapter III, many experts in the new generation have offered advice to the economic officials either through the projects of economic research entrusted by the economic bureaucracy or via the media, especially newspapers. The increasing importance of newspapers is reflected in the fact that the two publishers who own the biggest two private newspapers, *Chung-kuo shih-pao* and *Lien-ho-pao,* have become the members of the CSC since 1979. The prosperity of mass media also implies the increasing weight of the middle class and of public opinions.

In the following sections we are going to analyze how the change of the internal structuring of the KMT state and the evolution of the domestic social structure as well as of the international situation worked upon the formulation and execution of economic policy after the early 1960s.

Agricultural Policy

From a macro-perspective, the most dramatic change of the KMT's agricultural policy after the early 1960s was the shift from extracting resources from the agricultural sector to subsidizing the sector. During the 1950s, facilitated by the land reform and the development of agricultural technology, the farmers' income was greatly improved. Although the discriminating agricultural pricing policy removed agricultural production further from the hands of the farmers, they were still better off than many urban laborers. But with the acceleration of the industrial development in the early 1960s, the situation quickly changed. The income disparity between the agricultural and non-agricultural households was widening. In 1953, the income of farming households was about 75% of the non-farming households. The ratio declined to 61% in 1964 and 58% in 1968. While the average annual growth rate of industrial production increased from 11.7% for 1852-62 to 18.5% for 1963-72, the growth rate of agricultural production decreased from 4.8% to 4% (CEPD, 1986: 2). The result was an outflow of a large quantity of rural youth, which deteriorated the quality of farm labor and brought about the slowdown of rural development. The increasing disparity between the urban and rural sectors also provoked the farmers' resentment.

The KMT state began to perceive the problem in the late 1960s but was reluctant to take serious steps to solve it. In 1969, when the production of agriculture, for the first time after the war, shrank 2% more than the preceeding year, a "Review Outlines of Agricultural Policy" was announced to examine the problem. Fourteen solutions were proposed. Then in March, 1970, the KMT issued an "Outlines of the Present Stage Rural Reconstruction Program" in its plenary session of the Central Committee. The document acknowledged the critical situation of Taiwan's agriculture and urged the state to adopt necessary measures. In the meantime, attention to the problem was paid by local politicians, academics, and journalists. Based on these documents and suggestions, the state adopted some measures intending to lower fertilizer prices, promote farm mechanization, increase agricultural loan, and improve the marketing of agricultural products. These measures, however, was never seriously carried out. Moreover, the squeezing strategy was kept intact. The problem was continuously worsening (Wang, 1978: 86; Hsiao, 1981: 64-65).

A milestone of Taiwan's agricultural policy, the "Guidelines for Accelerating Rural Reconstruction," was announced in September, 1972, three months after Chiang Ching-kuo assumed his post as Premier. The program abolished the rice-fertilizer barter system and certain land surtax; improved the availability of the agricultural credit and loan; reduced price differentials discriminating agricultural products; set up special agricultural production zones; and increased investment in rural infrastructure. The "Agricultural Development Act" was enacted in August, 1973, stipulating the modernization of agriculture as a national policy. At the same time, rural reconstruction was stressed in the sixth Four-Year Economic Development Plan (1973-76). The reduction of the inequality between the rural-agricultural and urban-industrial sectors became one of the primary goals in the economic planning (EPC, 1974: 24-29). Then the Six Year Plan for Economic Development (1976-81) suggested to set guaranteed prices for certain crops (rice, corn, and sugar cane), expand the scale of farm operations, help farmers to purchase farmland and new farm machinery, and provide welfare programs such as medical care and farmers' insurance (EPC, 1976: 7). And since 1973 the KMT state significantly increased its investment in the agricultural sector (Hsiao, 1981: 65-68; Hsiung, 1984: 23). The agricultural policy gradually shifted from extraction to subsidy.

The new approach in the agricultural policy to a certain degree released the farmers' financial burden but did not effectively improve agricultural production. The average annual growth rate for 1973-85 declined to 2% (CEPD, 1986: 2). The ultimate source of trouble is the scale of the farm size. Due to the increase of the rural population, the average size of the farm at present is about only 1 hectare. The small scale of farm operations retarded the possibility to adopt more capital-intensive techniques for increasing labor productivity. Since the mid-1970s, the state has tried to encourage land consolidation but not been very successful. In addition to the farmers' strong attachment to and indentification with their own land, there were also some objections from the state and society lest the consolidation would damage the fairly equitable distribution of farmland resulted from the land reform. As a matter of fact, even if there had been no objections, it still seems unrealistic to increase the average land holding to 3 hectares, the ideal size of a farm in Taiwan suggested by some experts, in less than a couple of decades. This change means moving two-thirds of the current rural population out of agricultural activities (Thorbecke, 1979: 197). Therefore, the only way to improve the relative income standards of the farmers during the transitional period was the state's protective measures such as price-support programs and various subsidies. Some of these measures have been adopted by the KMT state since the mid-1970s.

There were some debates in the KMT state about what kinds of measures and to what degree that the state should protect and subsidize Taiwan's agriculture. For the neoclassical consulting economists and some economic officials, the decline of the importance of agriculture in the economy is a natural tendency for a developing country marching toward the advanced level of free economy. The share of agriculture in net domestic product had declined from 35.9% in 1952 to 7.0% in 1985 (CEPD, 1986: 39). The state needs not resist this tendency and in turn retard the whole economic development. They suggested to reduce the subsidies and open markets for foreign agricultural products in order to promote resource use. For another group of officials, the decline of agriculture is a regretable thing and the state should not let nature take its course because the agriculture had contributed Taiwan's economic development a lot and is still not insignificant in the economy. So far the state has leaned toward the latter (Hsing, 1986: 191-192).

The reason that the KMT's agricultural policy leans toward the protective approach is related to the internal structuring of the state apparatus. Different from other economic policies, the agricultural policy in Taiwan is basically formulated by the officials in the agency for agricultural development, i.e., the JCRR and the Council for Agricultural Planning and Development in the past and the Council of Agriculture at present. For the last thirty-seven years, especially in the fifties and sixties, under their management, Taiwan's agricultural development has been one of the most successful cases in the world. This unusual record makes it somewhat difficult to merely let the agriculture dwindle without taking some actions. At the same time, the relatively independent status of the agency in the stage apparatus allows these officials to cultivate a special *esprit de corps* among themselves. These factors together shape their attitude toward Taiwan's agricultural development. They believe that through certain state actions Taiwan's agriculture can still make considerable progress and become more productive in the future and that protective measures are necessary for maintaining the dynamics of agriculture during the transitional period. The weight of this view has been further enhanced when a former official of JCRR, Lee Teng-hui (Ph. D. in agricultural economics from Cornell University; had been specialist, consultant, and chief of Rural Economy Division of the JCRR, 1957-72; minister of state (without portfolio), 1972-78; mayor of Taipei, 1978-81; governor of Taiwan, 1981-84) became Vice President of the Republic of China in May, 1984. In addition, the laissez-faire approach would reduce the power and functions of the agricultural agency. For the officials in charge of agricultural development, this would surely be unwelcome.

Another decisive factor to determine the agricultural policy is the attitude of the top political leadership. The dramatic shift of Taiwan's agricultural policy in 1972 was clearly related to Chiang Ching-kuo's determination. When Taiwan was suffering the impact from the worldwide economic recession, only Chiang could make the decision to continue the program of rural reconstruction. Of course, for the top political leadership, agricultural policy is not only an economic issue. Taiwan's political stability in the 1950s and 1960s to a considerable extent should be attributed to a prosperous rural sector. The KMT had consistently won elections in the rural areas, while challenges had come from the large industrial cities. The measures to prevent the rural areas from severe depression were supposed to pacify the rural people. Moreover, self-sufficiency in food production is seen as a principle of national development. The measures for encouraging food production, especially rice, are therefore taken for granted.

The protective measures for encouraging agricultural production, nevertheless, have met with some external pressure in recent years. The pressure is mainly from the United States. Due to the trade surplus in favor of Taiwan, the U.S. demands greater access to Taiwan's market, including agricultural products. Under the pressure, the KMT state has already allowed American tobacco, wine, beer, and apples to enter Taiwan. More American agricultural products will be introduced on the island in the future. Some of the protective measures, such as the guaranteed price for corn, are likely to face serious challenges. Taiwan's agricultural policy might have to be revised to cope with the new situation.

Industrial Policy

A special feature of Taiwan's economic development after the early 1960s is the spatially dispersed and labor-intensive character of its industrialization. While the agricultural reforms in the early 1950s greatly contributed to the "growth with equity" on the island in the 1950s, the admirable performance of Taiwan after the early 1960s is largely attributable to the rapid development of the export-oriented labor-intensive industries which create job opportunities not only in the urban areas but also in the rural areas (Fei, Ranis and Kuo, 1979; Ho, 1979). The spatially dispersed and labor-intensive industrialization alleviates the impact on rural development of the slowdown in agriculture. Many farm families in today's Taiwan have their income mainly from rural industries. The proportion of income derived from non-agricultural productive activities in aggregate farm household income reached 72.6% in1980 whereas the percentage of full-time farmers dwindled to 10.2% of all farm households (CEPD, 1981: 20). In addition, rapid development of labor-intensive industries creates job opportunities particularly for unskilled labor. After Taiwan achieved full employment in the late 1960s, a strong demand for unskilled labor made the wages of unskilled labor increase even faster than the wages of skilled labor and therefore it improved income distribution. Moreover, due to the nature of labor-intensive industries, which requires neither huge capital nor advanced technology, the degree of industrial concentration on the island is now low. Taiwan's economy is characterized by hundreds of thousands of small- and medium-size enterprises rather than dominated by few large conglomerates. The low degree of industrial concentration considerably contributes to the income equality in Taiwan. This character makes the economy not only different from many LDCs in the world but also different from other newly industrializing countries at the similar developmental stage, such as South Korea, where the 10 largest industrial groups (*chaebol*) produce about 75% of the country's GDP. While the effects of the different approaches on economic growth is debatable, better income distribution in Taiwan than in South Korea is explained in terms of lesser industrial concentration (Lau, 1986: 9). Then, what is the relationship between the distinguishing feature of Taiwan's economy and the development strategy of the KMT state?

The labor-intensive character of Taiwan's industrialization is the consequence of intentional state actions. In the early 1960s, when the economic reforms during the turning-point period had been successfully carried out, there was a debate about the approach for promoting Taiwan's industrialization. The neoclassical consulting economists, such as Tsiang Sho-chieh and Liu Ta-chung, contended that in accordance with factor endowment and comparative advantage, Taiwan should focus on labor-intensive industries. They opposed the development of any capital-intensive industries which did not agree with comparative advantage at the time. In contrast to this view, some other scholars and economic bureaucrats, represented by Wang Tso-jung, held that in addition to labor-intensive industries, the state should adopt certain measures to propell industrial deepening and enlarge the economic scale of certain industries. They advocated the building of an integrated steel mill and develop petrochemical industry as soon as possible (Wang, 1978: 87-88; Wang, 1981: 38; Wang, 1983: 110; Chou, 1982b: 69).

For the 1960s, the KMT's industrial policy leaned toward the labor-intensive approach. The change of personnel composition of the economic policy makers might be a crucial factor to explain the victory of the labor-intensive approach. As we have mentioned, although both K. Y. Yin and K. T. Li agreed on the thesis of "create" comparative advantage for and jump to advanced industries by adopting certain types of state intervention, while Li tended to be more moderate and more likely to "follow" comparative advantage without rushing in higher level. Given his appreciation of the Japanese model of development, Yin would have probably adopted an approach closer to the viewpoint held by Wang Tso-jung if he did not die in the begining of 1963. After Yin's death, Li became the leading figure in determining industrial policy. Under his charge, the approach for promoting industrialization naturally leaned toward the approach suggested by the neoclassical consulting economists. The different views of K. T. Li and Wang Tso-jung on the way of Taiwan's economic development casued incompatibility between them and eventually resulted in Wang's leaving from the economic bureaucracy.

A concrete example of the implementation of the export-oriented labor-intensive approach of economic development during this period was the establishment of Export Processing Zones (EPZ). Pushed by K. T. Li, the state enacted the Statute for the Establishment and Management of Export Processing Zones in January, 1965. In December, 1966, the first EPZ was established in the southern port city of Kaohsiung. The EPZ combines the advantages of an industrial estate with those of a free port. Firms in the zone enjoy all privileges and tax incentives provided to export producers in Taiwan but without the red tape. Official transactions, from investment application to foreign exchange settlement, are handled by one agency. Furthermore, customs duties, commodity taxes, and sales taxes are not levied, thus bypassing the bureaucratic procedures of tax rebates. Not all kinds of firms are welcome at the EPZ. Only firms that can offer considerable job opportunities are allowed to operate in the zone. Based on the suggestion of the Standford Research Institute, an AID contracted American consulting company, in the late 1960s and early 1970s, precision, labor-using, and relatively high value-added industries (e.g., precision machinary, electronics components, transistor radios, optical equipment, and plastic products) were given priority for admission to the EPZ (Ho, 1978: 197; Ger, 1983: 8-11).

The response of transnational capitalists to the establishment of the EPZ was quite positive. Local capitalists, singly or in partnership with foreigners, invested actively as well. Facilitated by the operation of product cycle, many Americans and Japanese came to Taiwan to search for opportunities of investment. In addition, a lot of overseas Chinese were attracted by the investment climate in Taiwan, characterized by political stability and favorable tax incentives, which was better than the situation in their host countries. Table 7.1 illustrates the evolution of direct foreign investment in Taiwan. We can figure out three time periods. The first period runs from 1952 to 1959. During this period, Taiwan's political situation was still unsettled; Japanese corporations were still developing their domestic bases; and American firms were concentrating on rehabilitating Europe. Foreign investment was trivial. The second period extends from 1960, the time of promulgating the Statute for Encouragement of Investment, to 1966, the time of opening the Kaohsiung EPZ. During this period, the political and economic situation had stabilized and AID was pressing the KMT state to improve investment climate. More foreign capital came to Taiwan. The third period begins in 1967. The improved investment climate on the island, coupled with wage increases in the U.S. and Japan, urged great amounts of capital inflow to Taiwan. Between 1971-72, the diplomatic setback, i.e., Taiwan's explusion from the United Nations, Nixon's visit to the mainland, Japan's establishment of relations with the PRC, and the reemergence of the Chinese Communists on the world scene, buffetted the willingness of foreigners to commit capital. When Taiwan did not sink, investments rebounded in 1973. The next buffeting came from the oil crisis and the world recession, but investments continued to increase. In 1979, despite continued diplomatic setbacks, including loss of official relations with the U.S., approved investment reached a record 328.8 million U.S. dollars (Gold, 1981: 161-164). The demonstrated success of Kaohsiung EPZ led to the establishment of two more zones at Nantze and Taichung in the early 1970s.

Some problems were brought about by the remarkable success of the export-oriented and labor-intensive development strategy. Taiwan

Table 7.1
Private Foreign & Overseas Chinese Investment in Approvals—By year

Amount Unit: US$ 1,000

Year	Total		Overseas Chinese		U.S.A.	
	Case	Amount	Case	Amount	Case	Amount
1952	5	1,067	5	1,067	—	—
1953	14	3,695	12	1,654	1	1,881
1954	8	2,220	3	128	3	2,028
1955	5	4,599	3	176	2	4,423
1956	15	3,493	13	2,484	2	1,009
1957	14	1,622	10	1,574	1	11
1958	9	2,518	6	1,402	—	—
1959	2	965	—	820	1	100
1960	14	15,473	6	1,135	5	14,029
1961	29	14,304	24	8,340	1	4,288
1962	36	5,203	10	1,660	8	738
1963	38	18,050	22	7,703	9	8,734
1964	41	19,897	28	8,007	7	10,196
1965	66	41,610	30	6,470	17	31,104

1966	103	29,281	51	8,377	15	17,711
1967	212	57,006	105	18,340	18	15,714
1968	325	89,894	203	36,449	20	34,555
1969	201	109,437	90	27,499	30	27,862
1970	151	138,896	80	29,731	16	67,816
1971	130	162,956	86	37,808	17	43,736
1972	166	126,656	114	26,466	17	37,307
1973	351	248,854	201	55,166	29	66,876
1974	168	189,376	85	80,640	21	38,760
1975	85	118,175	44	47,235	12	41,165
1976	98	141,519	53	39,487	8	21,767
1977	102	163,909	52	68,723	17	24,242
1978	116	212,929	50	76,210	18	69,765
1979	123	328,835	50	147,352	19	80,375
1980	110	465,964	39	222,584	15	110,093
1981	105	395,757	32	39,463	25	203,213
1982	132	380,006	50	59,720	33	79,606
1983	149	404,468	49	29,086	35	93,294
1984	174	558,741	74	39,770	41	231,175
1985	174	702,406	67	41,757	42	332,760
Total	3,471	5,159,835	1,747	1,174,483	505	1,716,333

Source: CEPD, 1986: 262-264.

Table 7.1 (continued)
Private Foreign & Overseas Chinese Investment in Approvals—By Year

Amount Unit: US$ 1,000

Year	Japan		Europe		Others	
	Case	Amount	Case	Amount	Case	Amount
1952	—	—	—	—	—	—
1953	1	160	—	—	—	—
1954	1	14	—	—	1	5
1955	—	—	—	—	—	—
1956	—	—	—	—	—	—
1957	3	37	—	—	—	—
1958	3	1,116	—	—	—	—
1959	1	45	—	—	—	—
1960	3	309	—	—	—	—
1961	3	1,301	—	—	1	375
1962	16	2,664	—	—	2	141
1963	6	1,397	—	—	1	216
1964	2	728	1	150	3	816
1965	14	2,081	—	—	5	1,955

1966	35	2,447	2	746	—	—
1967	76	15,947	4	1,872	9	5,133
1968	96	14,855	2	1,762	4	2,273
1969	75	17,379	4	20,642	2	16,055
1970	51	28,530	3	10,713	1	2,106
1971	17	12,400	4	66,135	6	2,877
1972	26	7,728	4	6,842	5	48,313
1973	92	44,599	14	33,825	15	48,388
1974	50	38,901	3	14,761	9	16,314
1975	22	23,234	2	4,193	5	2,348
1976	26	30,760	2	32,796	9	16,709
1977	20	24,145	3	28,001	10	18,798
1978	43	50,336	1	4,468	4	12,150
1979	39	50,462	2	19,766	13	30,880
1980	35	86,081	11	14,428	10	32,778
1981	27	64,623	8	12,636	13	75,822
1982	24	152,164	11	46,570	14	41,946
1983	33	196,770	7	20,746	25	64,572
1984	28	113,978	15	92,242	16	81,576
1985	32	145,236	12	100,011	21	82,696
Total	900	1,130,427	115	533,305	204	605,287

Source: CEPD, 1986: 264.

began to feel insufficiency of infrastructure, especially in transportation, in the late 1960s. Full employment and a rising standard of living caused the rise of wages and made Taiwan lose the edge of cheap labor as compared with other LDCs. Taiwan's trading partners began to set up protectionist quotas against her exports (Gold, 1986: 94). Moreover, the impacts from international politics in the early 1970s urged the KMT to consider the necessity of enhancing the defense component in its economic development. The assertion of industrial deepening gradually won more support. The state also asked advice of Arthur D. Little, Incorporated. The American consulting firm suggested upgrading Taiwan's industrial structure by investment in petrochemicals, electrical machinery and equipment, advanced electronics, precision machine tools, and computer terminals and peripherals. Consequently, in contrast to the fairly labor-intensive character in the 1960s, the KMT's industrial policy since the early 1970s began to give more weight to capital- and technology-intensive industries. A best example of this change was the implementation of the Ten Major Development Projects.

The Ten Major Development Projects was announced in November, 1973 by Premier Chiang Ching-kuo. The projects, spanning 5 years, included a north-south freeway running through the island, electrification of the west coast trunkline trailway, a railway running through the east coast, an international airport, a commercial harbor in the middle of the west coast, an auxiliary harbor in the north-east, an integrated steel mill, a petrochemical complex, a shipyard, and three nuclear power plants. While the original estimates of the cost were $5 billion, the projects came out with a final price tag exceeding $8 billion. Domestic savings, mostly government investment, provided about 60% of the required funds; the other 40% was borrowed from foreign lenders. The projects comprised nearly 30% of the nation's total fixed capital formation in the mid- and late seventies and helped the economy ride out the first oil crisis (Li, 1980: 81-82; Gold, 1981: 256-258; Gold, 1986: 101).

The announcement of the Ten Projects was a bold decision by Chiang Ching-kuo. As early as the time when Chiang was inaugurated as Vice Premier and chairman of the CIECD in 1969, an ambitious plan for upgrading Taiwan's industrial structure was brewing. Wang Tso-jung was called back from Bangkok, where he served as the chief of the Industrial Studies Section of Economic Commission for Asia and the Far East of United Nations, to be a consultant on the CIECD. Chao Yao-tung was invited back from Singapore to be the director of the project for the integrated steel mill. When Taiwan began to suffer external political impacts in the begining of the 1970s and Chiang Chingkuo became Premier, the state decided to link several projects already underway as the Ten Major Development Projects to boost the self-confidence of the people and spur Taiwan's continued growth through the hard times. Before the projects were officially announced, some economic officials and scholars were worried about the adverse effects of the projects on the economy, such as financial burden and inflation. They suggested to break the projects down into a few smaller ones with different priorities and a longer time span to carry them out. But partly due to the insistance of Chiang Ching-kuo and partly due to the sudden outbreak of the oil crisis which changed the mind of some economic policy makers and bureaucrats, the Ten Projects were finally announced simultaneously as a package for accelerating Taiwan's economic transformation. Somewhat by coincidence, the implementation of the projects became effective measures to cushion the impact of the severe global recession and the rapid falling off in domestic investment and ease the transition to full recovery. In retrospect, the announcement of the Ten Projects was undoubtedly a timely remedy to overcome the economic crisis, but it is questionable whether that very same treatment would have been prescribed, if Premier Chiang had not been in charge.

Following the completion of the Ten Projects, the state announced the inauguration of Twelve New Projects in 1979: six in infrastructure, five in transportation, and the remaining one in nuclear power generation. Some of the new projects were actually the second stage of the earlier set of projects. A Fourteen Development Projects of a similar nature was further undertaken in 1985 (Li, 1985: 21). Moreover, the state tried to develop high-tech industry since the early 1980s. A Science-Based Industrial Park was established in 1980. It offered the same incentives as the EPZ, but only the firm producing high-tech products are welcome. In the course of the downward spiral in the international political situation, the people of Taiwan naturally experienced a crisis of confidence in the ability of the KMT state to control the island's fate. Many local capitalists hesitated to commit long-term investments in capital and technology-intensive industries. It became the state's responsibility to upgrade the industrial structure of the economy. Through the development projects noted above and the four-year and six-year plans, the state devised a flexible, multifaceted strategy to reduce Taiwan's vulnerability to the instability of the global economy, primarily by vertically integrating and deepending industry through the steel mill and petrochemical complex.

The state originally hoped to invent a local bourgeosie in the steel industry. Both the integrated steel mill and the shipyard were intended to be joint state-private enterprises for profit. But because one reason or another, most of the private investors backed out. They both finally became almost 100 percent state enterprises. Under the dynamic direction of Chao Yao-tung, who took the job with the understanding that he could operate the steel mill free of the bureaucratic red tape that paralyzed other state enterprises, the China Steel Corporation became very profitable. It was designed to supply domestic customers, but began exporting in the early 1980s (Gold, 1986: 101). In contrast to the steel mill, the shipyard turned out to be an unsuccessful case. Since the shipyard was built not only for economic purpose but also for the purpose of strengthening national defense, the managerial level of the shipyard was filled with retired admirals in order to develop the ability to produce warship. However, partly due to the inefficiency and corruption of those managers from the Navy and partly due to the recession of the world economy, which caused the slowdown of sea transportation and the setback of the shipbuilding industry, the shipyard continuously suffered huge deficit and triggered lost of critiques.

In addition to the steel mill and shipyard, the other manufacturing enterprisis in the Ten Projects is the petrochemical complex. Development of the petrochemical industry was envisioned as a means to integrate vertically two of Taiwan's major industries–synthetic textiles and plastics–and thereby locate domestically as many stages of the production process as possible. It was also expected to reduce vulnerability to price fluctuations in imported supplies. As in Brazil (Evans, 1979: 211-273; Evans, 1982: S226-S232), the petrochemical industry brought the state, transnational, and local capitalists together as equity partners. In addition to capital, foreign partners supplied technology and managerial expertise. Local partners, usually downstream and intermediate manufacturers, brought a captive market. The state, through a monopoly control of oil imports, ownership of all naphtha crackers, and its own petrochemical plants, supplied raw materials, infrastructure, incentives, and overall coordination. The two oil crises gave the industry a very hard time. In 1981, the private petrochemical producers asked the state to regulate the imports, production, and prices. The state's reply was to encourage the downstream sector to increase value added and the intermediate producers to invest overseas closer to the sources of raw materials. Formosa Plastics, the biggest private firm in petrochemical industry, therefore entered a joint venture as majority partner with the Louisiana Chemical and

Plastic Corporation to build a 240,000-ton per year, $168 million pvc plant in Texas. The industry was boosted back to normal capacity by the declin of the oil prices in recent years (Gold, 1986: 101-102).

For some economists (Little, 1979: 503-505), these capital- and technology-intensive industries do not match Taiwan's comparative advantage and the KMT state need not rush in urgently; for the state managers, however, these industries not only have their functions in the economy but also in national defense. As a matter of fact, a relatively strong sector of state enterprises is a special feature of Taiwan's economy. Although the share of the output of state enterprises in industrial production has continuously declined (56.6% in 1952, 47.9% in 1960, 27.7% in 1970, 18.7% in 1980, and 16.1% in 1985), the state enterprises are still very important in economic scale and supplies of energy, raw materials, and intermediate products. In 1980, Ministry of Economic Affairs owned 14 enterprises in petroleum, power, sugar, steel, shipbuilding, engineering, aluminum, fertilizer, petrochemicals, machinery, chemicals, mining, alkali, and phosphates. Their combined sales for 1980 approximated the combined sales of the top 62 private firms. In addition, the Ministry of Finance owned several banks and insurance companies and the Taiwan provincial government owned 6 enterprises in iron, paper, agricultural, ammonium sulfate, textiles, as well as tobacco and wine. The state control of big enterprises and banking system not only provides the state with powerful policy instruments to regulate the economy, but also facilitated the less industrial concentration and more economic equality in Taiwan (Liu and Tso, 1984).

The state enterprises have nevertheless faced increasing critiques in recent years. The main accusation is on their efficiency. Except for a few cases, such as China Steel Corporation, most of the state enterprises have efficiency problems. Along with the growth of the private sector, the pressure for better management or the sale of state enterprises has mounted. In fact, as early as the 19-point program was formulated, the sale of state enterprises was one major item in the program. Nevertheless, only a few smaller state enterprises in textiles, fishing, and petrochemicals were sold to local capitalists in the late 1960s under K. T. Li's charge. One obvious reason for this is that the state is reluctant to give up profitable enterprises, and the local capitalists are not interested in those with a deficit. In addition, the sale of state enterprises would cut down the positions for retired high ranking officials and officers as well as cause the problem of firing superfluous members. Moreover, the leverage of the economic officials to control the economy will be reduced after the sale. Most state officials in charge of the issue do not have the courage to break through the difficulties and the determination to get rid of the vested interests. Accordingly, the execution of the policy has been ineffective (Li and Ch'en, 1984b: 59-63).

Due to the increasing pressure from the local and transnational capitalists, as well as the consulting economists, the situation has been somewhat changed. The state has recently decided to allow local and transnational capitalists to run some businesses monopolized before by state enterprises, such as gas stations and the wine and tabacco businesses. The change signaled the rise of social forces on the island.

Fiscal and Monetary Policies

Following to the fundamental line of the 1950s, stability was still a major concern of the KMT's fiscal and monetary policies after the early 1960s. The overall slogan for economic development remained "growth with stability" or "stability in growth" (Wu, 1985: 24). A balanced budget and reasonable interest rates were the main measures to control the prices and encourage savings. Evan during the period of the Ten Projects, the state managed the budget such that it yielded a surplus. The continuity of monetary policy could also be learned from the continuity of the personnel of governor of the Central Bank of China. Since the early 1960s to the present, the post has been held by only three persons, namely, Hsu Peh-yuan, Yu Kuo-hwa, and Chang Chi-cheng. Among them, Yu Kuo-hwa had held the post for 15 years. If there was a change at all, it was perhaps a slightly greater emphasis on growth than before, impressed by the rapid growth of South Korea's economy. While there was no change in essence, there were two issues in the fiscal and monetary policies which are worth discussing here. The first is a tax reform program during 1968-70 and the second is a tripartite debate about the interest rate, money supply, and equity-debt ratio during 1981-82.

The tax reform program was a device to improve Taiwan's tax system and a prelude to raise more revenue for a series of development projects. As in many other LDCs, Taiwan's tax system was characterized by an excessive dependence on indirect taxes, which on the whole were not only regressive but also inelastic in yield as income rises. Ambiguity and obvious inequalities in the tax law also encouraged many business enterprises to evade the business income tax and thus keep its yield low. With income taxes relatively unproductive, indirect taxes produced nearly 80% of Taiwan's total tax revenue in the 1950s and 1960s. In the late 1960s, the state became convinced that if it was to play a more active role in the economy, especially if it was to affect savings or capital formation, the revenue system had to be improved and made more dependent on direct taxes (Ho, 1978: 241-242). At the same time, to upgrade the quality of human capital for the future economic development, the state decided to extend compulsory education from 6 years to 9 years since 1968, while a series of development projects, including several items in the Ten Projects, were being drafted. All of these needed a lot of money. A commission for reforming the tax system and increasing revenue was therefore set up in March, 1968.

The neoclassical consulting economists played an important role in the tax reform. In June, 1967, a conference on Taiwan's economic development was held in Taipei. Many American scholars, including the neoclassical consulting economists, were invited. Chiang Kai-shek payed much attention to it. After the meeting, Liu Ta-chung, Tsiang Sho-chieh, Anthony Koo, and John Fei were invited to stay in Taiwan for a few more weeks to study the current economic situation and offer their opinions directly to Chiang. President Chiang appreciated particularly the report by Liu Ta-chung about the regulation of national resources for economic development. Therefore, when C. K. Yen (Premier) recommended Liu to chair the Tax Reform Commission, the recommendation was not only agreed upon by K. T. Li (minister of Economic Affairs) and Yu Kuo-hwa (minister of Finance), but also supported by President Chiang (Li and Ch'en, 1984a: 181-182).

The Tax Reform Commission was set up as a super-ministry organization composed of the minister of Finance, the minister of Economic Affairs, the governor of the Central Bank of China, the vice chairman of the CIECD, and some other officials. Chiang Sho-chieh also participated in the commission. The reason to invite Liu from the United States back to Taiwan to chair the commission was to reduce the potential conflicts among the authorities concerned and make the reform program organizationally coherent. Just like the case of the Statute for Encouragement of Investment, the tax reform involved many different state departments with different interests. An outsider could take a more neutral stance. In addition, Liu had built a quantitative macroeconomic model for estimating economic growth and government budget, which could be applied on the tax reform. Moreover, with Chiang Kai-shek's trust in Liu, the tax reform could be carried out more effectively (Li and Ch'en, 1984b: 159-160).

The commission was dissolved in August, 1970 when it finished the task. Aside from 25 reform proposals and 19 research papers, the income tax law was revised and a new rate structure was promulgated. In effect, the tax reform reduced the tax burden on small businesses and individuals with relatively low income and increased the income tax on larger firms and persons with high income. More importantly, to reduce tax evasion, the state introduced a computerized system to process and scrutinize tax returns. As a result, the revenues from income taxes as a share of total revenue, after declining steadily for two decades, increased in the early 1970s. Partly because of the improved tax system, and partly because of the rapid expansion of manufacturing output and trade which increased the revenues from custom duties and commodity taxes, total tax revenue increased rapidly in the late 1960s and early 1970s (Ho, 1978: 242). Tables 7.2 and 7.3 illustrate these changes. The rise in revenue strengthened the confidence of the KMT state to embark on various development projects.

The tax reform both showed the strength and weakness of the KMT stae. On the one hand, it effectively improved the tax system to extract more revenues from rich tax payers while taking the burden off the poorer people. This clearly demonstrated the autonomy of the KMT state from the dominant classes and its capacity to control them. On the other hand, however, the state was not able to reform its tax administration successfully. Among the various proposals for tax reform, one crucial program was to raise significantly the salary of the tax administrators so as to increase the efficiency of tax collection and reduce corruption. But the proposal did not get much support due to the fear of stirring up anger in other state departments. Therefore, although the state was capable of coping with the opposition from those whom the tax reform affected (who tended to have higher economic status in the society), it seemed incapable of overcoming the obstruction within the very state apparatus.

The tripartite debate happened in a context when the world demand and the high energy prices were depressing Taiwan's external market and causing investments to lag on the island. The consulting economists were again the main actors. One side, led by Wang Tso-jung, advocated some relaxation of credit while professing concern for price stability and the undesirability of unbridled monetary expansion, arguing that the real rate of interest in Taiwan had been too high and had thus deterred investment. The other side, led by Tsiang Sho-chieh, stressed that the nominal rate of interest was high only because of continuing inflation, that inflation could not be controlled unless money supply was effectively curbed, that determination of the interest rate

Table 7.2
Tax and Monopoly Revenues

Unit: NT$ million

Fiscal Year	Total	Customs Duties	Commodity Tax	Income Tax	Others*
1954	4,352	1,041	409	388	2,514
1955	5,095	1,096	471	624	2,904
1956	5,879	1,209	583	532	3.555
1957	6,983	1,648	674	617	4,044
1958 **	7,538	1,823	802	749	4,164
1960 **	8,802	1,618	895	912	5,377
1961	9,554	1,823	1,066	981	5,684
1962	10,142	1,963	1,018	813	6,348
1963	11,254	2,242	1,452	768	6,792
1964	12,840	2,694	1,789	1,131	7,226
1965	15,247	3,477	2,074	1,365	8,331
1966	17,298	4,110	2,390	1,281	9,517
1967	19,531	4,447	2,936	1,376	10,772
1968	24,347	5,655	3,654	1,822	13,216
1969	32,760	7,405	5,657	2,547	17,151
1970	36,664	8,591	6,272	3,438	18,363

1971	40,685	9,059	6,999	4,517	20,110
1972	47,976	10,927	8,235	6,219	22,595
1973	60,727	14,364	11,419	7,732	27,212
1974	88,854	24,904	13,879	13,777	36,294
1975	97,504	23,527	14,018	16,373	43,596
1976	121,767	29,078	17,464	18,373	56,852
1977	139,306	32,023	19,538	22,527	65,218
1978	168,194	40,027	23,967	27,349	76,451
1979	220,521	53,597	32,761	35,694	98,469
1980	261,349	57,003	41,678	45,052	117,616
1981	315,049	57,781	49,202	58,147	149,919
1982	338,090	56,323	48,195	65,542	168,030
1983	342,379	55,570	48,171	65,016	173,622
1984	383,364	67,622	54,471	67,957	193,314
1985	394,846	66,873	54,573	75,889	197,511

* Other tax and monopoly revenues include salt tax, stamp tax, business tax, harbor dues, licence tax, land tax, slaughter tax, household tax, house tax, amusement tax, deeds tax, feast tax, and tobacco & wine monopoly revenue

** Fiscal year 1958 runs from July, 1958 to June, 1959 while fiscal year 1960 runs from July, 1960 due to the change in fiscal year system.

Source: CEPD, 1986: 167-168.

Table 7.3
Structure of Tax and Monopoly Revenues

Unit: %

Fiscal Year	Total	Customs Duties	Commodity Tax	Income Tax	Others*
1954	100.00	23.30	9.40	8.91	58.39
1955	100.00	21.51	9.36	12.25	56.88
1956	100.00	20.56	9.92	9.05	60.47
1957	100.00	23.60	9.65	8.84	57.91
1958 **	100.00	20.50	10.64	9.94	58.92
1960 **	100.00	18.38	10.17	10.36	61.09
1961	100.00	19.08	11.16	10.27	59.49
1962	100.00	19.36	10.03	8.02	62.59
1963	100.00	19.92	12.90	6.82	60.36
1964	100.00	20.98	13.93	8.81	56.28
1965	100.00	22.81	13.60	8.95	54.64
1966	100.00	23.76	13.82	7.41	55.01
1967	100.00	22.77	15.03	7.05	55.15
1968	100.00	23.23	15.01	7.48	54.28
1969	100.00	22.60	17.27	7.77	52.36
1970	100.00	23.43	17.10	9.38	50.09

1971	100.00	22.27	17.20	11.10	49.43
1972	100.00	22.78	17.16	12.96	47.10
1973	100.00	23.65	18.80	12.73	44.82
1974	100.00	28.03	15.62	15.51	40.84
1975	100.00	24.13	14.38	16.79	44.70
1976	100.00	23.88	14.34	15.09	46.69
1977	100.00	22.99	14.03	16.17	46.81
1978	100.00	23.80	14.25	16.26	45.69
1979	100.00	24.30	14.86	16.19	44.65
1980	100.00	21.81	15.95	17.24	45.00
1981	100.00	18.33	15.62	18.46	47.59
1982	100.00	16.66	14.26	19.39	49.69
1983	100.00	16.23	14.07	18.99	50.71
1984	100.00	17.64	14.21	17.73	50.42
1985	100.00	16.94	13.82	19.22	50.02

* Other tax and monopoly revenues include salt tax, stamp tax, business tax, harbor dues, licence tax, land tax, slaughter tax, household tax, house tax, amusement tax, deeds tax, feast tax, and tobacco & wine monopoly revenue.

** Fiscalyear 1958 runs from July, 1958 to June, 1959 while fiscal year 1960 runs from July, 1960 due to the change in fiscal year system.

Source: CEPD, 1986: 169-170.

should be left to the market, and that private investment would revive once inflation was arrested and the real rate of interest had fallen of its own accord. The latter group made two additional points: (1) Inflation has an uneven impact on persons at different levels of income, general speaking, favoring the rich; (2) Credit expansion would augment the debt-equity ratio of local firms, encourage local capitalists to borrow more money, largely from state-owned banks, for speculative activities rather than production, and hurt the principle of fair competition. Needless to say, most local capitalists supported the first group (Wang, 1983: 55-112; Tsiang, 1985: 65-152; Wu, 1985: 33).

The debate, originally raging in newspapers, eventually brought about an open forum on August 18, 1982, with a great deal of public fanfare and participation. *Kung-shang shih-pao* (Commercial Times), a branch of *Chung-kuo shih-pao,* sponsored the forum. Aside from Wang and Tsiang, 6 business leaders and 8 noted academic economists, including John Fei, were invited. The result was a report on the common understanding of both sides. In spite of some ambiguity and disagreements on certain issues, such as what specific industries should be encouraged through tax reductions and exemptions, when market forces alone should be allowed to determine the internal and external prices of money, the precise nature of the modern economic institutions to be established, and the relative roles of public versus private enterprises, they had consensus on the following aspects. Regarding industrial policy, they suggested that inducements of investment concentrate on production in order to promote productivity, that state control and protection on Taiwan's industries be replaced by free competition in order to strengthen competitiveness for exports, and that past vacillations of state policy in controlling exports and imports be replaced by an unambiguous and consistent policy toward free competition. Regarding fiscal policy, they advocated that the state keep striving to balance the budget, that the state expand the tax base, reduce the income tax rates, and grant selective tax exemption and reduction to enterprises, and that public spending be considered an appropriate short-run measure to stimulate aggregate demand. Regarding to monetary policy, they held that money supply should be controlled at 10 to 15 percent annually in order to arrest inflation, and that while the market conditions in Taiwan were yet unprepared, a perfectly competitive market could best determine interest and exchange rates and should be a long-term goal to aspire to. In sum, the two economists stressed the need for an appropriate social framework most compatible with economic development (The Commercial Times, 1982; Wu,

1985: 34-35).

The significance of this debate and its result was the surprising finding that there was in fact a vast ground on which the consulting economists were apparaently in agreement. Dramatically altering his previous view of upholding the state to intervene in the market with various fiscal and monetary instruments to promote economic transformation, Wang Tso-jung spoke in tune with the neoclassicalists by advising the stae to accelerate the pace for liberalizing the economy. For Wang, this change is actually consistent with his basic attitude twoard economic development, i.e., the state actions for facilitating economic transformation should correspond with the stages of national development. In the past, the KMT state was autonomous and capable enough to play a dominant role in developing the economy, so that the state should actively intervene in the market to create comparative advantage for the smaller local capitalists or even take part in the accumulation of capital by itself. Now since the society has grown and the private enterprises have demonstrated better efficiency, the state should reduce the intervention and shift its energy to establish and maintain an open economy allowing free and fair competition. The change in Wang's view to a certain extent portrays the evolution of, or at least express the expectation of many consulting economists and local capitalists on the relationship between the state and society on the island in recent years.

The state, however, has still enjoyed enough autonomy and capacities in its financial policy-making, by holding the banking system in its hands. The financial system in Taiwan is mainly composed of banks and non-bank financial institutions (such as investment and trust companies, bill finance companies, insurance companies, and the like). While the state controls almost all of the local banks, the non-bank financial institutions have largely remained private. But the non-bank financial institutions accounted for only 4.63% of the assets of Taiwan's major financial institutions by 1980. Besides, there were 21 branches of foreign banks at the end of 1980. Their scope of business, however, was strictly limited by the state and their assets accounted for only 3.96% of the assests of the major financial institutions (Chiu, 1983:326). The financial system is therefore dominated by the state-owned banks.

As Wade (1985b: 116-123) observes, there are several advantages for the state in controlling the financial sytem. It allows the state to tighten control over the flow of finance in and out of the country, to reduce financial instability, to guide sectoral mobility, and to build up the social coalitions needed to support the state's objectives. The cost, of course, is the inefficiency caused by the "rigidity" of its operation, as the situation in many other state-owned manufacturing enterprises. In parallell with the demand for sale of state enterprises, there has been a growing appeal for privatization of the banking system recently (Li and Ch'en, 1984b: 201-202). The state was nevertheless reluctant to do so. One main reason, according to Yu Kuo-hwa, was the fear of the very possibility that the banking sytem would fall in the hands of a few industrialists and become a tool for benefiting their own businesses (Ying, 1981). This philosophy of managing the economic transformation has still been relatively prevalent in the KMT state. Therefore, whereas South Korea denationalized most of its banks between 1980 and 1983, the KMT state has not shown signal of such a move in Taiwan so far. However, this by no means implies that the KMT state has never adopted any measure to liberalize the financial system.

The thrust of pushing the KMT state to liberalize the financial sytem mainly came from abroad. The growing surplus of foreign exchange reserve caused the crisis of excessive money supply as well as the wrath of Taiwan's major trading partner, namely, the United States. The coming reversion of Hong Kong to the PRC resulted in capital outflow and gave Taipei a chance to take over Hong Kong's status as the business center of East Asia in the future. Owing to these factors, the KMT state made several moves to cater to the new situation since 1982. The measures included an offshore banking unit, a unit trust scheme for allowing foreign capital to take equity positions indirectly in Taiwanese companies, a venture capital scheme, a market for bankers' acceptances, permission from the military to allow financial data to leave the country by high-speed computer transmission (this had long been resisted because it is difficult to monitor the content of what is sent by this method), and several other related schemes. In 1983, the Ministry of Finance announced that foreign banks could accept time deposits for up to six months in local currency, on condition that the amount of deposits accepted did not exceed 12.5 times the amount of capitalization already remitted into the country by the bank (Wade, 1985b: 114-115).

These moves did not effectively solve the problem of excessive foreign exchange reserve. Because of the continuous growth of exports and the stagnation of imports (mainly due to the decline of domestic capital accumulation which in turn resulted in the stagnation of the import of equipment and raw materials) the reserve mounted to $50 billion by 1986 and may reach to $70 billion, the world's largest, at the end of 1987. There was a heated appeal from the society and within the state apparatus for further loosening up the controls of foreign exchange. But a force within the state apparatus, mainly composed of the senior officials who were contemporaries of Chiang Kai-shek, opposed the lifting of the controls. Premier Yu apparently dared not fight against this force, so it was left to Chiang Ching-kuo to break through the question. On March 14, 1987, President Chiang ordered his top officials to speed the liberalization of Taiwan's financial policy. Two weeks later, Premier Yu announced a milestone of financial policy-that the state would lift the controls to allow foreign exchange retained by the people personally as well as in and out of the country freely (Shao, Holstein and Dryden, 1987: 47). Parelelling the liberalization of financial policy, there has also been a trend to liberalize the KMT's foreign trade policy which we are to discuss in the next section.

Foreign Trade Policy

An outward-oriented trade policy has been consistently and persistenly held by the KMT state since the early 1960s. After the Foreign Exchange and Trade Reform, which devalued the exchange rate and liberalized foreign trade, export expansion gradually became a decisive factor in Taiwan's economic growth. Since the early 1970s, its importance outweighed even domestic expansion. Increased market opportunities abroad, particularly for labor-intensive products, created hundreds of thousands of jobs, despite advancements in labor productivity, enabling Taiwan to reach full employment and create the miraculous achievement of "growth with equity" (Kuo, Ranis and Fei, 1981: 136). Although devaluation coupled with trade liberalization had obviously brought great success to the economy of Taiwan, there nevertheless remained an undercurrent of protectionism among the economic policy makers and bureaucrats.

According to Tsiang Sho-chieh, protectionist sentiment was particularly prevalent among the industrial policymakers, most of whom were engineers by training. For these officials, the development of a new industry at home constituted a worthy achievement in and of itself, regardless of its overall economic contributions and opportunity costs. Considerations of comparative costs meant little to them. They did not regard the spectacular increase in the volume of trade and real income as the results of the exchange reforms and trade liberalization, but attributed the success entirely to exogenous causes, such as unprecedented worldwide prosperity in the 1960s, etc. Because of the existence of such a strong protectionist undercurrent among the economic policy makers and bureaucrats, any liberalizing reform introduced upon the recommendations of outside experts tended to be compromised or adulterated with protectionist measures (Tsiang, Chen and Hsieh, 1985: 6). Although his argument might be one-sided and the gains and losses of the policy are debatable, Tsiang is right in pointing out the fact that there was an undercurrent of protectionism in the KMT state's foreign trade policy.

Since 1962 tariff barriers and non-tariff barriers have replaced foreign exchange control as the most powerful instruments of trade policy. When substantial devaluations of the exchange rate were carried out through the reform during the turning-point period, the very high tariff structure in Taiwan was essentially untouched. Furthermore, the abolition of quota restrictions on permissible imports in 1958 was countered in July, 1960 with the promulgation of the Criteria Governing the Control of Imports by the FETCC. Article 4 of the criteria specified that under the following conditions the FETCC could reclassify any commodity, which was produced domestically in sufficient quantity to meet domestic demand, from a permissible import to a controlled import for the purpose of economizing on the nation's foreign exchange spending: (1) The quality of the domestic product met international standards or the Chinese national standard as ascertained by official inspection; (2) The ex-factory price of the domestic product was not higher than the cost of importing similar products by a certain specified percentage (this percentage was 25% in 1960, 15% in 1964, 10% in 1968, 6% in 1971, and was finally eliminated in 1979); (3) The cost of imported raw materials required for the manufacture of the product did not exceed 70% of the total production cost (Tsiang, Chen and Hsieh, 1985: 7).

For a neoclassical economist like Chiang Sho-chieh, this was a very pernicious regulation because it would enable any domestic industry big enough to supply the whole domestic market to shut out foreign competion that would terribly distort resource use. Fortunately, petitions for the reclassification of imports from the permissible to the controlled category have remained subject to the administrative approval of the relevant authorities, and so far there have not been signs of gross abuse of this discretionary power. The ratio of controlled and prohibited imports to total imports in terms of number of items was 44.0% in 1960, 45.7% in 1966, and 42.9% in 1970. It sharply declined to 17.9% in 1972, 2.3% in 1974, and roughly maintained at the same level thereafter. The sharp decline in the number of controlled and prohibited imports after 1970 was due mainly to the trade surplus and to an emerging worldwide shortage of industrial raw materials both of which had the effect to stir up inflation and pushed the state to loosen up the control (Tsiang, Chen and Hsieh, 1985: 7-8).

It must be noted that all permissible imports were not, all still are not, really permitted to be imported freely without a license from the Ministry of Economic Affairs or the agencies it delegates to issue import licenses. In some cases, approval for permissible imports is automatic upon petition; in other cases, it is by no means automatic and without delay. Some of the permissible items imported from Japan, the country enjoying largest surplus in the bilateral trade with Taiwan, such as automobiles, trucks, forklifts, portland cement, rubber tires, and electronic products, for example, have been put under control from time to time. In the same vein, when the economic policymakers began to switch the strategy for economic development from the labor-intensive approach to capital- and technology-intensive approach, some of the capital- and technology-intensive manufacturing goods were shifted from permissible to controlled or prohibited categories.

Both the economic officials and local capitalists lobbied for employing non-tariff barriers, though the economic policy makers and bureaucrats seem to have more leverage. A quantitative study on the political-economic aspects of trade policy formulation in Taiwan discovers that for those imported goods that are used as raw materials, intermediate input, and equipment, or have a higher share of labor cost in value-added, the non-tariff barrier protection is low. In contrast, for those imported goods that have a higher import penetration, or are in the categories of public enterprises and primary sector, the non-tariff barrier protection is high. The study also reports that those local capitalists who had special connections with high level state officials seemed to play an effective role in influencing policy formulation concerning non-tariff protection. However, the state still maintained a certain degree of autonomy in adopting non-tariff protection, reflected by the fact that the state attempted to benefit the majority of the producers rather than favoring the few biggest firms (Chang, 1986: 170-172).

In addition to the outright measures of import control, tariff barriers have also been used as a more subtle way to protect Taiwan's domestic industries. As mentioned earlier, when the KMT state substantially devalued the New Taiwan dollar in the late 1950s and early 1960s, tariff protection was kept intact. As a matter of fact, when the state dramatically reduced the number of controlled import goods in the early 1970s, it raised the tariff rates on those decontrolled commodities while simultaneously offseting the effect of the reduction. In an aggregate perspective, the tariff protection has been gradually lowered since the early 1960s. The average tariff burden on imports, as measured by the ratio of total tariff revenue to the total value of imports before tariffs, was as high as 31.1% in 1958, but thereafter declined steadily. It became 16.8% in 1960, 16.5% in 1965, 16.1% in 1970, 12.4% in 1975, 9.6% in 1980, and 7.1% in 1984 (Tsiang, Chen and Hsieh, 1985: 11-13).

The decline of the ratio on the average tariff burden, however, is not entirely satisfactory as an indicator of tariff protection, because the average burden measured in this way is a weighted average of the tariff rates, with the volume of each import item as the weight. Therefore if a tariff rate is so high as to cut off the import of the item completely, the weight will be 0 and the strong protective effect will not be shown in the ratio. A more detailed study, which examines the frequency distribution of actual tariffs on all permissible import items, reveals that there has been an undeniable trend toward a more liberal trade policy, but the change is less significant than the effect shown by the average tariff burden (Tsiang, Chen and Hsieh, 1985: 12-15).

In contrast to the case of non-tariff barriers, the employment of tariff barriers is dominated by the economic officials whereas the influence of local capitalists is nonsignificant, according to the quantitative study. The structure of tariff protection is that the higher the ratio of products used as final demand, and the higher the export share are, the more likely it is that protection will occur. Inversely, the higher the ratio of import goods used as intermediate input and capital formation, labor share in value-added and import penetration is, the less likely protection will be employed. The few biggest firms concerned, special political connection, and transnational capitalists have no significant weight in shaping the tariff structure. One explanation of the findings is that the decision-making process for the tariff barriers concerns the authorities more, whereas import control is basically managed singly by the FETCC before and the Ministry of Economic Affairs later and is easier to penetrate. Also, the policy-making concerning tariff structure had been kept secret until 1982, while the public has been able to apply for non-tariff barriers for a long time (Chang, 1985: 170-172).

Roughly speaking, we can conclude that the KMT state formulated trade policy rather autonomously, especially that concerned with tariff protection, and did not act as the instrument of either local capitalists or transnational capitalists. Nevertheless, there has been some signals implying the increase of the influence of local capitalists on tariff protection. Due to the rapid increase of trade surplus since around 1984, many experts, including the neoclassicialists and Wang Tso-jung, have begun to urge the state to accelerate the pace of trade liberalization, especially to lower tariff rates. But the authorities concerned responded to the appeal rather slowly and reluctantly. In addition to the considerations of tariff revenue and economic stability by the state officials, it seems quite obvious that the resistance also came from the local capitalists benefiting from tariff protection.

The pressure from the United States again plays a major role in pushing the KMT state to accelerate trade liberalization. Since the early 1980s, through a series of trade negotiations, the U.S. had demanded that Taiwan lower tariff rates and open the market to U.S. agricultural products and service industries, such as banking, advertising, marketing, insurance, management, and investment service. American beer, wine, and tabacco, as well as service industries, such as insurance, supermarket, and fast food, have thus entered the island in recent years. In addition, under the pressure of the U.S., the KMT state took action to protect intellectual and industrial property rights and eliminated counterfeiting products. Taiwan also dispatches buying teams to the U.S. to purchase agricultural products, consumer goods, and equipment (Hsu, 1985: 8-9). But the measures so far have not effectively reduced the trade surplus in favor of Taiwan. Consequently, Taiwan becomes the No. 2 target, after Japan, of the American campaign for eliminating "unfair trade." American officials accuse Taiwan of deliberately protecting its market mainly through unreasonable high tariff rates. They threat to impose higher import duties on Taiwan's products as a revenge. They also demand the raise of the exchange rate of the New Taiwan dollar to the U.S. dollar. Public opinion in Taiwan, including the consulting economists, some new blood in the Legislative Yuan, and the exporting businessmen, are very worried and blame the authorities concerned for their inefficacy in coping with the problem. As a result, the state has speed the pace for lowering tariff rates in order to alleviate the pressure from the U.S. since late 1986.

The KMT State's Changing Role in Taiwan's Economic Transformation

The role of the KMT state in Taiwan's economic transformation has changed significantly, particularly in the recent years. For the last thirty-seven years, the KMT state had basically acted as an autonomous corporate body in regulating Taiwan's development. Under its governance, the people on the island created many miraculous accomplishments. However, as Rueschemeyer and Evans (1985: 49) argue, the success of the state in building its role as a corporate actor may undercut its ability to remain autonomous and effective state intervention may increase the extent to which the state becomes an arena of social conflict. There are strong antinomies in the interaction between increasing state intervention, state autonomy, and state capacity. Indeed, in the case of Taiwan, we discover the validity of this statement. In this section, we would like to show its significance by investigating the evolution of the role of the KMT state after the early sixties in terms of the extent to which the state realized its role as corporate actor, the degree to which it may be considered autonomous from the dominant class, and its efficacy as an agent of economic transformation.

The Change of the KMT State As a Corporate Actor

Roughly speaking, the KMT state's economic policy-making structure after the early sixties can be divided into three periods: the 1960s, the 1970s, and the 1980s. In the 1960s, based on the foundation and following the broad lines set up by the reforms during the turning-point period, the economy moved forward speedily and smoothly. International political and economic situations were conducive to the KMT's outward-oriented and labor-intensive development strategy. In the state apparatus, the deaths of K. Y. Yin and Ch'en Ch'eng somehow dampened the vigor of the KMT state in managing Taiwan's economic transformation. But Chiang Kai-shek still stood firmly at the center of power and backed the economic policy makers. Meanwhile, with C. K. Yen's help, Chiang Ching-kuo gradually emerged as a new leader of the state. The American advisors left with the termination of U.S. aid but American private consulting companies somehow succeed them in role of advisors. The neoclassical consulting economists played an important role in advocating the labor-intensive approach for economic development and carrying out the tax reform. In the society, a group of local capitalists mainly in textiles and electrical machinery were emerging with the rapid development of export-oriented industrialization. Because of the labor-intensive nature, most of the local firms were small- and medium-size enterprises. The capacity of the state in dominating the society and controlling the local capitalists was shown in the tax reform, which was made to extract more revenues from the rich while alleviating the burden of the poor. Transnational capitalists entered the arena during the latter half of the 1960s, while the state was strong enough to confine their operation. Favorable external circumstances, an autonomous and capable state, and a docile society made up the context in which economic policies were formulated and executed.

External political and economic circumstances began a turn for the worse the early 1970s. The turmoil of the world economy and diplomatic frustration gave the island a series of shocks. Under the strong leadership of Chiang Ching-kuo, the state and society cooperated reasonably well to overcome the challenges. Somewhat at odds with the neoclassicialists, the state revised the development strategy by putting more weight on capital- and technology-intensive industries. The revision was a reflection of the top politicala leadership's expectation to boost the morale of the people amid the increasingly disadvantageous external environment and his ambition to accelerate Taiwan's economic transformation. The revision also reflected the growing strength of the economy. In contrast to South Korea where the state actively intervened in the creation of chaebol (Kim, 1987a; Kim, 1987b), the KMT state on Taiwan managed the revised strategy less aggressively. The labor-intensive small- and medium-size enterprises were allowed to thrive, while the state tried to invent local entrepreneurs in certain heavy industries, such as steel and shipbuilding. The attempt did not succeed partly owing to the external impacts and not-very-bright prospects of the industries which deterred local capitalists from commiting long-term investment, and partly owing to some economic policy makers' distrust in large private enterprises. The KMT state gradually changed its policy in the agricultural sector from extraction to subsidy. Transnational capitalists kept coming to the island despite Taiwan's increasing diplomatic isolation. For this period, the economic policies were formulated and executed in the context of a changeable and increasingly unfavorable external environment, a stronger but controllable society, and a state which was still autonomous and capable enough to regulate the economy.

Both the internal structuring of the state and surrounding social structure have undergone remarkable changes since Taiwan entered the

1980s. Due to his health, Chiang Ching-kuo has no longer taken charge of day-to-day affairs of the state since the late 1970s. The power of economic policy-making was delegated to his top aides in economic and financial affairs, namely, Sun Yun-suan, Yu Kuo-hwa, and K. T. Li. The KMT state's economic policy-making demonstrated reasonable activeness and coherence under Premier Sun's charge. The economic policy-making became slow and less coherent in Yu's cabinet. In addition to Yu's conservativeness and indecision, a more important factor was the tremendous change of the surrounding social structure intra-nationally and internationally.

Internationally, the threat from the other side of the Taiwan Strait, the stalemate of diplomatic isolation in the world politics, the protectionism from important trading partners, and the intensified competition from other LDCs made the external environment even more disadvantageous than the 1970s and added more challenges to the state. In the meantime, as mentioned above, the force of transnational capitalists has shown a tendency to be stronger. Their presence was seen as a means to break through Taiwan's diplomatic isolation and upgrade Taiwan's industrial structure. These functions gave them more leverage in bargaining with the KMT state, though they were not so significant in capital formation given Taiwan's abundant domestic savings.

Intra-nationally, local capitalists clearly demonstrated their strength in recent years. Through the accumulation of wealth, the enlargement of election, the establishment of various pressure groups, and certain special connection with high ranking economic officials, the local capitalists increasingly exerted upon their influence on economic policy-making. The concrete example was an *ad hoc* Economic Reform Committee during April to November, 1985. Facing the decline in private investment, the impact of the Cathay scandal, the intensified competition and protection in the international market, the KMT state set up the committee, composed of state officials, scholars, and businessmen, to seek solutions collectively.

The committee was divided into 5 subcommittees: Tax, Finance, Industry, Trade, and Economic Administration. Two leading entrepreneurs, Wang Yung-ch'ing (chairman of Board of Directors of Formosa Plastics Corporation; Formosa Chemical & Fiber Corporation; Cyma Plywood & Lumber Company; and Ming-chi Institute of Technology) and Koo Chen-fu (member of CSC; chairman and president of Taiwan Cement Corporation; chairman of Chinese Investment & Trust Company; Taiwan Polypropylene Company; and Chinese National Association of Industry and Commerce) were invited to chair the Subcommittees of Industry and Trade respectively. In addition, many business leaders attended the meetings. Their criticism of state policies were fully exposed to the public through mass media and aroused heated response; many of their opinions for economic development were accepted as reform proposals. This was a sharp contrast to the situation in the 1950s and 60s and clearly reflected the changing status and weight of local capitalists in the society and economic policy-making.

Apart from the local capitalists, the consulting economists were another active group in the Economic Reform Committee. Tsiang Sho-chieh was invited to chair the Subcommittee of Tax and Wang Tso-jung was one of the attendants who attracted most attention. Many other scholars also used this opportunity to express their viewpoints. In fact, as noted earlier, the influence of the consulting economists has extended due to the rapid development of mass media. The tripartite debate about the interest rate, money supply, and equity-debt ratio during 1981-82 was another evidence.

In parallel with the rise of local capitalists and consulting economists, other social forces have also been emerging on the island and gradually increasing their weight on economic policy-making. These forces included the middle class and the workers.

There have been some debates on the size of the middle class on Taiwan due to different definitions, but all scholars agree that a middle class exists on the island and has been getting stronger (Wen, 1985; Hsiao, 1986). Roughly speaking, they shared about one-third of the labor force in recent years. Since they enjoyed a better life than most lower class people, they were the supporters of the existent sociopolitical sturcture. Basically they constituted a stabilizing force in Taiwan's socioeconomic transformation. But their higher expectation concerning the quality of life on the other hand led them to be a force of moderate reform. The rise of social movements for consumerism and environmental conservation since the early 1980s implied the growth of this social force.

The people on Taiwan had payed little attention to the idea of consumer rights before the late 1970s. In 1973, Sun Yun-suan, the minister of Economic Affairs at the time, wrote an article promoting consumerism. This was the first important printed comment about consumerism on Taiwan. But it did not arouse much attention and the state did not have further action to continue this appeal. In 1979, a case of food-poisoning which affected hundreds of people was exposed by the media; the cause of the food-poisoning accident was a chemical ingredient, which, although strictly limited in many countries, was still abused by Taiwan's businessmen in many products. The case arouse a lot of attention. The arrogant attitude of the local firms and authorities concerned in dealing with the case provoked widespread resentment in society. Facilitated by the reports and comments of the mass media, consumerism became a hot public issue. In November, 1980, the private Consumer's Foundation of the Republic of China was set up. Many scholars, lawyers, and professionals participated in the foundation. It then became one of most active social organizations in the Taiwanese society (Hsiao, Chen and Lei, 1982).

The KMT state's attitude toward the movement of consumerism was first cool and then more ethusiastic. Originally, the KMT state was worried that the movement would result in more conflicts between the producer and the consumer, which in turn many have a serious impacts on social stability. At the same time, some of the KMT officials suspected that the movement might be manipulated by the opposition force. And the state agencies responsible for the control of the quality of consumer goods felt that some of the functions of the Consumers' Foundation invaded their authority. However, when the KMT realized that the movement had won widespread support in society, it gradually changed its attitude. Therefore, when the National Health Administration and some local food manufacturers accused the Consumers' Foundation of acting beyond its authority in late 1984, the KMT kept a neutral stance in the dispute. The suggestion to disband the foundation by a KMT member in the Legislative Yuan was rejected. Several KMT members in the Legislative Yuan, the Taiwan Provincial Assembly, and the Taipei City Council spoke in favor of the foundation. And the KMT also allowed the party-owned newspapers and television networks to give favorable comments on the foundation's activities.

The appeal of environmental conservation was another social movement started only in recent years. Its impact was even stronger than the consumerism. While the interests of the state and the consumer were not very difficult to combine, the environmental conservation movement not only contradicted the interests of many local and transnational capitalists but also some of the state's development projects. A concrete example of this clash was the cancellation of a plan to build the fourth nuclear power plant on Taiwan. By May, 1984, Taiwan had built three nuclear power plants and the state had planned to build a fourth one. At the same time, influenced by the environmental conservation movement in the advanced industrial countries, there was an appeal in society for limiting the building of nuclear power plants.

The appeal went through the mass media, the Control Yuan, and the Legislative Yuan. The state officials made efforts to convince the representatives in the elective offices and the public that the building of a fourth nuclear power plant was necessary to ensure a steady supply of electricity and to maintain economic development. They also assured the people that nuclear power plants in Taiwan were absolutely safe. However, on July 7, 1985, a fire broke out at a nuclear power plant is southern Taiwan. The cause of the fire was a faulty turbine in a generator installed by the General Electric Company of the United States. No one was injured by the fire, but it provoked tremendous criticism in society. State officials still tried to continue the plan, but they eventually gave up because of society's strong objection. In addition to the state officials, another loser in the event was the American firms involved in the plan. Due to the depression of the business in the U.S., some American nuclear power companies were eager for this opportunity. They tried to push forward the plan through various channels, including through American politicians who had good relations with Taipei. Yet their influence was overwhelmed by the public opinion in the Taiwanese society in this case.

Still another example shows the strength of the environmental conservation movement. This time the main object was the U.S. company Du Pont. The American company was planning to build a titanium dioxide plant in the middle of Taiwan's west coast in 1985. Construction of the $ 168 million plant was scheduled to start in early 1986. This was the biggest foreign investment application case in recent years. Even though it was welcomed by the economic policy makers, the local people were afraid of the pollution the plant may bring about. Do Pont tried to convince local people about the safety of the plant by many measures, but did not succeed. In June, 1986, hundreds of people rallied to protest the plan. The residents also picketed government offices in Taipei, and handed out leaflets denouncing transnational corporations. Many politicians, especially the opposition force, took advantage of the protests to make propoganda. Amid the decline of domestic capital formation, the KMT state originally was inclined to support Do Pont, although it then changed its attitude when the opposition to the plant grew stronger. Following the protests, it stressed its commitment to pollution control by announcing that the state would quadruple its spending on environmental conservation in the next budget year. Do Pont finally gave up the plan in late 1986. It is said that one of the forces involved in the event was Wang Yung-ch'ing, the owner of Formosa Plastics and the biggest conglomarate on Taiwan. He was planning at the same time to build a titanium dioxide plant in cooperation with another American firm, Kerr Mcgee. The withdrawal of Du Pont could make his plan proceed easier. Having started as a middle class movement, environmental conservation has now become a force blended with a variety of social groups. Many lower class people also took part in the movement to protect their residential environment.

Along with the movements for consumer rights and environmental conservation, the labor movement has been getting stronger since the early 1980s. Labor movement on Taiwan was under right control of the KMT state (Galenson, 1979; Johnson, 1985: 76). To provide a favorable investment climate for local and transnational capitalists, the KMT state actively intervened in the labor-management relationship. Strikes and collective bargaining were prohibited under martial law; the labor unions were under strong KMT supervision, including party controls over the selection of the union leaders and all union activities. In addition, to prevent the Taiwanese society from the penetration of communism, the KMT state suppressed any discussion encouraging class consciousness or struggle. Based on Sun Yat-senism, it upheld an idea that all of the social groups or classes should cooperate with each other and that the state is the guardian of the universal interests of the whole society. This effort of eliminating class consciousness, accompanied with high social mobility for the proletariat to attain middle-class or even bourgeoisie status through the "growth with equity," deeply affected Taiwan's political culture. There was no class-based political activity on the island (Gold, 1986: 119). Moreover, the high turnover rate, the high proportion of female labor, the part-time farmer's status, and the conservative character inherited from small-farmer's family retarded the activism of Taiwan's workers. Consequently, Taiwan's economic development was relatively free from the conflict between the worker and the employer. This situation had lasted for more than two decades since 1949.

The rapid economic development began to affect the stable labor-management relationship in the early 1970s. Because of the growth of urban workers and the spread of education, interest in unionism and labor-management dispute incrased. The economic recession caused by the first oil crisis made the problem more manifest. The KMT state recognized this change and intended to do something to deal with the problem. In 1974, the Legislative Yuan asked the Executive Yuan to draft a Labor Standards Law. The Executive Yuan Council in turn assigned the task to the Ministry of the Interior, which was in charge of labor affairs. The law was expected to provide minimum standards of labor conditions as well as protect workers' rights and interests. The Ministry of the Interior finished the draft by the end of 1974. Owing to the opposition of the economic bureaucracy, which was worried about the impact of this law on investment climate, the draft did not get sent to the Legislative Yuan immediately. From 1975 to 1982, there was a struggle for the enactment of the law in the state apparatus. The Ministry of the Interior and some legislators elected by labor unions repeatedly urged the Executive Yuan to send the draft to the Legislative Yuan. But the economic bureaucracy and some other legislators tried to halt the bill in the Executive Yuan. During this period, Taiwan's economy underwent further development and another recession caused by the second oil crisis. The impact of unemployment and labor-management dispute resulting from economic recession became more severe this time. Meanwhile, the politicians of the opposition were backed by the workers. Facing the pressure, the KMT state finally increased its coalition with the workers and balance of the force of capitalists. In early 1982, the bill was sent to the Legislative Yuan.

The discussion of the Labor Standard Law in the Legislative Yuan entailed the rivalry between different state units and social forces. The officials from the Ministry of the Interior, the legislators elected by the labor unions, and some scholars advocated the protection of workers' rights and interests. The officials from the economic bureaucracy, the legislators representing the local capitalists, and some other scholars tried to lower those standards. Many local capitalists appealed to the authorities concerned and to the mass media to slow the process of lawmaking. After a few revisions and several delays, the law was eventually promulgated on August 1, 1984. Hence, the KMT state showed its determination to care for the workers, but it also made a compromise with the local capitalists about certain terms in the law.

Further important actions to win the workers' allegiance were adopted by the KMT state following the enactment of the Labor Standards Law. The lawmaking greatly aroused the workers' consciousness about their rights and interests. In addition to the benefits provided by the law, they then asked for more autonomy for their unions. In October, 1986, President Chiang Ching-kuo announced that due to the progress of social conditions on Taiwan, the KMT state planned to lift the martial law, which had been in effect since 1949. After the lifting of martial law in 1987, workers will have the right to strike. But Taiwan's workers wanted more. At the end of 1986, the KMT lost two seats for workers' representative in the National Assembly to the opposition force, the newly formed Democratic Progressive Party. The two candidates nominated by the KMT were party-arranged leaders of labor unions. The defeat shocked the KMT. As a result, the KMT decided to separate the authority concerning labor affairs from the Ministry of the Interior and upgrade it to a special council with ministry status. There are also signals that the KMT will loosen up its intervention in unions' activities. The force of labor unions is expected to extend remarkably in the near future.

After thirty years of playing the role of the corporate actor, the KMT state has since the early 1980 gradually became an arena of social conflict. In the past, as a bourgeoisie, a proletariat, and a modern intelligentsia emerged, the KMT incorporated them into party-dominated associations or prevented them from forming class consciousness or spontaneously organizing (Gold, 1986: 127-128). These efforts had been quite successful. But as Rueschemeyer and Evans (1985: 69) point out, increased penetration of civil society by the state activates political responses and increases the likelihood that societal interests will attempt to invade and divide the state. In other words, as the state more deeply penetrates civil society, the contradictions of civil society will undermine the state's coherence as a corporate actor. According to the events mentioned above and corresponding actions by the KMT state, we do discover this tendency amid the rise of various social forces on Taiwan in recent years.

The Decrease of the KMT State's Autonomy

The KMT state's successful intervention in promoting Taiwan's economic transformation has led to the decrease of its autonomy from the dominant class on the island. Now it has become clearer that various social forces have been able to penetrate the formulation and to distort the execution of economic policy to a certain degree, the influence of the dominant class deserve more attention. After all, they are supposed to be the most powerful group in influencing state policy. Two recent events show the strength of the local capitalists.

The first case was the change of state policy concerning the development of the automobile industry. Beginning in 1980, impressed by the development of automobile industry in South Korea, the state attempted to create a comparative advantage for Taiwan in automobiles, following the example of Japan and Korea. By that time, there were already six car makers on the island, though each was too small to benefit from efficient mass production. While the Korean government had limited the number of car makers in South Korea to three large producers, the KMT state was not able to do so on Taiwan. Therefore, the plan was to build another big automobile plant with the capacity to produce three hundred thousand cars a year. The state negotiated with several Japanese makers to set up a tri-pe-style joint venture with China Steel Corporation and private interests. In December, 1982, the auto deal was closed with Toyota. The minister of Economic Affairs Chao Yao-tung supported the plan strongly.

The deal naturally provoked the opposition of the existing car makers and their foreign partners. Through their spokesmen in the state apparatus and the mass media, they launched a series of lobby actions to obstruct the plan. Partly due to some disagreements over the terms of cooperation, but largely due to the opposition from other units in the state apparatus and the local car makers, the deal was broken off in the summer of 1984. In contrast to the development of the textile industry in the 1950s, the effort to create an automobile industry was frustrated. Moreover, Chao was shifted to CEPD in the midst of negotiations. The move was seen as a promotion in appearance but a demotion in fact. Similar to the case of K. Y. Yin, Chao's aggressive style made enemies in the state and society. In addition to Premier Yu's dislike, his transfer was believed to be somewhat related to the opposition from the local capitalists.

The second example was the scandal related to the bankruptcy of Cathay Plastics. The Cathay conglomerate was one of the leading private enterprises on Taiwan, owned by the Ts'ai family. Its business covered real estate, construction, hotel, insurance, and plastics. The major figure in this scandal was Ts'ai Ch'en-chou, a KMT member in the Legislative Yuan and the owner of Cathay Plastics. Ts'ai's capital for running the plastic plant was mainly from a local credit cooperative controlled by his family. Since the late 1970s, he began to make money by various illegal measures to make up for the loss in his plastics plant. The authorities concerned learned of his doings in 1979 and administrated punishment; however, owing to his connections with some high ranking party cadres and state officials, the punishment was trivial. He still continued his operations and extended his connection with party cadres and state officials through bribes. The authorities had warned him again and again but never really adopted any serious measures. Meanwhile, the losses of Cathay Plastics became larger and larger. He then decided to participate in politics to consolidate his influence in the party and the state. In 1983, he was nominated by the KMT and then elected legislator for Taipei City. In the Legislative Yuan, he organized a small faction with the other twelve newly-elected legislators. They tried to revise the law concerning the regulation of the banking system in order to save his business. Due to the opposition of the old members, their plan did not succeed.

The scandal was disclosed finally in the early 1985. The cooperative was taken over by the Ministry of Finance and Ts'ai Ch'en-chou was arrested. The investigation discovered that the debt of the plastic plant and illegal loans of the credit cooperative amounted to about 300 million U.S. dollars. Thousands of investors and hundreds of employees of the cooperative and the plant were hurt by the bankruptcy. This bankruptcy was the biggest disaster since the retreat of the KMT state to Taiwan. What is even worse was that a number of high ranking officials were involved in the scandal. No timely measures to prevent the problem from getting worse had been adopted due to the interference of these officials. The scandal consequently resulted in the ousting of the secretary-general of the KMT, the ministers of Finance, the minister of Economic Affairs, and several lower-ranking officials. The scandal was seen as a signal of the crisis of the KMT state's autonomy from the local capitalists.

Although the scandal exposed the problem of the decrease of the KMT state's autonomy, it also showed that the KMT state's autonomy was only partly eroded. In spite of the warnings, Ts'ai was too confident of his connections in the state apparatus to worry. But he apparently overestimated his influence, for the KMT state was still autonomous enough to terminate his adventure. It is said that the KMT state also intended to use the case of Ts'ai to warn those haughty and lawless local capitalists. In fact, as we have reiterated, government-business relations on Taiwan differed substantially from those in Japan and Korea. On the one hand, Johnson (1982) is right in arguing that Taiwan has followed the Japanese model, which differs from the communist dictatorship model of development as well as from the Western market economies. In this model, the "state's role in the economy is shared with the private sector, and both the public and private sectors have perfected means to make the market work for developmental goals" (Johnson, 1982: viii). On the other hand, the KMT state has made considerable modifications in applying this developmental model on the island. Whereas regularized consultations between the MITI and industry representatives helped to determine economic policy in Japan and the Korean government employed a more commandist approach to regulate Korea's economy, the KMT state's economic policy makers retained a relatively aloof posture. Although economic officials did meet with the local capitalists to push state policy or pick some favorites, Taiwan's private sector has been much more anarchic and self-directed than its counterpats in Japan or South Korea. In this sense, when the rise of social forces reduced the KMT state's autonomy, the momentum to make the KMT state an arena of social conflict was stronger than the momentum towards making it an instrument of the dominant class.

The Change of the KMT State as an Agent of Economic Transformation

Accompanying the decrease of state autonomy, the capacities of the KMT state in regulating Taiwan's economic transformation has shrunk *vis-a-vis* the rise of social forces. In addition to the examples noted above, such as the cancellation of the fourth nuclear power plant and the auto deal, some more examples demonstrate the incapacity of the KMT state to direct Taiwan's economy in recent years.

The first one was the effort to persuade Taiwan's businessmen to merge companies. Impressed by the Korean government's success in promoting competitiveness through the merging of companies. Taiwan's officials believed that the island could be more competitive if enterprises would merge and form bigger, more efficient units. But the effort has had little success so far. Aside from the case of the automobile industry noted above, another case was that of the steel industry. As chairman of the state-run China Steel Corp. in the late 1970s, Chao Yao-tung tried to persuade the operators of some 200 local steel furnaces to combine into three or four large plants. After many meetings stretching over two years, Chao finally gave up. None of the businessmen would relinquish his independence. One obstacle was Taiwan's rugged individualism. Most people on the island wanted to be their own boss. Another factor was that the KMT state lacked effective policy instrument to regulate and Taiwan's small- and medium-size enterprises. Most of the small- and medium-size enterprises did not rely on the state-owned banking system for their capital. They borrowed from their relatives, friends, or black market money changers. The strong saving capacity in the Taiwanese society, derived from the "growth with equity," provided these local firms with abundant idle capital. Although the interest rates usually were higher than the public loans, the private loans were free from the red tape of the banks.

Moreover, owing to the rise of the opposition force on the island and the increasing pressure from the other side of the Taiwan Strait, the KMT state had cruples to adopt radical measures that could lead to strong resentment. Economic stability and social order were always the KMT state's overriding objectives.

Similar situations developed in other cases. For example, in 1984, the economic bureaucracy attempted to curtail expansion by the polyester-fiber industry. Its exports were booming because of the growing illicit trade with Mainland China via Hong Kong and other countries. State officials tried to convince the businessmen of the dangers of rapid expansion by offering related market information. But the businessmen refused to cooperate with the state and continued to expand their business. The economic bureaucracy discovered that it had no way to stop them, whereas its Korean counterpart would just freeze the loans of the disobedient businessmen. At the same time, the economic policy makers felt that carrying out transformative policy had become problematic. More and more people learned how to bargain with the state through elective offices, the mass media, or other channels. The people on the island were no longer ignorant and docile. They wanted more and knew how to fight for their objectives.

Indeed, the dominance of the KMT state over the Taiwanese society has gradually decreased. As the economy grew and joined the international markets, society became increasingly complex and difficult to manage. At the same, the state had trouble in absorbing human and financial resources. More and more well-educated people were attracted by the better conditions offered by private enterprises. The private sector became bigger than the public sector in both production and consumption. A trend of social pluralization emerged with the economic development. Businessmen and professionals required more freedom to pursue their careers in and outside the country as well as to enjoy direct channels with their decision makers. Workers wanted more autonomy for their union activities to extend their rights and interests. Farmers also appealed to the state for protecting their falling business. The improvement of the standard of living and educational level caused higher social and political participation. Interest groups were set up and opposition political forces were organized. While the KMT was still the major political force on the island, it became less authoritarian and more election-oriented. It gradually accepted the existence of an opposition force and allowed a Western pluralist democratic system to take root on the island.

The autonomy of the state and party from society was reduced by the trend of "Taiwanization" also. The mass education system and open social mobility integrated the generation born after 1949. The lines between the mainlanders and the Taiwanese significantly reduced. Young Taiwanese had not experienced the 2-28 Incident personally nor had they even heard of it. They not only wanted economic power but also political power. The enlargement of election and the policy of "Taiwanization" provided them with good opportunities to enter the state apparatus. The old division of labor, whereby the mainlanders ran national politics and enforced their will while the Taiwanese made money in business and channelled their political ambitions into local contests, was breaking down. A similar trend was noticed in the party. Among the two million members of the KMT in recent years, most of them were Taiwanese. The KMT had effectively absorbed emerging social forces into its organization. But it had also become too large to function as a vanguard elite. The complexity of its membership made the party's order difficult to carry out throughly. And many younger members were too independent-minded to submit to its centralist discipline (Gold, 1986: 119).

All of these changes reshaped the KMT state's relationship to the Taiwanese society and weakened its role as an agent of economic transformation. For the last thirty-seven years, the KMT state had greatly transformed Taiwan's economy while it had, in turn, also been considerably transformed by the changes in the Taiwanese society. In a sense, we may say that the "KMT party-state fell victim to its own success" (Gold, 1985: 128). As Rueschemeyer and Evans (1985: 69) argue, when state action moves beyond guaranteeing minimal institutional conditions of social and economic life in the direction of substantial intervention in socioeconomic processes, the state's own character as well as its relation to civil society will change fundamentally. The success of the state in regulating economic development might diminish autonomy and internal coherence of the state and reduce its capacities as an agent of economic transformation. The case of Taiwan demonstrated the validity of this argument.

CHAPTER 8

CONCLUSION

Explaining Policy-making in Taiwan's Economic Transformation

We have so far examined Taiwan's economic transformation after 1949 by means of a conceptual framework derived from the state-centric approach. We have assumed throughout that in order to understand the island's accomplishments, we must consider the role of the KMT state. The reason that Taiwan's socioeconomic development occurred at rates and forms different from many other LDCs was mainly due to the KMT state's distinctive development policies. There is no doubt that Taiwan's development enjoyed special advantages, i.e., the Japanese legacy, U.S. aid, favorable timing of the world economy, Confucianism, and size, but it was the effective economic policy-making of the KMT state that brought these advantages fully into play and broke through disadvantages, like the lack of natural resources, small economic scale, high population density, heavy national defense burden, serious inflation during the earlier period, and diplomatic isolation in recent years. To grasp the dynamics underlying Taiwan's economic transformation, we must put the KMT state at a pivotal position in the analytical framework and probe into the formulation and execution of development policy.

A variety of the KMT state's policy decisions concerning economic development are reviewed in this dissertation. Specific policies include the land reform, the reorganization of the farmers' associations, the extractive pricing policy before the late 1960s, and the relieving policy after the early 1970s for agricultural development; the entrustment scheme in the textile sector, the Export Processing Zones, the Ten Major Development Projects, the state control of basic industries, and the transfer of state enterprises for industrial development; the high-interest policy, the balance of government budget, the Statute for Encouragement of Investment, the tax reform, and the state control of banking system as well as its liberalization in fiscal and monetary policies; and the early import control, the foreign exchange and trade reform, the protective tariff structure, as well as the recent opening of domestic market for foreign trade. In addition, there is also the overall Nineteen-Point Program of Economic and Financial Reform. These policies can be roughly subsumed under a few broad development strategies: promoting industrialization from a solid base of agriculture; orderly development of industry in accordance with comparative advantage; great emphasis on economic stability; and encouragement of exports. Above all, we can discern a general trend toward a liberalization of the economy along with the process of development.

Through these development measures, the KMT state played an active role in regulating Taiwan's economic transformation. It led Taiwan's economy to overcome several crises and create the experience of "growth with equity." Although it progressively loosened up the control over the economy to include the operation of market forces, it did not just get the prices right. It still intervened directly in the economy by channelling funds for investment, devising indicative plans, improving the physical and psychological investment climate, and guiding Taiwan's incorporation into the world capitalist system (Gold, 1986: 122).

Of course, not all of these development measures were unquestionably contributive to Taiwan's success story. As a matter of fact, not even all of them were effectively formulated or executed. There are different and often contradictory goals in economic development, such as growth, equality, stability, independence, and environmental conservation. Evaluation of the effects of the various development strategies and policies depends on value preferences and theoretical logic. For instance, for those who emphasize the importance of opportunity costs and trust the functions of the invisible hand, the strategy of orderly development of industry in accordance with comparative advantage should win applause. For those who stress the possibility of creating comparative advantage by state intervention, this strategy is too timid and short-sighted. For those who prefer economic equality and stability, the state control of basic industries and financial system is a necessary policy, but for those who prefer economic efficiency and growth, this policy should be abandoned as soon as possible. The growth of exports has brought about unprecedented prosperity to Taiwan's economy, but for the critics it results in the crisis of extraordinary trade dependency. Our discussion, however, did not attempt to settle these arguments. Instead, the analysis in this dissertation has focused on the following questions: Why and how were these strategies and policies formulated? Why were they successfully or unsuccessfully executed? What were their effects on Taiwan's social structure? And what were their effects on subsequent economic policy-making? Furthermore, in a comparative sense, we tried to explain why the KMT state was able to exercise its intervention more effectively than the states in other developing countries.

We discovered that to answer these questions we had to pay attention to a number of issues. First, we had to bring the wider international economic and geo-political context into discussion. Second, the cultural and structural characteristics of the Taiwanese society had to be depicted. Third, we had to probe into the internal structuring of the KMT state. And finally, the interactions among these components were linked. By examining the structures and evolutions of the KMT state apparatus, the Taiwanese society, the international environment, and the linkages among them in terms of the concepts of *state autonomy* and *state capacities,* we have provided our answer to the above puzzle. The analysis can be summarized as follows.

The International Political-Economic Environment

The most important feature of the wider political-economic environment in which Taiwan's economy evolved was a particular international geo-political context dominated by the United States. Taiwan was incorporated into the American hegemonic system for containing communist expansion soon after the outbreak of the Korean War in June, 1950, far earlier than its incorporation into the world capitalist system in the mid-1960s. For the whole 1950s and the first half of the 1960s, Taiwan was cocooned within American hegemony both geo-politically and economically. One of the main effects of this situation on Taiwan's economic transformation was of course the enormous U.S. aid to the island. It not only helped Taiwan alleviate its defense burden, balance government budget, arrest inflation, and accumulate capital, but also enhanced the confidence and willingness of investment on the island. Moreover, in contrast to the dependency assumptions that foreign aid might have the effect of restricting the social changes necessary for pursuing economic growth or equality by reinforcing the interests of transnational capitalists or preserving traditional elites in power, the geo-political context of U.S. aid to Taiwan meant that aid promoted social change rather than holding it back. First of all, American aid had little to do with the interests of U.S. transnational corporations and much of the aid were grants instead of loans. At the same time, while the aid undoubtedly aimed at preserving the political status quo in Taiwan, it strengthened the KMT state's capacity to implement the land reform and thus remove the force of traditional elites, i.e., the landlords, rather than restricting the possibility of change. U.S. aid also strengthened the capacity of the KMT state to foster local capitalists and regulate their activities (Evans, 1984: 10-11).

Another effect of this particular geo-political context on Taiwan's economic transformation was the influence of the American advisors on the KMT state's economic policy-making. Controlling the crucial resources for the KMT state, the U.S. AID Mission to China played a weighty role in Taiwan's earlier development. In addition to providing suggestions by its own staff members and independent experts, the mission also helped the KMT state to create the initial developmental institutions, such as the CUSA, the JCRR, the ESB, and the FETCC. The American advisors consistently urged the KMT state to pay more attention to economic development. They supported the pro-development pragmatists in their clash with the return-to-the-mainland ideologues. They saw to the fostering of a private sector and Taiwanese participation in it. They also encouraged the KMT state to liberalize the control over the economy. Under their initiative and assistance, the 19-Point Program of Economic and Financial Reform was formulated; this plan symbolized the victory of the developmentalists and laid down the fundamental lines for Taiwan's subsequent development.

Furthermore, the geo-political context defined by the United States led to the rearrangement of the KMT state's priority for national development. While the Defense Treaty between the United States and the Republic of China shielded Taiwan from the invasion of the CCP, at the same time it restricted the military action of the KMT. The reluctance of the U.S. government to support an armed attack on the mainland blocked the way for the KMT state to recover the lost teritory by strengthening military might. This basic situation coupled with the influence of the American advisors considerably shifted the KMT's attention from military buildup to economic development. Of course, the lack of confrontation between the KMT and CCP also exerted its weight upon the priority shift. Victory in the offshore islands conflict and the subsequent calmness in the Taiwan Strait alleviated the pressure of military buildup.

The second noticeable feature of the wider political-economic environment was a favorable timing of the world economy. U.S. aid had insulated Taiwan's economy from external forces during the 1950s. American financial and commodity assistance alleviated the necessity for Taiwan to rush into the capitalist world system. In the meantime, there was little TNC interest in the island. Taiwan was small, poor, had no natural resources, and faced the threat from the CCP. By the early 1960s, however, the market in the advanced industrial societies, especially the United States, after having experienced high growth, increase of wage rates, and the loss of competitiveness in labor-intensive manufactured goods, was readily accessible to manufactured exports from the LDCs. The switch of the KMT state's development strategy from import substitution to export expansion and its efforts to improve Taiwan's investment climate meshed this favorable timing somewhat by coincidence. The product cycle brought foreign capital from Japan and the U.S. to the island. The timely arrival of the foreign private capital made up for the phasing out of U.S. aid. All the while the CCP was obssesed with the Cultural Revolution in the mainland. Taiwan's export-led industrialization thus started in a good external environment. The favorable international economic situation lasted for about a decade. Facilitated by the prosperous world economy and enjoying preferential tariff rates in American markets, Taiwan's foreign trade and light industries of consumer goods grew rapidly and steadily.

Not only did Taiwan take advantage of a favorable timing in the international market, it also benefitted from its status as a latecomer in the world capitalist system, a "concrete situation of dependence" different from that of many other LDCs (Evans, 1984: 5). In the 1950s and early 1960s, due to the reason noted above, the presence of transnational capitalists on Taiwan had hardly been felt. Given American assistance, the KMT state had more range to determine its economic relations with the outside world. The KMT state, on the one hand, dominated the heights of the economy and accounted for a sizable portion of the industrial production. On the other hand it fostered the supply of consumer goods through various measures of encouragement and protection of local capitalists. The result was that when U.S. aid stopped and Taiwan had to incorporate herself into the world capitalist system, she had already developed a prospering local bourgeoisie and a strong state which played the most weighty role among the three partners of the "triple alliance." In contrast to Latin American countries, where TNCs had been penetrating in for a long time and played a significant role in shaping consumption patterns as well as the structure of the productive apparatus, the transnational capitalists in Taiwan were under the control of strict rules laid down by the KMT state. Basically they were confined in the export sector and not able to form an entrenched enclave given the shallow historical depth of their investment on the island as well as the close supervision by the KMT state.

Taiwan's economy was incorporated deeply into the world capitalist system due to the rapid growth of her foreign trade and export-oriented industries. The boom of trade brought about unprecedented prosperity on the island but also brought in the influence of other economies, especially the influence of the two major trading partners, namely, the United States and Japan. As a result, the involvement in the world economy deepened Taiwan's trade dependency and exposed Taiwan to the competition with other countries in the international market. At the same time, the change of the global political situation, particularly the change of U.S. diplomatic policy, constituted another major factor influencing the KMT state's development strategies. Since the early 1970s onward, the KMT state's economic policy-making to a certain degree has actually been a response to the challenges from the international political-economic environment.

The first impact of the international political-economic environment after the early 1970s was the diplomatic setback of the withdrawal from the United Nations and the first oil crisis. The response of the KMT state to the impact was the Ten Major Development Projects. The second major external impact was the second oil crisis, coupled with the intensified competition from other LDCs in the international market, and the loss of diplomatic relations with the United States. The KMT state's response was the revision of its economic plan to pay more attention to industries with high intersectorial linkages, high technology-intensiveness, high value added, low energy coefficiency, capacity for increased use of locally produced raw materials, good market ability, and capability for consolidating the development base of national defense (CEPD, 1978: 24-25; CEPD, 1981: 46-47). In the meantime, the KMT state had to assume more responsibility in capital accumulation to make up for the decline of private investment which had resulted from the deterioration of the external political situation. Finally, recent pressure asking for opening markets, lowering tariffs, and adjusting exchange rate from the U.S. was also a consequence of the international situation. It pushed the KMT state to accelerate the pace of economic liberalization.

In sum, for the last thirty-seven years, Taiwan has undergone a big change of status in the changeable international political-economic environment. Economically, she climbed from the bottom of the world capitalist system to the middle level as a newly industrializing semi-peripheral country. Her economy shifted from a closed system insulated from the external forces to a highly open system deeply involved in the international market. She also changed her status from an aid recipient to an active exporter earning a huge surplus. Politically, contrasting to her rising status in the world economy, she was demoted from an original member of the United Nations to an isolated political entity in the world. Her role in American global strategy changed from the legitimate representative of China and a showcase of free economy strongly backed by the U.S. to "a part of China" having no official relations with Washington. All of these changes influenced the KMT state's economic policy-making.

The Taiwanese Society and Its Relationship to the KMT State

The colonial experience and the oppressive Nationalist takeover during 1945-47 deeply influenced the character of the Taiwanese society. Japanese occupation and fifties years as a second-class race had accustomed the Taiwanese to repression and limited aspirations. It made most people on the island relatively docile. The "2-28 Incident" eliminated the stratum of Taiwanese intellectuals and weakened the force of the social elites. It also made the Taiwanese society leaderless, atomized, quiescent, and apolitical. This situation plus the "exogenous" status of the KMT state to the Taiwanese society resulted in a particular historical and structural condition of high *state autonomy*. Because of both the retrocession of Taiwan to the ROC in 1945 and the retreat of the Nationalist central government in 1949, most people from the mainland were either servicemen or civilian government employees; they occupied the positions in various state bureaucracies and the military. Most state and party cadres and military officers were accordingly mainlanders having no property or connections in Taiwan. At the same time, leading Mainlander capitalists and those state managers having extensive connections with businessmen, such as T. V. Soong and H. H. Kung, did not follow Chiang Kai-shek to Taiwan but fled to Hong Kong or the United States. The separate existence of the state elites and the social elites thus made the KMT state highly autonomous from Taiwanese society.

This extraordinary *state autonomy* allowed the KMT state to formulate transformative policies and pursue developmental goals different from the interests of the social dominant classes. The most striking example was the implementation of the land reform. In order to secure the loyalty of the peasants and to combat the communist intrigue of using the illness of the tenancy structure to instigate agrarian uprisings as in the mainland, the KMT state carried out a "revolution from above" to equalize land ownership. The reform turned many tenants into owner-cultivators and removed the landlord class from Taiwanese society. In addition, the KMT state penetrated the rural areas through the reorganization of the farmer's associations. Collaborating with the

American advisors, Chinese officials changed the role of the associations from that of an instrument manipulated by landlords and the local gentry for usury and commission earning to that of an agency controlled over by the state with the goal of facilitating agricultural production and extracting agricultural surplus. After the land reform and the reorganization of the farmers' associations, Taiwan's rural areas became a relatively cohesive and stable society consisting of numerous small owner-cultivators. This land ownership structure has not changed too much since then.

The farmers did not play an active role in formulating economic policy. Enjoying the benefits from the land reform and the reorganization of the farmers associations, they were obssesed with the new opportunities to improve their living standards in the 1950s and early 1960s. The slowdown of rural development since the late 1960s provoked farmers' resentment, but the switch of state policies from extraction to subsidy was mainly a decision made from above rather than from below. The farmers' associations did help the rural people to express their opinions on agricultural policy-making, but the associations acted more like a state agency than like a social interest group. More importantly, the decrease of agricultural population, especially full-time farmers, led to the decline of the rural people as a social force when compared with the other social classes or groups. And the import of American agricultural products further weakened the bargaining power of the Taiwanese farmers.

In contrast to the farmers, the local capitalists extended their influence along with Taiwan's economic transformation. The local capitalists were few and feeble in the beginning of Taiwan's postwar development. Under Japanese colonialism, the Taiwanese were excluded from the more important industries. They could only engage in small manufacturing plants and handicraft shops. There was a small group of mainlander capitalists who followed Chiang Kai-shek to move to Taiwan. But they were reluctant to invest because of the political uncertainty and soaring inflation. Through a variety of state policies, such as the entrustment scheme in the textile sector, the industrial projects supported by U.S. aid, the transfer of the four state enterprises, and various measures of protection and encouragement, a bourgeoisie gradually emerged and continuously expanded their businesses. In addition, accompanying the arrival of foreign capital since the mid-1960s, a group of local entrepreneurs was formed from the cooperation with the transnational capitalists. Moreover, a huge number of small- and medium-size enterprises emerged with the boom of exports. These people apparently formed the new dominant class in the Taiwanese society.

The different fractions of the new dominant class had varied influence on the KMT state's economic policy-making. A few mainlander capitalists in textiles and food processing seemed to enjoy special advantages in running their business in the earlier period. Some former landlords had benefited from government contracts and protection after taking over the state enterprises. Other Taiwanese gained assistance from the state through the projects supported by U.S. aid. Many local firms took advantage of the import control and protective tariff structure. Large private enterprises usually had a much better chance to get loans in preferential terms from the state-owned banks than the small- and medium-size enterprises. And the economic policy makers maintained close links with the leading businessmen through a couple of informal channels, such as the Chinese National Association of Industry and Commerce. The expansion of the private sector and the emergence of big enterprises have gradually undercut the autonomy of the KMT state in formulating and executing economic policy.

For most time and cases, however, the local capitalists did not play a decisive role in the KMT state's economic policy-making. The KMT state consistently kept relatively high autonomy from the new dominant class. Different from the situation in Japan and Korea, the state-business relations were relatively "distant" and "cool" in Taiwan. Exchange between the state and the bourgeoisie was infrequent. So far not one local capitalist has been recruited as the member of the Executive Yuan Council or the economic bureaucracy. The CSC had no representative from the local capitalists until 1981. At the same itme, it is not easy to find many retired economic officials in private enterprises. The economic policy makers and bureaucrats usually did not consult social groups prior to policy shifts. They analyzed problems and options and then devised incentives based on what they believed the local and transnational capitalists would respond to (Gold, 1986: 127). Although in some cases the local capitalists were solicited for opinions, the economic policy makers still played the role of final judge.

A special feature of the KMT state's economic policy-making was the influence of the consulting economists. Among them a small group of neoclassical scholars, members of the Academia Sinica, were most influential. Owing to their close relationship with the economic policy makers, they exerted considerable weight on the KMT state's economic policy-making. Their views to a certain degree contributed to the Foreign Exchange and Trade Reform. They helped the KMT state to improve Taiwan's revenue system. The orderly development of industry in accordance with comparative advantage and the emphasis on economic stability were partly due to their advice. For the last three decades, they consistently urged the KMT state to reduce its direct intervention in Taiwan's economy. Their influence also went through their friends, students, and subordinates in Taiwan's universities and research institutes.

In addition to these neoclassicalists, there were some other voices from a number of professors and columnists. Some of them had engaged in economic planning before and some of them were economic bureaucrats concurrently. Their views varied from the extreme of upholding laissez-faire to the extreme of advocating strong state intervention. They might not have had the same weight as the neoclassicialists in the economic policy-making, but they had certain influence on public opinion. Their arguments sometimes also drew the attention of the top political leadership and economic policy makers. Along with the rapid growth of mass media, the influence of the consulting economists has greatly extended. Roughly speaking, their comments on economic matters or policy-making were independent from any social force and had the functions of balancing the influence of the dominant class. In recent years, a consensus of reducing state protection and regulation in the economy has been formed among the consulting economists. Their assertion plus the pressure from the U.S. constituted a strong force in pushing the KMT state to accelerate the pace of economic liberalization.

Moreover, the middle class and the workers showed their strength in the recent years. The emergence of social movements for consumerism and environmental conservation since the early 1980s implied the growth of the middle class. The enactment of the Labor Standard Law reflected the increasing weight of the workers. Consequently, the rise of various social forces on Taiwan has undermined the KMT state's character as a corporate actor and made it more like an arena of social conflict.

Aside from the structural features, cultural characteristics played a noticeable role. As mentioned in the introductory chapter, some of the Confucian cultural elements, such as thrift, diligence, respect for educational achievement, avoidance of overt conflict in social relations, loyalty to hierarchy and authority, and stress on order and harmony, are believed to have something to do with Taiwan's economic transformation. More specifically, the relatively distant relationship between state elites and local capitalists was somehow related to the Chinese cultural tradition of objecting to an intimate relationship between the state and the bourgeoisie. The relatively strong influence of the consulting economists could be partly attributed to the cultural value of respecting educational achievement. In Confucianism, intellectuals are expected to contribute their knowledge to the state and the state is supposed to respect intellectuals and listen to their advice. Moreover, the cultural elements, such as avoidance of social conflict, loyalty to hierarchy and authority, and stress on order and harmony, helped the KMT state to govern the Taiwanese society in a paternalistic style of leadership. In this system the state tried to nurture a spirit of national consensus and to encourage cooperation among all elements of society. The people were taught to accept a moralistic authoritarian state and to conform to state policies. This feature reduced dissent from society on economic reform or policy shift.

In sum, the KMT state's effectiveness in economic policy-making partly derived from the structural and cultural characteristics of the Taiwanese society, especially the state's relations to the surrounding social structure. The colonial occupation, the "2-28 Incident," the "exogenous" status of the KMT state, the land reform, the consulting economists, as well as the cultural tradition jointly weakened the "pact of domination." In the course of Taiwan's economic transformation, the KMT state acted as a relatively autonomous apparatus pursuing developmental goals defined by itself rather than as an instrument of domination manipulated by certain social classes or groups.

The Internal Structuring of the KMT State

The relocation of the Nationalist central government in Taipei brought a relatively capable state onto Taiwan. The influx of experienced mainlander professionals and administrators filled the vacancies left by the Japanese, since the Taiwanese did not have the required training and experience to take over most of these positions. The KMT state became much more cohesive and less corrupt after the retreat. Most disobedient persons did not follow Chiang Kai-shek moving to the island. A reform program further expelled those who were corrupt and weakened the factional forces. Learning a lesson from the defeat in the mainland, the KMT state became more prudent. The strong motivation of wiping out the shame at the loss of the mainland as well as of safeguarding the last bastion led the KMT elites to devote themselves completely to national buildup.

Several factors contributed to the KMT state's effectiveness in formulating and executing economic policy. The colonial administration had left to the KMT state a number of powerful policy instruments, such as the banking system and the big enterprises. Not only did U.S. aid extend the KMT state's financial resources, but the American advisors helped the KMT officials improve their administrative skills as well. The party control over the state made the economic policy involving different departments more easily formulated and executed. In addition, Sun Yat-senism provided the KMT elites with a relatively practical, tolerant, and flexible ideological framework for undertaking the state-led economic development. It enabled the KMT state to avoid severe ideological clash and facilitated the coherence of policy formulation. With its assertion that the state should pursue the general interests of the people as a whole rather than of any particular social group or class, Sun Yat-senism also made the KMT state somewhat self-conscious about maintaining *state autonomy*.

Constitutionally, the KMT state's economic policy-making structure was composed of four organizations: the economic bureaucracy was responsible for drafting policy proposals and executing policy decisions; the Executive Yuan Council was in charge of coordinating proposed economic policy with other national policies; the CSC represented the ruling party and held the supremacy of making final decisions; and the Legislative Yuan representing the people, bore the responsibilities of deciding on the statutory bills submitted by the Executive Yuan.

The configuration of these components showed some distinctive organizational features which were conducive to the ability of the KMT state to regulate economic transformation. Regarding *state autonomy*, all of the organizations were highly autonomous from society in terms of the connections with the dominant class. Regarding *state capacities*, under the control of the ruling party, all of the organizations individually enjoyed a certain degree of internal cohesiveness on the one hand and were integrated into a coherent network with the CSC as the pivot on the other. Moreover, to cope with the extraordinary situation in the early stage of Taiwan's postwar development, to utilize U.S. aid efficiently, and to handle the subsequent development of Taiwan's economy, the KMT state created a number of supra-ministry and relatively independent organizations for economic transformation, such as the CUSA, the JCRR, the FETCC, the TPB, the ESB, the CIECD, the EPC, and the CEPD. Several organizational features of these state agencies contributed to the efficacy of economic policy-making. First, the overlap of personnel at the top echelon of the economic bureaucracy removed the boundaries of different state units. It reduced the conflicts between different agencies and made the process of economic policy-making more coherent. Second, the financial independence of the economic bureaucracy enabled the economic officials to get rid of bureaucratic redundancy and act speedily on development projects. Finally, the higher salaries of the economic bureaucrats motivated honesty and devotion to their duty.

However, a careful study discovered that there are many important features of the KMT state's economic policy-making which are not apparent when only examining the constitutional structure. For example, while the CSC formally performed the role of supreme judge in economic policy-making, in practice it did not contribute substantive functions to policy decision. The analysis of the changing composition of the CSC's members in terms of their ethnic and professional backgrounds revealed that the shifts of the KMT state's development priorities and strategies took place far earlier than the personnel change of the CSC. In other words, the policy shifts were not due to the change of the CSC's members representing different factional or social forces. Instead, it was the policy shifts that in turn led to the personnel change of the CSC. Actually, as we further observed, the final resolution to policy proposal in the KMT state's policy-making process was usually given by the few real power-holders' decision, rather than by the votes of the CSC's members. The decisive steps in making many important economic policies were determined by the top political leadership and some economic policy makers outside the jurisdiction of the CSC. Moreover, the policy-making in the KMT state, especially in the earlier stages of Taiwan's postwar development, was fashioned by the rule of certain men rather than by law or bureaucratic regulations. Many economic policies were fomented and decided in the interactions among certain state elites that did not wholly correspond with the constitutional structure of making economic policy.

Based on the previous findings, we constructed an operational economic policy-making structure by probing into the actualities underneath the constitutional structure. In this structure, the top political leadership, the economic policy makers, and the economic bureaucrats constituted the three major components which determined the economic policies within the KMT state apparatus.

A strong and stable political leadership resided at the top of the policy-making structure. It refers to Chiang Kai-shek and Ch'en Ch'eng for the fifties and sixties as well as Chiang Ching-kuo since the early seventies. They were the real-power holders in leading the KMT state and Taiwanese society. The general acceptance of them as national leaders was an important factor for political stability on the island. Although their paternalistic style of leadership was somewhat out of tune with modern democratic institutions, they managed to maintain the stable socil-political circumstance that allowed Taiwan to bring about economic progress and in turn political democratization.

The top political leaders were the final decision makers for arranging the priorities for national development and regulating Taiwan's economic transformation. Their attitude toward national development, mainly based on their experience of defeat in the mainland and their assessment on situational imperatives, were the main factors explaining the basic development strategies and important strategy shifts. For example, taking the lesson of losing the mainland, they insisted on carrying out the land reform in order to secure the loyalty of the peasants and to combat the Chinese Communists' intrigue for using the weakaness of the tenancy structure to instigate agrarian uprisings. To maintain political order in the rural areas, the agricultural policy was shifted from extraction to subsidy. Their concern with the control of inflation made economic stability an overriding objective of Taiwan's economic development. Although their initial motivation behind development was short term, i.e., to build Taiwan into a bastion for counterattacking the mainland, they rearranged the priorities for national development from military buildup to economic growth when they realized that an armed attack on the mainland would be impracticable and the sojourn on Taiwan would be lengthy.

The ability of the top political leadership to control its subordinates contributed greatly to the KMT state's efficacy. It facilitated the internal coherence of the state apparatus and led the KMT state to act as a well-organized corporate actor. Retaining broad powers to appoint, dismiss, or transfer officials, the top political leadership firmly controlled the chains of command in the state, party, military, and security. Residing at the apex of the power pyramid, the top political leadership was immune from the power or ideological struggle among its subordinates. Under its supervision, the conflicts between the economic policy makers and the officials in other state departments (e.g., the tension between the return-to-the-mainland ideologues and the pro-development pragmatists) as well as between the economic policy makers themselves (e.g., the tension between the state-intervention-oriented cadres and the free-market-oriented officials) never affected the organizational coherence of the state.

The top political leadership at the same time helped the KMT state maintain its autonomy. Not only was the top political leadership immune from the conflicts of state officials, but it was also immune from the influence of dominant social forces. Putting itself as an example of frugality and incorruptibility, it kept its distance from businessmen. Under its supervision, the government-business relationship on Taiwan was relatively remote. In certain cases, the top political leadership intervended in economic policy-making to counter the excessive influence of local capitalists and the corruption of state officials, such as the case of Cathay Plastics.

The most important contribution of the top political leaders toward Taiwan's economic transformation has been their ability to recruit competent persons to manage the economy. Although both Chiang Kai-shek and Ch'en Ch'eng were servicemen themselves, they established a civilian government and kept the economy off the hands of the military. Chiang Ching-kuo further raised the status and power of economic officials in the state apparatus. Partly due to the influence of U.S. aid which separated economic assistance from military assistance and limited the role of the military in economic sphere, partly due to the fact that the military had its own production facilities independent from economic development projects, but mainly due to the decision of the top political leaders, the military was largely insulated from economic policy-making. The top political leaders selected a group of non-military officials to take charge of economic development and showed respect for these officials' expertise. With their support, the economic officials effectively formulated and executed a series of transformative policies. While the top political leadership had the supremacy for determining the state's priorities and policy orientation for national development in principle, Taiwan's economic transformation in practice was propelled mainly by these economic policy makers.

The economic policy makers were a group of technocrats having their training mostly in engineering and science. Since they had higher educational degrees and more experience in studying abroad, they seemed to be more cosmopolitan-minded than other leading state officials. Many of them were in charge of technical affairs in the economic bureaucracy and state enterprises before taking charge of economic policy-making. Due to their distinctive training background and career paths, they took a practical view toward national development and managed Taiwan's economic transformation by trial and error rather than by following any specific school of economics. They interpreted Sun Yat-senism as a non-dogmatic pragmatism and tried to avoid ideological constraints. Along with the growth of Taiwan's economy and the accumulation of knowledge about economic activities, these policy makers progressively adjusted their policy-making for economic development.

The opinions of the economic policy makers on the strategies for economic development were not uniform. There were conflicts among them. The rise and fall of the different factions of the economic policy makers influenced directly the KMT state's economic policy formulation. In the first half of the fifties, all the economic policy makers were inclined to control the economy by strict state intervention. A split between those who favored continued state dominance of the economy and those who advocated more range for the private sector took place during the late 1950s. The victory of the latter resulted in the economic reforms during the turning-point period. Since the mid-sixties, partly because of the gorwth of the economy and partly because of the pressure from the United States, a consensus of economic liberalization has gradually come to the fore. Nevertheless, there have still been disagreements about the ways and pace for liberalizing the economy among the economic policy makers. These disagreements were somehow reflected in the issues of lowering tariff protection, opening domestic market, and transferring state enterprises.

The economic policy makers were enthusiastic in fostering the private sector but did not serve as an instrument of the bourgeoisie. Most of them came from middle class families without extensive connections with the local or foreign capitalists. While they made contact frequently with businessmen, they were dedicated to their career in the state apparatus and showed little interest in developing their own private business. Basically, their policy decisions aimed at promoting the whole economy rather than a few enterprises. Most of them were known to be clean, honest, and capable.

The economic policy makers played a pivotal role in the economic policy-making process and took the major responsibility in policy formulation and execution. Backed by the top political leadership and the American advisors, they initiated various economic reforms. Due to their advice and to pressure from the Americans, the top political leadership rearranged the state's priorities and paid more attention to economic development. Generally speaking, they were quick and clear in responding to the change of international and intra-national economic situations. They were also interested in hearing the opinions and demands of society but autonomous in making their decisions.

The autonomy and capacity of the economic policy makers have been undercut in recent years, however. Owing to the rise of the private sector, the policy instruments that can be used by the economic policy makers, such as the state enterprises and banking system, have become less effective. Through the elective offices, the mass media, and personal contact, various social forces, especially the local capitalists, have been able to exert more influence upon economic policy-making. The cancellation of the plans to build the fourth nuclear power plant, to introduce Du Pont's titanium dioxide plant, to develop the automobile industry, to merge local steel furnaces, and to curtail the expansion of the polyester-fiber industry signaled the change.

There has also been some change regarding the training background of the economic policy makers. While the KMT state's economic policy-making had been dominated by engineers and scientists for more than three decades, there have been more economists, lawyers, and political scientists joining the cast of the economic policy makers recently. One main reason for this change is that a group of senior economic bureaucrats, who had their training in economics, law, or political science, have now become mature enough to take charge of economic policy-making. Many of this new cohort of economic policy makers were actually the former aides of the senior economic policy makers.

The economic policy makers were assisted by a competent staff. Enjoying the advantage of higher paying salaries and not being subject to civil service regulations, the core agencies of the economic bureaucracy were staffed with a group of loyal and skilled officials. They cultivated a strong *esprit de corps* and worked quite hard. These economic bureaucrats, comprising many American-trained economists, contributed to the KMT state's economic policy-making by providing the economic policy makers with their expertise in economic and technical development. They took charge of analyzing the economic situation, drafting policy proposals, and mapping out a series of economic development plans. Although these bureaucrats did not have power to determine policy decisions, some of them had substantive influence on the economic policy makers' decision-making.

Similar to the case of the economic policy makers, a majority of the economic bureaucrats in the earlier stage of Taiwan's postwar development were engineers rather than economists by training. Nevertheless, this situation has been reversed since the mid-seventies, implying the change of the KMT state's role in economic transformation. In the earlier stage, when the economic bureaucracy intervened directly in the development of various industries and the state enterprises played the leading actor of economic activities, engineers were needed to take charge of the technical affairs. Along with the growth of the economy and the expansion of the private sector, more economists are now needed to analyze the economic situation and smooth the market mechanism. The increase of number and power of economists in the economic bureaucracy has contributed to the trend toward economic liberalization.

Because managerial capabilities in the private sector have improved so fast, the capacity of the economic bureaucrats to manage the economy has declined somewhat. In contrast to the previous situation where talented people assembled in the economic bureaucracy, more and more well-educated people were attracted by the better conditions offered by private enterprises. As a result, the dominance of the economic bureaucracy over the economy has gradually decreased. Although many economic bureaucrats were lured away by private enterprises in recent years, the exchange between the KMT state and the bourgeoisie was still relatively infrequent. It somehow helped the economic bureaucracy slow down the decline of *state autonomy*.

The composition and change of personnel in this internal structuring had significant impact on economic policy-making, especially in the earlier stage. For instance, K. Y. Yin was the key figure in explaining Taiwan's industrial development during the fifties and early sixties. The entrustment scheme in the textile sector was his masterpiece; his resignation caused the oscillation of economic policy during the period 1955-57; and his aggressiveness coupled with Ch'en Ch'eng's support constituted the main dynamics of the reforms during the turning-point period. In addition, the coherence of the "Yin-Yen-Yang" cast facilitated the implementation of these reforms. Moreover, the less aggressive development strategy as well as the slowdown of economic reform in the latter three quarters of the 1960s should largely be attributed to the deaths of Ch'en Ch'eng and K. Y. Yin.

Similarly, the inauguration of Chiang Ching-kuo as Premier was an important factor in explaining the announcement of the ambitious Ten Major Development Projects. The evolution of economic policy-making since the early 1970s was related to the change of power configuration of K. T. Li, Sun Yun-suan, and Yu Kuo-hwa. Nevertheless, since the KMT has held the reign continuously, the change of personnel was relatively infrequent. The continuity of personnel enabled the economic officials to accumulate experience and build consensus on managing Taiwan's economic transformation. It also enabled the economic officials to switch development policies without organizational disruption.

The continuity of personnel and organization, on the other hand, resulted in some inertia. The persistance of the protective trade policy and agricultural policy somehow reflected this problem. In addition, some ineffectiveness of the KMT state's economic policy-making was mainly related to the vested interests in the state apparatus. The attempts of the state itself or the various departments in the state apparatus to maintain or expand existent power and interests limited the effects of some reform programs. The implementation of the 19-Point Reform Program, the proposal to reform tax administration, and the transfer of state enterprises were the examples.

In sum, facilitated by a number of advantages, the strong capacities of the KMT state in economic policy-making largely derived from its internal structuring. This consisted of an impregnable leadership who recruited competent officials to take charge of economic development and maintained internal coherence of the state apparatus; a group of clean, honest, and capable economic policy makers who played a pivotal role in synthesizing the various opinions and demands of the different parties within or outside the state apparatus; and a company of skilled and loyal economic bureaucrats who offered required expertise and worked hard. Surrounded by the various favorable or unfavorable conditions in the Taiwanese society and the international political-economic environment, they played the major role in formulating the executing various development policies for regulating Taiwan's economic transformation.

What Can Be Learned from the Taiwan Case?

Taiwan's enviable performance for the last thirty-seven years was a result of many factors. Some of them were decisive; the others were auxiliary. In this dissertation, through an analytical framework derived from the state-centric approach, we discover that the most crucial factor determining Taiwan's economic development was a relatively capable and autonomous state. All of the other factors contributing to the miraculous accomplishments on the island could to a certain degree and in a certain way be linked to this pivotal factor. To understand better why Taiwan's economic transformation occurred at different rates and in different forms than in many other LDCs, the KMT state on Taiwan is the best place to start with.

Both economists and sociologists would agree that economic development in the LDC is mainly determined by the state's economic policy. There have been many studies by economists telling us about the rationality (or sometimes irrationality) of the economic policies for Taiwan's development. As sociologists, however, we want to stress that policy-making for economic development is not simply a matter of economic rationality. It is also a political issue involving conflict and compromise as well as the domination and subordination of the different forces within and outside state apparatus. To grasp the dynamics of Taiwan's economic transformation, we should not forget this sociopolitical aspect. Therefore, when Hal Myint (1982), a British economist, made a comment on the lesson of Taiwan's experience to other LDCs, he said, "I think perhaps that it is more fruitful to concentrate on the conjuncture of economic and political circumstances, including the overcoming of the vested interests, which enabled Taiwan to switch over effectively from the import-substitution to expansion policies rather than try to construct an elaborate sequence of phases or subphases of economic development from her experience" (Mint, 1982: 78). We discover that the cornerstone of this conjuncture was an autonomous and capable state.

Indeed, Taiwan's experience tells us that to promote economic development, we need a state which is autonomous and capable enough to formulate and execute transformative policy effectively. This is the key to unravel the puzzle of Taiwan's success in carrying out those development policies, such as the land reform and the strategy switch from import substitution to export expansion. A capable and automous state is crucial even in the case of reducing state intervention in the economy. It is correct to indicate that one rationality in the KMT state's economic policy-making was its determination to reduce progressively its intervention in the market in accordance with the growth of the economy. But it is also true that economic liberalization cannot be effectively carried out by simply defaulting the state's functions. On the contrary, it requires autonomous and capable state action to overcome the obstruction of the vested interests in the previous stage and establish an orderly market with less state control. The successful and unsuccessful records in Taiwan's experience of economic liberalization confirm this argument. Therefore, for those LDCs attempting to initiate certain economic reform programs, the autonomy and capacities of the state to implement these programs should deserve at least equal attention as the rationality of the programs *perse*.

The Taiwan case also tells us that for a LDC, transnational linkages need not be tantamount to turning the nation over to foreign masters (Evans, 1985; Gold, 1986: 133). It is no doubt that Taiwan's specific situation of dependency evolved through a series of unique or nonduplicable phenomena, such as the shallow history of TNCs and U.S. protection and assistance in the earlier period. But a more important point is that the KMT state played a decisive role in guiding the incorporation of Taiwan's economy into the world system and avoiding many adverse effects of transnational linkages argued by the mechanistic dependency theses. Therefore, for those LDCs attempting to reduce existent or avoid future destructive effects of dependency, the role of the state remains a crux.

Although many elements contributing to the autonomy and capacities of the KMT state were derived from particular historical-structural conjuncture and cultural traits that may be difficult to replicate, some organizational features and developmental strategies adopted by the KMT state are not beyond the ability of most states in the LDCs. For instance, creation of special commission with supra-ministry status and attractive offer for economic transformation is a duplicable component that can strengthen the state's capacity in managing the economy. Establishment of such organization as Taiwan's farmers' associations will help the LDCs develop a solid base of agriculture for industrialization. Elimination of distortion in exchange rate and suitable control of the import of luxurious consumer goods are conducive to the expansion of foreign trade and balance of international payments. In addition, encouragement of rural industry and orderly development of industry in accordance with comparative advantages will facilitate the evolution of "growth with equity." Of course, to carry out these policies effectively, a state apparatus that is cohesive and relatively insulated from dominant social elites is still required.

In sum, we believe that for any case or comparative study of national development, the role of the state is a crucial component that should never be dismissed. Taiwan's economic transformation is a good example of this assertion.

APPENDIX A

CAPSULE BIOGRAHPIES OF POLICY MAKERS

Top Political Leadership

Ch'en Ch'eng
Born in Chekiang, 1897. Died 1965. Education: Paoting Militray Academy. Career: commander, 18th Army Corps, 1930-34; commander-in-chief, 3rd Route Army, 1934; commander-in-chief, 6th and 9th War Area and concurrently governor of Hepeh, 1939-44; minister of War, 1944-45; chief of General Staff and concurrently commander-in-chief, Chinese Navy, 1946-48; chairman, CUSA, 1949 and 1958-63; governor of Taiwan, 1949-50; member, Central Reform Committee, 1950-52; member, CSC, 1953-54; Premier, 1950-54 and 1958-63; Vice Tsungtsai, KMT, 1954-65; Vice President of the Republic of China, 1954-65.

Chiang Kai-shek
Born in Chekiang, 1887. Died 1975. Education: Paoting Military Academy, 1907; Tokyo Military Academy, 1908-10. Joined Tung Meng Hui, 1908; participated in 1911 Revolution. Career: president, Whampoa Military Academy, 1924; commander-in-chief, Revolutionary Armies, 1926; between 1928 and 1931, held at different periods posts of Premier and minister of Education; president of National Military Council, 1932-46; at certain periods between 1932 and 1947 was concurrently chief of general staff, Premier, chairman of Supreme National Council, governor of Szechwan; member, Central Executive Committee, KMT, 1926-50; *Tsungtsai* (Director-General), KMT, 1938-75; supreme commander of Allied Forces in China Theater during World War II; President of the Republic of China, 1948-75.

Chiang Ching-kuo
Born in Chekiang, 1910. Died 1988. Education: Sun Yat-sen University, Moscow; USSR Military & Political Institute. Career: commisoner for Southern Kiangsi 1939-45; special foreign affair commissioner for Northeastern China, 1945-47; deputy economic control supervisor for Shanghai, 1948; chairman, KMT Taiwan Provincial Headquarters, 1949-50; member, Central Reform Committee, 1950-52; member, CSC, 1953-76, Chairman, KMT, 1976-; director, General Political Depart-

ment, Ministry of National Defense, 1950-54; chairman, Vocational Assistance Commission for Retired Servicemen, 1957-64; vice minister of National Defense, 1964-65; deputy sectray-general, National Defense Council, 1954-67; minister of National Defense, 1965-69; Vice Premier & concurrently chairman of the CIECD, 1967-72; director, Chinese Youth Corps, 1952-73; Premier, 1972-78; President of the Republic of China, 1978-1988.

Key Economic Policy Makers

Chiang Monlin
Born in Chekiang, 1886. Died 1964. Education: B.L., University of California, 1912; Ph. D., Education, Columbia University, 1917. Career: editor, Chinese Free Press, San Francisco, 1910-12; editor, the New Education, Shanghai, 1918-20; professor of education, National Peking University, 1919-28; acting chancellor, National Peking University, 1923-27; president, National Peking University, 1928-29; minister of Education, 1928-30; chancellor, National Peking University, 1930-45; president, Chinese Red Cross Society, 1942-50; secretary-general, Executive Yuan, 1945-47; state councilor, Nationalist Government, 1947-48; chairman, Board of Trustees on Rehabilitation Affairs, 1948-49; commissioner and chairman, JCRR, 1948-64; chairman, Shihmen Development Committee, 1958-64; chairman, board of trustees, China Foundation for the Promotion of Education & Culture, 1940-64.

Hsu Peh-yuan
Born in Chekiang, 1902. Died 1980. Education: College of Commerce, National Southeastern University; advanced study in finance at the University of ILLinois and the University of California. Career: general manager, China Electric Corp., 1933; deputy director-general, Postal Remittances and Saving Bank, 1934-35; manager, Bank of Communications, 1935-39; member, People's Political Council, 1938-40; deputy secretary-general and secretary-general, joint board of Four Government Banks, 1939-48; vice minister of Finance, 1946-48; deputy governor, Central Bank of China, 1949-50; chairman, board of directors, Bank of Taiwan, 1951-52; commissioner of Finance, Taiwan provincial government, 1953-54; minister of Finance, 1954-58; chairman, FETCC, 1955-58 and 1963-69; chairman, board of directors, Bank of China, 1948-69; governor, Central Bank of China, 1960-69.

Li Kwoh-ting (K. T. Li)
Born in Nanking, 1910. Education: B.S., National Central University, Nanking, 1930; advanced study in physics at Cambridge University, England, 1934-37. Career: professor, National Wuhan University, 1937-40; engineer, National Resources Commission, 1941-48; vice president and later president, Taiwan Shipbuilding Corp., 1949-53; member, IDC of ESB, 1953-58; secretary-general, CUSA , 1958-63; vice chairman, CIECD, 1963-73; minister of Economic Affairs, 1965-69; minister of Finance, 1969-76; minister of state (without portfolio?, 1976-; member, National Science Council; member, CSC, 1969-.

Shen Tsung-han (T.H. Shen)
Born in Chekiang, 1895. Died 1984. Education: National Agricultural College, Peking; M.S., State University of Georgia, 1924; Ph. D., Agriculture, Cornell University, 1928; professor of plant breeding, College of Agriculture, University of Nanking, 1934-37; concurrently chief technician, National Agricultural Research Bureau, Ministry of Industry; vice director and later director, National Agricultural Research Bureau, Ministry of Agriculture and Forestry, 1938-50; director, National Tabacco Improvement Bureau, 1947-49; head, Agricultural Division, Central Planning Board, Chungking, 1943-46; chairman, borad of directors, Agricultural Association of China, 1956-57; deputy head, China Section, the Joint China-US Agricultural Mission, 1946; commissioner, JCRR, 1948-73; chairman, JCRR, 1964-73.

Sun Yun-suan
Born in Shantung, 1913. Education: B.S., Electrical Engineering, Harbin Polytechnic Institute, 1934; received engineer training in Tennessee Valley Authority, USA, 1943-45. Career: engineer, National Resources Commission, 1937-40; superintendent, Tienshui Electric Power Plant, 1940-43; head engineer, Electric & Mechanical Department, Taiwan Power Co., 1946-50; chief engineer, Taiwan Power Co., 1950-53; vice president and chief engineer, Taiwan Power Co., 1953-62; president, Taiwan Power Co., 1962-64; chief executive officer & general manager, Electricity Corp. of Nigeria, 1964-67; minister of Communication, 1967-69; minister of Economic Affairs, 1969-78; Premier, 1978-83; member, CSC, 1969-; senior advisor to the President, 1984-.

Yang Chi-tseng
Born in Anhwei, 1898. Education: Diploma, (Mechanical) Engineer, Technische Hochschuele, Charlottenburg, Germany, 1926. Career:

chief of Ordance, Ministry of National Defense, 1944-49; vice minister of National Defense, 1950; vice minister of Economic Affairs, 1950; president, Taiwan Sugar Corp., 1950-58; minister of Economic Affairs; 1958-65.

Yen Chia-kan (C. K. Yen)
Born in Kiangsu, 1905. Education: B.S., Chemistry, St. John's University, Shanghai, 1926. Career: member & reconstruction commissioner, Fukien provincial government, 1938-39; member and Finance commissioner, Fukien provincial government, concurrently chairman, Fukien Provincial Bank, 1939-45; director of procurement, War Production Board, Central Government, 1945; commissioner of Communication, Taiwan provincial government, 1945-46; member & Finance commissioner, Taiwan provincial government, concurrently chairman of the Bank of Taiwan, 1946-49; minister of Economic Affairs, 1950; minister of Finance, concurrently vice chairman, CUSA, 1950-54; governor of Taiwan, 1954-57; minister of state (without portfolio), concurrently chairman, CUSA, 1957-58; minister of Finance, 1958-63; vice chairman, CUSA, 1963; Premier, 1963-72; chairman, CIECD, 1963-69; Vice President of the Republic of China, 1966-75; President of the Republic of China, 1975-78; member, CSC, 1964-.

Yin Chung-jung (K. Y. Yin)
Born in Hunan, 1903. Died 1963. Education: B.S., Electric Engineering, 1925. Career: assistant manager, China Development Finance Corp., 1936-40; director, Chinese Foreign Trade Office, New York, 1941-46; executive director, Hwainan Mining and Railway Co., 1947-49; deputy chairman, TPB, 1949-54; president, Central Trust of China, 1950-55; convener, IDC of ESB, 1953-55; minister of Economic Affairs, 1954-55; member and secretary-general, ESB, 1957-58; vice chairman, CUSA, 1958-63; chairman, FETCC, 1958-63; chairman of board, Bank of Taiwan, 1960-63.

Yu Kuo-hwa
Born in Chekiang, 1914. Education: B.A., Political Science, Tsinghua University, 1934; advanced study in finance and economics at the Graduate School, Harvard University, 1944-46 and London School of Economics, 1946-47. Career: secretary to the President, National Military Council, 1936-44; alternative executive director, International Bank for Reconstruction & Development, 1947-50; president, Central Trust of China, 1955-61; managing director, Chinese Development

Corp. 1959-67; chairman, board of directors, Bank of China, 1961-67; chairman, board of directors, Chinese Insurance Co., Ltd., 1961-67; minister of Finance, 1967-69; governor, International Bank for Reconstruction & Development for the ROC, 1967-69; governor, Central Bank of China, 1969-84; minister of state (without portfolio), 1969-84; governor, International Monetary Fund for the ROC, 1969-80; governor, Asian Development Bank for the ROC, 1969-84; chairman, CEPD, 1977-84; Premier, 1984-; member, CSC, 1979-.

Yui Hung-chun (O. K. Yui)
Born in Kwangtung, 1902. Died 1960. Education: B.A., Foreign Language and Literature, St. John's University, Shanghai. Career: secretary-general, Shanghai municipal government, 1930-37; mayor of Shanghai, 1937; managing director, Central Trust of China, 1938-40; vice minister of Finance, 1941-44; minister of Finance, 1944-48; managing director, Bank of China 1946-60; governor, Central Bank of China, 1948-49 and 1950-60; chairman, board of directors, Bank of Communications, 1950-60; chairman and president, Philippine Bank of Communications, 1951-60; chairman, board of directors, Bank of Taiwan, 1952; governor of Taiwan, 1953-54; Premier, 1954-58; member, CSC, 1953-60.

Other Policy Makers

Chang Chi-cheng
Born in Szechwan, 1918. Education: B.S., Civil Engineering, National Tungchi University; Ph. D., Civil Engineering, Cornell University. Career: professor, National Szechwan University, 1944-46; professor, National Taiwan University, 1953-58; senior expert, IDC of ESB, 1953-58; chief, General Affairs Division, CUSA, 1958-60; chief, 2nd Division, CUSA, 1960-63; secretary-general, CIECD, 1963-65 & 69; vice minister of Economic Affairs, 1965-69; minister of Communications, 1969-72; vice chairman and secretary-general, CIECD, 1972-73; chairman, EPC, 1973-76; secretary-general, Executive Yuan, 1976-78; minister of Finance, 1978-81; chairman of the board, Central Trust of China, 1981-84; governor, Central Bank of China, 1984-; national policy advisor to the President, 1981-.

Chang Hsien-ch'iu
Born in Peking, 1915. Education: B.S., Nanking University; M.S., Kan-

sas State College; Ph. D., Iowa State College. Career: assistant agronomist, National Rice and Wheat Improvement Bureau, 1937-38; assistant agronomist and later agronomist, National Agricultural Research Bureau, 1938-39 & 1944-47; senior specialist, Plant Industry Division, JCRR, 1948-53; chief, Plant Industry Division, JCRR, 1945-61; secretary-general JCRR; chairman, Council for Agricultural Planning and Development, 1981-84.

Chang Kwang-shih
Born in Kiangsu, 1913. Education: B.S., Chemistry, National Tsinghua University, Peking. Career: general manager, Marketing & Transportation Division, China Petroleum Corporation, 1948-56; vice president, China Petroleum Corporation, 1956-69; vice minister of Economic Affairs, 1969-78; minister of Economic Affairs, 1978-81.

Chang Tse-k'ai
Born in Kwangtung, 1900. Education: M.B.A. New York University, 1932. Career: deputy director, Industrial and Mining Readjustment Administration, Ministry of Economic Affairs, 1938-44; director of Materials War Production Board, 1944-45; general manager, China Petroleum Corporation, 1947-49; vice minister of Finance, 1950-51; executive vice president and general manager, Philippine Bank of Communications, 1951-52; minister of Economic Affairs, 1952-54; chairman, board of directors, Bank of Taiwan, 1953-60.

Chao Yao-tung
Born in Shanghai, 1915. Education: B.S., Mechanical Engineering, National Wuhan University, 1940; M.S., Mechanical Engineering, MIT, 1945. Career: factory manager, Tientsin Machine Works, 1946-48; chief engineer, Jong-been Textile Co., 1949-52; acting general manager, Jong-been Textile Co., 1953-58; project manager, Vietnam Textile Co., 1959-63; project manager, Sicovina Danang, Vietnam, 1962-63; project manager, Singapore Textile Ind. Ltd., 1964-66; deputy chairman, Leader Textile & Fiber Ind., 1967-68; director, Still Mill Project, Ministry of Economic Affairs, 1968-70; general manager, China Steel Corp., 1971-78; chairman, board of directors, China Steel Corp., 1978-81; minister of Economic Affairs, 1981-84; chairman, CEPD, 1984-; minister of state (without portfolio), 1984-.

Ch'en Ch'ing-yu
Born in Kiangsu, 1900. Education: B.A., Economics, National

Southeastern University. Career: commissioner of Reconstruction, Shensi provincial government; commissioner of Finance, Shensi provincial government; manager, Nanking Branch, Central Bank of China; director, Department of National Treasury, Minister of Finance; vice minister of Finance; secretary-general, Executive Yuan, 1954-58; comptroller-general, Executive Yuan, 1958-63; minister of Finance, 1963-67.

Chiang Piao
Education: Diploma, Mechanical Engineering, Munich University, Germany, 1924. Career: secretary-general, Resources Supply Commission, Executive Yuan; vice minister of National Defense, 1954-55; minister of Economic Affairs, 1955-58.

Ch'ien Ch'un
Born in Chekiang, 1928. Education: B.A., Economics, National Taiwan University; M.A., University of Minnesota, 1955-57. Career: director, Economic Research Department, Bank of China, 1963-68; executive secretary, Tax Reform Commission, Executive Yuan, 1968-70; director, Secretariat, Central Bank of China, 1970-73; general manager, Bank Department, Central Bank of China, 1973-77; deputy governor, Central Bank of China, 1978-85; minister of Finance, 1985-.

Ch'ien T'ien-ho
Born in Chekiang, 1893. Education: M.S., Agriculture, Cornell University, 1918. Career: assistant professor, Nanking University, 1919-23; director, Social Education Department, Ministry of Education, 1927-29; director, Metropolitan Museum of National History, Academia Sinica, 1929-32; vice director, National Agricultural Research Bureau, Ministry of Industries, 1932-37; director, Agriculture and Forestry Department, Ministry of Economic Affairs, 1933-40; vice minister of Agriculture and Forestry, 1940-47; regional advisor, FAO, 1947-48; chief, Agricultural Improvement Division, JCRR, 1948-51; commissioner, JCRR, 1951-61.

Fei Hwa
Born in Kiangsu, 1912. Education: B.S., Civil Engineering, Chiaotung University; M.S., Civil Engineering, Cornell University. Career: director and chief engineer, Taiwan Public Works Administration, 1945-47; deputy director, Taiwan Railway Administration, 1947-53; member, IDC of ESB, 1953-58; director, Transportation & Public Works,

CUSA, 1958-60; vice minister of Communications, 1960-69; chairman, China Tourism Development Corp., 1969; vice chairman and secretary-general, CIECD, 1969-72; secretary-general, Executive Yuan, 1972-76; minister of Finance, 1976-78; governor, International Bank for Reconstruction and Development Association, 1976-78; minister of state (without portfolio), 1978-84, member, CSC, 1976-79.

Hsu Li-teh
Born in Honan, 1931. Education: M.A., Political Science, National Chengchi University. Career: director, Department of Personnel, Ministry of Economic Affairs; director, 5th Department, Executive Yuan; vice minister of Finance, 1976-78; commissioner of Finance, Taiwan provincial government, 1978-81; minister of Finance, 1981-84; minister of Economic Affairs, 1984-85.

Lee Ch'ung-tao
Born in Shanghai, 1923. Education: B.S., National Kwangsi University; Ph. D., Agriculture, Cornell University. Career: chief, Vaccine Room, Taiwan Provincial Veterinary Serum Institute, 1947-50; senior specialist, JCRR, 1950-62; chief, Animal Industry Division, JCRR, 1962-1970 and 1977-81; secretary-general, JCRR, 1970-73; chairman, JCRR, 1973-79; professor, National Taiwan University and National Chunghsing University, 1962-73 and 1977-81; chairman, Council for Agricultural Planning and Development, 1979-81; president, National Chunghsing University, 1981-84; member, Examination Yuan, 1984-.

Lee Ta-hai
Born in Liaoning, 1919. Education: B.S., Chemistry, National Southwest Associate University. Career: chief, Engineering Department, Kaohsiung Refinery, 1955-61; chief engineer, Kaohsiung Refinery, 1961-66; deputy general manager, Kaohsiung Refinery, 1966-72; general manager, Kaohsiung Refinery, 1966-72; general manager, Kaohsiung Refinery, 1972-76; president, China Petroleum Corp., 1976-82; chairman of board, China Petroleum Corp., 1982-85; minister of Economic Affairs, 1985-.

Lee Teng-hui
Born in Taiwan, 1923. Education: Kyoto Imperial University, Japan, 1946; B.S., National Taiwan University, 1948; M.A., Iowa State University, 1953; Ph. D., Agricultural Economics, Cornell University, 1968. Career: teaching assistant, National Taiwan University,

1948-51; instructor, National Taiwan University, 1953-55; associate professor, National Taiwan University, 1956-58; research fellow, Provincial Cooperative Bank, 1957-61; specialist, JCRR, 1957-61; senior specialist and consultant, JCRR, 1961-70; chief, Rural Economic Division, JCRR, 1970-72; minister of state (without portfolio), 1972-78; professor, National Chengchi University, 1958-78; mayor of Taipei, 1978-81; governor of Taiwan, 1981-84; member, CSC, 1979-; chairman, KMT, 1988-; Vice President of the Republic of China, 1984-1988; President of the Republic of China, 1988-.

Lu Jun-k'ang
Education: M.A., Law, Soochow University. Career: secretary, Ministry of Finance; secretary, Ministry of Economic Affairs; director, Taxation Bureau of Taipei City; vice minister of Finance, minister of Finance, 1984-85.

T'ao Sheng-yang
Born in Shanghai, 1919. Died 1969. Education: B.A., Civil Engineering, St. John's University, Shanghai; Dipl-Ing., Technische Hochschule, Career: designing and research engineer in various German Plants, 1942-45; engineer, department head, and director of Technology Division, 10th Arsenal, 1946-47; professor, Taiwan College of Engineer, 1947-52; chief end-use investigator,ICA Mission to China, 1953-58; senior specialist, and deputy division chief, CUSA, 1958-60; executive secretary, Industrial Development and Investment Center, 1960-63; deputy secretary-general, CIECD, 1963-65; secretary-general, CIECD, 1965-69; minister of Economic Affairs, 1969.

Tsiang Yien-si
Born in Chekiang, 1915. Education: Ph. D., Agriculture, the University of Minnesota, 1942. Career: instructor, Minnesota University, 1942-45; advisor, Chinese Delegation to U.N. Food and Agriculture Organization, 1946; professor, Nanking University, 1947; chief, Department of Miscelleneous and Specialist Corp., National Agricultural Research Bureau, 1948; executive officer, JCRR, 1948-52; secretary-general, JCRR, 1952-61; commissioner, JCRR, 1961-78; secretary-general, Executive Yuan, 1967-72; minister of Education, 1972-77; secretary-general, Office of the President, 1978; minister of Foreign Affairs, 1978-79; secretary-general, KMT, 1979-84; national policy advisor to the President, 1984-; vice chairman, Committee for Science Development, National Science Council, 1966-; member, Atomic

Energy Council, 1966-; councilor, Academia Sinica, 1963-; member, CSC, 1969-79.

Wang You-tsao
Born in Fukien, 1925. Education: B.S., National Taiwan University; M.S. and Ph. D., Agriculture, Iowa University. Career: assistant professor to professor, National Taiwan University, 1954-73; specialist to chief of Rural Economic Division, JCRR, 1960-71; chief, Office of Planning & Programming, JCRR, 1971-72; deputy secretary-general, JCRR, 1972-73; secretary-general, UCRR, 1973-79; secretary-general, Council for Agricultural Planning and Development, 1979; vice chairman, Council for Agricultural Planning and Development, 1979-84; vice chairman, Council for Agricultural Planning and Development, 1984; chairman, Council of Agriculture, 1984-.

Yang Chia-lin
Born in Yunnan, 1910. Education: Fuhtan University; combined operation class, National War College. Career: director, Yunnan Land Bureau, 1943-47; member, Legislative Yuan, 1948-65; deputy chairman, Central Planning & Screening Committee, 1954-65; deputy delegate, 17th Session of UN Economic Commission for Asia and the Far East, 1966; chief delegate, Commission on Industry and National Resources, 1968; vice minister of Economic Affairs, 1965-69; professor, National War College, 1962-72; member, CIECD, 1969-72; chairman, Administration Research & Evaluation Commission, Executive Yuan, 1972-76; chairman, EPC, 1976-77.

Economic Bureaucrats

Kuo Wan-jung (Shirley W. Y. Kuo)
Born in Taiwan, 1930. Education: B.A., National Taiwan University; M.S., MIT; Doctor, Economics, Kobe University, Japan. Career: lecturer and associate professor, National Taiwan University; Ful Bright-Hays exchange professor, MIT, 1971-72; vice chairman, EPC, 1973-77; vice chairman, CEPD, 1977-79; deputy governor, Central Bank of China, 1979; professor, National Taiwan University, 1966-.

Shieh Shen-chung
Born in Kwangtung, 1924. Education: B.S. and M.S., National Central University; Ph. D., Agricultural Economics, University of Min-

nesota. Career: specialist, chief, and secretary-general, JCRR, 1951-65; professor, National Taiwan University, 1950-60; visiting professor, University of Philippines, 1965-67; director, Department of Projects, Asian Development Bank, 1967-81; vice chairman, CEPD, 1981-83; chairman of the board, Bank of Communications, 1983-; member, board of directors, Central Bank of China, 1983-.

Sun Chen
Born in Shangtung, 1934. Education: B.A. and M.A., National Taiwan University, 1956 and 1959; Ph. D., Oklahoma University, 1970. Career: teaching assistant, National Taiwan University, 1957-59; instructor, National Taiwan University, 1964-68; associate professor, National Taiwan University, 1968-71; professor, National Taiwan University, 1971-; vice chairman, EPC, 1973-77; vice chairman, CEPD, 1978-84; president, National Taiwan University, 1984-.

Tsui Tsu-k'an
Born in Peking, 1920. Education: B.S., Purdue University; M.S., Chemical Engineering, Polytechnic Institute of New York. Career: deputy secretary-general, CIECD, 1963-73; secretary-general, EPC, 1973-77; secretary-general, CEPD, 1977-83; vice chairman, CEPD, 1984-.

Wang Chang-ch'ing
Born in Hupeh, 1920. Education: B.C.E., National Chiaotung University: M.S., Environment Engineering, Johns Hopkins University, 1966. Career: senior engineer and concurrently division chief, Department of Communications, Taiwan provincial government, 1949-58; director, Public Works Bureau, Taiwan provincial government, 1958-69; director, Department of Public Works, Taipei city government, 1967-69; vice minister of Communications, 1969-77; vice chairman, CEPD, 1977-84; secretary-general, Executive Yuan, 1984-.

Wang Chou-ming
Born in Fukien, 1920. Education: Bachelor of Laws, Soochow University; Armed Forces University. Career: secretary-general, Ministry of Economic Affairs, 1965-69; secretary-general, Ministry of Finance, 1969-72; director, Department of Finance, Taipei city government, 1972-75; director, Department of Custom, Ministry of Finance, 1975-78; vice minister of Finance, 1978-81; vice minister of Economic Affairs, 1981-84; vice chairman, CEPD, 1984-.

Wang Tso-jung
Born in Hopeh, 1919. Education: B.A., National Central University, 1943; M.A., University of Washington, 1949; M.A., Vanderbilt University, 1958. Career: counselor and director, Economic Research Center, CUSA, 1959-63; director, 3rd Division, CIECD, 1963-65; advisor, CIECD, 1965-66; chief, Industrial Studies Section, U.N. Economic Commission for Asia and the Far East, 1967-70; professors, National Taiwan University, 1970-; member, Examination Yuan, 1984-; editor-writer, China Times and Commercial Times.

Yeh Wan-an
Born in Nanking, 1924. Education: B.A., Banking, National Shanghai Institute of Commerce; advanced research, International Monetary Found Institute; advanced research, Economic Development Institute, World Bank. Career: specialist, IDC of ESB, 1953-58; senior oficer, CUSA, 1958-63; director, Economic Research Division, CIECD, 1963-73; director, Economic Research Division, EPC, 1973-77; vice chairman, CEPD, 1977-.

Consulting Economists

Chow, Chi-chong (Gregory C. C. Chow)
Born in Kwangtung, 1930. Education: B.A., Cornell University; M.A. and Ph. D., University of Chicago. Career: assistant professor, MIT, 1955-59; associate professor, Cornell University, 1959-62; research staff, IBM Research Center, 1962-70; visiting professor, Cornell University, 1964-65; Harvard University, 1967; Rutgers University, 1969; adjunct professor, Columbia University, 1965-71; professor, Princeton University, 1970-; director, Econometric Research Program, Princeton University; member, Academia Sinica.

Fei, Ching-han (John C. H. Fei)
Born in Peking, 1923. Education: B.A., Economics, Yenching University; M.A., Economics, University of Washington; Ph. D., Economics, MIT. Career: assistant professor, Harvard University, 1952-55; associate professor and professor, Antioch College, Ohio, 1955-62; professor, Yale University, 1962-65; professor, Cornell University, 1965-69; professor, Yale University, 1969-; member, Academia Sinica; consultant, A.I.D. and N.P.A., 1964-.

Hsing Mo-huan
Education: B.A., Economics, National Central University; advanced studies, Chicago University; advanced research, Harvard University. Career: professor, National Taiwan University; advisor, National Science Council; research fellow and director, Institute of Economics, Academia Sinica; distinguished professor, Chinese University, Hong Kong; dean, School of Social Sciences, Chinese University, Hong Kong; dean, Graduate School, Chinese University, Hong Kong; emeritus professor, Chinese University, Hong Kong; member, Academia Sinica.

Koo, Ying-chang (Athony Y. C. Koo)
Born in Shanghai, 1918. Education: B.A., St. John's University; M.S., University of Illinois; M.A. and Ph. D., Harvard University. Career: assistant professor, associate professor, and professor, Michigan State University; the Distinguished Faculty Award of Michigan State University; member, Academia Sinica.

Liu Ta-chung
Born in Peking, 1914. Died, 1975. Education: M.S., National Chiaotung University; M.C.E., Cornell University; Ph. D., Economics, Cornell University. Career: professor, National Tsinghua University, 1946-48; economist, International Monetary Fund, 1949-58; visiting lecture, Johns' Hopking University, 1949-58; professor, Cornell University, 1958-75; member, Academia Sinica.

Tsiang Sho-chieh
Born in Hupeh, 1918. Education: B.S. and Ph. D., Economics, London School of Economics and Political Science; Doctor of Science, London University. Career: professor, National Peking University, 1946-48; professor, National Taiwan University, 1949; economist, International Monetary Found, 1949-60; professor, Rochester University, 1960-69; Guggenheim fellow, 1966-67; visiting senior research fellow, Jesus College, Oxford University, 1966-67; commissioner, National Reconstruction Planning Committee, National Science Council, 1967-68; commissioner, Tax Reform Committee, 1970-72; visiting fellow, Nuffield College, Oxford University, 1976-77; member, Academia Sinica, 1958-; president, Chung-hua Institute for Economic Research; emeritus professor, Cornell University.

APPENDIX B

EVOLUTION OF ORGANIZATION AND PERSONNEL FOR ECONOMIC POLICY-MAKING, 1950-85 (DIVIDED BY THE CHANGE OF THE PREMIERS)

March, 1950 to June, 1954
President: Chiang Kai-shek
Premier: Ch'en Ch'eng
    TPB (before 06/53): Wu Kuo-cheng (chairman)
                                 K. Y. Yin (vice chairman)
    ESB (after 06/53): O. K. Yui (chairman)
    CUSA: Ch'en Ch'eng (chairman)
    JCRR: Chiang Monlin (chairman)
    Ministry of Economic Affairs: Cheng Tao-ju (minister, before 05/52)
                                           Chang Tse-k'ai (minister, after 05/52)
    Ministry of Finance: C. K. Yen (minister)
    Bank of Taiwan: Hsu Peh-yuan (chairman of board, 1951-52)
                      O. K. Yui (chairman of board, 1952-53)
                      Chang Tse-k'ai (chairman of board, 1953-)

July, 1954 to July, 1958
President: Chiang Kai-shek
Vice President: Ch'en Ch'eng
Premier: O. K. Yui
    ESB: C. K. Yen (chairman)
    CUSA: O. K. Yui (chairman, before 08/57)
             C. K. Yen (chairman, after 08/57)
    FETCC: Hsu Peh-yuan (chairman, before 08/57)
    JCRR: Chiang Monlin (chairman)
    Ministry of Economic Affairs: K. Y. Yin (minister, before 12/55)
                                           Chiang Piao (minister, after 12/55)
    Ministry of Finance: Hsu Peh-yuan (minister)
    Bank of Taiwan: Chang Tse-k'ai (chairman of board)

July, 1958 to December, 1963
President: Chiang Kai-shek
Vice President: Ch'en Ch'eng
Premier: Ch'en Ch'eng
  CUSA: Ch'en Cheng (chairman)
        K. Y. Yin (vice chairman, before 01/63)
        C. K. Yen (vice chairman, after 01/63)
        K. T. Li (secretary-general)
  FETCC: K. Y. Yin (chairman, before 01/63)
        Hsu Peh-yuan (chairman, after 01/63)
  JCRR: Chiang Monlin (chairman)
  Ministry of Economic Affairs: Yang Chi-tseng (minister)
  Bank of Taiwan: K. Y. Yin (chairman of board, 07/60 to 01/63)
  Central Bank of China: Hsu Peh-yuan (governor, 07/60-)

December, 1963 to June, 1972
President: Chiang Kai-shek
Vice President: Ch'en Ch'eng (before 05/65)
            C. K. Yen (after 05/65)
Premier: C. K. Yen
  CIECD: C. K. Yen (chairman, before 08/69)
        Chiang Ching-kuo (chairman, after 08/69)
        K. T. Li (vice chairman, before 10/69)
        Fei Hwa (vice chairman and secrtary-general, after 10/69)
        Chang Chi-cheng (secretary-general, 12/63 to 01/65) and
            08/69 to 10/69)
        T'ao Sheng-cheng (secretary-general, 01/65 to 08/69)
  FETCC (dissolved in 1969): Hsu Peh-yuan (chairman)
  JCRR: Chiang Monlin (chairman, before 06/64)
        T. H. Shen (chairman, after 06/64)
  Ministry of Economic Affairs: Yang Chi-tseng (before 01/65)
  (minister)   K. T. Li (01/65 to 07/69)
                          T'ao Sheng-yang (07/69 to 10/69)
                          Sun Yun-suan (after 10/69)
  Ministry of Finance: Ch'en Ch'ing-yu (before 12/67)
  (minister)   Yu Kuo-hwa (12/67 to 07/69)
                    K. T. Li (after 07/69)
  Central Bank of China: Hsu Peh-yuan (before 06/69)
  (governor)   Yu Kuo-hwa (after 07/69)

June, 1972 to May, 1978
President: Chiang Kai-shek (before 04/75)
　　　　　C. K. Yen (after 04/74)
Vice President: C. K. Yen (before 04/75)
Premier: Chiang Ching-kuo
　CIECD (before 07/73): Chiang Ching-kuo (chairman)
　　　　　　　　　　　Chang Chi-cheng (vice chairman and
　　　　　　　　　　　　　　　　　　secretary-general)
　　EPC (07/73 to 12/77): Chang Chi-cheng (chairman, before 06/76)
　　　　　　　　　　　　Yang Chia-lin (chairman, after 06/76)
　　　　　　　　　　　　Sirley W. H. Kuo (vice chairman)
　　　　　　　　　　　　Sun Chen (vice chairman)
　　　　　　　　　　　　Tsui Tsu-k'an (secretary-general)
　CEPD (after 12/77): Yu Kwo-hwa (chairman)
　　　　　　　　　　　Wang Chang-ch'ing (vice chairman)
　　　　　　　　　　　Sun Chen (vice chairman)
　　　　　　　　　　　Shieh Shen-chung (vice chairman)
　JCRR: T. H. Shen (chairman, before 05/73)
　　　　Lee Ch'ung-tao (chairman, before 05/73)
　Ministry of Economic Affairs: Sun Yun-suan (minister)
　Ministry of Finance: K. T. Li (minister, before 06/76)
　　　　　　　　　　　Fei Hwa (minister, after 06/76)
　Central Bank of China: Yu Kuo-hwa (governor)

May, 1978 to May, 1984
President: Chiang Ching-kuo
Vice President: Shieh Tung-min
Premier: Sun Yun-suan
  CEPD: Yu Kuo-hwa (chairman)
        Wang Chang-ch'ing (vice chairman)
        Sun Chen (vice chairman)
        Shieh Shen-chung (vice chairman)
  JCRR (before 1979): Lee Ch'ung-tao (chairman)
  Council for Agricultural Planning and Development (after 1979):
        Lee Ch'ung-tao (chairman, before 07/81)
        Chang Hsien-ch'iu (chairman, after 07/81)
  Ministry of Economic Affairs:
        Chang Kwang-shih (minister, before 12/81)
        Chao Yao-tung (minister, after 12/81)
  Ministry of Finance: Chang Chi-cheng (minister, before 12/81)
        Hsu Li-teh (minister, after 12/81)
  Central Bank of China: Yu Kuo-hwa (governor)

May, 1984 to May, 1987
President: Chiang Ching-kuo
Vice President: Lee Teng-hui
Premier: Yu Kuo-hwa
  CEPD: Chao Yao-tung (chairman)
      Wang Chou-ming (vice chairman)
      Yeh Wan-an (vice chairman)
      Tsui Tsu-k'an (vice chairman)
  Council of Agriculture: Wang You-tsao (chairman)
  Ministry of Economic Affairs: Hsu Li-teh (Minister, before 03/85)
        Li Ta-hai (minister, after 03/85)
  Ministry of Finance: Lu Jun-k'ang (minister, before 03/85)
        Ch'ien Ch'un (minister, after 03/85)
  Central Bank of China: Chang Chi-cheng (governor)

BIBLIOGRAPHY

1. English

Adelman, Irma and Cynthia Taft Morris. 1973. *Economic Growth and Social Equality in Developing Countries.* Standford, CA: Standford University Press.

Almond, Gabriel. 1965. "A Developmental Approach to Political System." *World Politics.* 16: 183-214.

Althusser, Luis. 1969. For Marx, translated by Ben Brewster. New York: Pantheon.

Althusser, Luis and E. Balibar. 1970. *Reading Capital,* translated by Ben Brewster. London: New Left Books.

Amin, Samir. 1976. *Unequal Development: An Essay on the Social Formations of Peripheral Capitalism.* New York: Monthly Review Press.

Amsden, Alice H. 1979. "Taiwan's Economic History: A Case of Etatisme and a Challenge to Dependency Theory." *Modern China.* 5(3): 341-373.

Amsden, Alice H. 1985. "The State and Taiwan's Economic Development." Pp. 78-106, in *Bringing the State Back In,* edited by Peter B. Evans, Dietrich Rueschemeyer and Theda Skocpol. New York: Cambridge University Press.

Anderson, W. A. 1950. *Farmers Associations in Taiwan.* Taipei: Joint Commission of Rural Reconstruction.

Barrett, Richard E. 1980. "State Intervention in the Taiwanese Economy in the 1960's." Paper presented at the *Taiwan Political Economy Workshop,* East Asian Institute, Columbia University, New York, December, 1980.

Barrett, Richard E. 1983. "State and Economy on Taiwan, 1960-1980." Unpublished ms.

Barrett, Richard E. and Martin King Whyte. 1982. "Dependency Theory and Taiwan: Analysis of a Deviant Case." *American Journal of Sociology.* 87(5): 1064-1089.

Bates, Robert H. 1981. *Markets and States in Tropical Africa: The Political Basis of Agricultural Policies.* Berkeley, CA: University of California Press.

Becker, David G. 1983. *The New Bourgeiosie and the Limits of Dependency: Mining, Class and Power in Revolutionary Peru.* Princeton, NJ: Princeton University Press.

Berger, Peter L. 1983. "Secularity–West and East." Mimeo.
Binder, Leonard, et al. 1971. *Crises and Sequences in Political Development*. Princeton, NJ: Princeton University Press.
Canak, William L. 1983. "The Peripheral State Debate: Bureaucratic Authoritarianism and State Capitalism." *Latin American Research Review* 19(1):3-36.
Cardoso, Fernando H. and Enzo Faletto. 1979. *Dependency and Development in Latin America,* translated by Marjory M. Urquidi. Berkeley, CA: University of California Press.
Carnoy, Martin. 1984. *The State and Political Theory.* Princeton, NJ: Princeton University Press.
CEPD. 1978. *Revised Plan for the Second Three-Year Period (1979-1981) of the Six-Year Plan for the Economic Development of Taiwan, Republic of China.* Taipei: Council for Economic Planning and Development, Executive Yuan.
CEPD. 1981. *Four-Year Economic Development Plan for Taiwan, Republic of China (1982-1985).* Taipei: Council for Economic Planning and Development, Executive Yuan.
CEPD. 1986. *Taiwan Statistical Data Book 1986.* Taipei: Council for Economic Planning and Development, Executive Yuan.
CEPD. 1989. *Taiwan Statistical Data Book 1986.* Taipei: Council for Economic Planning and Development, Executive Yuan.
CEPD. 1991. *Taiwan Statistical Data Book 1986.* Taipei: Council for Economic Planning and Development, Executive Yuan.
Chang, Jui-meng. 1986. *The Political Economy of Taiwan's Trade Policy.* Ph. D. dissertation. New York: Columbia University.
Chao, Kang. 1982. *The Economic Development of Manchuria: The Rise of a Frontier Economy.* Ann Arbor, MI: Center for Chinese Studies. The University Michigan.
Ch'en, Ch'eng. 1961. *Land Reform in Taiwan.* Taipei: China Publishing Co.
Ch'en, Yu-hsi. 1981. *Dependent Development and Its Sociopolitical Consequence: A Case Study of Taiwan.* Ph. D. dissertation. Hawaii: The University of Hawaii.
Chiang, Kai-shek. 1954. "Chapters on National Fecundity, Social Welfare, Education and Health and Happiness." Pp. 213-329, in Sun Yat-sen, *San Min Chu I,* translated by Durham S. F. Chen. Taipei: China Publishing Co.
China Handbook. 1956-57. Taipei: China Publishing Co.
China Yearbook. 1957-58. Taipei: China Publishing Co.
China Yearbook. 1960-61. Taipei: China Publishing Co.

China Yearbook. 1963-64. Taipei: China Publishing Co.
Chiu, Paul C. H. 1983. "Performance of Financial Institutions in Taiwan." Pp. 313-334, in *Experiences and Lessons of Economic Development in Taiwan,* edited by Kwoh-ting Li and Tzong-shian Yu. Taipei: Institute of Economics, Academia Sinica.
Chiu, Hun-dah (ed.) 1973. *China and the Question of Taiwan: Documents and Analysis.* New York: Praeger.
Clough, Ralph N. 1978. *Island China.* Cambridge, MA: Harvard University Press.
Copper, John Franklin. 1984. "Political Development in the Republic of China, 1949-1981." Pp. 119-155, in *China: Seventy Years After the 1911 Hsin-hai Revolution,* edited by Hungdah Chiu and Shao-chuan Leng. Charlottesville, VA: University Press of Virginia.
Cumings, Bruce. 1984. "The Origins and Development of the Northeast Asian Political Economy: Industrial Sectors, Product Cycles, and Political Consequences." *International Organization.* 38(1): 1-40.
DGBAS. 1990. *Social Indicators in Taiwan Area of the Republic of China 1989.* Taipei: Directorate-General of Budget, Accounting and Statistics, Executive Yuan.
Domhoff, G. W. 1967. *Who Rules America.* Englewood Cliffs, NJ: Prentice-Hall.
Dos Santos, Theotonio. 1970. "The Structure of Dependcence." *American Economic Review.* 60(2): 231-236.
Dupuy, Alex and Barry Truchill. 1979. "Problems in the Theory of State Capitalism." *Theory and Society.* 8: 1-38.
Easten, David. 1957. "An Approach to the Analysis of Political System." *World Politics.* 9: 383-400.
EPC. 1974. *The Republic of China's Sixth Four-Year Plan for Economic Development of Taiwan 1973-1976.* Taipei: Economic Planning Council, Executive Yuan.
EPC. 1976. *The Republic of China's Six Year Plan for Economic Development of Taiwan 1976-1981.* Tapiei: Economic Planning Council, Executive Yuan.
Evans, Peter B. 1979. *Dependent Development: The Alliance of Multinational, State and Local Capital in Brazil.* Princeton, NJ: Princeton University Press.
Evans, Peter B. 1981. "Collectivized Capitalism: Integrated Petrochemical Complexes and Capital Accumulation in Brazil." Pp. 85-126, in *Authoritarian Capitalism: Brazil's Contemporary Political and Economic Development,* edited by T. Bruneau and P. Faucher. Boulder, CO: Westview Press.

Evans, Peter B. 1982. "reinventing the Bourgeoisie: State Entrepreneurship and Class Formation in Dependent Capitalist Development." *American Journal of Sociology.* 88(Supplement): S210-S247.

Evans, Peter B. 1984. "Class State, and Dependence in East Asia: Lessons for Latin Americanists." Manuscript prepared for *The Political Economy of the New Asian Industrialism,* edited by Frederick Deyo. Ithaca, NYL: Cornell University Press.

Evans, Peter B. 1985. "Transnational Linkages and the Economic Role of the State: An Analysis of Developing and Industrialized Nations in the Post-World War II Period." Ph. 192-226, in *Bringing the State Back In,* edited by Peter B. Evans, Dietrich Rue-schemeyer, and Theda Skocpol. New York: Cambridge University Press.

Evans, Peter B., Dietrich Rueschemeyer and Theda Skocpol. 1985. "On the Road toward a More Adequate Understanding of the State." Pp. 347-366, in *Bringing the State Back In,* edited by Peter B. Evans, Dietrich Rueschemeyer, and Theda Skocpol. New York: Cambridge University Press.

Fainsod, Merle. 1963. "Bureaucracy and Modernization: The Russian and Soviet Case." Pp. 233-267, in *Bureaucracy and Political Development,* edited by Joseph LaPalombara. Princeton, NJ: Princeton University Press.

Fei, John C. H. 1982. "Ideology of Economic Development in Taiwan." Pp. 83-99, in *Experiences and Lessoms of Economic Development in Taiwan,* edited by Kwoh-ting Li and Tzong-shian Yu. Taipei: Institute of Economics, Academia Sinica.

Fei, John C. H. 1984. "Policy Evolution in the Development Process." In K. T. Li, *Analysis of Transition Growth and Policy Evolution: The Case of the ROC.* Manuscript to be published by Yale University Press, New Haven, Connecticut.

Fei, John C. H., Gustav Ranis, and Shirley W.Y. Kuo. 1979. *Growth with Equity: The Taiwan Case.* New York: Oxford University Press.

Fitzgerald, E. V. K. 1976. *The State and Economic Development: Peru Since 1968.* New York: Cambridge University Press.

Frank, Andre Gunder. 1967. *Capitalism and Underdevelopment in Latin America.* New York: Monthly Review Press.

Frank, Andre Gunder. 1969. *Latin America: Underdevelopment or Revolution.* New York: Monthly Review Press.

Galenson, Walter (ed.) 1979. *Economic Growth and Structural Change in Taiwan: The Postwar Experience of the Republic of China.*

Ithaca, NY: Cornell University Press.
Galenson, Walter. 1979. "The Labor Force, Wages, and Living Standards." Pp. 384-447, in *Economic Growth and Structural Change in Taiwan: The Postwar Experience of the Republic of China,* edited by Walter Galenson. Ithaca, NY: Cornell University Press.
Cates, Hill. 1981. "Ethnicity and Social Class." Pp. 241-281, in *The Anthropology of Taiwanese Society,* edited by Emily Martin Ahern and Hill Gates. Standford, CA: Standford University Press.
Gerschenkron, Alexander. 1979. *Economic Backwardness in Historical Perspective.* Cambridge, MA: Belknap.
Giddens, Anthony. 1973. *The Class Structure of the Advanced Societies.* Lodon: Hutchinson.
Gold, David A., Clarence Y. H. Lo, and Eric O. Wright. 1975. "Recent Development in marxist Theories of the Capitalist State." *Monthly Review.* 27(5): 29-43 and 27(6): 36-51.
Gold, Thomas B. 1981. *Dependent Development in Taiwan.* Ph. D. dissertation. Cambridge, MA: Harvard University.
Gold, Thomas B. 1986. *State and Society in the Taiwan Miracle.* Armonk, NY: M. E. Sharpe.
Gregory, James A., Maria Hsia Chang, and Andrew B. Zimmerman. 1981. *Ideology and Development: Sun Yat-sen and the Economic History of Taiwan.* Berkeley, CA: Institute of East Asian Studies, University of California, Berkeley.
Hamilton, Nora. 1983. *The Limits of State Autonomy: Post-Revolutionary Mexico.* Princeton, NJ: Princeton University Press.
Hirschman, Albert O. 1958. *Strategy of Economic Development.* New Haven, CT: Yale University Press.
Ho, Samuel P. S. 1975. "The Economic Development of Colonial Taiwan: Evidence and Interpretation." *Journal of Asian Studies.* 34(2): 417-430.
Ho, Samuel P. S. 1978. *Economic Development of Taiwan, 1860-1970.* New Haven, CT: Yale University Press.
Hofheinz, Jr., Roy and Kent E. Calder. 1982. *The Eastasia Edge.* New York: Basic Books.
Hoh, Chih-hsiang. 1971. *The Constitution of the Republic of China.* Taipei: Shang-wu Publishing Co.
Holland, Stuart (ed.) 1972. *The State as Entrepreneur.* London: Weidenfeld and Nicolson.
Hou, Chi-ming, 1985. "The Sturcturalists, the Neoclassicalists, and Industrial Upgrading in the Republic of China." *Industry of Free China.* 63(2): 9-25.

Hsiao, Hsin-huang Michael. 1981. *Government Agricultural Strategies in Taiwan and South Korea: A Macrosociological Assessment.* Taipei: Institute of Ethnology, Academia Sinica.

Hsiao, Hsin-huang Michael. 1985. "An East Asian Development Model: Empirical Overview." Paper presented in the Symposium *In Search of an East Asian Development,* jointly sponsored by Asia and World Institute (Taipei) and Council on Religion and International Affairs (New York), Merrill House, New York City, June 28-30, 1985.

Hsu, L. T. 1985. "ROC-USA Economic and Trade Relations: Problems and Opportunities" *Industry of Free China.* 63(3): 7-11.

Hsu, Wen-hsiung. 1980a. "From Aboriginal Island to Chinese Frontier: The Development of Taiwan Before 1683." Pp. 3-29, in *China's Island Frontier,* edited by Ronald G. Knapp. Honolulu, Hawaii: University Press of Hawaii and Research Corporation of the University of Hawaii.

Hsu, Wen-hsiung. 1980b. "Frontier Social Organization and Social Disorder in Ch'ing Taiwan." Pp. 87-105, in *China's Island Frontier,* edited by Ronald G. Knapp. Honolulu, Hawaii: University Press of Hawaii and Research Corporation of the University of Hawaii.

Israel, John. 1964. "Politics on Formosa." Pp. 59-67, in *Formosa Today,* edited by Mark Mancall. New York: Frederick A. Praeger.

Jacoby, Neil H. 1966. *U.S. Aid to Taiwan: A Study of Foreign Aid, Self-help and Development.* New York: Praeger.

Jessop, Bob. 1977. "Recent Theories of the Capitalist State." *Cambridge Journal of Economics.* 1: 353-373.

Johnson, Chalmers. 1982. *MITI and the Japanese Miracle: The Growth of Industrial Policy, 1925-1975.* Standford, CA: Standford University Press.

Johnson, Chalmers. 1985. "Political Institutions and Economic Performance: The Government-Business Relationship in Japan, South Korea, and Taiwan." Pp. 63-89, in *Asian Economic Development–Present and Future,* edited by Robert A. Scalapino, Seizaburo Sato, and Jusfu Wanand. Berkeley, CA: Institute of Asian Studies, University of California.

Kahn, Herman. 1979. *World Economic Development, 1979 and Beyond.* Boulder, CO: Westview Press.

Kau, Ying-mao. 1984. "The Changing Power Configuration and Its Implications for the Republic of China." Paper presented at the Conference on *Changing International Relations in Asia,* spon-

sored by the Institute of Asian Studies, St. John's University, New York City, October 26-27, 1984.
Kerr, George H. 1965. *Formosa Betrayed.* Boston: Houghton-Mifflin.
Keynes, John Maynard. 1964. *The General Theory of Employment, Interest, and Money.* New York: A Harbinger Book.
Kim, Eun Mee. 1987a. *From Dominance to Symbiosis: State and Chaebol in the Korean Economy, 1960-1985.* Ph. D. dissertation. Providence, RI: Brown University.
Kim, Myoung Soo. 1987b. *The Making of the Korean Society: The Role of the State in the Republic of Korea (1948-1979).* Ph. D. dissertation. Providenced, RI: Brown University.
Koo, Anthony Y. C. 1968. *The Role of Land Reform in Economic Development: A Case Study of Taiwan.* New York: Prager.
Krasner, Stephen D. 1978. *Defending the National Interests: Raw Materials Investments and U.S. Foreign Policy.* Princeton, NJ: Princeton University Press.
Krasner, Stephen D. 1984. "Apporaches to the State: Alternative Conceptions and Historical Dynamics." *Comparative Politics. (January)* 1984: 223-246.
Kuo, Shirley W. Y. 1983. *The Taiwan Economy in Transition.* Boulder, CO: Westview Press.
Kuo, Shirley W. Y., Gustav Ranis and John C. H. Fei. 1981. *The Taiwan Success Story: Rapid Growth with Improved Distribution in the Public of China, 1952-1979.* Boulder, CO: Westview Press.
Kuo, Ting-yee. 1973. "The Internal Development and Modernization of Taiwan." Pp. 171-240, in *Taiwan in Modern Times,* edited by Paul K. T. Sih. New York: St. John's University Press.
Kuznets, Simon. 1955. "Economic Growth and Income Inequality." *American Economic Review.* 45: 1-28.
Kuzents, Simon. 1979. "Growth and Structural Shifts." Pp. 15-131, in *Economic Growth and Structural Change in Taiwan: The Postwar Experience of the Republic of China,* edited by Walter Galenson. Ithaca, NY: Cornell University Press.
Lamley, Harry J. 1981. "Subethnic Rivalry in the Ch'ing Period." Pp. 282-318, in *The Anthropology of Taiwanese Society,* edited by Emily Martin Ahern and Hill Gates. Standford, CA: Standford University Press.
LaPalombara, Joseph (ed.) 1963. *Bureaucrary and Political Development.* Princeton, NJ: Princeton University Press.
Lasswell, Harold D. 1960. *Psychopathology and Politics.* New York: The Viking Press.

Lau, Lawrence J. 1986. "Introduction." Pp. 1-11, in *Models of Development: A Comparative Study of Economic Growth in South Korea and Taiwan,* edited by Lawrence J. Lau. San Francisco: Institute for Contemporary Studies.

Lee, Teng-hui. 1971. *Intersectoral Capital Flows in the Economic Development of Taiwan, 1895-1960.* Ithaca, NY: Cornell University Press.

Lewis, W. Arthur. 1955. *A Theory of Economic Growth.* London: Allen & Unwin.

Li, K. T. 1976. *The Experience of Dynamic Economic Growth on Taiwan.* Taipei: Meiya Publications.

Li, K. T. 1980. *My Views on Taiwan's Economic Development: A Collection of Essays from 1975-1980.* Taipei.

Li, K. T. 1985. *Prospects for Taiwan's Economic Development: A collection of Essays from 1980-1984.* Taipei.

Li, K. T. 1986a. "Economic Development and Ethical Standards." *Industry of Free China.* 64(4): 1-10.

Li, Kwoh-ting and Yeh Wang-an. 1982. "Economic Planning in the Republic of China." Pp. 103-129, in *Experience and Lessons of Economic Development in Taiwan,* edited by Li Kwoh-ting and Yu Tsong-shian. Taipei: Institute of Economics, Academia Sinica.

Lin, Ching-yuan. 1973. *Industrialization in Taiwan, 1946-72: Trade and Import-Substitution Policies for Developing Countries.* New York: Praeger.

Linebarger, Paul Myron Anthony. 1937. *The Political Doctrines of Sun Yat-sen: An Exposition of the San Min Chu I.* Wesport, CT: Greenwood Press.

Little, Ian M. D. 1979. "An Economic Reconnaissance." Pp. 448-507, in *Economic Growth and Structural Change in Taiwan: The Postwar Experience of the Republic of China,* edited by Walter Galenson. Ithaca, NY: Cornell University Press.

Liu, Alan P. L. 1986. *Phoenix and the Lame Lion: Modernization in Taiwan and Mainland China, 1950-1980.* Manuscript to be published by Hoover Institute Press, Standford, California.

Lundberg, Erik. 1979. "Fiscal and Monetary Policy." Pp. 263-307, in *Economic Growth and Structural Change in Taiwan: The Postwar Experience in the Republic of China,* edited by Walter Galenson. Ithaca, NY: Cornell University Press.

March, James G. and Herbert A. Simn. 1958. *Organizations.* New York: John Wiely & Sons.

McCoy, Al. 1971. "Land Reform as Counter-Revolution: U.S. Foreign

Policy and the Tenent Farmers of Asia." *Bulletin of Concerned Asian Scholars.* 3:1.
Miliband, Ralph. 1969. *The State in Capitalist Society.* New York: Basic Books.
Myers, Ramon H. 1973. "The Economic Development." Pp. 28-73, in *China and the Question of Taiwan: Documents and Analysis,* edited by Chiu Hun-dah. New York: Praeger.
Myers. Ramon H. 1986. "The Economic Development of the Republic of China on Taiwan, 1965-1981." Pp. 13-64, in *Models of Development,* edited by Lawrence J. Lau. San Francisco: ICS Press.
Myers, Ramon H. and Adrienne Ching. 1964. "Agricultural Development in Taiwan under Japanese Colonial Rule." *Journal of Asian Studies.* 23: 555-570.
Myint, Hal. 1982. "Comparative Analysis of Taiwan's Economic Development with other Countries" Pp. 59-81, in *Experiences and Lessons of Economic Development in Taiwan,* edited by Kwohting Li and Tzong-shian Yu. Taipei: Institute of Economics, Academia Sinica.
Myrdal, Gunnar. 1957. *Economic Theory and Underdeveloped Regions.* London: Duckworth.
Nordlinger, Eric A. 1981. *On the Autonomy of the Democratic State.* Cambridge, MA: Harvard University Press.
North, Douglass C. 1979. *Structure and Change in Economic History.* New York: W. W. Norton & Company
Nurkse, Ragnar. 1953. *Problems of Capital Formation in Underdeveloped Countries.* Oxford: Basil Blackwell.
O'Donnell, Guillermo. 1973. *Modernization and Bureaucratic-Authoritarianism: Studies in South American Politics.* Berkeley, CA: Institute of International Studies, University of California, Berkeley.
O'Donnell, Guillermo. 1978. "Reflections on the Patterns of Change in the Bureaucratic-Authoritarian State." *Latin American Research Review.* 13(1): 3-38.
Offe, Claus. 1973. "The Capitalist State and the Problems of Policy Formation." In *Stress and Contradition in Modern Capitalism,* Leon N Lindberg, Robert Alford, Colin Crouch, and Claus Offe. Lexington, MA: D. C. Heath.
Offe, Claus. 1974. "Structural Problems of the Capitalist State: Class Rule and the Political System on the Selectiveness of Political Institutions." In *German Politics Studies. Vol. 1,* edited by Klaus

Von Beyme. Beverly Hills, CA: Sage.
Olson, Mancur. 1977. *The Logic of Collective Action: Public Goods and the Theory of Groups.* Cambridge, MA: Harvard University Press.
Polanyi, Karl. 1944. *The Great Transformation.* New York: Rinehart.
Poulantzas, Nicos. 1969. "The Problem of the Capitalist State." *New Left Review.* 58: 67-78.
Poulantzas, Nicos. 1973. *Political Power and Social Classes,* translated by Timothy O'Hagen. London: New Left Books.
Poulantzas, Nicos. 1978. State, Power, Socialism. London: New Left Books.
Prebisch, Raul. 1950. *The Economic Development of Latin America and Its Principle Problems.* New York: United Nations.
Prybyla, Jan S. 1979. "Economic Development in Taiwan." Pp. 77-126, in *China and the Taiwan Issue,* edited by Hungdah Chiu. New York: Praeger.
Pye, Lucian W. 1985. "The New Asian Capitalism: A Political Portrait." Paper for the symposium *In Search of an East Asian Development Model,* sponsored by the Council on Religion and International Affairs and the Asia and World Institute, New York City, June 27-30, 1985.
Rabbins, Lord. 1983. "Stagflation." Pp. 21-33, in *Experiences and Lessons of Economic Development in Taiwan,* edited by Kwoh-ting Li and Tzong-shian Yu. Taipei: Institute of Economics, Academia Sinica.
Ranis, Gustav. 1979. "Industrial Development." Pp. 206-262, in *Economic Growth and Structural Change in Taiwan: The Postwar Experience of the Republic of China,* edited by Walter Galenson. Ithaca, NY: Cornell University Press.
Republic of China 1986: A Reference Book. 1986. Taipei: Hilit Publishing Co.
Riggs, Fred W. 1952. *Formosa Under Chinese Nationalist Rule.* New York: Macmillan.
Rosenstein-Rodan, P. N. 1943. "Problems of Industrialization of Eastern and Southeastern Europe." *Economic Journal.* June-September.
Rueschemeyer, Dietrich and Peter B. Evans. 1982. "The State and Economic Transformation: Towards an Analysis of the Conditions Underlying Effective Intervention." Pp. 44-77, in *Bringing the State Back In,* edited by Peter B. Evans, Dietrich Rueschemeyer and Theda Skocpol. New York: Cambrdige University Press.

Schurmann, Franz. 1974. *The Logic of Power.* New York: Pantheon.
Scott, Maurice. 1979. "Foreign Trade." Pp. 308-383, in *Economic Growth and Structural Change in Taiwan: The Postwar Experience of the Republic of China,* edited by Walter Galenson. Ithaca, NY: Cornell University Press.
Shao, Maria, William J. Holstein and Steven J. Dryden. 1987. "Taiwan's Wealth Crisis: Its $53 Billion Cash Hoard is Economic Poison." *Business Week.* April 13: 46-47.
Shen, T. H. 1970. *The Sino-American Joint Commission on Rural Reconstruction: 20 Years of Cooperation for Agricultural Development.* Ithaca, NY: Cornell University Press.
Shiau, Chyuan-jeng. 1985. "The Functions and Development of the Farmers' Associations in the Republic of China." Paper presented at the 27th annual meeting of the *American Association for Chinese Studies,* University of California, Berkeley, November 22-24, 1985.
Singer, Hans W. 1954. "Problems of Industrialization of Underdeveloped Countries." *International Social Science Bulletin.* 6(2).
Skocpol, Theda. 1979. *States and Social Revolutions in France, Russia and China.* New York: Cambridge University Press.
Skocpol, Theda. 1985. "Bring the State Back in: Strategies of Analysis in Current Research." Pp. 3-37, in *Bringing the State Back In,* edited by Peter B. Evans, Dietrich Rueschemeyer and Theda Skocpol. New York: Cambridge University Press.
Stepan, Alfred. 1978. *The State and Society: Peru in Comparative Perspective.* Princeton, NJ: Princeton University Press.
Sun, Yat-sen. 1922. *The International Development of China.* Taipei: China Cultural Service.
Sun, Yat-sen. 1924. *San Min Chu I (The Three Princilpe of the People),* translated by Frank Price. Taipei: China Publishing Co.
Sunkel, Osvaldo. 1973. "Transnational Capitalism and National Disintegration in Latin America." *Social and Economic Studies.* 22: 132-176.
Thorbecke, Erik. 1979. "Agricultural Development." Pp. 132-205, in *Economic Growth and Structural Change in Taiwan: The Poswar Experience of the Republic of China,* edited by Walter Galenson. Ithaca, NY: Cornell University Press.
Trimberger, Ellen Kay. 1978. *Revolution from Above: Military Bureaucrats and Development in Japan, Turkey, Egypt and Peru.* New Brunswick, NJ: Transaction Books.
Tsiang, S. C. 1984. "Taiwan's Economic Miracle: Lessons in Economic

Developmet." Pp. 301-326, in *World Economic Growth,* edited by Arnold C. Harberger. San Francisco: ICS Press.

Tsiang, S. C., Wen Lang Chen and Alvin Hsieh. 1985. "Progress in Trade Liberalization: Taiwan, Republic of China." *Industry of Free China.* 63(6): 1-15.

Truman, David B. 1951. *The Government Process.* New York: Alfred A. Knopf.

Wade, Robert. 1984. "Dirigisme Taiwan-Style." *IDS Bullentin.* 15(2): 65-70.

Wade, Robert. 1985a. "Taiwan." ESRC Newsletter. (Economic and Social Research Council, UK). 54: 12-15.

Wade, Robert. 1985b. "East Asian Financial Systems as a Challenge to Economics: Lessons from Taiwan." *California Management Review.* 27(4): 106-127.

Wallerstein, Immanuel. 1979. *The Capitalist World-Economy.* New York: Cambridge University Press.

Weber, Max. 1946. "Politics as a Vocation." Pp. 77-128, in *From Max Weber: Essays in Sociology,* translated and edited by H. H. Gerth and C. Wright Mills. New York: Oxford University Press.

Weber, Max. 1968. *Economy and Society: An Outline of Interpretive Sociology,* edited by Guenther Roth and Claus Wittich. Vol. 3 New York: Bedminster Press.

Wei, Yung. 1973. "Political Development in the Republic of China on Taiwan." Pp. 74-111, in *China and Question of Taiwan: Documents and Analysis,* edited by Chiu Hun-dah. New York: Praeger.

Wei, Yung. 1976. "Modernization Process in Taiwan: An Allocative Analysis." *Asian Survey.* 16(3): 249-269.

Weir, Margaret and Theda Skocpol. 1985. "State Structure and the Possibilities for 'Keynesian' Responses to the Great Depression in Sweden, Britain, and the United States." Pp. 107-163, in *Bringing the State Back In,* edited by Peter B. Evans, Dietrich Rueschemeyer and Theda Skocpol. New York: Cambridge University Press.

Wickberg, Edgar. 1970. "Late Nineteenth Century Land Tenure in North Taiwan." Pp. 78-92, in *Taiwan: Studies in Chinese Local History,* edited by Leonard H. D. Gordon. New York: Columbia University Press.

Wickberg, Edgar. 1981. "Continuities in Land Tenure, 1900-1940." Pp. 212-238, in *The Anthropolocy of Taiwanese Society,* edited by Emily Martin Ahern and Hill Gates. Standford, CA: Stand-

ford University Press.
Winckler, Edwin A. 1980a. "State Struggle and Class Conflict on Taiwan." Paper presented at the *Taiwan Political Economy Workshop,* East Asian Institute, Columbia University, New York, December, 1980.
Winckler, Edwin A. 1980b. "State System and Class Incorporation on Taiwan." Paper presented at the *Taiwan Political Economy Workshop,* East Asian Institute, Columbia University, New York, December, 1980.
Winckler, Edwin A. 1981a. "National, Regional and Local Politics." Pp. 13-37, in *The Anthropology of Taiwanese Society,* edited by Emily Martin Ahern and Hill Gates. Standford, CA: Standford University Press.
Winckler, Edwin A. 1981b. "Roles Linking State and Society." Pp. 50-86, in *The Anthropology of Taiwanese Society,* edited by Emily Martin Ahern and Hill Gates. Standford, CA: Standford University Press.
Wright, Erick Olin. 1978. *Class, Crisis, and the State.* London: New Left Books.
Wu, Yuan-li. 1985. *Becoming an Industrialized Nation: ROC's Development on Taiwan.* New York: Praeger.
Yang, Martin M. C. 1970. *Socio-Economic Results of Land Reform in Taiwan.* Honolulu, Hawaii: East-West Center Press.
Yen, C. K. 1982. "The Fundamentals and Conditions of Postwar Economic Development in Taiwan." Pp. 3-10, in *Experiences and Lessons of Economic Development in Taiwan,* edited by Kwoh-ting Li and Tzong-shian Yu. Taipei: Institute of Economics, Academia Sinica.

II. Chinese

Chang, Chung-han. 1980. *Kuang-fu-ch'ien Taiwan chih kung-yeh-hua* (The Industrialization on Taiwan before Retrocession). Taipei: Lien-ching.
Chao, Chi-ch'ang. 1985. *Mei-yuan ti yuun-yung* (The Utilization of U.S. Aid). Taipei: Lien-ching.
Ch'en, Ch'ao-p'ing. 1982. "Chin-ch'ien, cheng-k'e, shih" (Money, Politicians, and Corruption). *Lien-ho yueh-k'an (United Monthly).* 10: 16-21.
Ch'en, Hoh. 1985. "Kuomintang p'ai-hsi fu-eh'en liu-shih-nien" (The Rise and Fall of the Factions in the Kuomintang for the last Sixty

Years). Pp. 133-172, in *P'ou-hsi Kuomintang p'ai-hsi* (An Analysis of the Factions in the Kuomintang). Taipei: Tung-hsiang ts'ung-k'an.

CEPD. 1982. "Chung-mei ching-chi she-hui fa-chan chi-chin chih yun-yung" (The Utilization of Sino-American Fund for Economic and Social Development). *Tsu-yu chung-kuo chih kung-yeh* (Industry of Free China). 57(4): 19-31.

Chiang, Kai-shek. 1958. *Tsungtsai yeh-lun hsuan-chi* (Selected Speeches of Tsungtsai). Taipei: Chung-kuo Kuomintang tang-shih wei-yuan-hui.

Chiang, Kai-shek. 1963. "Chung-kuo ching-chi hsueh-shuo" (The Theory of the Chinese Economy). In *Chiang tsung-t'ung chi* (Collected Works of President Chiang Kai-shek). Vol. 1. Taipei: Kuo-fang yen-chiu yuan.

Chiang, Nan. 1984. *Chiang Ching-kuo chuan* (Biography of Chiang Ching-kuo). Los Angeles: Mei-kuo lun-t'an pao.

Ch'in, Hsiao-yi (ed.). 1966. *Tsung-t'ung yen-lun-chi* (President Chiang's Speeches). Vol. 1. Taipei: Chung-hua wen-hua ch'u-pen shih-yeh she.

Chou, Yu-kou. 1982a. "Hsi-shu t'sai-ching shou-ching ti pei-ching" (A Detailed Account of the Backgrounds of the Leading Economic Officials). Pp. 5-33, in *Ch'eng-chang ti t'ung-k'u* (Growing Pains). Taipei: Commonwealth Publishing Co.

Chou, Yu-kou. 1982b. "Wang Tso-yung chiao-shou" (Professor Wang Tso-yung). *T'ien-hsia tsa-chih* (Commonwealth). 10: 68-71.

Chung-hua min-kuo nien-chien 1950 (1950 Yearbook of the Republic of China). 1951. Taipei: Chung-hua min-kuo nien-chien she.

Commercial Times. 1982. *Ching-chi cheng-ts'e ta-pien-lun* (A Great Debate on Economic Policy). Taipei: China Times.

Commonwealth. 1986. "Kao Ti-min t'an" (An Interview with Thomas Gold). Pp. 70-79, in *T'ai-ping-yang shih-chi ti chu-jen* (People of the Pacific Century). edited by Diane Ying. Taipei: Commonwealth Publishing Co.

Fei, John C. H. 1982. "Wang Tso-jung hsien-sheng ho wo ti shih-er ta kuan-nien tui-li" (The Twelve Ideological Disagreements between Mr. Wang Tso-jung and Me). *Lien-ho yueh-k'an* (United Monthly). 14: 60-65.

Fei, John C. H. 1986. "Ch'uan-t'ung chung-kuo wen-hua chia-chih ho hsien-tai-hua ching-chi fa-chan chih kuan-hsi" (The Relationship between Traditional Chinese Cultural Value and Modern Economic Development). *Chiu-chou hsueh-k'an*. 1: 123-136.

FETCC. 1969. *Wai-mao-hui shih-szu nien* (Fourteen Years of the FETCC). Taipei: Foreigns Exchange and Trade Controlling Commission.
Fu, Ch'i-hsueh. 1976. *Chung-shan szu-hsiang pen-i* (The Essentials of Sun Yat-sen's Thought). Taipei: Kuo-fu i-chiao yen-chiu hui.
Fu, Li-hsi. 1982. "Ch'i-yeh-chieh ju-ho ying-hsiang cheng-fu chueh-ch'e" (How the Private Enterprise Influences State Policies). *Lien-ho yueh-k'an* (United Monthly). 13: 8-13.
Ger, Cheng-ou. 1983. *Chia-kung ch'u-k'ou-ch'u ti ch'uang-she* (The Creation of the Export Processing Zones). Taipei: Lien-ching.
Ger, Yeong-kuang. 1980. *Chung jih han cheng-tang pi-chiao yen-chiu* (A Comparative Study of the Political Parties in Taiwan, South Korea, and Japan). Master thesis. Taipei: Taiwan University.
Ho, Fei-p'eng. 1986. "Wo-men kai chi-ch'u shen-mo" (What Sould We Remember). *Cho-yueh tsa-chih* (Execellence). 21: 14-21.
Hsiao, Hsin-huang Michael. 1986. "Taiwan she-hui chieh-kou chuan-hsing ti tsai-t'an-shuo" (A Reexamination of Taiwan's Social Structural Transformation). *Chung-kuo lun-t'an* (China Forum). 248: 21-30.
Hsiao, Hsin-huang Michael, Cheng You-p'ing and Lei Ch'ien. 1982. *Taiwan ti hsiao-fei-che yun-tung: Li-lun yu shih-chi* (Consumerism on Taiwan: Theory and Practice). Taipei: China Times.
Hsing, Mo-huan. 1986. *T'ung-shu ching-chi chiang-hua: Kuan-nien yu cheng-ts'e* (Popular Lectures on Economics: Ideas and Policies). Taipei: San-min Books.
Hsiung, Chung-kuo. 1984. *Nung-yeh fa-chan ts'e-lueh* (Agricultural Development Strategy). Taipei: Lien-ching.
Hsu, Fu-ming. 1984. *Chung-kuo Kuomintang ti kai-tsao (1950-1952)* (The Reform of the Koumintang, 1950-1952). Master thesis. Taipei: Taiwan University.
Hsu, Peh-yuan. 1969. "Hsu-yen" (Preface). Pp. 1-9, in *Wai-mao-hui shih-szu nien* (Fourteen Years of the FETCC). Taipei: Foreign Exchange and Trade Controlling Commission.
Hu, Kuang-piao. 1964. *P'o-chu liu-shih nien* (Weaving in a Turbulent Era). Hong Kong: Hsin-wen t'ien-ti she.
Kau, Hsi-chun. 1982. "Ts'ai-ching shou-chang ti chieh-pan-jen tsai na-li" (Where are the Successors of the Leading Economic Officials). Pp. 34-39, in *Ch'eng-chang ti t'ung-k'u* (Growing Pains). Taipei: Commonwealth Publishing Co.
King, Ambrose Yao-chi. 1981. "Chung-kuo hsien-tai-hua ti tung-hsiang" (The Orientation of China's Modernization). Pp. 3-34,

in *Chung-kuo hsein-tai-hua ti li-ch'eng* (The Porcess of China's Modernization), edited by Chu Yun-han and P'eng Huai-en. Taipei: China Times.

King, Ambrose Yao-chi. 1985. "Ju-chia lun-li yu ching-chi fa-chan: Weber hsueh-shou ti ch'ung-t'an" (Confucian Ethics and Economic Development: A Reexamination of Weber's Theory). Pp. 29-55, in *Hsien-tai-hua yu chung-kuo-hua lun-chi* (Essays on Modernization and Sinization), edited by Lee Yi-yuan, Yang Kuo-shou and Wen Ch'ung-yi. Taipei: Kuei-kuan.

Li, K. T. 1986b. *Fei ching-chi ying-su tui ching-chi fa-chan ti ying-hsiang* (The Effects of Non-economic Factors on Economic Development). Taipei.

Li, K. T. and Ch'en Mu-tsai. 1984a. *Chung-kuo ching-chi fa-chan ch'e-lueh tsung-lun* (Introduction to the Development Policies of Chinese Economy). Vol. 1. Manuscript to be published by Lien-ching Publishing Co., Taipei.

Li, K. T. and Ch'en Mu-tsai. 1984b. *Chung-kuo ching-chi fa-chan ch'e-lueh tsung-lun* (Introduction to the Development Policies of Chinese Economy). Vol. 2. Manuscript to be published by Lien-ching Publishing Co., Taipei.

Liao, Meng-ch'ien. 1986a. "Taiwan chih-kung-chieh ti ti-yi-k'e t'ien-wang-hsing" (The First Super Star in Taiwan's Monetary System). Pp. 86-95, in *T'ou-shih ts'ai-ching jen-mai* (A Study of the Personnel in Taiwan's Economy). Taipei: Ts'ai-hsun tsa-chih she.

Liao, Pen-yuan. 1986b. "Ch'en Ch'eng wei Taiwan ch'i-yeh ming-ying-hua tien-chi" (Ch'en Ch'eng Lays the Fundation of the Enlargement of Private Sector in Taiwan). Pp. 62-71, in *T'ou-shih ts'ai-ching jen-mai* (A Study of the Personnel in Taiwan's Economy). Taipei: Ts'ai-hsun tsa-chih she.

Liao, Te-jun. 1986c. "Chung-kuo chih-jung chih-tu ti kai-lu hsien-feng" (The Pioneers of the Establishment of China's Monetary Institution). Pp. 40-51, in *T'ou-shih ts'ai-ching jen-mai* (A Study of the Personnel in Taiwan's Economy). Taipei: Ts'ai-hsun tsa-chih she.

Liao, Te-jun. 1986d. "Ch'en Ch'eng wei Taiwan ching-chi pa-cho jen-ch'ai" (Ch'en Ch'eng Recruited Talented People for Taiwan's Economy.). Pp. 52-61, in *T'ou-shih ts'ai-ching jen-mai* (A Study of the Personnel in Taiwan's Economy). Taipei: Ts'ai-hsun tsa-chih she.

Liu, Ch'ing-jui. 1960. *Chung-hua ming-kuo hsien-fa yao-yi* (Essentials of the Constitution of the Republic of China). Taipei: San-min

Books.

Liu, Feng-wen. 1957. *Kai-shan wai-hui chih-tu ch'u-i* (My Humble View for the Improvement of the Foreign Exchange System). Unpublished manuscript.

Liu, Feng-wen. 1980. *Wai-hui mao-i cheng-ts'e yu mao-i k'uo-chan* Foreign Exchange and Trade Policies and Trade Expansion). Taipei: Lien-ching.

Liu, Min-ch'eng and Hung-t'au Tso. 1983. *Kai-shan t'ou-tzu huan-ching* (Improvement of the Investment Climate). Taipei: Lien-ching.

Lung, Cheng-p'ing. 1982. "Tang-wai, yu-lun, kung-shang-chieh: Chien-tu cheng-fu ti san-tsung shih-li" (Tang-wai, Public Opinions, and Businessmen: The Three Social Forces to Monitor the Government). *Lien-ho yueh-k'an* (United Monthly). 10: 54-56.

P'an, Chih-chia. 1983. *Ming-ying ch'i-yeh ti fa-chan* (Development of the Private Enterprise). Taipei: Lien-ching.

Pang, Chien-kuo. 1980. *San Min Chu I tui she-hui pien-chi'ien ti chih-tau kung-neng* (The Guiding Functions of San Yat-senism on Social Change). Master thesis. Taipei: Taiwan University.

P'eng, Huai-en. 1985. *Chung-hua-ming-kuo cheng-chih t'i-hsi ti fen-hsi* (Analysis of the Political System of the Republic of China). Taipei: China Times.

Sah, Meng-wu. 1974. *Chung-kuo hsien-fa hsin-lun* (A New Review of China's Constitution). Taipei: San-min Books.

Shen, Yun-lung. 1972. *Yin Chung-jung hsien-sheng nien-p'u ch'u-kao* Biography of K. Y. Yin). Taipei: Chuan-chi wen'hsueh.

Sun, Chen. 1981. *Min-sheng chu-i ti ching-chi cheng-ts'e* (Economic Plicies of the Min-sheng Principle). Taipei: Cheng-chung Books.

Sun, Chen. 1984. *Mai-hsiang fu-er hao-li ti she-hui* (Toward a Rich and Courteous Society). Taipei: Commenwealth Publishing Co.

Szuma, Hsiaok-ch'ing. 1986a. "Kuan-ch'ang t'ai-tou Yen Chia-kan" C. K. Yen: A Leading Authority in the Officialdom). Pp. 20-31, in *T'ou-shih ts'ai-ching jen-mai* (A Study of the Personnel in Taiwan's Economy). Taipei: T'sai-hsun tsa-chih she.

Szuma, Hsiao-ch'ing. 1986. "Taiwan ch'i-yeh-chieh ti liang-ta chung-ch'ang-wei" (The Two Taiwanese Enterpreneurs in the CSC). Pp. 260-269, in *T'ou-shih ts'ai-ching jen-mai* (A Study of the Personnel in Taiwan Economy). Taipei: Ts'ai-hsun tsa-chih she.

Tsiang, Sho-chieh. 1985. *Taiwan ching-chi fa-chan ti ch'i-shih* (Lessons from the Economic Development of Taiwan). Taipei: Commonwealth Publishing Co.

Tung, Hsien-kuan. 1967. *Chiang Tsung-t'ung chuan* (Biography of President Chiang Kai-shek). Taipei: Chung-hua ta-tien pien-yin hui.

Wang, Tso-jung. 1972. "Postscript." Pp. 1-13, in Yun-lung Shen, *Yin Chung-jung hsien-sheng nien-p'u* (Biography of K. Y. Yin). Taipei: Chuan-chi wen-hsueh.

Wang, Tso-jung. 1978. *Wo-men ju-ho ch'uang-chao-le ching-chi ch'i-chi* (How We Great the Economic Miracle). Taipei: China Times.

Wang, Tso-jung. 1981. *Taiwan ching-chi fa-chan lun-wen shuan-chi* (Selected Essays on Taiwan's Economic Development). Taipei: China Times.

Wang, Tzouh-rong. 1983. *Chang-wo tang-ch'ien fan-hsiang* (The Contemporary Economic Trends in Taiwan). Taipei: Commonwealth Publishing Co.

Wang, Tso-jung. 1984. "ching-chi yin tsu-yu-hua yu kuo-chi-hua" (The Economy Should March Toward Liberalization and Internationalization). *T'ien-hsia tsa-chih* (Commonwealth). 42: 30-37.

Wen, Hsien-shen. 1984. "Ching-chien-hui ti kuo-ch'u, hsien-tsai, yu wei-lai" (Past, Present and Future of the CEPD). *T'ien-hsia tsa-chih* (Commonwealth). 42: 12-25.

Wen, Ch'ung-i. 1985. "Taiwan ti kung-yeh-hua yu she-hui pien-ch'ien" (Taiwan's Industrialization and Social Change). Pp. 1-40, in *Taiwan ti-ch'u she-hui pien-ch'ien yu wen-hua fa-chan* (Social Change and Cultural Development in Taiwan Area), edited by China Forum. Taipei: Lien-ching.

Wu, Rong-I, Wang-lien Ch'ang-fu, Chou T'ien-ch'eng, Li Chao-k'ao. 1980. *Mei-shang t'ou-tzu tui wo-kuo ching-chi ti ying-hsiang* (The Impact of the Investment of American Businessman on Taiwan's Economy). Taipei: Institute of American Culture, Academia Sinica.

Yang, Chi-wei. 1986. "Hsing-hsien i-lai cheng fu tsung-t'ung yu ke-k'uei ti ch'uan-li kuan-hsi" (The Power Relationships between President, Vice President, and Premier since the Promulgation of the Constitution). Pp. 127-180, in *Taiwan wei-lai lin-hsiu* (The Leadership of Taiwan in the Future). Taipei: Feng-yun lun-t'ang she.

Yang, Hsu-sheng. 1984. "Taiwan ching-chi ti lin-hang-jen" (The Pilots of Taiwan's Economy). Pp. 147-165, in *T'ou-shih ching-chi ch'iang-jen* (Gaining a Perspective of the Economic Strong Men). Taipei: Ching'chi-jen tsa-chih she.

Yin, K. Y. 1973a. *Wo-tui Taiwan ching-chi ti k'an-fa* (My Views on

Taiwan's Economy). Vol. 1. Taipei: Economic Planning Council.
Yin, K. Y. 1973b. *Wo-tui Taiwan ching-chi ti k'an-fa* (My Views on Taiwan's Economy). Vol. 2. Taipei: Economic Planning Council.
Yin, K. Y. 1973c. *Wo-tui Taiwan ching-chi ti k'an-fa* (My Views on Taiwan's Economy). Vol. 3. Taipei: Economic Planning Council.
Yin, K. Y. 1973d. *Wo-tui Taiwan ching-chi ti k'an-fa* (My Views on Taiwan's Economy). Vol. 4. Taipei: Economic Planning Council.
Ying, Diane. 1981. "Yu tsung-ts'ai t'an" (An Interview with Governor Yu Kuo-hwa). *T'ien-hsia tsa-chih* (Commonwealth). 1: 26-30.
Yu, Tzong-shian. 1976. *Taiwan Ching-chi fa-chan chung-yao wen-hsien* (Important Documents on Taiwan's Economic Development). Taipei: Lien-ching.
Yu, Tzong-shian. 1983. "Chung-kuo wen-hua tui Taiwan ching-chi chen-chang ti ying-hsiang" (The Effect of Chinese Culture on Taiwan's Economic Growth). Pp. 1-17, in *Taiwan yu Hong Kong ti ching-chi fa-chan* (Economic Developments on Taiwan and Hong Kong), edited by Yu Tzong-shian, Liu K'e-chih and Lin Ch-ung-piao. Taipei: Institute of Economics, Academia Sinica.

INDEX

Accelerated Economic Growth Program, 184-185
Administrative Reform Committee, 179
Agency for International Development (of the United States). *See* AID
Agricultural Development Act, 211
AID, 51, 110-112, 150, 177-178, 180-185, 186
Anderson, W. A., 132
Arthur D. Little Incorporated, 221

bombarment of Quemoy, 164
Brent, Joseph L., 112

Cathay Plastics, 249, 269
CCP, 37, 203, 258-259
Central Bank of China, 52, 55, 57, 59, 153, 179
Central Reform Committee (of the KMT), 83, 88
Central Standing Committee (of the KMT). *See* CSC
CEPD, 55, 57, 60, 207, 266
Chang Chi-cheng, 206, 207, 208, 225
Chang Chun, 183
Chang Kwang-shih, 207
Chang Tse-k'ai, 127
Chao Yao-tung, 207, 208, 221, 223, 249, 251
Ch'en Ch'eng, 53, 62, 70, 80, 81, 82, 86-87, 89, 100, 103, 120, 127, 128, 138, 160, 175, 181-183, 189, 194, 205, 240, 267, 269, 272
Ch'en Yi, 42
Cheng Ch'eng-kung, 37
Chiang Ching-kuo, 54, 59, 62, 63, 70, 80, 81, 87-89, 100, 103, 120, 205-206, 213, 221-222, 235, 240, 241, 242, 247, 267, 269, 272
Chiang Kai-shek, 45, 46, 47, 62, 63, 70, 72, 80, 81-86, 89, 100, 127, 128, 131, 138, 147, 160, 165, 175, 179, 182-184, 186, 194, 211, 226, 240, 261, 262, 265, 267, 269
Chiang Monlin, 90, 130, 131, 170
Chiang Piao, 175

Ch'ien Ch'un, 208
Chien T'ien-ho, 130
China Aid Act, 51
China Steel Corporation, 223, 224, 249
Chinese Communist Party. *See* CCP
Chinese National Association of Industry and Commerce, 114, 263
Chou En-lai, 203
Chow Chi-chong (Gregory C. C. Chow), 107-108
CIECD, 51, 54, 59, 205-206, 221, 266
class struggle thesis, 12
colonial occupation of Japan, 39-42, 265
Confucianism, 35-36, 264-265
Consumer's Foundation of the Republic of China, 244
Control Yuan, 45, 114, 194
Council for Agricultural Planning and Development, 52, 212
Council for Economic Planning and Development. *See* CEPD
Council for International Economic Cooperation and Development. *See* CIECD
Council for United States Aid. *See* CUSA.
Council of Agriculture, 52, 212
Criteria Governing the Control of Imports, 236
CSC, 43, 62-71, 74, 77, 89, 90, 113, 190, 209, 263, 266, 267
Cultural Revolution, 259
CUSA, 51, 52, 53, 54, 57, 59, 189, 195, 258, 266

Democratic Progressive Party, 248
Dillon, C. Douglas, 180
Do Pont, 245-246
Dulles, John F., 165

Economic Reform Committee, 242-243
Economic Planning Council. *See* EPC
Economic Settlement Certificate. *See* ESC
Economic Stablization Board. *See* ESB
entrustment scheme in the textile sector, 148-150

EPC, 54-55, 57, 59, 206-207, 266
EPZ, 191, 204, 215-216
ESB, 53-54, 59, 60, 152, 160, 258, 266
ESC, 158-159
Evans, Peter, 2, 4, 7, 14, 47, 150, 240, 248, 253
Executive Yuan, 45, 246-247
Executive Yuan Council, 61-62, 73-74, 113, 122, 184, 189-190, 246, 263, 266
Export Processing Zone. *See* EPZ

farmer's associations, 132-134, 146, 262
Fei Ching-han (John C. H. Fei), 107-108, 226, 232-233
FETCC, 51-52, 57, 59, 160, 167, 174-175, 176, 195, 206, 236, 238, 258, 266
Five-man Finance and Economic Group, 206
First Sino-Japanese War, 39
Foreign Exchange and Trade Control Commission. *See* FETCC
Formosa Plastics, 223-224
Fourteen Development Projects, 222

Gang of Four, 204
GATT (General Agreement on Tariffs and Trade), 157
Geneva talks, 164
Great Leap Forward, 166
Guidelines for Accelerating Rural Reconstruction, 211

Haraldson, Wesley C., 112, 181-185
historical-structural perspective, 17
Hsing Mo-huan, 102, 107-108, 173
Hsu Li-teh, 207, 208
Hsu Peh-yuan, 90, 128, 160, 175, 205-206, 225

IDC, 53
Industrial Development Commission of ESB. *See* IDC
instrumentalism, 12

Japanese legacy, 22, 34, 47
JCRR, 52, 57, 129-132, 134, 138, 146, 212, 258, 266
Joint Commission on Rural Reconstruction, (Sino-American). *See* JCRR
Judicial Yuan, 45

Killough, H. B., 112
Kissinger, Henry, 203
KMT, 1, 43
KMT state, autonomy of the, 46, 74, 117, 191-197, 208-209, 233, 250-251, 251-253, 261, 266, 272
  capacities of the, 47, 74, 117, 191-197, 208-209, 233-234, 241, 251-253, 257, 266
Koo Chen-fu, 242
Koo Ying-ch'ang (Anthony Y. C. Koo), 107-108, 226
Korean War, 51, 123-124, 127, 257
Kung, H. H., 82, 94, 261
Kuomintang (Chinese Nationalist Party). *See* KMT

land reform, 134-142, 262, 265
land-to-the-tiller program, 135, 136
labor movement (in Taiwan), 246-248
Labor Standards Law, 246-247
Lee Ta-hai, 208
Lee Teng-hui, 213
Legislative Yuan, 45, 71-73, 77, 114, 122, 185-186, 190, 239, 246-247
Li Kwoh-ting (K. T. Li), 1, 18, 90, 94, 98-99, 101, 106, 107, 114, 120, 168, 182-183, 185, 186, 194, 205-208, 215-216, 224, 226, 242, 272
Li Tsung-jen, 127
Liu Feng-wen, 173
Liu Ming-chuan, 39
Liu Shao-ch'i, 166
Liu Ta-chung, 107-108, 173, 214-215, 226
Lu Jun-k'ang, 207, 208

Mao Tse-tung, 166
Middle East War in October, 1973, 200
Ministry of Economic Affairs, 51, 52, 54, 55, 57, 59, 167, 172, 224, 237, 238
Ministry of Finance, 51, 52, 55, 57, 59, 189-190, 224, 234
Ministry of the Interior, 246-247
Min-sheng Principle, 83, 118-119, 135
movement of consumerism (in Taiwan), 243-244

movement of environmental conservation (in Taiwan), 244-246
Mutual Defense Treaty (between the United States and the Republic of China), 124, 203, 258

National Assembly, 45, 247
New Taiwan Dollar Reform, 153
Nixon, Richard M., 124, 203

Outlines of the Present Stage Rural Reconstruction Program, 210

Parsons, Howard L., 112
pluralist approach, 10-11
Policy Coordination Commission (of the KMT), 63-64, 185, 190
preferential interest savings deposits, 153
Review Outlines of Agricultural Policy, 210
rice-fertilizer barter system, 143-144
Roosevelt, Franklin D., 123
Rueschemeyer, Dietrich, 2, 4, 14, 47, 240, 248, 253

Saccio, Leonard, 180-181
San Min Chu I. See Sun Yat-senism
Science-Based Industrial Park, 222
Second Shanghai Communique, 203
Shanghai Communique, 203
Shen Tsung-han (T. H. Shen), 90, 130, 131
society-centered approach, 10-13
Soong, T. V., 82, 94, 96, 261
stagflation, 201
state, characteristics of the, 14
    definition of the, 14
state autonomy, 17, 46, 48
state capacities, 17, 48
state-centric approach, 1, 2, 10, 11-12, 13
Statute for Investment of Foreigners, 188
Statute for Investment of Overseas Chinese, 188
structuralism, 12
Sun Chen, 106-107
Sun Yat-sen, 43, 81, 83, 135
Sun Yat-senism, 46, 47, 83, 117-119, 165, 179, 266
Sun Yun-suan, 62, 89, 90, 103, 120, 206-207, 242, 243, 272

Taiwan Production Board. See TPB
Taiwan Relations Act, 203
Taiwanization, 253
T'ao Sheng-yang, 206
Tax Reform Commission, 226-227
Temporary Provisions Effective During the Period of Communist Rebellion, 127
Ten Major Development Projects, 221-222, 260
Teng Hsiao-p'ing, 166
TNCs, 152, 209, 259
TPB, 51, 53, 57, 148, 160, 174, 266
Transnational Corporations. See TNCs
Truman, Harry S., 124
Ts'ai Ch'en-chou, 249-250
Tsiang Sho-chieh, 107-108, 173, 214-215, 226, 227, 232-233, 235, 236, 243
Tsiang Yien-si, 131
Twelve New Projects, 222
2-28 Incident, 42-43, 46, 126, 142, 253, 261, 265

unevenness of state capacities, 61
United Nations, 203, 260
U.S. aid, 34, 47, 60, 75, 110-112, 138, 148, 157, 162, 163, 166, 170-172, 178, 187, 188, 203, 257, 262, 263, 266, 269
U.S. Aid Mission to China, 51, 52, 110-112, 130, 132, 133, 150, 178, 258
U.S. Hoover Committee, 179

Vietnam War, 202

Wang Chou-ming, 107
Wang Tso-jung, 18, 105-106, 107, 109, 187, 194, 197, 215, 221, 227, 232-233, 243
Wang Yun-wu, 179
Wang yung-ch'ing, 242, 245
Wu Kuo-cheng, 53

Yang Chi-tseng, 90, 194
Yeh Wan-an, 106, 107
Yen Chia-kan (C. K. Yen), 62, 82, 90, 99-101, 103, 120, 127, 128, 174, 175, 182-183, 190, 194, 205, 226, 240

Yin Chung-jung (K. Y. Yin), 53, 90, 9-98, 99, 101, 105, 106, 107, 114, 120, 127, 128, 148-149, 152, 160, 168-170, 171-172, 173-175, 176, 205 182-185, 186, 189, 191-197, 215, 240, 272
Yu Kuo-hwa, 62, 89, 90, 103, 120, 206-208, 225, 226, 234, 235, 242, 272
Yui Hung-chun (O. K. Yui), 53, 62, 90, 103, 128, 169, 175, 194